for Oral and
Written Review

French
for Oral and Written Review
Third Edition

Charles Carlut   Walter Meiden

THE OHIO STATE UNIVERSITY

Holt, Rinehart and Winston

NEW YORK   CHICAGO   PHILADELPHIA   SAN FRANCISCO   MONTREAL
TORONTO   LONDON   SYDNEY   TOKYO   MEXICO CITY
RIO DE JANEIRO   MADRID

Permission for readings in the text are on page xv.

PUBLISHER: Rita Pérez
DEVELOPMENTAL EDITOR: Marilyn C. Hofer
SENIOR PROJECT EDITOR: Arthur J. Morgan
PRODUCTION MANAGER: Annette Mayeski
DESIGN SUPERVISOR: Gloria Gentile
TEXT DESIGN: Ben Kann

Library of Congress Cataloging in Publication Data

Carlut, Charles, 1911–
  French for oral and written review.

  Includes index.
  1. French language—Grammar—1950-   . I. Meiden,
Walter, 1907-   . II. Title.
PC2112.C3 1983   448.2'421   82–11721
ISBN 0-03-062318-9

CBS COLLEGE PUBLISHING
Holt, Rinehart and Winston
The Dryden Press
Saunders College Publishing

Contents

To the Teacher   ix

To the Student   xii

CHAPTER 1

Interrogatives   1

    Une soirée perdue, *René Goscinny*   1
I.   Interrogative Adjectives   2
II.   Interrogative Pronouns   4
    Problem Words: *actually, advice, again, agree*   9

CHAPTER 2

Adjectives   13

    Lever de soleil, *Michel Tournier*   13
I.   Formation of Adjectives   14
II.   Comparison of Adjectives   18
III.   Position of Adjectives   20
    Problem Words: *become, better, bring, can*   23

CHAPTER 3

Adverbs   27

    Les chiens, *Jacques Lacarrière*   27
I.   Formation of Adverbs   28
II.   Position of Adverbs   30
III.   Negative Constructions   32
    Problem Words: *change, character, day (morning, evening)*   37

CHAPTER 4

Use of Tenses   41

    Le petit coq noir, *Marcel Aymé*   41
I.   The Present   42
II.   The Future   44
III.   The Conditional   45
IV.   The Pluperfect and Related Tenses   46

V.   The Future Perfect   48
VI.   Conditional Sentences   49
    Problem Words: *early, end, escape, every*   52

CHAPTER 5

Personal Pronouns   56

    Un écrivain âgé considère la vie et la mort, *Jacques Chancel,*
        Maurice Genevoix   56
I.   Object Pronouns and Their Uses   58
II.   Position of Object Pronouns   60
III.   Disjunctive Pronouns   61
    Problem Words: *expect, fail, feel, get*   66

CHAPTER 6

Past Tenses in Narration   71

    Textes variés du dix-neuvième et du vingtième siècle (*Camus,*
        Chateaubriand, Dumas, Simenon)   71
    Problem Words: *go, happen, bear*   79

CHAPTER 7

Possessives   84

    Le souterrain, *Françoise Mallet-Joris*   84
I.   Possessive Adjectives   86
II.   Possessive Adjectives with Nouns (Parts of the Body)   87
III.   Possessive Pronouns   90
    Problem Words: *intend, introduce, a knock, know*   92

CHAPTER 8

Participles   95

    Pages blanches, *Romain Gary*   95
I.   The Past Participle   97
II.   The Present Participle   102
    Problem Words: *lack, last night, late, leave*   106

CHAPTER 9

Demonstratives   111

    Le tableau soluble, *Claude Spaak*   111
I.   The Demonstrative Adjective   113
II.   The Indefinite Demonstrative Pronouns   114

III. The Definite Demonstrative Pronouns   115
IV. The Demonstrative Pronoun *ce*   117
The Indefinite *ce*   117
The Introductory *ce*   118
Problem Words: *little, live, long, make*   121

CHAPTER 10

Relatives   125

Manifestation au lycée de Lausanne, *Jacques Chessex*   125
Problem Words: *marry, miss, more, next*   132

CHAPTER 11

The Subjunctive   136

Villes d'Amerique, *Jean-Paul Sartre*   136
Problem Words: *notice, opportunity, paper, people*   152

CHAPTER 12

The Article   156

Moi, le plus heureux des Français?, *Georges Brassens*   156
Problem Words: *piece, place, rather, reason*   167

CHAPTER 13

Indefinite Nouns   171

La maison, *André Maurois*   171
Problem Words: *return, room, save, sit*   179

CHAPTER 14

The Passive Voice and the Causative Construction   184

Émancipation, *Françoise Sagan*   184
I. The Passive Voice   186
II. The Causative Construction   192
Problem Words: *soon, spend, stop, such*   195

CHAPTER 15

The Verb *devoir*   199

Souvenirs du Canada, *Gabrielle Roy*   199
Problem Words: *take, teach, time*   205

CHAPTER 16

Constructions with Prepositions   211

Pourquoi j'ai choisi d'écrire, *Simone de Beauvoir*   211

I.   Prepositions of Place   212
   To, In, At   212
   From   215
II.   Verb + Preposition + Infinitive   216
III.   The *à* + *de* Verbs   219
IV.   Verb (+ Preposition) + Noun   220
V.   The *It is* + Adjective + Infinitive Constructions   222
VI.   Verbal Constructions after Prepositions: Constructions
   with *pour*   223
   Problem Words: *very much, visit, while, wish*   227

CHAPTER 17

Problem Prepositions   231

Contre remboursement, *Félicien Marceau*   231

I.   English Words that are both Prepositions and Conjunctions   233
II.   Other English Prepositions that Pose Problems in French   238
   Problem Words: *would, year, yes, young men*   249

Verbs   253

The Organization of the French Verb   253
The Conjugation of the Verb   256
Verbs with Spelling Changes   274

Vocabularies   277

French-English Vocabulary   277
English-French Vocabulary   309

Index   325

To the teacher

This text is designed to review all the common elements of French grammar, both orally and in written French. To that end it is provided with numerous all-French exercises and English-to-French translations on various phases of the French language and with a set of tapes containing numerous structure drills.

The organization of the chapters

Each chapter deals with a specific grammatical topic. The chapters are divided into short sections, each one of which takes up a particular aspect of the subject under consideration. After one or several sections treating related topics there are written exercises that afford practice on the material of the preceding paragraphs. At the end of the grammatical parts of the chapter are review exercises that give additional practice on the topics taken up in the chapter. Each chapter ends with three or four problem words and a verb review.

This type of organization allows for great flexibility: it permits teachers who so desire to assign a limited amount of grammar each day with reading from other texts; it permits those using the book in a pure grammar review course to adjust the number of sections and exercises to the needs of the class; topics can easily be omitted without disturbing the unity of the whole. For those wishing exercises that offer practice on all aspects of a grammatical topic, there are *exercices d'ensemble* at the end of each chapter.

The grammar is presented in a sequence designed to make its study graduated in difficulty. The first three chapters take up relatively uncomplicated topics: interrogatives, adjectives, and adverbs. In Chapter 4 the use of most tenses is studied; other aspects of the verb are presented in Chapters 6, 8, 11, and 14, so that not too much material on verbs is taken up consecutively. Since no chapter depends on any preceding one, however, the chapters may be taken up in any order the instructor prefers.

The "textes"

Each chapter except the sixth begins with a selection from some twentieth-century author with italicized examples of the grammar presented in the chapter. The sixth includes a number of selections from well-known nineteenth- and twentieth-century authors. Most texts have been slightly modified to make them more readable at the intermediate level and to permit the presentation of the grammatical topics taken up in the chapter. For those who wish, these selections may be used for class discussion in French or for grammatical analysis of the examples they contain.

In the Exercise Manual there are two questions based on each text that suggest a topic of composition for the students.

The structure drills

Along with the grammar is a set of tapes with a complete set of structure drills dealing with each aspect of the chapter except those that do not lend themselves to oral drill. These drills consist of simple rather than complex sentences so that the students can remember them long enough to repeat them and to internalize the structure. For maximum benefit students should hear these drills but not see them. They should go to the laboratory and listen to and repeat each drill until they can do it automatically and without any hesitation.

A complete tapescript of the structure drills is available to the instructor upon request to the publisher.

The Exercise Manual

To supplement the text is an Exercise Manual. It consists of two parts: 1) written exercises on all phases of French grammar; 2) an outline of the taped structure drills, which give the directions to each drill and the model sentence preceding each drill. These directions and model sentences are also heard on the tapes.

The written exercises in the Manual are different from those in the text. Many of them encourage the students to show their understanding of grammatical points by completing a statement or answering a question. In certain exercises choices of several possible answers must be made. These all-French exercises provide additional drill on grammatical topics in a somewhat more imaginative form than those in the text. They are designed to add a further dimension to the study of French—an opportunity for personalized work and self-expression.

Ways in which the book may be adjusted to fit the needs of different types of courses

Where the number of recitations in a course is limited, parts of the book or parts of a chapter may be omitted without affecting the study of the parts that are assigned, for each chapter and each section (with the exception of certain sections in Chapter 11) is an independent unit.

For the shorter grammar course, the PROBLEM WORDS, the *Exercices d'ensemble* at the end of the chapters, and Chapter 17 dealing with Problem Prepositions could be omitted at the discretion of the instructor.

Some schools that are on the shorter quarter system take up the majority of the chapters of *French for Oral and Written Review* in their grammar review course and use the rest of them as the grammatical portion of one or more conversation–composition courses.

For the course where an emphasis on the proper use of words if paramount, the core of the study could be built around the PROBLEM WORDS and, where necessary, certain grammatical sections might be omitted.

Innovations in the third edition

The following changes have been made in this third edition:

1. Each chapter except Chapter 6 begins with a selection from twentieth-century literature containing italicized examples of the grammar points discussed in the chapter. Chapter 6 includes selections from nineteenth- and twentieth-century literature.

2. The chapter order has been rearranged so that the verb is taken up earlier in the text and so that chapters on verbs are alternated with chapter on other topics.

3. The grammatical sections of each chapter are followed by review exercises.

4. Rules have been rewritten so as to be more readily understandable.

5. Notes have been added.

6. Long exercises have been divided into two or more shorter exercises so that they are easier to assign.

To the student

Grammar is an organized study of the usages of the various aspects of a language. This study usually consists of a series of principles or rules.

A rule is simply a statement of usage in a generalized form.

To formulate a rule to govern any French grammatical construction, one looks for as many examples as possible of this construction in both written and spoken French, and, after carefully examining how the construction is expressed, one tells how it is expressed in generalized form.

In a small way, you should try to make your own rules by studying the examples of the constructions found in this book.

To that end, each section of a chapter begins with a question on some type of French construction. There follow examples of the construction. Study these examples carefully in light of the question that precedes them. From what you observe, try to derive a generalization that will answer the question and will then constitute your own rule for that construction. To permit you to check the accuracy of your generalization, the answer to the question follows the examples. This answer is likewise in form of a generalization and constitutes a rule.

It is not necessary to learn these rules verbatim, but it is valuable to understand the principle at hand and to be able to state it accurately and clearly as a generalization.

Naturally, a knowledge of French grammar will not be of much use to you unless you can apply it in speaking and writing. For that reason, each grammatical unit is followed by exercises that will give you the opportunity to apply what you have learned in the unit, and for each chapter there are oral structure drills to be listened to in the laboratory. Practice the oral exercises and work out the written exercises in the Exercise Manual as your teacher directs. If you have access to a laboratory, listen carefully to the tapes and repeat with the indicated changes during the intervals of silence until you can say the pattern in question without hesitation.

But a knowledge of grammatical principles and the ability to apply them will not alone give you a mastery of French, even if you learn to say the patterns automatically. In addition, you must know how to use the common words of the language properly.

In English and French, there are a certain number of common words and ideas that are expressed in several ways in each language, but their usages do not correspond. Let us consider two examples:

Example 1: The French word **temps**

Je n'ai pas beaucoup de **temps.**   *I don't have much* time.
Le **temps** est splendide aujour-   *The* weather *is marvelous to-*
d'hui.   *day.*

In each sentence, we find the French word **temps**. But English expresses **temps** of the first sentence by *time*, of the seond sentence by *weather*.

Example 2: The English word *time*

Je n'ai pas beaucoup de **temps.**	*I don't have much* time.
Je vous ai appelé trois **fois.**	*I called you three* times.
Quelle **heure** est-il?	*What* time *is it?*
Que faites-vous en ce **moment?**	*What are you doing at this* time?
A cette **époque**-là, j'étais très jeune.	*At that* time *I was very young.*
Vous êtes-vous amusé à cette soirée?	Did you have a good time *at that party?*

In each sentence, English has used the same word—*time*. But French has used successively **temps, fois, heure, moment,** and **époque** to express the English word *time,* and in the last sentence it uses the verb **s'amuser** to convey the idea of *having a good time.*

It is very important to know when French uses one word and when another to express a given English word, for often the various French words that express the same English word cannot be interchanged. To teach you how to deal with such words, there is at the end of each lesson a group of some three or four "problem words." Through the examples, explanations, and exercises, familiarize yourself with all aspects of the words given.

A thorough knowledge of the forms of the most used tenses of regular and irregular verbs is essential if you wish to speak and write French correctly. For that reason, two verbs are reviewed at the end of each lesson. On pages 253–55 you are shown how you can organize your knowledge of the verb by deriving its tenses from the five principal parts.

Acknowledgments

We are very indebted to the many teachers who have made suggestions which have led to the changes in this third edition. We are especially grateful to the following, who have made detailed suggestions:

Pierre Astier, Ohio State University
Dorothy M. Betz, Georgetown University
Diane Birckbichler, Ohio State University
Jean-Hugues Boisset, Pennsylvania State University
Barbara T. Cooper, University of New Hampshire
Dean Detrich, Michigan State University
Richard Grant, University of Texas
Mario Iglesias, Ohio State University
Robert Kreiter, University of the Pacific
Leona B. LeBlanc, Florida State University
Judith E. Preckshot, University of Minnesota
Robert P. Shupp, University of Houston
Paul Socken, Waterloo University

Charles Carlut
Walter Meiden

Permissions

French
for Oral and
Written Review

CHAPTER 1

Interrogatives

Une soirée perdue

Il est question, ces jours-ci, d'arrêts de travail à la télévision, et cela m'a remis en mémoire la première grève que j'ai subie en tant que télé-spectateur[1].

5 Dès le palier[2], avant d'ouvrir la porte de mon appartement, ce soir-là, j'avais été surpris par un grand silence. D'ordinaire, dans l'ascenseur, je perçois déjà des bruits de la télévision, paroles ou musiquette[3]. Mais là, rien. *Qu'est-ce que* cela signifiait? Inquiet, j'entrai chez moi et je restai sidéré[4] par l'étrange spectacle qui m'attendait: les lumières étaient allu-mées dans la salle à manger; c'était pourtant l'heure du dîner. *Qu'est-ce*
10 *qui* pouvait bien se passer? J'ouvrai la porte et demandai, angoissé:

—*Qui* est malade?

—Ben[5], c'est la grève. Tu ne lis pas les journaux?

C'est vrai, à force d'y collaborer, je les lis de moins en moins. Je ne lis que ce que j'y écris, pour y corriger, trop tard, le passé simple de mes
15 verbes, que je n'ai jamais su utiliser correctement.

—Et alors, demandai-je, *qu'*allons-nous faire?

—Nous allons manger, me répondit-on.

Je n'avais pas faim. Une boule[6] d'angoisse obstruait ma gorge, et la lumière crue qui baignait[7] les aliments me les rendait étranges, hostiles
20 et peu appétissants. Nous commençâmes le dîner dans un silence inha-bituel, troublé seulement par le bruit des fourchettes et des couteaux, qui prenait alors une importance considérable. De temps en temps nous tournions la tête vers le petit écran[8], sombre et muet, témoin mort de notre triste repas . . .
25 Nous essayâmes d'engager une conversation. Mais de *quoi* parler? N'étant pas téléspectateurs passifs, c'est le petit écran, encore, qui nous

---

[1] *television viewer*   [2] *landing*   [3] *light music*   [4] *flabbergasted*   [5] eh bien [bɛ̃] (*colloquial*)   [6] boule d'angoisse *pang of anguish*   [7] baignait les aliments *fell on the food*   [8] *screen*

fournissait des sujets de discussion. Nous étions tous nerveux, comme des intoxiqués privés de drogue . . .

Après le dîner, nous allâmes nous asseoir dans le «living», dans les
30 fauteuils placés autour de la table[9] basse où tout le monde se cogne les genoux. Et justement, ils étaient là, les fauteuils, à leur place, autour de la table basse, alors que, tous les soirs, ils sont disposés en rang, face au récepteur. *Lequel* d'entre nous aurait pensé à autre chose qu'à regarder les programmes? Nous nous trouvâmes mal assis, mal[10] dans notre peau,
35 gênés d'être face à face, bêtement . . .

—*Qu'est-ce que* nous pourrions bien faire? dis-je.

—On pourrait jouer aux cartes, à n'importe quoi.

Mais le seul jeu que nous possédons a un défaut. Il[11] manque un coin au valet de cœur. Or, il n'existe aucun jeu qui puisse se passer de valet
40 de cœur. Nous ne pûmes donc pas jouer aux cartes.

J'essayai de faire des mots croisés, mais j'abandonnai bien vite devant un petit champignon de douze lettres. Je tournai en rond, je me cognai le genou contre la table basse, j'allumai et j'éteignis plusieurs fois le récepteur; *quel* fol espoir m'animait, vite déçu, évidemment?

45 —*Qui* veut aller au cinéma? demandai-je. Mais il pleuvait si fort que c'eût[12] été de la folie de sortir.

Il fallait faire quelque chose, je ne pouvais pas rester comme ça . . . Mais *que* faire?

Alors, tant pis, je pris un livre, et je commençai à lire.

D'après René Goscinny, humoriste, auteur, avec Albert Uderzo, de la célèbre série *Astérix,* qui raconte l'histoire de France à leur manière. («Grève», in *Interludes,* Denoël, 1966)

---

[9] *coffee table*   [10] mal dans notre peau *ill at ease*   [11] Il manque un coin au valet de cœur *A corner is missing from the Jack of Hearts*   [12] *that would have been*

I. Interrogative Adjectives

An interrogative adjective is one that modifies a noun and asks a question. In English the interrogative adjectives are *which?* and *what?*

1. What are the French interrogative adjectives and how are they used before a noun?

Quel livre lisez vous?	Which *book are you reading?*
Quelles leçons préparent-ils?	Which *lessons are they preparing?*
Quel homme! **Quels** beaux enfants!	What *a man!* What *good-looking children!*

The interrogative adjectives are:

	Masculine	Feminine
Singular	**quel**	**quelle**
Plural	**quels**	**quelles**

Interrogative adjectives precede their noun and its modifiers directly and agree with it in gender and number.

The interrogative **quel** is also used in an exclamation and is then the equivalent of the English *what . . .* ! or *what a . . .* !

NOTE: The interrogative adjective *Whose . . . ?* is usually expressed by **De qui . . . ?** Ex.: **De qui** portez-vous la cravate? (*or*) Vous portez la cravate **de qui?** (Whose *tie are you wearing?*)

In sentences in which the French equivalent of *Whose . . . ?* is used with a form of **être** it is expressed by **De qui . . . ?** except when *Whose . . . ?* denotes possession. Ex.: **De qui** est-il le fils? (Whose *son is he?*) **De qui** est ce livre? (Whose *book is that?* = Who *is the author* of *that book?*)

But when *Whose . . .* + **être** . . . indicates possession, **À qui . . . ?** is used. Ex.: **À qui** est cette radio? (Whose *radio is that?*)

2. Under what circumstances is the interrogative *quel* used before some form of the verb *être*?

Quelle est la route la plus directe? — Which *is the shortest route?*

Quels sont ces hommes en noir? — Who *are these men in black?*

NOTE: It is also possible to say: «**Qui** sont ces hommes en noir?» But by using **Quels** the nature of the question is changed slightly to mean: *What sort of . . . ?*

The interrogative adjective is used before a form of the verb **être** to ask which of a number of possible answers is the case and to ask the nature of a person or thing.

A. Remplacez les tirets par la forme convenable de l'adjectif interrogatif.

1. *Quelle* est la vraie raison de votre départ?   2. Dans *quelle* rue habitent vos amis?   3. *quel* est votre acteur préféré?
4. *quels* pays étrangers avez-vous visités?   5. *quelles* sont les plus belles villes des États-Unis?   6. *quel* professeur!
7. *quelle* heure est-il?   8. *quelles* sont les dernières nouvelles?

B. Traduisez en français.

1. *(tu)* What dress do you want to wear?   2. Which is the best car this[1] year?   3. *(vous)* What are your favorite[2] songs?   4. *(tu)* What programs interest you the most?   5. What a catastrophe! 6. What is that girl's telephone number[3]?   7. *(tu)* What animals do you prefer, dogs[4] or cats[4]?

[1]de cette année   [2]The normal position for descriptive adjectives in French is treated fully on pages 20–22.   [3]numéro de téléphone   [4]Use the proper form of the definite article with these nouns.

II. Interrogative Pronouns

An interrogative pronoun is one that asks a question. In English, the interrogative pronouns are *who? whose? whom? which? what? which one?*

3. What interrogative pronoun is used in French to refer to persons?

Qui a ouvert la porte?	Who *opened the door?*
Qui avez-vous vu?	Whom *did you see?*
Avec **qui** êtes-vous sorti?	*With* whom *did you go out?*

In French, **qui** is the interrogative pronoun which refers to persons.

NOTE: For **qui** as the subject, the longer form **qui est-ce qui** may be used; for **qui** as the object, the longer form **qui est-ce que** may be used. But since the longer forms sometimes entail a change in word order, students are advised to use the shorter for the present.

4. When *qui* is the object of the sentence, what word order is used when the subject of the sentence is a pronoun? a noun?

Qui voyez-vous là-bas?	Whom *do you see over there?*
Qui Jacques voit-il là-bas?	Whom *does Jack see over there?*

When **qui** is the direct object of the sentence, note the word order:

Qui + VERB + PRONOUN SUBJECT
Qui + NOUN SUBJECT + VERB + PRONOUN SUBJECT

5. Which interrogative pronouns are used to refer to things in French?

Qu'est-ce qui est sur la table?	What *is on the table?*
Que faites-vous?	What *are you doing?*
Qu'est-ce que vous faites?	
Avec **quoi** avez-vous ouvert la boîte?	*With* what *did you open the box?*

The four French interrogative pronouns referring to things are **qu'est-ce qui, que, qu'est-ce que,** and **quoi.** Their use depends on their function in the sentence.

6. **When is** *que* **and when is** *qu'est-ce que* **used as the object of the sentence to refer to a thing?**

Que voyez-vous?
Qu'est-ce que vous voyez? } *What do you see?*

Que fait Françoise?
Qu'est-ce que Françoise fait? } *What does Frances do?*

When the direct object is a thing, either **que** or **qu'est-ce que** may be used, but notice the difference in word order:

Que + verb + subject	and	**Qu'est-ce que** + subject + verb

NOTE: In a question such as *What is John doing?*, where the subject of the sentence is a noun and the interrogative object is *what?*, the above word order must be used. Incorrect is "**Que** + noun subject + verb." WRONG: Que Jean fait-il là-bas? RIGHT: **Que fait Jean là-bas?** (*or*) **Qu'est-ce que Jean fait là-bas?**

7. **What are the various uses of the word** *quoi?*

De **quoi** parlez-vous?   *Of* what *are you speaking?*

—Ah! je vois quelque chose.   *"Oh, I see something."*
—**Quoi?**   *"What?"*

Je ne sais pas **quoi** faire.   *I don't know* what *to do.*

Quoi!
Comment! } Vous partez?   What! *You're leaving?*

The word **quoi** is used to refer to a thing after a preposition, it is used when asking *"What?"* alone, it is often used instead of **que** before an infinitive, especially in a negative sentence, and it is used to express the exclamatory *What!* **Comment!** may also be used to express *What!*

—Allez chercher le dossier du   *"Go and get the candidate's*
candidat.   *file."*
—**Comment?**   *"What?"*

In English, when we do not hear or do not understand what someone has said, we normally ask: *"What?"* The French normally ask «**Comment?**» rather than «**Quoi?**» under such circumstances. However, «**Quoi?**» is often used by children who have not yet learned the amenities and by certain uneducated people.

8. How can the interrogative pronouns be presented in graphic tabular form?

Function	Persons	Things
Subject	**qui**	**qu'est-ce qui**
Object	**qui**	$\begin{cases}\textbf{que} \\ \textbf{qu'est-ce que}\end{cases}$
After preposition	**qui**	**quoi**

C. Remplacez le mot anglais par son équivalent français.

1. (*Whom*) avez-vous vu en allant à la bibliothèque?   **2.** De (*what*) avez-vous parlé pendant mon absence?   **3.** À (*whom*) donc écrivez-vous toutes ces lettres?   **4.** (*What*) doit-on faire dans ce cas? **5.** (*What*) vous trouvez de si difficile dans ce devoir?   **6.** (*Who*) me montrera le chemin?   **7.** De (*whom*) est le roman que vous avez acheté?   **8.** (*What*) vous intéresse le plus dans ce livre?   **9.** (*What*) vous aimeriez faire maintenant?   **10.** (*What*) est sur votre bureau? **11.** Je vais vous faire un petit cadeau. (*What?*)

D. Traduisez en français.

1. Who took my ballpoint pen?   **2.** (*vous*) We don't have any[1] vase. In[2] what do you want to put these flowers?   **3.** (*tu*) What makes you laugh?   **4.** (*tu*) With whom are you going to the movies? **5.** (*vous*) What are you going to read?   **6.** (*tu*) Whom did your brother meet[3] at the station?   **7.** (*vous*) He seems[4] angry. What did you say to him?   **8.** Whom will Maurice and Marie see?   **9.** (*tu*) "I'd like to tell you something." "What?"   **10.** (*tu*) What! You're crying?

[1] **de**   [2] **dans**   [3] Use a form of **aller chercher.**   [4] Use a form of **avoir l'air.**

9. When is a form of *lequel* used to ask *which one* in French? What are the forms of *lequel*?

J'ai trois stylos. **Lequel** voulez-vous?	*I have three fountain pens. Which one do you want?*
Laquelle de ces personnes parle français?	*Which one of these persons speaks French?*

The interrogative *which one*, referring to a definite object already mentioned or mentioned immediately after *which one of,* is expressed by the following:

	Masculine	Feminine
Singular	**lequel**	**laquelle**
Plural	**lesquels**	**lesquelles**

These pronouns contract with **à** and **de** forming: **auquel, auxquels, auxquelles; duquel, desquels, desquelles.**

10. When must *qui, que,* or *qu'est-ce que* be used to express *which one*?

Que préférez-vous, le français ou l'italien?
Qu'est-ce que vous préférez, le français ou l'italien?

Which one *do you prefer, French or Italian?*

When asking a question about something which has not yet been mentioned, *which one* must be expressed by **qui . . . ?** (referring to persons), or **que . . . ?** or **qu'est-ce que . . . ?** (referring to things) except that *which one of* + THE OBJECT is expressed by a form of **lequel de** + THE OBJECT. Ex. **Lesquels de ces livres** est à vous?

E. Remplacez les tirets par la forme convenable de *lequel*. Faites les contractions nécessaires.

1. _____ de vous deux veut bien me prêter sa voiture?
2. —Votre ami est très original. —De _____ parlez-vous?
3. —Voyez-vous ces deux dames? — _____? 4. _____ de ses filles va épouser Henri? 5. Tous ces exercices sont bons, mais _____ sont les plus utiles?

F. Traduisez en français.

1. These watches are[1] expensive; I do not know which one to buy.
2. "There will be many difficulties." "Which?" 3. Which of the two roads[2] must we take? 4. (*vous*) Which do you prefer, tea[3] or coffee[3]? 5. (*tu*) I like Italian films a great deal[4]. Which ones do you prefer? 6. (*vous*) There are several programs this afternoon. Which one do you wish to see?

[1] Use a form of **coûter cher**. [2] routes [3] Either the definite or the partitive article is possible, depending on the meaning. [4] The adverb comes immediately after the verb.

11. When does French use a variation of *quel est . . .* to express *what is . . .* or *what are . . .*?

Quelle est la capitale de la Belgique?

What is *the capital of Belgium?*

Quels sont les produits les plus importants de ce pays?

What are *the most important products of that country?*

When *what is* ... or *what are* ... ask "which of a number of possibilities," French uses **quel est . . .** or some variation of it.

12. How does French express *what is . . .* **or** *what are . . .* **when asking a definition?**

> **Qu'est-ce que** la philosophie?   What is *philosophy?*
> **Qu'est-ce que c'est que** le   What is *communism?*
> communisme?
> **Qu'est-ce que c'est que** les   What are *mathematics?*
> mathématiques?

When *what is* ... or *what are* ... ask for a definition of a word, French uses either **qu'est-ce que . . .** or **qu'est-ce que c'est que . . .** + DEFINITE ARTICLE + that word.

G. Remplacez les tirets par l'équivalent de ***what is*** ou ***what are*** selon le cas.

1. _____ un programmateur?   2. _____ les présidents des États-Unis les plus connus?   3. _____ la biologie?   4. _____ votre fleur favorite?   5. _____ le meilleur système de gouvernement?

H. Traduisez en français.

1. What is the longest river in[1] the United States?   2. What is the Louvre?   3. What are the qualities of a good teacher?   4. What is democracy?   5. (*vous*) What is the aim of your work?

[1] Not «dans»

Exercices d'ensemble

I. Remplacez les mots anglais par leur équivalent français.

1. (*Which*) sorte de jeune fille Jacques veut-il épouser?   2. (*Who*) est là?   3. (*Which one*) aimez-vous le mieux, votre secrétaire ou la mienne?   4. (*What*) nous ferons cet après-midi?   5. Chez (*whom*) passerez-vous le week-end?   6. (*What*) l'empêche de venir?   7. (*What*) dites-vous?   8. (*What*) sont les fruits les plus nourrissants?   9. Avec (*whom*) allez-vous jouer au bridge?   10. (*Who*) est ce monsieur à la barbe blanche?   11. (*What is*) un mythe?   12. (*What*) vous me donnerez en échange?   13. (*What*) regardez-vous?   14. Avec (*what*) a-t-il fait cette réparation?   15. (*Whom*) êtes-vous allé voir?   16. Nous ne savons pas (*what*) faire.

J. Mettez les phrases suivantes à la forme interrogative, remplaçant les mots en italique par un pronom ou un adjectif interrogatif selon le cas.

MODEL: *Marie* a fermé la fenêtre. *Qui* a fermé la fenêtre?
Marie a fermé *cette* fenêtre. *Quelle* fenêtre Marie a-t-elle fermée?

1. *La cathédrale* se trouve au centre de la ville. 2. Il faut absolument voir *ce* film. 3. Paul a laissé *son courrier* sur mon bureau. 4. *Monsieur Galand* arrivera demain. 5. *Votre* client a téléphoné il y a une heure. 6. Ils ont ouvert la porte avec *un passe-partout.* 7. Pierre a rencontré *leur fils* dans la rue ce matin. 8. Il a trouvé *son* portefeuille dans la voiture. 9. Les autres comptent sur *Charles* pour les tirer d'affaire. 10. Il a enfin rendu *ce* livre à la bibliothèque. 11. Nos voisins vendront *leur maison* l'année prochaine.

K. Traduisez en français.

1. "What is the smallest state in[1] the United States?" "What?"[2] 2. What is a computer? 3. Who has just gone out? 4. To whom shall we give our old sofa? 5. Which are the most useful languages? 6. (*vous*) What sort of plays do you like to see? 7. Whom did the policeman arrest? 8. (*tu*) What are you speaking of? 9. (*vous*) What did your friends do last evening? 10. What is making that noise? 11. (*tu*) "What did you learn during your trip?" "Which one?" 12. What! Paul isn't here?

[1] Not «dans» [2] This "What?" indicates that the second speaker did not hear or understand the question.

Problem Words

1. actually

(a) When *actually* = *really*

Avez-vous **réellement** vu
l'accident?
Avez-vous **vraiment** vu
l'accident?

Did you actually *see the accident?*

When *actually* means *really,* it may be expressed by **vraiment, véritablement,** or **réellement,** depending on the sentence.

(b) When *actually* = *as a matter of fact*

Il caresse vos chats, mais **en fait**
il en a peur.
Il caresse vos chats, mais **à vrai
dire,** il en a peur.

He pets your cats, but actually *he is afraid of them.*

When *actually* means *as a matter of fact* and contradicts what seems to be the case, it may be expressed by **en fait** or **à vrai dire.**

CAUTION: Do NOT use «actuellement» for *actually*. It means *at present*.

2. advice

(a) How to say *a piece of advice*

Donnez-moi **un conseil.**	*Give me* a piece of advice.

The singular **un conseil** means *some advice* or *a piece of advice.*

(b) How to say *advice*

J'ai toujours écouté **les conseils** de mon vieux maître.	*I always listened to* the advice *of my old teacher.*

The word *advice* is expressed by the plural form, **les conseils.**

CAUTION: The French word **avis** means *opinion*. Do NOT use it for *advice*.

3. again

(a) The prefix **re-** + VERB = *again*

Voulez-vous **relire** cette phrase?	*Will you* read *that sentence* again?
Je te **retéléphonerai** tout de suite.	*I'll* telephone *you* again *right away.*

(b) **encore, encore une fois, de nouveau,** and **à nouveau** = *again*

Mon avocat m'a parlé **de nouveau** à ce sujet.	*My lawyer talked to me about that matter* again.
Est-ce que nous allons **encore** avoir la guerre?	*Are we going to have a war* again?
Faites cela **encore une fois.**	*Do that* again.

In affirmative sentences, *again* is expressed by **encore une fois,** and **de nouveau** and only occasionally by **à nouveau** and **encore.**

NOTE: The word **encore** usually means *still*, although it occasionally means *again*. Ex.: Je regrette d'être en retard. Je ne croyais pas que vous seriez **encore** ici.

(c) In negative sentences **ne . . . plus** = *again*

Je **ne** le ferai **plus.**	I *will* not *do it* again.

In negative sentences, *not . . . again* is often expressed by **ne . . . plus,** but it may also be expressed by **ne . . . re-** + VERB when **re-** + VERB exists.

4. agree

(a) When *agree to = consent to*

Monsieur Pommier **a consenti**
à venir parler devant notre
groupe.
Monsieur Pommier **a accepté**
de venir parler devant notre
groupe.

Mr. Pommier has agreed to
come and speak to our
group.

When *agree to* means *consent to,* it may be expressed by **consentir**
à or by **accepter de.**

(b) When *agree = be in agreement*

Ma femme et moi **sommes**
d'accord sur l'éducation de
nos enfants.

My wife and I agree on the
bringing-up of our children.

When *agree* means *be in agreement,* it may be expressed by **être**
d'accord.

(c) When *agreed = OK*

—Voulez-vous venir à six
heures?
—**C'est entendu.**

"Do you want to come at six
o'clock?"
"Agreed."

The English *agreed,* indicating assent, may be rendered by: **c'est en-**
tendu or by: **entendu,** or: **d'accord.**

(d) When *agree* is a grammatical term

L'adjectif **s'accorde** avec le
nom qu'il modifie.

The adjective agrees with the
noun it modifies.

Grammatical agreement is expressed by forms of the verb **s'accor-**
der.

CAUTION: DO NOT use «agréer» for *agree.* French use **agréer** only in
special situations, and it normally means *accept.*

L. Remplacez les mots anglais par leur équivalent français.

1. Jacques est (*again*) en retard. **2.** Est-ce que le participe passé
(*agrees*) avec le sujet? **3.** Vos (*advice*) sont toujours très utiles.
4. Il paraît que Marcel est (*actually*) très malade. **5.** Le patron
(*agreed to*) vous voir ce soir après cinq heures. **6.** Je vous répète
(*again*) que vous regretterez cette action. **7.** (*Actually*), j'aimerais
mieux ne pas aller voir cet opéra. **8.** (*Advice*) ne servent à rien à
la plupart des gens. **9.** Il faut (*begin the lesson again*).
10. —Voulez-vous venir me chercher à midi? —(*Agreed*).
11. Je (*agree*) avec vous sur la politique actuelle.

M. Traduisez en français. Attention aux mots en italique.

1. (*vous*) Copy that exercise *again*.   2. He *agreed* to write a letter of recommendation for me.   3. (*tu*) Do you want me to give you a piece of good *advice?*   4. John says he works hard, but *actually* he wastes a great deal of time.   5. (*vous*) You should follow my *advice*.   6. Jack told me that he would not smoke *again*. 7. (*vous*) We all *agree* that you must leave immediately.   8. (tu) Did you *actually* go to the movies yesterday evening?   9. (*tu*) Tell me *again* what you want.   10. Does the present participle *agree* with the noun it modifies?   11. I heard that noise *again* last night. 12. (*vous*) You don't see them? Look *again*.

Verb Review

Review the verbs **parler** and **finir** according to the outline on page 253.

CHAPTER

2

Adjectives

L'auteur imagine une nouvelle version de *Robinson Crusoé*. Après vingt-huit ans, un navire anglais, le Whitebird, fait escale dans son île. Robinson dîne et passe la soirée sur ce bateau, mais au lieu de partir il décide de rester dans son île, baptisée par lui Speranza. Le Whitebird est maintenant parti.

Lever de soleil

L'aube était blême[1] encore lorsque Robinson descendit de son arbre. Il avait pris l'habitude de dormir jusqu'aux *dernières* minutes qui précèdent le lever du soleil, afin de réduire autant que possible cette période *atone*[2], *la plus déshéritée*[3] de la journée . . . Mais les viandes *inhabi-*
5 *tuelles,* les vins et aussi une *sourde*[4] angoisse[5] lui avaient donné un sommeil *fiévreux*[6]. Couché, enveloppé de ténèbres[7], il avait été la proie[8] sans défense d'idées *fixes* et d'obsessions *torturantes.* Il avait eu hâte de se lever pour secouer cette meute[9] *imaginaire.*

Il fit *quelques* pas sur la plage. L'eau était grise sous le ciel *décoloré*[10].
10 Une rosée[11] *abondante* alourdissait[12] les plantes qui se courbaient *éplorées*[13] sous cette lumière *pâle, navrée*[14]. Les oiseaux observaient un silence *glacé* . . . Sur la grève une vague s'étirait[15] mollement[16], jouait un peu avec un crabe *mort,* et se retirait, *déçue.* Dans *quelques* minutes le soleil se lèverait et regonflerait[17] de vie et de joie *toutes* choses et
15 Robinson lui-même.

Le soleil lança ses *premières* flèches. Une cigale grinça[18]. Une mouette[19] tournoya dans l'air et se laissa tomber sur le miroir d'eau. Elle rebondit à sa surface et s'éleva à *grands* coups d'ailes, un poisson d'argent en

---

[1] *very pale*   [2] *colorless*   [3] *wretched*   [4] *numb*   [5] *anguish*   [6] *feverish*   [7] *shadows*
[8] *prey*   [9] *pack*   [10] *colorless*   [11] *dew*   [12] *weighted down*   [13] *in tears*   [14] *heart-rending*   [15] *stretched*   [16] *gently*   [17] *would pump life into*   [18] *chirped*   [19] *gull*

13

travers du bec. En un instant le ciel devint céruléen[20]. Les fleurs
20 pivotèrent[21] toutes ensemble sur leurs tiges en ouvrant leurs pétales du
côté du levant[22]. Les oiseaux et les insectes emplirent l'espace d'un concert *unanime* . . . Redressant[23] sa *haute* taille, Robinson faisait face à
l'extase *solaire*[24] avec une joie presque *douloureuse.* Le rayonnement[25]
qui l'enveloppait le lavait des souillures[26] *mortelles* de la journée *pré-*
25 *cédente* et de la nuit. Un glaive[27] de feu entrait en lui . . . Speranza se
dégageait[28] des voiles de la brume, *vierge* et *intacte.* En vérité cette
longue agonie, ce *noir* cauchemar[29] n'avaient jamais eu lieu . . . Une
profonde inspiration l'emplit d'un sentiment d'assouvissement[30] *total.*
Sa poitrine bombait[31] comme un bouclier[32] d'airain. Ses jambes
30 prenaient[33] appui sur le roc, *massives* et *inébranlables*[34] comme des
colonnes. La lumière *fauve*[35] le revêtait[36] d'une armure[37] de jeunesse
inaltérable . . . Enfin l'astre-dieu[38] déploya[39] tout *entière* sa couronne
de cheveux *rouges* dans des explosions de cymbales et des stridences[40]
de trompettes.

D'après Michel Tournier, membre de l'Académie Goncourt, poète, philosophe,
un des premiers écrivains d'aujourd'hui. (*Vendredi ou Les Limbes du Pacifique,*
Gallimard, 1967)

---

[20] *bluish*   [21] *turned around*   [22] *rising sun*   [23] *straightening up*   [24] *of the sun*
[25] *radiance*   [26] *impurities*   [27] *sword*   [28] *was coming out*   [29] *nightmare*
[30] *fulfillment*   [31] *bulged*   [32] bouclier d'airain *brass shield*   [33] prenait appui *got a*
footing   [34] *immovable*   [35] *fawn-colored*   [36] *clothed*   [37] *armor*   [38] *the star god*
(i.e., the sun)   [39] *unfurled*   [40] *shrieking*

An adjective is a word that modifies a noun or pronoun. Ex.: the *green*
house; the *tall* tree; the *interesting* letter. The house is *green.* The trees
were *tall.* The letter will be *interesting.*

I.   The Formation of Adjectives

In English, adjectives have one form only. In French, they usually have
four forms: masculine singular, feminine singular, masculine plural, feminine plural.

PLURAL OF ADJECTIVES

1. How do most French adjectives form their masculine plural?

petit   petit**s**

Most French adjectives form their masculine plural by adding **-s** to the
masculine singular.

2. **What about the masculine plural of adjectives whose masculine singular ends in *-s, -x,* or *-z?***

gris	gris
heureu**x**	heureu**x**

Adjectives whose masculine singular ends in **-s, -x,** or **-z** do not change in the masculine plural.

3. **What about the masculine plural of adjectives whose masculine singular ends in *-eau?***

nouv**eau**   nouv**eaux**

Adjectives whose masculine singular ends in **-eau** add **-x** to form the masculine plural.

4. **What about the masculine plural of adjectives whose masculine singular ends in *-al?***

nation**al**   nation**aux**

Most adjectives whose masculine singular ends in **-al** change the **-al** to **-aux** in the masculine plural.

5. **How is the feminine plural of adjectives formed?**

petite	petite**s**
grise	grise**s**
nouvelle	nouvelle**s**
nationale	nationale**s**

Feminine adjectives normally form their plural by adding **-s** to the feminine singular form.

A. Écrivez le pluriel de l'adjectif indiqué.

1. des chats (gris)   2. de (nouveau) livres   3. de (grand) événements   4. des enfants très (gentil)   5. deux (gros) garçons 6. des personnes (distingué)   7. de (riche) touristes   8. de (mauvais) livres   9. des hôtels (élégant)   10. de (vieux) amis 11. des amis (loyal)   12. de (beau) musées

FEMININE OF ADJECTIVES

English adjectives have no feminine form. French adjectives have a special feminine form. The forms of the examples that follow are given in this order:

masculine singular; feminine singular;
masculine plural; feminine plural.

6. How do most adjectives form their feminine singular and plural?

petit	petite		petits	petites
fermé	fermée		fermés	fermées

Most adjectives form their feminine singular by adding **-e** to the masculine singular form.

7. What about adjectives whose masculine form ends in unaccented -e?

difficile	difficile	difficiles difficiles

Adjectives whose masculine form ends in unaccented **-e** do not change in the feminine.

8. What about certain adjectives whose masculine form ends in -e- + CONSONANT?

premier	première	,	premiers	premières
étranger	étrangère		étrangers	étrangères
complet	complète		complets	complètes

Certain adjectives whose masculine form ends in **-e- +** CONSONANT place a grave accent **(`)** over this **-e-** as well as adding the regular **-e** to form the feminine.

9. What about adjectives whose masculine form ends in -f?

actif	active	actifs	actives
neuf	neuve	neufs	neuves

Adjectives whose masculine form ends in **-f** change the **-f** to **-ve** in the feminine.

10. What about adjectives whose masculine form ends in -x?

nombreux	nombreuse	nombreux	nombreuses
heureux	heureuse	heureux	heureuses

Adjectives whose masculine form ends in **-x** change the **-x** to **-se** in the feminine.

11. What about adjectives whose masculine form ends in -el, -eil, -ien, -as, and -os?

quel	quelle	quels	quelles
pareil	pareille	pareils	pareilles
ancien	ancienne	anciens	anciennes
bas	basse	bas	basses
gros	grosse	gros	grosses

Adjectives whose masculine form ends in **-el, -eil, -ien, -as,** and **-os** double the final consonant before adding **-e.**

12. What are the irregular feminine forms of the adjectives *blanc, bon, doux, épais, faux, frais, gentil, grec, long, public,* and *sec*?

blanc	**blanche**	blancs	**blanches**	*white*
bon	**bonne**	bons	**bonnes**	*good*
doux	**douce**	doux	**douces**	*soft, sweet*
épais	**épaisse**	épais	**épaisses**	*thick*
faux	**fausse**	faux	**fausses**	*false*
frais	**fraîche**	frais	**fraîches**	*fresh*
gentil	**gentille**	gentils	**gentilles**	*nice*
grec	**grecque**	grecs	**grecques**	*Greek*
long	**longue**	longs	**longues**	*long*
public	**publique**	publics	**publiques**	*public*
sec	**sèche**	secs	**sèches**	*dry*

B. Écrivez la forme féminine de l'adjectif indiqué.

1. une leçon (difficile)   **2.** des femmes (actif)   **3.** la semaine (dernier)   **4.** deux robes (pareil)   **5.** une (long) histoire   **6.** les familles (nombreux)   **7.** des chaussures (usé)   **8.** la maison (blanc)   **9.** des chansons (italien)   **10.** les populations (natif)   **11.** des années (heureux)   **12.** une armoire (massif)   **13.** une nuit (frais)   **14.** des jeunes filles (sérieux)

13. What are the masculine and feminine singular and plural forms of the adjectives *beau, fou, mou, nouveau,* and *vieux,* and when is the second masculine form used?

SINGULAR			PLURAL		
MASCULINE					
(before consonant)	*(before vowel)*	FEMININE	MASCULINE	FEMININE	
beau	**bel**	belle	beaux	belles	*beautiful*
fou	**fol**	folle	fous	folles	*foolish*
mou	**mol**	molle	mous	molles	*soft*
nouveau	**nouvel**	nouvelle	nouveaux	nouvelles	*new*
vieux	**vieil**	vieille	vieux	vieilles	*old*

Some adjectives have two masculine singular forms, one of which is used when the word it directly precedes begins with a consonant, the other when the word it directly precedes begins with a vowel or a mute **h.** In the plural, they have only one form for the masculine and one for the feminine.

C. Écrivez la forme convenable de l'adjectif indiqué.

1. de (vieux) rues   **2.** la (nouveau) mode   **3.** un très (beau) homme   **4.** le (nouveau) an   **5.** une vitesse (fou)   **6.** une personne un peu (mou)   **7.** de (vieux) souvenirs   **8.** les (beau) quartiers   **9.** un (vieux) oncle   **10.** de (vieux) dames   **11.** un (beau) arbre

II.   Comparison of Adjectives

In English, adjectives are compared with *more* or *less* (comparative degree) and *most* and *least* (superlative degree) if they have more than two syllables.

POSITIVE	COMPARATIVE	SUPERLATIVE
beautiful	*more* beautiful	*most* beautiful
interesting	*less* interesting	*least* interesting

French adjectives are compared in somewhat the same way.

14. How are French adjectives compared?

POSITIVE	COMPARATIVE	SUPERLATIVE
cher	**plus** cher	**le plus** cher
difficile	**moins** difficile	**le moins** difficile

The comparative form of the French adjective is formed by placing **plus** (*more*) or **moins** (*less*) before the positive form. The superlative form is reached by placing the definite article (**le, la, les**) before the comparative form.

15. How are the adjectives *bon, mauvais,* and *petit* compared?

POSITIVE	COMPARATIVE	SUPERLATIVE
bon	**meilleur**	**le meilleur**
mauvais	{ **plus mauvais** { **pire**	{ **le plus mauvais** { **le pire**
petit	{ **plus petit** { **moindre**	{ **le plus petit** { **le moindre**

The adjective **bon** is always compared irregularly, the adjectives **mauvais** and **petit** have a regular and irregular comparative form. The form **moindre** is ordinarily used in the superlative and means *slightest*.

16. How is *than* expressed in French?

Les hivers sont plus froids que les autres saisons.

After a comparative, *than* is expressed by **que**.

BUT

Nous avons **plus de vingt** pages à lire.
Vous avez **moins de dix** minutes pour y arriver.

After **plus** and **moins** before a numeral *than* is expressed by **de**.

17. When the superlative form of an adjective follows its noun, what is the sign of the superlative?

Pour moi le russe est la langue <u>**la plus difficile**</u> á apprendre.

When the superlative form of an adjective follows its noun, the definite article must always directly precede **plus** or **moins.**

18. What preposition regularly follows the French superlative?

La France et la Russie sont les pays les plus grands **d'**Europe.	*France and Russia are the largest countries* in *Europe.*
Quel est le meilleur élève **de** la classe?	*Who is the best pupil* in *the class?*

In English, the superlative is usually followed by *in.* But in French, **de** is regularly used after the superlative.

19. How is the *as . . . as* **comparative expressed in French?**

Jacques est **aussi** consciencieux **que** Paul.	*Jacques is as conscientious as Paul.*
Le français n'est **pas aussi** difficile **que** le latin.	*French is not as hard as Latin.*

The comparison with *as . . . as* is called the comparative of equality. In French this comparative is formed with **aussi . . . que.** In present-day French, the negative is expressed by **pas aussi . . . que.**

D. Remplacez les adjectifs indiqués entre parenthèses par le comparatif ou le superlatif de l'adjectif, selon le cas. Faites l'accord de l'adjectif avec le nom.

1. Robert est l'élève (vif) de la classe.   **2.** Est-ce que les hommes sont (curieux) que les femmes?   **3.** L'étoile du Berger est (brillant) des étoiles.   **4.** Les automobiles françaises sont (petit) que les américaines.   **5.** Quels sont les livres (récent) de votre bibliothèque?   **6.** Je trouve les poires (savoureux) que les pommes. **7.** Mon chien est mon (bon) ami.   **8.** Le tennis est bien (fatigant) que le ping-pong.   **9.** Les (beau) années sont souvent celles de la jeunesse.   **10.** Il travaille plus et pourtant ses résultats sont (mauvais) que l'année dernière.

E. Remplacez les mots anglais par leur équivalent français.

1. Voici les meilleurs élèves (*in*) la classe.   **2.** Il habite dans la plus belle maison (*in*) la ville.   **3.** Je vais vous montrer le timbre le plus rare (*in*) ma collection.   **4.** Nous avons moins (*than*) cent dollars pour faire le voyage.   **5.** Qui est plus chargé de responsabilités (*than*) le président?   **6.** Ce chien est (*as*) méchant (*as*) un loup. **7.** Les routes sont (*as*) bonnes en France (*as*) en Angleterre.   **8.** Les prix des repas ne sont pas (*as*) élevés en Espagne (*as*) en Italie.

F. Traduisez en français.

1. What is the largest city in Canada?   **2.** He refuses to read even the most interesting books.   **3.** I never have more than five dollars with[1] me.   4. He has nothing, but he is as happy as a king.   5. His closest friends do not understand his attitude.   6. A conversation[2] class is too large if there are more than twelve students.   7. (*vous*) I waited for you more than half an hour.   8. Motorcycles are more dangerous than cars.   9. The shortest answers are sometimes the best.   10. He allows[3] himself to be stopped by the slightest difficulty.   11. The richest people are often the least generous.

[1] sur   [2] classe de conversation   [3] Use a form of se laisser arrêter.

III.   Position of Adjectives

In English, adjectives precede their nouns. Ex.: *bad* weather, *disagreeable* work.

20. What is the normal position of a descriptive adjective in French?

Il m'a fait une proposition **intéressante.**
C'est une maison **blanche.**
Quelles sont les couleurs du drapeau **français?**
Voulez-vous du pain **grillé?**

In French, descriptive adjectives normally follow their nouns. They distinguish the object under consideration from others of its kind. Adjectives of color, nationality, and religion and past participles almost always follow their noun.

21. Why are descriptive adjectives sometimes placed before their noun?

Il a été victime d'un **terrible accident.**
M. Garet est un **excellent professeur.**
Chenonceaux est un **magnifique château** de la Renaissance.
Elle oubliait la **triste soirée** de la veille.

Many descriptive adjectives may precede their noun for stylistic effect. In such cases, the adjective, which usually indicates a quality inherent in the noun, adorns its noun rather than distinguishing it from other objects of its kind.

22. When an adjective has both a literal and a figurative meaning, where is the adjective usually placed to denote its figurative meaning?

une **porte étroite**	un **lac profond**
une **étroite amitié**	un **profond sentiment**
une **boisson amère**	un **chat maigre**
un **amer reproche**	un **maigre salaire**

Certain adjectives are sometimes placed before and sometimes after their noun. They usually have a literal meaning when they follow their noun and take on a figurative meaning when they precede the noun.

23. What is the meaning of the following adjectives when they precede and when they follow their noun?

MEANING WHEN PRECEDING NOUN	ADJECTIVE	MEANING WHEN FOLLOWING NOUN
former	**ancien**	*old, ancient*
fine, good (referring to a person)	**brave**	*brave* (but usually the word **courageux** is used instead)
certain (one of many)	**certain**	*certain (sure)*
dear, beloved	**cher**	*dear, expensive*
last (of a series)	**dernier**	*last* (used with time element to indicate the one just passed)
different, various	**différent**	*different (unlike)*
same	**même**	*very*
many different kinds	**nombreux**	*many of the same kind*
poor (unfortunate)	**pauvre**	*poor (not rich)* (ordinarily used with **très**)
next (in a series)	**prochain**	*next* (used with time element to indicate one about to come)
own	**propre**	*clean*
darned, confounded	**sacré**	*sacred*
ugly, bad	**sale**	*dirty*
only	**seul**	*alone*
mere	**simple**	*simple in character*
real	**vrai**	*true*

NOTE: Exceptionally, in the expression **le sacré coeur** the word **sacré** means *sacred* even though it precedes its noun.

24. What is the position of limiting adjectives in French?

deux leçons	**ces** journaux	**son** père
quelles difficultés	**plusieurs** personnes	**quelques** amis

Numerals, both cardinal and ordinal, and demonstrative, interrogative, possessive, and indefinite adjectives regularly precede their noun. These are called LIMITING ADJECTIVES, for they limit the meaning of the noun.

25. What about the position of the short, common descriptive adjectives?

une **autre** femme	un **beau** rêve	une **bonne** solution
une **grande** ville	un **jeune** enfant	une **jolie** maison
une **longue** histoire	un **mauvais** tour	une **petit** bouche

A number of commonly used short adjectives regularly precede their noun. The most common of these are: **autre, bon, gentil, grand, gros, haut, jeune, long, mauvais, méchant, meilleur, moindre, nouveau, petit, vieux,** and **vilain.**

NOTE: The superlative of most of these short adjectives is formed by **le (la, les)** + **plus** + ADJECTIVE. The superlative forms of <u>these</u> particular adjectives only may either precede or follow the noun. Ex.: C'est **la plus longue** rue de la ville. (*or*) C'est la rue **la plus longue** de la ville.

G. Mettez l'adjectif à la position convenable, en faisant l'accord de l'adjectif.

1. (rouge) une fleur   2. (inestimable) des trésors   3. (difficile) une leçon   4. (mauvais) une route   5. (anglican) l'église   6. (gentil) un garçon   7. (social) les conflits   8. (bruyant) une salle   9. (insupportable) des enfants   10. (noir) le drapeau   11. (usé) des souliers   12. (profond) un puits   13. (absolu) un monarque   14. (réussi) un spectacle   15. (vert) des volets   16. (secondaire) les écoles   17. (indien) des étoffes

H. Traduisez en français. Faites attention à l'accord et à la position de l'adjectif.

1. We saw a terrible[1] accident.   2. There are American tourists in every country in[2] the world.   3. There is a real hero.   4. There are still certain[3] difficulties.   5. We want a free country. 6. Those fine people don't have any luck.   7. It was a somber story.   8. High[4] mountains separate those two countries.   9. (*tu*) You always make the same mistakes.   10. There is a slight difference between those two words.   11. (*vous*) Take[5] a course with that excellent professor.   12. Paul has a bad cold.   13. I like illustrated magazines.   14. (*vous*) Have you seen those elegant models?   15. I should like a good warm meal.   16. That book made a deep impression on the students.   17. (*vous*) Next week you will write your last résumé.

[1] Consider this as an adjective used to adorn its noun for stylistic effect, as described in §21.   [2] du   [3] Do not use the partitive or any substitute for it here.   [4] Use a form of **haut**. Place **de** in front of **haut**.   [5] Use a form of **suivre**.

Exercices d'ensemble

I. Remplacez les tirets par le mot convenable.

1. Louise est la meilleure pianiste _____ groupe.   2. Paul dispose-t-il de plus de temps _____ vous?   3. Nous avons moins _____ trois heures à passer à Dijon.   4. Je ne suis pas _____ riche que mon partenaire.   5. La Russie est-elle plus grande _____ le Canada?   6. Le chinois est une des langues les plus difficiles _____ monde.   7. Monsieur Blanc a perdu plus _____ la moitié de sa fortune à la bourse.

J. Introduisez les adjectifs indiqués dans la phrase pour modifier le nom en italique. Faites l'accord de l'adjectif avec le nom.

1. (merveilleux)[1] J'aimerais revoir ces *paysages* de Grèce.
2. (méchant) Cet *animal* devrait être attaché.   **3.** (propre) Avez-vous votre *rasoir*?   **4.** (public) L'*opinion* favorise ce changement.
5. (humble) Je suis votre *serviteur,* comme on disait autrefois.
6. (amer) Vous devriez goûter le *sirop* que je prends le soir.
7. (sacré) Ce *chien*! Il aboie tout le temps.   **8.** (vrai) Ce vieux bonhomme est un *avare*.   **9.** (maigre) On nous a servi un *repas*.
10. (grave)[1] Demain nous discuterons cette *affaire*.
11. (intéressant)[1] Cette *hypothèse* a été condamnée par l'expérience.
12. (profond) Avez-vous remarqué le *malaise* qui règne dans ce pays?

[1] Consider this as an adjective used to adorn its noun for stylistic effect as described in §21.

K. Traduisez en français. Attention aux adjectifs.

1. I find her much prettier than her sister.   **2.** (*tu*) Will you finish your studies next month?   **3.** The most expensive products are not always the best.   **4.** The young people were exchanging ardent glances.   **5.** (*vous*) You sent me some beautiful carnations.
6. We made the trip more than ten years ago.   **7.** Certain[2] pupils do not work enough.   **8.** (*tu*) I like your nice apartment.   **9.** The Italians are one of the most musical peoples in the world.   **10.** They are richer than we, but are they happier?   **11.** (*vous*) Do you write to your former teacher from time to time?   **12.** (*tu*) My examinations are harder than yours.

[1] Consider this adjective as being used to adorn its noun for stylistic effect.   [2] Do not use the partitive or any substitute for it here.

Problem Words

5. become

(a) When *become* is followed by a NOUN

Jacques **est devenu officier.**   *Jack* became an officer.

The verb *become* is **devenir,** and when a noun follows *become,* the French usually employ a form of **devenir.**

(b) When *become* is followed by an ADJECTIVE

Ne **vous fâchez** pas si je vous dis cela.

Don't become angry *if I tell you that.*

Le patron **s'est impatienté** en vous attendant.

The boss became impatient while waiting for you.

French often uses the reflexive form of a verb where English uses *become* + ADJECTIVE.

(c) How to express *became* in certain idiomatic expressions

Tout à coup **il a fait** très **chaud.**	*Suddenly* it became *very* warm.
Vers onze heures **j'ai eu** très **sommeil.**	*About eleven o'clock* I became *very* sleepy.

The English *became* + ADJECTIVE is often expressed in French by using the simple past or the compound past of the verb. This is especially true in the case of idiomatic expressions with **avoir** and **faire.**

CAUTION: Avoid using **devenir** + ADJECTIVE. To express *become* + ADJECTIVE, French occasionally does use **devenir** + ADJECTIVE, but far more often it uses a reflexive verb or a past tense of **avoir** or **être.**

6. better

(a) When *better* is an adjective

Je cherche une **meilleure** solution.	*I am looking for a* better *solution.*

As an adjective, *better* is normally expressed by **meilleur.**

Ces peintures sont **mieux** que les autres.	*These paintings are* better *than the others.*

However, when the English adjective *better* is to be expressed after a form of **être,** French sometimes uses **mieux.** In such cases, a form of **meilleur** could also be used.

(b) When *better* is an adverb

Jacques lit **mieux** que Jean.	*Jack reads* better *than John.*

The adverb *better* is expressed by **mieux.**

(c) How to say *much better*

Le livre est **bien meilleur** que le film. Le livre est **beaucoup mieux** que le film.	*The book is* much better *than the film.*

After forms of **être,** *much better* may be expressed by **bien meilleur, bien mieux,** or **beaucoup mieux.** But the French do not say «beaucoup meilleur».

Cet élève comprend { **bien** **beaucoup** } **mieux** l'algèbre maintenant.	*This pupil understands algebra* much better *now.*

As an adverb, *much better* is either **beaucoup mieux** or **bien mieux.**

CAUTION: When expressing *better* in French, determine whether it is used as an adjective or an adverb. DO NOT use «meilleur» as an adverb.

CAUTION: DO NOT use «beaucoup meilleur» for *much better*. This combination does not exist in French.

7. bring

(a) How to say *bring a thing*

Apportez-moi ce livre.   Bring *me that book.*

When it is a question of *bringing a thing,* French usually employs a form of **apporter.**

(b) How to say *bring a person*

Est-ce que je pourrais **amener**   *Could I* bring *my husband?*
mon mari?

When it is a question of *bringing a person,* a form of **amener** is used. But **amener** is also used for taking a person somewhere.

CAUTION: DO NOT use «apporter» when it is a question of bringing a *person.*

8. can

(a) When *can = be able*

Vous ne **pouvez** pas porter cela   *You can*not *carry that all alone.*
tout seul. Laissez-moi vous   *Let me help you.*
aider.

The English *can* (= *be able*) is ordinarily expressed by **pouvoir.**

(b) When *can = may*

Vous **pouvez** partir si vous
voulez.   *You* $\left\{ \begin{array}{l} can \\ may \end{array} \right.$ *leave if you wish.*

Careful speakers of English distinguish between *can* and *may*. In French, the verb *pouvoir* is used for both ideas.

(c) When to use **je peux** and when **je puis**

Je peux vous accompagner de-   I can *go with you tomorrow.*
main.
Puis-je vous voir à huit heures?   Can I *see you at eight o'clock?*

The **je** form of the present tense of **pouvoir** is both **peux** and **puis.** In non-interrogative sentences **je peux** is normally used. When an interrogative sentence has inverted word order, **puis-je** is used, but this form is mainly literary.

(d) When *can* = *know how to*

Est-ce que Thérèse **sait**   Can *Theresa drive?*
conduire?

When *can* = *know how to,* French often uses a form of **savoir** rather than of **pouvoir.**

L. Remplacez les mots anglais par leur équivalent français.

1. Il a fallu à Georges plusieurs années d'études pour (*become*) pharmacien.   **2.** N'hésitez pas à (*bring*) votre frère; nous serons très heureux de faire sa connaissance.   **3.** La représentation des *Femmes savantes* était bien, mais celle du *Misanthrope* était (*better*). **4.** Les programmes du dimanche sont (*much better*) que ceux de la semaine.   **5.** (*Can*) -vous me dire l'heure?   **6.** Quand la lumière s'est éteinte, tout le monde (*became frightened*[1]).   **7.** Les résultats de cet étudiant sont (*better*) ce trimestre.   **8.** Finis tes études avant de te marier, ce serait (*much better*).   **9.** (*Can*) -on traverser l'Atlantique en moins de trois heures?   **10.** Prenez plutôt cette route; elle est (*better*) que l'autre.   **11.** On (*becomes tired*) à faire toujours la même chose.   **12.** Claude nous (*brings*) toujours des chocolats quand il vient nous voir.   **13.** François a beaucoup souffert ces derniers jours, mais maintenant il se sent (*better*). **14.** Les repas dans ce petit bistrot sont (*much better*) que dans les autres restaurants du quartier.

[1] Use a form of **avoir peur.**

M. Traduisez en français. Attention aux mots en italique.

1. The climate of the Riviera would be *much better* for them. **2.** (*vous*) Could you explain this problem to me?   **3.** Henry *became* interested in that writer after hearing his lecture[1].   **4.** (*tu*) If these stamps interest you, I'll *bring* you my collection next week. **5.** The day[2] was warm, but it *became* cold as soon as the sun set. **6.** (*vous*) Can your fiancée play the[3] piano?   **7.** (*vous*) It is in Paris that you will find the *best* perfumes.   **8.** Mr. Borel *became* one of the directors of the company[4].   **9.** *Can* I *bring* my friend Roger to the next meeting of our club?   **10.** Pierrette finally *brought* us the snapshots of her family.   **11.** (*vous*) *Bring* me what you have just written.   **12.** (*tu*) *Can* you type?

[1] Not «lecture»   [2] journée   [3] Not «le»   [4] société

Verb Review

Review the verbs **dormir** and **perdre** according to the outline on page 253.

CHAPTER
3

Adverbs

L'auteur, ayant couché dans la grange de fermiers dans un hameau au centre de la France, repart à l'aube pour continuer sa marche de mille kilomètres à travers le pays. Il parle ici de ses rencontres avec les chiens.

Les chiens

Dès l'orée[1] du village, le sentier grimpe[2] au flanc d'une colline raide[3] en longeant une longue forêt. Dans un grand pré, juste à côté, une femme garde *tranquillement* ses vaches. Près d'elle un chien au museau[4] noir hésite, hargneux[5]: qui est cet intrus, ce vagabond, cet homme bon à
5 mordre avec ses mollets[6] bien dodus[7]? Des chiens, j'en ai vu des centaines au cours de ce voyage. À l'exception de quelques cas, ces rencontres se placèrent toutes sous le signe d'une incompréhension totale—et sans doute réciproque. Est-ce le bâton que je prends *parfois (pas toujours d'ailleurs* car il est *plutôt* gênant[8] dans les montées[9] et je
10 l'envoie[10] *bien souvent* promener) est-ce *donc* ce bâton ou la seule vue d'un inconnu qui agace les chiens? *Généralement,* ils se contentaient de me suivre à distance respectueuse et sans *trop* empiéter[11] sur ma route. Moi, j'avançais *négligemment* comme si je *n'*avais *rien* remarqué. Les gens[12] malins—et ceux qui savent *toujours* tout—vous diront qu'un chien
15 *n'*attaque *jamais* un passant hors de son propre territoire. Erreur. J'en ai fait l'expérience maintes fois . . . D'autres vous expliqueront qu'il suffit de *ne pas* avoir peur (*personnellement,* je *n'*ai *jamais* eu peur, j'ai éprouvé *seulement* des inquiétudes pour mes mollets), de les approcher *gentiment,* de leur parler, de les flatter, d'attendre qu'ils vous flairent[13] et se
20 calment. Erreur *aussi.* Ce *n'*est *pas toujours* vrai. Non. Quiconque envisage une marche à pied à travers la France doit savoir que son problème

---

[1] *edge*   [2] *climb*   [3] *steep*   [4] *snout*   [5] *snarling*   [6] *calf (of the leg)*   [7] *plump*
[8] *bothersome*   [9] *slopes*   [10] l'envoie promener *throw it away*   [11] *encroach*   [12] les
gens malins *the "wise guys"*   [13] *sniff*

27

numéro un *ne* sera *ni* la faim, *ni* la soif, *ni* la fatigue, *ni* les entorses[14], *ni* les marécages[15] . . . mais LES CHIENS. On *n*'imagine *pas* le nombre de chiens qu'il peut y avoir en France. J'en ai rencontré *partout* . . .

25   Il y a quelques jours, je me trouvai sur une route de montagne sur le chemin d'un chien errant[16] qui décida que je *ne* ferais *pas* un pas *de plus*—et cela dans un paysage *entièrement* dépourvu[17] de trace d'habitation et d'être humain. Je *ne* sus *que* faire. Impossible d'avancer d'un pas: le fauve[18] l'emboîtait. *De plus,* c'était un chien-loup, de belle taille,

30   à l'oeil rouge et aux crocs[19] bien visibles, si furieux, si hurlant contre moi que je le crus un moment enragé[20]. Il se tenait à un mètre, gueule[21] ouverte, prêt à bondir. *Stoïquement,* je lui tournai le dos, essayant de continuer ma route. Mais je dus m'arrêter. Je le sentais sur mes mollets, prêt à me mordre. Impossible de continuer *ainsi* . . . Je restai au milieu

35   de la route, indécis, dans l'espoir que quelqu'un passerait et qu'à[22] deux, on trouverait sans doute une solution. Mais *personne ne* se montra, *aussi* adoptai-je une nouvelle tactique. Je posai mon sac sur la route, *lentement,* et je m'assis *dessus. Puis,* je tendis ma main à l'animal, en lui[23] prodiguant les noms les plus flatteurs (et les moins mérités). Il cessa d'aboyer un

40   instant, m'observa, *puis* aboya de[24] plus belle. J'insistai. *Alors,* toujours grognant[25], il s'approcha *lentement,* flaira *longtemps* ma main tendue *puis* d'un coup partit *droit* dans la direction opposée.

D'après Jacques Lacarrière, grand voyageur, à travers la France comme ici, et dans le monde méditerranéen, la Grèce notamment, sur laquelle il a écrit les plus beaux livres. (*Chemin faisant,* Fayard, 1974)

---

[14] *sprains*   [15] *marshes*   [16] *roving*   [17] dépourvu de *without*   [18] le fauve l'emboîtait *the beast followed step by step*   [19] crocs [kro] *fangs*   [20] *mad, rabid*   [21] *mouth (of an animal)*   [22] à deux *together*   [23] lui prodiguant *lavishing on him*   [24] de plus belle *even more*   [25] *growling*

An adverb is a word that modifies a verb, an adjective, or another adverb. Ex.: He writes *clearly*. They have a *very* difficult lesson. He speaks *somewhat* slowly.

I.   Formation of Adverbs

1. How are adverbs usually formed from adjectives?

| rapide | rapide**ment** | | sérieux | sérieuse**ment** |
| vrai | vrai**ment** | | naturel | naturelle**ment** |

Many French adverbs are formed by adding **-ment** to the masculine form of adjectives that end in a vowel and to the feminine form of adjectives whose masculine form ends in a consonant.

NOTE: A certain number of adverbs have an **-é-** before **-ment**. The most common of these are: **aveuglément, commodément, conformément, énormément, obscurément, précisément, profondément.**

To the adjective **gentil** corresponds the adverb **gentiment**, to **bref** the adverb **brièvement.** The adjective **bon** has not only the very common adverb **bien** (meaning *well*) but also **bonnement** (meaning *simply*).

A certain number of adjectives do not have a corresponding adverbial form. Such adjectives may be used adverbially in a phrase. For instance, **charmant** and **amusant** have no adverbial form. But one can say: Elle a agi **d'une façon charmante.** Il a parlé **d'une façon amusante.**

2. How are adverbs formed from adjectives ending in *-ant* and *-ent*?

suffisant   suffis**amment**   récent   réc**emment**

Adjectives in **-ant** and **-ent** usually have adverbial forms in **-amment** and **-emment.** These suffixes are both pronounced [amã].

But the adjective **lent** has the corresponding adverb **lentement.**

3. Which adjectives have irregular adverbial forms?

bon **bien**   meilleur **mieux**   petit **peu**   mauvais **mal**

NOTE 1: The adjective *quick* is most often expressed in French by **rapide,** whereas the adverb *quickly* is rendered in French by **rapidement** and **vite** («vitement» does not exist) or in certain cases by the popular expression **en vitesse.** The French equivalent of the exclamatory *Quick!* is **Vite!**

NOTE 2: The verb **sentir** (meaning *smell*) is followed by the masculine singular form of an adjective.

Ces fleurs sentent **bon.**   *These flowers smell* good.
Cette médecine sent **mauvais.**   *This medicine smells* bad.

The verb **se sentir** (meaning *feel*) is modified by an adverb.

Marie se sent **bien.**   *Marie feels* good.
Paul se sent très **mal.**   *Paul feels very* bad.

A. Écrivez les adverbes qui correspondent aux adjectifs suivants.

1. clair   2. heureux   3. rare   4. évident   5. faux
6. constant   7. discret   8. patient   9. profond   10. ardent
11. bruyant   12. mauvais   13. triste   14. bon   15. sage
16. savant   17. tendre   18. violent   19. élégant

II.   Position of Adverbs

4. What is the usual position of the adverb in a sentence with a simple verb?

Jean sait **aussi** le français.   *John* also *knows French.*

The adverb usually follows a simple verb directly.

5. What is the position of most common adverbs in sentences with compound tenses?

Nous avons **beaucoup** travaillé.

We worked a great deal.

Il a **bien** compris la phrase.

He understood the sentence well.

Vous n'avez pas **encore** remis votre devoir.

You have not yet *handed in your exercise.*

In sentences with compound tenses, most common adverbs not ending in **-ment** are placed between the auxiliary verb and the past participle and after **pas.** But sometimes the position of these adverbs is changed because the speaker wishes to stress a certain word. Also, see §7.

NOTE: When an adverb modifies an infinitive it normally precedes that infinitive.
Ex.: Il faudrait venir sans **trop tarder.** (*You should come without waiting too long.*) Alice a pu **beaucoup travailler** quand il n'y avait personne. (*Alice could work* a great deal *when no one was around.*)

6. Where are adverbs in -ment placed?

Nous avons soulevé ce poids **facilement.**

We lifted this weight easily.

Il a **complètement** oublié mon nom.

He completely forgot my name.

Vous avez **probablement** oublié d'envoyer cette lettre.

You probably *forgot to send this letter.*

Évidemment vos amis se sont trompés de route.

Obviously *your friends took the wrong road.*

Nous avons marché **lentement** jusqu'à la poste.

We walked slowly *up to the post office.*

Some adverbs in **-ment** come between the auxiliary verb and the past participle, some follow the past participle directly and some follow the noun object of the sentence. Certain ones of these adverbs in **-ment** may also begin a sentence. The length of the adverb in **-ment** does not determine its position in sentences with compound tenses. The position of each adverb in **-ment** must be learned.

7. What is the position of adverbs of place and time?

Jean est venu me voir **hier.**	*John came to see me* yesterday.
Aujourd'hui, nous avons parlé avec votre mère.	Today *we spoke with your mother.*
M. Dupont est arrivé **ici** après un long voyage.	*Mr. Dupont arrived* here *after a long trip.*

The adverbs of time and place **aujourd'hui, hier, demain, autrefois, tôt, tard, ici, là, ailleurs,** and **partout** never come between the auxiliary verb and the past participle. They normally follow the past participle, but not always directly. The adverbs of time **aujourd'hui, hier, demain,** and **autrefois** often begin or end the sentence.

8. When a sentence begins with *peut-être* or *à peine*, what word order follows?

Peut-être est-il déjà parti. **Peut-être** qu'il est déjà parti. Il est **peut-être** déjà parti.	Perhaps *he has already left.*
À peine était-il parti que les autres ont commencé à parler. Il était **à peine** parti que les autres ont commencé à parler.	Scarcely *had he left when the others began to speak.*

After **peut-être** and **à peine** when placed at the beginning of the sentence, the subject and the verb are inverted. After **peut-être** this construction is normally found only in written literary style. In conversational French, the usual word order is **peut-être que** + SUBJECT + VERB.

However, **peut-être** and **à peine** do not have to come at the beginning of the sentence. They often come immediately after a simple verb or after the auxiliary of a compound verb, and in that case the word order is not inverted.

9. What does *aussi* mean when it begins a sentence, and what kind of word order is used in that case?

Jean est jaloux. **Aussi** a-t-il perdu ses amis.	*John is jealous.* Therefore *he lost his friends.*
Noël approche. **Aussi** Michel est-il très occupé.	*Christmas is getting near.* So *Michael is very busy.*

When **aussi** has the meaning of *therefore,* it must come first in its clause, and it is usually followed by inverted word order. For that reason, **aussi** meaning *also* must NEVER come first in a sentence.

However, **Aussi . . .** = *So/Therefore* is literary. To express this idea in conversation, a word such as **Alors** or **Et alors** would be used. Ex.: **Alors** il a perdu ses amis. (So *he lost his friends.*)

B. Introduisez les adverbes indiqués pour qu'ils modifient le verbe en italique.

MODEL: (vite) Il *a fermé* la porte. **Il a vite fermé la porte.**

1. (trop) Il *travaille;* il se rendra malade.   **2.** (toujours) Le vice *est* puni et la vertu aussi. (Flaubert)   **3.** (attentivement) *Avez*-vous *lu* cette page?   **4.** (immédiatement) Pourquoi *est*-il *parti* après la conférence?   **5.** (peut-être) Vous *devriez* voir un docteur. **6.** (déjà) Il *a raconté* cette histoire aux enfants.   **7.** (follement) Elle l'*a aimé* dans sa jeunesse.   **8.** (continuellement) Le pauvre *se plaint* de ses douleurs.   **9.** (à peine) Je dois m'en aller; j'*ai* le temps de manger.   **10.** (lentement) Ils *se sont promenés* le long de la rivière. **11.** (demain) Je vous *enverrai* la lettre.   **12.** (tôt) Marie *est arrivée* à la maison.   **13.** (enfin) Il *s'est arrêté* de parler.

C. Traduisez en français.

1. He would have liked to see me at[1] length tomorrow.   **2.** (*vous*) You received him well at your house.   **3.** (*tu*) Have you read a good book recently?   **4.** I often wonder what John was writing. **5.** He spoke brilliantly.   **6.** (*vous*) You have scarcely arrived, and you already wish to leave.   **7.** It rained so much[2] that I could[3] not come.   **8.** Man always seeks happiness.   **9.** So[4] he often finds what he wants.   **10.** We haven't received any[5] news from him; perhaps he is dead.

[1] longuement   [2] tellement [3] Use a form of the passé composé.   [4] Write first in conversational, then in literary, French.   [5] *any news from him* = de ses nouvelles

III.   Negative Constructions

10. What is the normal position of the *ne . . . pas* in a negative statement with a simple verb?

Je **ne** parle **pas** allemand.   Paul **ne** le lui montrera **pas**.
Il **ne** me donnera **pas** ce livre.   Ce jeune homme **ne** me salue **pas**.

The word order is:

$$\boxed{\text{SUBJECT}^* + \textbf{ne} + \genfrac{}{}{0pt}{}{\text{PRONOUN}}{\text{OBJECT}^{**}} + \text{VERB} + \textbf{pas}}$$

*that is, the subject with all its modifiers
**The pronoun-object comes here if there is one. Many sentences do not have a pronoun-object.

11. What is the position of *ne ... pas* in interrogative sentences with a simple verb?

Ne parle-t-il **pas** allemand?
Ne me donnera-t-il **pas** ce livre?

Paul **ne** le lui montrera-t-il **pas?**
Ce jeune homme **ne** vous salue-t-il **pas?**

In sentences with a pronoun-subject, negative interrogative order is:

$$\textbf{Ne} + \text{PRONOUN OBJECT}^{**} + \text{VERB} + \text{PRONOUN SUBJECT} + \textbf{pas} + \text{following words}$$

In questions with a noun-subject, negative interrogative word order is:

$$\text{NOUN SUBJECT}^{*} + \textbf{ne} + \text{PRONOUN OBJECT}^{**} + \text{VERB} + \text{PRONOUN SUBJECT} + \textbf{pas} + \text{following words}$$

* that is, the subject with all its modifiers
** The pronoun-object comes here if there is one. Many sentences do not have a pronoun-object.

12. What is the position of *ne ... pas* in sentences with compound verbs?

Je **n**'ai **pas** parlé allemand.

Il **ne** m'a **pas** donné ce livre.

N'avez-vous **pas** parlé allemand?

Paul **ne** le lui a-t-il **pas** montré?

In sentences with verbs in compound tenses, the auxiliary verb only is regarded as the verb as far as the position of negative words is concerned. In other words, the words order in §§10–11 is followed, but **pas** comes directly after the auxiliary verb.

D. Mettez les phrases suivantes au négatif.

1. Je partirai avant son retour.   2. Il lui a donné beaucoup d'argent.
3. Êtes-vous allé en Europe l'année dernière?   4. Pourquoi venez-vous me voir?   5. Il a cru ce que vous avez dit.   6. Se décidera-t-il à venir?   7. Les questions de grammaire m'intéressent.

E. Traduisez en français.

1. This news[1] did not surprise me a great deal.   2. Isn't it difficult to learn Russian?   3. He doesn't go to[2] Florida[3] every winter.
4. These events do not worry me.   5. (*tu*) Didn't this painter make your portrait?   6. He didn't continue his work.   7. Doesn't the Rhone[3] cross Lyons[3]?   8. (*vous*) Didn't you buy that car last year?

[1] Use the singular to indicate *piece of news*.   [2] **en**   [3] The French spelling is slightly different.

13. What other negative combinations are there?

ne . . . aucun	*no, not* *any*	**ne . . . plus**	*no longer,* *no more*
ne . . . guère	*scarcely*	**ne . . . point**	*not at all*
ne . . . jamais	*never*	**ne . . . que**	*only*
ne . . . ni . . . ni	*neither* *. . . nor*	**ne . . . rien**	*nothing*
		ne . . . pas	*neither*
ne . . . personne	*no one*	**. . . non plus**	

In addition to **ne . . . pas** these are the negative combinations often used in French.

14. What word order is used with *ne . . . guère, ne . . . jamais, ne . . . plus,* **and** *ne . . . point?*

Je **ne** le vois **jamais.**   N'avez-vous **jamais** visité la Suisse?

Il **ne** vient **plus** ici.   Paul **n'**a-t-il **jamais** vu son oncle?

In all negative sentences, **ne** comes exactly where it would if used with **pas.** (See §§10–12)

The negatives **guère, jamais, plus,** and **point** follow the same rules for position as **pas.** (See §§10–12)

15. What is the word order of *personne* **and** *rien* **in sentences with a simple tense?**

Personne ne viendra.   **Rien ne** le sauvera.

Je **ne** connais **personne** dans ce quartier.   Ces élèves **ne** font **rien.**

In sentences with a simple tense, **personne** and **rien** come where they would in the corresponding English sentence.

16. Where are *personne* **and** *rien* **placed when they are used as the direct object in sentences with compound tenses?**

Je **n'**ai vu **personne.**   Ils **n'**ont **rien** compris.

In sentences with compound tenses, **personne** as the direct object follows the past participle; **rien** as the direct object comes between the auxiliary verb and the past participle.

17. What is the position of *que* **in the** *ne . . . que* (only) **construction?**

Il **n'**a vu **que** trois élèves.   Nous **n'**avons écrit **que** dix pages.

The **que** of the **ne . . . que** construction follows the entire verb.

18. Where does the negative adjective *aucun* come in a sentence?

Nous **n**'avons trouvé **aucune** trace de lui.

Aucun étudiant **ne** travaille suffisamment.

The negative **aucun** is an adjective and comes directly before its noun. The **ne** comes before the verb and before the preceding pronoun objects if there are any.

19. How is *neither . . . nor* expressed in French, and what is the position of *ni*?

Nous **n**'avons trouvé **ni** le journal **ni** la revue dont vous avez parlé.

N'avez-vous apporté **ni** papier **ni** stylo pour votre travail?

The negative adverbs **ni . . . ni** precede their noun immediately. If these nouns are indefinite, they follow **ni . . . ni** without any article. (See page 175, §9)

20. When it refers to the subject of the sentence, how is *neither (not . . . either)* expressed in French?

Je partirai **aussi.**

—George travaille beaucoup.

—Nous **aussi.**

Je **ne** partirai **pas non plus.**

—George ne travaille pas beaucoup.

—Nous **non plus.**

When the English *neither (not . . . either)* refers to the subject of the sentence and has a negative implication, it is expressed in French by **non plus** and comes at the end of the sentence. In such cases it is the negative of **aussi** (= *too*). When **non plus** ends a sentence with a verb, both **ne** and **pas** are used to make the sentence negative.

21. When negative words are used in a sentence without a verb, what happens to *ne*?

—Qui a-t-il trouvé?
—**Personne.**

—Puis-je boire du café, docteur?
—Non, **plus** de café.

—Quand le ferez-vous?
—**Jamais.**

—Combien de fautes avez-vous trouvées?
—**Aucune.**

When negative words are used in a sentence without a verb, the **ne** disappears.

F. Mettez au négatif le mot en italique. Faites les changements nécessaires dans la phrase.

MODEL: Je vais au cinéma *quelquefois.* **Je ne vais jamais au cinéma.**

1. —Y allez-vous souvent? —*Quelquefois.* **2.** J'ai vu *quelqu'un* dans le jardin. **3.** —Je partirai demain.[1] —Moi *aussi.* **4.** Il y avait *quelques indications*² dans la lettre.   **5.** Laurent a trouvé *quelque chose* sur la plage.   **6.** Nous connaissons Mme Dufour *aussi*.   **7.** Jean-Jacques arrive *toujours* en retard.   **8.** *Quelqu'un* est entré dans la chambre de Marguerite.   **9.** Il y avait *quelqu'un* dans mon bureau.   **10.** Ces jeunes garçons ont *des*³ *disques et des*³ *cassettes*.   **11.** *Quelque chose* est arrivé aux voyageurs du vol 907.   **12.** —Qui est là? —*Quelqu'un*.   **13.** —Qu'est-ce que vous avez fait ce matin? —*Quelque chose* d'intéressant.

¹ Make this sentence negative also.   ² Put in the singular with the negative.   ³ What happens to this partitive when the sentence is negative?

G. Traduisez en français.

1. I like movies¹ very much, but I no longer have the time to² go there.   **2.** Edward has neither money nor friends.   **3.** "Who knocked at the door?" "No one."   **4.** In any case, I didn't hear anything.   **5.** I don't like tea¹, and I don't like coffee¹ either. —Then what do you want?   **6.** No gift gave³ me so much pleasure.   **7.** I won't stay in this town any longer. —And I won't either.

¹ Use the definite article.   ² d'   ³ Use a form of faire.

Exercices d'ensemble

H. Complétez la seconde phrase avec l'adverbe qui correspond à l'adjectif de la première phrase.

1. Il est patient. Il attend _____ .   **2.** Ils sont sérieux. Ils travaillent _____ .   **3.** Il est amoureux. Il la regarde _____ .   **4.** Il est triste. Il se promène _____ .   **5.** Elle est élégante. Elle s'habille _____ .   **6.** Il est violent. Il a réagi _____ .   **8.** Il est affreux. Il s'est conduit _____ .   **9.** Elle est polie. Elle répond _____ .   **10.** Il est furieux. Il s'est débattu _____ .   **11.** Ils sont sévères. Ils jugent tout _____ .   **12.** Elle est simple. Elle s'habille _____ .   **13.** Il est énorme. Il mange _____ .   **14.** Ils sont attentifs. Ils écoutent _____ .   **15.** Il est tranquille. Il explique les choses _____ .

I. Introduisez dans les phrases suivantes les adverbes entre parenthèses.

1. (beaucoup) Nous nous sommes amusés à cette soirée.   **2.** (mal) Vos camarades ont compris vos intentions.   **3.** (encore) Guy n'a pas acheté ma vieille motocyclette.   **4.** (lentement) Il faut traverser ce vieux pont.   **5.** (évidemment) Ces travailleurs sont entrés chez nous sans passeports.   **6.** (hier) Il a plu toute la journée.   **7.** (là-bas) J'arriverai vers dix heures au plus tard.   **8.** (ailleurs) Allez faire ce bruit! 9. (partout) Nous avons vu de belles fleurs. 10. (tard) Georges est-il rentré cette nuit? 11. (peut-être) Solange est allée au cinéma. 12. (à peine) Pierrette a seize ans et elle veut sortir seule. 13. (déjà) Avez-vous payé la note? 14. (souvent) Nous avons visité l'Italie. 15. (toujours) Les alpinistes retenaient le même guide. 16. (suffisamment) Avez-vous étudié la question? 17. (rarement) Mon oncle nous a donné de bons conseils. 18. (récemment) Il a neigé; nous aurons un rude hiver.

J. Traduisez les phrases suivantes en français. Attention aux mots en italique.

1. *Obviously* they will no longer travel in Europe. 2. John asked me for some stamps, but I didn't have *any at all*. 3. The doctor *always* told me to[1] take two aspirins at bedtime. 4. (*vous*) When will I be able to see[2] you again? —*Never*. 5. *Yesterday* we sold our car. 6. Helen saw *no one* in the corridor. 7. Our friends don't often look at television[3] and we don't *either*. 8. I looked for[4] a long time, but I found *nothing*. 9. There are *only* twelve pupils in the class. 10. (*vous*) *Neither* you *nor* I know[5] anything about it[6]. 11. We read *only* half of the book last week.

[1] de [2] Use a form of revoir. [3] Use the definite article. [4] Either omit or express by pendant. [5] This verb must be in the first person plural. [6] en

Problem Words

9. change

(a) How to say *a change*

Avez-vous remarqué **un changement** en entrant?	*Did you notice* a change *when you came in?*
Ces dernières années il y a eu de grands **changements** dans le monde.	*In these last few years there have been great* changes *in the world.*

The ordinary French word for *change* is **le changement.**

CAUTION: DO NOT use «le change» for *change*. The French **le change** is used for financial transactions in expressions such as **le cours du change** (*the rate of exchange*), **l'office des changes** (*office dealing with foreign exchange*), **agent de change** (*stock broker*), etc.

(b) How to say *small change*

Je n'aime pas avoir toute cette **monnaie** dans ma poche.	*I don't like to have all this* change *in my pocket.*

When *change = small change*, French uses **la monnaie.**

(c) How to say that *someone* or *something changes*

Cécile **a** beaucoup **changé** depuis l'année dernière.

Cecilia has changed *a great deal since last year.*

The English *to change* is expressed by **changer.**

(d) When **changer** has a direct object

J'**ai changé mes projets de voyage** au dernier moment.

I changed my travel plans *the last minute.*

The verb **changer** + OBJECT means *to alter something*.

(e) When **changer de** is used

Tous les combien **change**-t-on **de serviettes** dans cet hôtel?

How often do they change towels *in this hotel?*

The expression **changer de quelque chose** means *to replace things of the same kind.*

(f) When **se changer** is used

Vous êtes tout mouillé; allez vite **vous changer.**

You're all wet; quick, go and change your clothes.

The reflexive **se changer** = *change one's clothes*.

(g) When to use **échanger**

Je voudrais **échanger** ma moto contre une voiture.

I'd like to exchange *my motorcycle for a car.*

The verb **échanger** means *exchange,* and to *exchange one thing for another* is **échanger une chose contre une autre.**

10. character

(a) How to say a *character* (in a literary work)

Combien de **personnages** y a-t-il dans cette pièce?

How many characters *are there in that play?*

A *character* in a literary work is **un personnage.**

(b) How to speak of *a person's character*

Georges est intelligent, mais je n'aime pas beaucoup son **caractère.**

George is intelligent, but I don't care much for his character.

One's personal attributes or one's *character* is **le caractère.**

NOTE: The French equivalent of *character* as used in the sentence "He's a *character*" is **numéro,** referring to either men or women, and **type** or **drôle de type,** referring only to men. Ex. C'est un **numéro!** C'est un **type!** C'est un **drôle de type!**

CAUTION: Do NOT use «le caractère» to indicate *a character* in a novel or play.

11. day (morning, evening)

(a) The ordinary way of saying *day*

Nous avons passé trois **jours** à Rome.	*We spent three* days *in Rome.*

The common word for *day* is **jour,** for *morning* is **matin,** for *evening* is **soir.**

(b) When the **-ée** forms are used

Toute la **journée** nous avons visité des églises et des musées.	*The whole* day *we visited churches and museums.*

The word **la journée** is used to indicate *day* when the speaker wishes to emphasize the duration of the time during the day and what happened during that time. The same distinction applies to **la matinée** and **la soirée,** but **la soirée** has the additional meaning of *evening gathering* or *evening party.*

(c) When **tous les jours** and when **toute la journée** are used

Note the following:

toute la journée = *the whole day*	**tous les jours** = *every day*
toute la matinée = *the whole morning*	**tous les matins** = *every morning*
toute la soirée = *the whole evening*	**tous les soirs** = *every evening*

K. Remplacez les mots anglais par leur équivalent français.

1. Pierre a cessé de fumer, mais cela influe sur son (*character*). 2. Il faut comprendre que les gens (*change*). 3. J'ai peu dormi cette nuit et j'ai eu sommeil (*the whole day*). 4. Avec quelques (*changes*), notre salle de séjour serait beaucoup mieux. 5. Pour réussir, une pièce ne doit pas avoir trop de (*characters*). 6. C'est ennuyeux de (*change clothes*) juste pour leur dire bonjour et au revoir. 7. En hiver il fait sombre à six heures (*in[1] the evening*). 8. Il serait bon de (*exchange*) nos vues sur la question. 9. J'ai toujours (*change*) sur moi quand je prends l'autobus. 10. J'ai passé (*the whole evening*) à rédiger cette composition. 11. Suzanne a la manie de tout (*change*) au dernier moment. 12. Jean a si mauvais (*character*) qu'on ne peut rien lui dire sans qu'il se fâche. 13. La traversée en bateau a duré cinq (*days*). 14. Qu'est-ce qui a pu

(*change*) Paul comme cela?   **15**. À midi je prends mon repas au restaurant, (*in²   the evening*) je dîne chez moi.   **16**. Va (*change*) chaussures si tu veux aller à la pêche.   **17**. Roland organise (*an evening party*) la semaine prochaine.

¹ How is *in* expressed after the time of day? See pages 242–43. ² How is *in* expressed with units of time? See pages 242–43.

L. Traduisez en français. Attention aux mots en italique.

1. I spoke of it to Daniel two *days* ago.   **2**. That author had to make many *changes* in his book in order to have¹ it published. **3**. At Christmas everyone *exchanges* gifts.   **4**. Who are the main *characters* in² that play?   **5**. (*tu*) Where did you spend the *day?* **6**. (*vous*) Do you have any *change* to buy a newspaper?   **7**. Which *characters* of Molière have become most famous?   **8**. The Carrels³ will come to play bridge tomorrow *evening*.   **9**. Mrs. Doré has *changed* chauffeurs⁴ again.   **10**. How can a person *change* in that way?   **11**. I must *change clothes* in order to go out this *evening*.

¹ **le faire publier**   ² *in* = **de**   ³ French proper names do not take an -s in the plural. ⁴ Use the singular form.

Verb Review

Review the verbs **recevoir** and **avoir** according to the outline on page 253.

Use of Tenses

Le petit coq noir est à la recherche du renard qui vient trop souvent rôder autour du poulailler[1] et auquel il veut «donner une leçon». Pour mieux observer la forêt, il est monté sur un acacia. Le renard l'a vu et arrive au pied de l'arbre.

Le petit coq noir

Le renard regardait le coq perché sur une haute branche et il voulait le manger. Il ne[2] s'en cachait pas du tout.

—Tu ne *sais* pas, dit-il au coq, ce que j'ai appris hier soir en passant sous les fenêtres de la ferme? J'ai appris que les maîtres allaient te faire
5 cuire dans une sauce au vin pour te servir dimanche prochain au repas de midi. Tu n'*imagines* pas combien l'annonce de cette nouvelle a pu me peiner.

—Mon Dieu! Ils me *feraient* cuire dans une sauce au vin!

—Je ne l'*aurais* pas *cru* si je ne les *avais* pas *entendus* moi-même!
10 Mais, *sais*-tu ce que tu *feras,* si tu *veux* leur jouer un bon tour? Tu *descendras* de ton arbre, et moi je te *mangerai.* Alors, eux, ils[3] *seront* bien attrapés.

Mais le coq ne voulait pas descendre. Il disait qu'il *aimerait* mieux être mangé par ses maîtres que par le renard.

15 —Tu en *penseras* ce que tu *voudras,* mais je *préfère* mourir de ma mort naturelle, être mangé par mes maîtres.

—Que tu *es* bête! Mais la mort naturelle, ce n'*est* pas ça du tout!

—Tu ne *sais* pas ce que tu *dis,* renard. Il *faut* bien que les maîtres nous tuent un jour ou l'autre. C'*est* la loi commune. Il n'y *a* personne
20 qui puisse y échapper. . .

—Mais, coq, suppose que les maîtres ne vous mangent pas . . . tu *vivrais* toujours, sans inquiétude. C'*est* ce que je voulais te faire com-

---

[1] *chicken coop*   [2] ne s'en cachait pas *made no secret of it*   [3] ils seront bien attrapés *that will fix them*

prendre. Tu n'*aurais* pas le souci, au réveil, de te demander si tu ne *serais* pas saigné dans le courant de la journée. Oui, je *sais,* tu *vas* encore
25 me *parler* de tes maîtres. Et[4] si tu n'avais pas de maîtres?

—Pas de maîtres? dit le coq. Et, d'étonnement, il resta le bec ouvert.

—On *peut* très bien vivre sans maîtres . . . Moi, je n'ai jamais regretté une seule fois d'être libre! Et comment le *regretterais*-je? Si j'*avais accepté* comme toi d'avoir des maîtres, il y a longtemps que je *serais*
30 mangé.

Le coq l'écoutait, et il était perplexe. Il se demandait s'il *serait* vraiment fait pour mener cette vie-là.

—Je *vais* y *réfléchir,* dit-il; car, me *vois*-tu errant par les bois à la recherche de ma nourriture? Je n'*aurais* pas ce beau jabot[5] plein avec
35 lequel tu me *vois* aujourd'hui, sans[6] compter que je m'*ennuierais,* dans cette grande forêt, tout[7] seul de mon espèce.

—Mon Dieu, que le souci de la nourriture ne t'occupe pas! Il *suffit* de se baisser pour gober[8] les plus délicieux vers[9] de terre, et je *connais* des coins[10] d'avoines folles où tu[11] *seras* à ton affaire. Je *craindrais* plutôt
40 pour toi le désagrément[12] de la solitude. Mais je vois à cela un remède bien simple: décider tous les coqs, toutes les poules du village à suivre ton exemple. La cause *est* si belle qu'elle *intéressera* d'abord, et ton éloquence *fera* le reste. Alors quelle satisfaction pour toi d'avoir guidé ta race vers une existence meilleure. Quelle gloire tu en *auras*! Et quelle ·
45 délivrance aussi pour vous tous de mener une vie sans fin, exempte de soucis, dans la verdure et le soleil!

D'après Marcel Aymé. Avec humour et sévérité il a mis dans ses romans et ses pièces ses observations des gens et des mœurs. Conteur, il était le meilleur «fabuliste» moderne. («Le petit coq noir», dans *Les Contes du chat perché,* Gallimard, 1939)

---

[4] Et si tu n'avais pas de maîtres? *What if you didn't have any masters?*   [5] *crop (of a bird)*   [6] sans compter que *not to mention that*   [7] tout seul de mon espèce *the only one of my kind*   [8] *gulp up*   [9] vers de terre *earthworms*   [10] coins d'avoines folles *patches of wild oats*   [11] tu seras à ton affaire *you'll have just what you want*
[12] *unpleasantness*

I.   The Present

1. What use of the simple present tense is exactly the same in French and English?

Jean **travaille** beaucoup.   *John* works *a great deal.*
Hélène **lit** un peu tous les jours.   *Helen* reads *a little every day.*

In both French and English, the SIMPLE PRESENT tense is used to state a general truth.

2. How does French express the English progressive present, that is, the present in *-ing*?

Jean **travaille** maintenant.	*John* is working *now.*
Hélène **lit** le journal en ce moment.	*Helen* is reading *the newspaper right now.*
Je **suis en train de corriger** mes fautes.	I am correcting *my mistakes.*

In general, French expresses the English progressive present by a simple present. But if French wishes to insist on the progressive nature of an action, it then uses a form of **être en train de** + INFINITIVE.

3. When may the French present tense express a future idea?

Demain nous **partons** pour Paris.	Tomorrow *we* leave *for Paris.*

The present is occasionally used to express an action in the immediate future when some other word in the sentence indicates futurity.

NOTE: The student should recognize this use of the present for the future but use it very sparingly, for it can be used only in certain cases.

4. When is the present tense used in French to express an action that would be expressed in the present perfect in English?

Nous **apprenons** le français **depuis** deux ans.	*We* have been learning *French* for *two years.*
Il y a trois jours **qu'il pleut.**	It has been raining for *three days.*
Voilà un an **que** Marc **habite** ici.	*Mark* has been living *here* for *a year.*

When an action which began in the past is still continuing in the present, French uses the *present tense* with **depuis, il y a . . . que, voici . . . que,** and **voilà . . . que.** English generally uses the progressive form of the present perfect with *for* to express the same concept.

In this type of sentence, **Il y a . . . que, Voici . . . que,** and **Voilà . . . que** normally come at the beginning of the sentence, whereas **depuis** + TIME EXPRESSION usually comes at the end of the sentence.

NOTE 1. But in a negative sentence with **depuis, voici . . . que, voilà . . . que,** and **il y a . . . que,** the *passé composé* is used because the action does not continue up to the present. Ex. Je **n'ai pas vu** Guy **depuis** trois jours. (*I* haven't seen *Guy* for *three days.*) **Voilà** deux mois que Mme Simon **n'a pas payé** son loyer. (*Mrs. Simon* hasn't paid *her rent* for *two months.*)

NOTE 2. If an action took place over a definite period of time in the past, the verb is in the *passé composé* and *for* is expressed by **pendant.** Ex. Nous **avons appris** le français **pendant** deux ans. Il **a plu pendant** trois jours.

A. Traduisez en français.

1. Peter drives very well.   2. He has been going out with her for[1] a long time.   3. Lucy is talking on[2] the telephone.   4. The day after tomorrow I will give[3] them my resignation.   5. (*tu*) Leave me alone[4]; I'm working.   6. Albert has had this letter in his pocket for[5] five days.   7. We have been waiting for her for[6] an hour. 8. This evening I'll pack[3] my suitcase.   9. He has refused to see me for[7] two days.   10. Tomorrow we'll go[3] to the movies.

[1] Use depuis.[2] *on the* = au   [3] Express this action by the present.   [4] tranquille   [5] Use **il y a . . . que.**   [6] Use **voilà . . . que.**   [7] Use **voici . . . que.**

II.   The Future

5. In what two ways does French usually express the future?

Un de ces jours j'**achèterai** un chien.	*One of these days* I'll buy *a dog.*
Je **vais partir** bientôt pour Rome.	*Soon I*'ll leave *for Rome.*

French usually expresses the future with the FUTURE TENSE or with the present of **aller** + INFINITIVE. This normally parallels English usage, but in certain cases of an immediate future French tends to use **aller** + INFINITIVE where English might use the future.

6. When do the French use the future tense where the present would be used in English?

Quand vous **saurez** le français, nous irons en France ensemble.	When *you* know *French, we'll go to France together.*
Dès que je **recevrai** sa lettre, je vous l'enverrai.	As soon as *I* receive *his letter, I'll send it to you.*
Tant que vous **parlerez** ainsi, vous aurez des ennuis.	As long as *you* speak *this way, you'll have trouble.*

In French, the future is used after **quand, lorsque, dès que, aussitôt que,** and **tant que** if the action will take place at some future time. English uses the present in such constructions.

B. Traduisez en français.

1. I'll[1] inquire about that immediately.   2. We'll[2] inquire about the cost[3] of the trip next week.   3. (*vous*) When you go to Paris,

send me a postcard.   4. As soon as I get my passport, we'll leave.
5. When it is warm, we'll spend the afternoon at the swimming
pool.   6. (*tu*) As soon as you arrive, telephone me.   7. As long
as there are men, there will be wars.   8. (*tu*) When I see you, I'll
tell you what happened.

[1] Because it is an immediate future, French uses **aller** + INFINITIVE here.   [2] Because this is
not an immediate future, French does not use **aller** + INFINITIVE here.   [3] **le prix**

III. The Conditional

7. When is the conditional used to indicate a future action?

Richard croyait que Georges le **ferait.**	*Richard thought that George* would do *it.*
Je lui ai demandé s'il **partirait** bientôt.	*I asked him if he* would leave *soon.*

When the main clause of a sentence is in a past tense, the CONDITIONAL
is often used in the dependent clause to indicate a future action.

NOTE: English uses the same sort of construction. Compare:

He says he will leave.   *He said he* would leave.
I think it will rain.   *I thought it* would rain.

8. How is the conditional used in polite requests or questions?

Je **voudrais** un verre d'eau.	*I would like a glass of water.*
Aimeriez-vous sortir avec moi?	Would *you* like *to go out with me?*

The conditional is sometimes used to soften a statement or question
which would be somewhat direct and blunt if stated in the present tense.

NOTE: Compare the politeness of the above examples to the bluntness of the
same sentences stated in the present, e.g., *I want a glass of water. Do you
want to go out with me?*

C. Traduisez en français.

1. I would prefer to leave at once.   2. Her parents told me that
she would come today.   3. Our friends thought that we would
spend the day at their place.   4. I heard[1] that the airplane would
be[2] late.   5. Claude asked Martha if she would go out with him
the next[3] day.   6. (*vous*) Would you like to go to England?

[1] *to hear that* = **entendre dire que**   [2] *to be late* = **avoir du retard**   [3] *the next day* =
le jour suivant *or* **le lendemain**

IV.   The Pluperfect and Related Tenses*

9. What is the basic use of the pluperfect?

J'**avais fini** mon travail quand Pierre est arrivé.

I had finished my work when Peter arrived.

Colette **était** déjà **sortie** quand il a commencé à pleuvoir.

Colette had already left when it began to rain.

The PLUPERFECT indicates a past action that took place before the beginning of another past action.

10. What tense does French use in cases when an action begins at a certain time in the past and continues until another time in the past?

Monsieur Lenoir **travaillait depuis** dix ans quand il a découvert ce nouveau procédé.

Mr. Lenoir had been working for ten years when he discovered that new process.

Il y avait un an **qu'il apprenait** le français quand il est parti pour l'Afrique.

He had been learning French for one year when he left for Africa.

When an action that begins in the past and continues up to a certain point in the past is interrupted by another action, stated or implied, the French express the first action by the IMPERFECT with **depuis** or **il y avait . . . que.** In such cases, English uses the pluperfect and usually the progressive form of the pluperfect.

D. Remplacez les mots anglais entre parenthèses par l'équivalent français.

1. Quand nous avons voulu l'acheter, nos voisins (*had sold*) leur auto.   2. (*He had been trying[1] for a year*) à s'évader quand l'occasion s'est enfin présentée.   3. Vous a-t-il demandé où vous (*had found*) le portefeuille?   4. Nous (*had been reading*) depuis une heure quand quelqu'un a frappé à la porte.   5. Il y avait une heure que Julie (*had been*) chez Nicole quand son ami est venu la chercher.   6. Jean-Paul (*had found*) une bonne place quand il a dû faire son service militaire.   7. Jacques et Paulette (*had been going out*) ensemble depuis trois semaines quand ils ont décidé de se marier.   8. Il y avait longtemps qu'il nous (*had been calling*) quand nous l'avons enfin entendu.

[1]Use a form of **chercher**.

11. In French, the pluperfect cannot be used to express the underlined *had finished* in a sentence such as *When I had finished my work yes-*

---

* The uses of the imperfect and the *passé composé* will be taken up in Chapter 6 (pp. 71–75).

terday, I went out. **How can such an English pluperfect be expressed in French?**

1. by the **passé composé** in conversation

    Quand j'**ai fini** mon travail hier soir, je **suis sorti.**
    Dès que Louis **a écrit** la lettre, il l'**a mise** à la poste.

When a past action introduced by **quand, lorsque, dès que, aussitôt que,** or **après que** immediately precedes a second past action which is in the compound past, the first action may be expressed by the compound past also. The use of the compound past here is not elegant but it is heard. In any case, the first action cannot be in the pluperfect.

2. by the **passé surcomposé** in conversation

    Quand j'**ai eu fini** mon travail hier soir, je **suis sorti.**
    Dès que Louis **a eu écrit** la lettre, il l'**a mise** à la poste.

When a past action introduced by **quand, lorsque, dès que, aussitôt que,** or **après que** immediately precedes a second past action which is in the compound past, the first action is usually in the **passé surcomposé.** It cannot be in the pluperfect.

NOTE: The **passé surcomposé,** which is relatively infrequent, is formed as follows:

> **passé surcomposé** = compound past of auxiliary + past participle

Reflexive verbs are not used in the **passé surcomposé.**

3. by the **passé antérieur** in literary French

    Quand j'**eus fini** mon travail, je **sortis.**
    Dès que Louis **eut écrit** la lettre, il la **mit** à la poste.

When a past action introduced by **quand, lorsque, dès que, aussitôt que,** or **après que** immediately precedes a second past action which is in the simple past, the first action must be in the **passé antérieur.** It cannot be in the pluperfect. The **passé antérieur,** which is used only in literary French and generally with **quand, lorsque, dès que, aussitôt que,** and **après que,** is formed as follows:

> **passé antérieur** = simple past of auxiliary + past participle

4. by **après** + PAST INFINITIVE under certain conditions

    Quand j'ai eu fini mon travail   **Après avoir fini** mon travail
      hier, **je** suis sorti.   hier, **je** suis sorti.
    Après qu'il a eu écrit la lettre,   **Après avoir écrit** la lettre,
      Louis l'a mise à la poste.   **Louis** l'a mise à la poste.

When the subject of a clause beginning with **quand, lorsque,** or **après que** refers to the same person as the subject of the main clause, and when the main clause is in the **passé composé,** then **après** + PAST INFINITIVE may be used instead of a **quand, lorsque,** or **après que** clause.

NOTE: The past infinitive = infinitive of auxiliary verb + past participle
Ex. **finir**—avoir fini; **sortir**—être sorti; **se laver**—s'être lavé

E. Remplacez les mots anglais entre parenthèses par l'équivalent français, en employant une des méthodes indiquées ci-dessus pour éviter le plus-que-parfait français dans la proposition subordonnée.

1. Dès que (*I had begun my work*), le téléphone a sonné. 2. Quand Michel (*had visited*) le musée, il nous a rejoints au restaurant.   3. Dès que nous (*had eaten*), le garçon a débarrassé la table.   4. Après que nos nouveaux voisins (*had seen*) notre maison, nous les avons menés au jardin.   5. Jean a prévenu Marc dès que nous (*had arrived*).   6. Luc est tombé malade après que nous (*had bought*)[1] les billets.

[1] Express by a form of **prendre.**

F. Traduisez en français en employant une des méthodes indiquées ci-dessus pour éviter le plus-que-parfait français dans la proposition subordonnée.

1. After I had lost my job, I had[1] to move.   2. When I had signed the letter, Maurice mailed it.   3. Jack left after he had watched television with us.   4. After I had gone to bed, I read for[2] an hour. 5. As soon as we heard the news, we telephoned Mr. Lesage[3].

[1] Use a form of être obligé de.   [2] pendant   [3] This is an indirect object in French.

V.   The Future Perfect

12. What French use of the future perfect corresponds to the English use?

J'**aurai vu** ton professeur quand tu rentreras.

I will have seen *your teacher when you get back.*

In French, as in English, the FUTURE PERFECT describes an action which will have taken place before another future action.

NOTE: The FUTURE PERFECT (**futur antérieur**) is made up of the future of the AUXILIARY + THE PAST PARTICIPLE of the verb. Ex.: j'**aurai parlé,** je **serai sorti.**

13. When is the future perfect used in French where the English might use the present perfect?

Quand Albert **aura écrit** la lettre, je vous la montrerai.	When *Albert* has written *the letter, I'll show it to you.*

The FUTURE PERFECT is used in French with adverbial conjunctions of time such as **quand, lorsque, dès que, aussitôt que,** and **après que** to express an action which will have taken place before another future action. English generally uses the present perfect in such cases.

G. Traduisez en français.

1. (*vous*) That family will have already left when you arrive in Tours.
2. (*tu*) When you have finished that report, send it to me.   3. (*vous*) When we have bought our new car, come and[1] see it.   4. As soon as they have arrived, we'll go for a walk.   5. Jack will learn to play[2] the violin after his brother has learned to play[2] the piano.
6. When I have received my check, I'll cash it immediately.   7. (*tu*) Come back as soon as you get out of the meeting.

[1] Translate: *Come to see it.*   [2] Omit *to play* in translation.

VI.   Conditional Sentences

14. What are the most common types of French conditional sentences?

(a) Si nous **travaillons,** nous **gagnerons** de l'argent.	*If we* work, *we* will earn *some money.*
(b) Si nous **étions** riches, nous **irions** en France.	*If we* were *rich, we* would go *to France.*
(c) Si vous **aviez parlé** français, Marie-Claire vous **aurait compris.**	*If you* had spoken *French, Marie-Claire* would have understood *you.*

The three most common tense sequences in conditional sentences are:

si-(*if*)-Clause	Conclusion
present	future
imperfect	conditional
pluperfect	past conditional

H. Remplacez les infinitifs par la forme convenable du verbe.

1. Si Philippe partait, il (falloir) lui demander pourquoi.   2. Si vous me (poser) la question, je vous aurais répondu.   3. S'il le faut, nous

(se battre).   **4.** Je (être) très content si mon frère réussissait.   **5.** Si je (savoir) cela, je n'y serais pas allé.   **6.** Je (partir) si vous continuez à me regarder comme cela.   **7.** Si l'auto ne marche pas, nous (prendre) l'autobus.   **8.** S'il avait fait beau, nous (aller) vous voir.   **9.** Si Anna (parler) français, vous n'auriez pas besoin d'un interprète.

I. Traduisez en français.

1. (*tu*) If you do what I tell you, everything will come[1] out all right.   **2.** I would be glad if I could retire[2] next year.   **3.** If I were free, I'd accept their invitation.   **4.** If he would speak louder, one could hear what he is saying.   **5.** (*vous*) You would have seen our slides if you had come sooner.   **6.** If I earned more,[3] I'd look for a larger apartment.   **7.** If I go to Paris now, I will not come back until[4] Easter.   **8.** I would have answered him if I had heard him call.   **9.** If the mayor had not been sick, he would have attended the lecture.

[1] *come out* = aboutir   [2] prendre ma retraite   [3] davantage   [4] avant

15. **What other tense sequences exist in conditional sentences?**

PLUPERFECT + CONDITIONAL

Si vous **aviez fait** votre travail, vous **pourriez** venir avec nous aujourd'hui.

If you had done *your work, you* could come with us today.

PRESENT + PRESENT

S'il **pleut**, je **reste** à la maison.

If it rains, I stay *home.*

PLUPERFECT + CONDITIONAL

Si nous **avions pris** des précautions, nous n'**aurions** pas ces ennuis maintenant.

If we had taken *precautions, we* wouldn't *have* this trouble *now.*

PASSÉ COMPOSÉ + FUTURE

S'ils **ont pris** l'avion, ils **seront** bientôt ici.

If they have taken *the airplane, they* will *soon* be *here.*

Almost any tense sequence that is possible in English conditional sentences is also possible in French conditional sentences. However:

Si vous **faites** votre travail, vous **gagnerez** beaucoup d'argent.

If *you* will do *your work, you* will earn *a lot of money.*

Si elle **écoutait** ses parents, elle ne **sortirait** jamais.

If *she* would obey *her parents, she* would *never* go out.

In French, neither the future nor the conditional can ever be used after **si** when **si** means *if*.

Je ne sais pas **si** Jean **viendra.**   *I don't know* whether *John will come.*

When **si** means *whether,* the French future and conditional may follow it.

J. Traduisez en français.

1. (*vous*) If you had left earlier, you would already be in Cannes.
2. If the children have gone to bed, they must be[1] asleep now.
3. If the students spent a lot of money, they always managed to[2] get more.   4. (*vous*) If you listen carefully, you will be able to follow his thought.   5. If he would paint his car, he could keep it another[3] year.   6. (*tu*) If you like football, come and[4] see the game[5] with me.   7. (*vous*) You mustn't hesitate to tell me if you are bored.
8. If he has found[6] that out, he must be furious.

[1] *be asleep* = dormir   [2] pour en avoir davantage   [3] encore un an   [4] Not «et»   [5] le match   [6] *find out* = apprendre

Exercices d'ensemble

K. Remplacez l'infinitif par la forme convenable du verbe.

1. Quand ils ne (être) plus là, je ne sais pas ce que je ferai.   2. Voilà un mois que vous (avoir) mon livre. Pouvez-vous me le rendre?
3. Quel sale temps! Il (pleuvoir) depuis ce matin.   4. Nous (préparer) un excellent dîner quand les invités ont téléphoné qu'ils ne pouvaient pas venir.   5. Georges (aller) obtenir son diplôme quand il est tombé malade.   6. Je garderai cette grammaire quand je (finir) mon cours.   7. Si tu (épouser) cette jeune fille, tes parents seraient très heureux.   8. J'ai toujours pensé que cela (finir) mal.
9. Je lirai ce roman quand je (avoir) le temps.

L. Remplacez l'infinitif par la forme convenable du verbe.

1. Il avait cru qu'elle (pouvoir) nous aider le lendemain.   2. Dès que je (apprendre) cela, je suis parti.   3. Donnez-moi la main si vous (avoir) peur.   4. Encore un mot et je (s'en aller).   5. Quand vous lui (écrire), faites-lui mes amitiés.   6. Si j'avais su, je (agir) tout autrement.   7. Je (s'endormir) déjà[1] quand ses cris m'ont réveillé.
8. Elle s'est trouvée mieux dès qu'elle (prendre) ce remède.
9. Quand ils (partir), je vous montrerai quelque chose d'intéressant.
10. Si vous (écouter) ses conseils, vous n'en seriez pas là.

[1] Where will **déjà** come in the compound tense of a verb?

M. Traduisez en français. Indiquez oralement la raison de chaque temps.

1. I must hurry; I am leaving this evening.   2. I wrote them that we would go to see them Sunday.   3. They had already washed the car when it began to rain.   4. (*vous*) Tell me what she says[1] to you as soon as you have seen her.   5. (*vous*) If you were willing to see him, he would be very happy.   6. When I came into the living room, everyone had already left.   7. He has been studying Russian for two years, but he does not know it very well.   8. He will be horrified when he learns what has happened.   9. If she had understood me, things[2] would have been very different.

[1] Does this verb express something happening now or something that will happen?   [2] Use the definite article.

N. Traduisez en français. Indiquez oralement la raison de chaque temps.

1. As soon as she had won the contest, she left for Paris.   2. (*vous*) Did you tell him that we would not be home tomorrow?   3. I'll speak to him of that matter as soon as I see him.   4. We had finished our meal when we heard the newscast.   5. I will travel when I have saved enough.[1]   6. If the weather[2] is good, I always take a walk.   7. (*tu*) What are you doing tonight?   8. (*tu*) When you speak to him, be very polite.   9. When he realized that he was wrong, he changed his mind.   10. (*vous*) I'll talk to him only if you come with me.

[1] *save enough* = faire assez d'économies   [2] Use an idiomatic expression with **faire**.

Problem Words

12. early

(a) When *early* means *early in a certain period of time*

Est-ce que vous vous couchez **tôt?**
Est-ce que vous vous couchez **de bonne heure?** } *Do you go to bed* early?

Ne venez pas trop **tôt.**   *Don't come too* early.

Both **tôt** and **de bonne heure** mean *early* in a given period of time.

(b) When *early = ahead of time*

Il y aura beaucoup de monde; il vaut mieux arriver **en avance.**   *There will be a lot of people there; it is better to arrive* early.

Early, meaning *ahead of time,* is expressed by **en avance,** which is the opposite of **en retard.**

Sometimes **d'avance** and **à l'avance** are also used to express *early = ahead of time,* but it is rather difficult to indicate just when one of these expressions is used rather than the other.

Prenez vos billets $\left\{ \begin{array}{l} \textbf{d'avance} \\ \textbf{à l'avance} \end{array} \right.$ si vous ne voulez pas faire la queue au guichet.

Get your tickets in advance *if you don't want to stand in line at the ticket window.*

13. end

(a) When *end* is the opposite of *beginning*

C'est **la fin** de la leçon.   *It is* the end *of the lesson.*

The word **la fin** means *end* when it implies the opposite of *beginning.*

(b) When *end* means *tip* or *extremity*

Ne touchez pas **le bout** de ce fil.

Don't touch the end *of this wire.*

Il y a un cinéma au **bout** de la rue.

There is a movie at the end *of the street.*

The French uses **le bout** to express *end* meaning *tip* or *extremity.*

(c) How to say *at the end of* + PERIOD OF TIME

À la fin du mois il ne me reste jamais rien.

At the end of *the month I don't ever have anything left.*

Au bout de trois mois M. Roux a donné sa démission.

At the end of three *months Mr. Roux resigned.*

Au bout de quelques semaines j'en ai eu assez.

At the end of some *weeks I had enough (of it).*

French expresses *at the end of the* + PERIOD OF TIME by **à la fin de** + DEFINITE ARTICLE + PERIOD OF TIME. On the other hand, when the period of time is accompanied by a numeral or by some other adjective indicating quantity, **au bout de . . .** is used.

14. escape

(a) When *escape* means *avoid*

Le criminel a réussi à **échapper à** la police.

The criminal succeeded in escaping *the police.*

The non-reflexive form **échapper à** is used to indicate that one has avoided or escaped someone or something that one has not yet confronted.

(b) When *escape* means *get out of*

Ce voleur réussit toujours à **s'échapper de** prison.	*That thief always succeeds in* escaping from *prison.*

The reflexive form **s'échapper de** is used to indicate that one has succeeded in getting away from a person or thing that one has confronted.

In the first example, the thief evaded the police, therefore, never came in contact with them, whereas in the second he was in prison and got out of it.

15. every

(a) How to express *every* by **chaque**

Chaque fois que je vois Paul, il me parle de ses ennuis.	Every *time I see Paul, he talks to me of his troubles.*

The adjective **chaque** means *every* or *each*.

(b) How to express *every* by **tous les . . .**

Tous les matins nous sortons de bonne heure et **tous les soirs** nous rentrons tard.	Every morning *we leave early and* every evening *we return home late.*

The English *every* is frequently expressed by **tous les** + UNIT OF TIME (**toutes les** + UNIT OF TIME). This formula is more common with units of time than **chaque,** although **chaque** is not incorrect.

(c) How to say *everyone*

Tout le monde est parti.	Everyone *has left.*

The pronoun *everyone* is expressed by **tout le monde,** which is singular and which must be followed by a singular verb.

CAUTION: DO NOT use a plural verb after **tout le monde.**

(d) How to say *everything*

Tout est perdu.	Everything *is lost.*
J'ai **tout** oublié.	*I've forgotten* everything.

The pronoun *everything* is expressed by **tout.** In the compound tenses, **tout** comes between the auxiliary and the past participle.

(e) How to say *everything that*

Tout ce qui est sur la table est à Jean.	Everything that *is on the table is John's.*
Donnez-moi **tout ce que** vous pouvez.	*Give me* everything that *you can.*

In French, *everything* used as the subject of its clause = **tout ce qui;** *everything* used as the object of its clause = **tout ce que.**

CAUTION: The indefinite **ce** must come between **tout** and the relative pronoun. Do NOT write «tout qui» or «tout que».

O. Remplacez les mots anglais par leur équivalent français.

1. Sauve qui peut! Un lion (*has escaped from*) sa cage.   2. Il me reste tant de travail à faire que je n'en vois pas (*the end*).   3. Je préfère travailler le soir; je n'aime pas me lever (*early*).   4. Voilà le menu; commande (*everything that*) tu veux.   5. (*Everyone laughed*) quand Pierre a raconté ses aventures.   6. (*At the end*) du deuxième acte, la situation semblait inextricable.   7. Jacques fait une période militaire (*every summer*).   8. Nous avons eu de la chance de (*escape*) cette épidémie.   9. (*Everything that*) vous dites est très juste.   10. Vous arrivez trop (*early*), Jacques n'est pas encore rentré.   11. —Où se trouve le bureau de tabac? —(*At the end*) de la rue, à droite.   12. Il y aura un cadeau pour (*every*) invité. 13. Saluez (*everyone*) de ma part.   14. Il vaudrait mieux arriver (*early*) au théâtre; sinon, nous ne trouverons plus de places. 15. Leurs enfants aiment (*everything that*) fait du bruit.

P. Traduisez en français. Attention aux mots en italique.

1. Nicole likes *everything that* is beautiful.   2. The airplane will not wait for us; it is better to arrive *early* than[1] to be late.   3. At the *end* of the book I finally understood what the author meant. 4. *Every* time that he gets angry, he regrets it.   5. We are invited for seven o'clock; we must not arrive too *early*.   6. If I am caught[2], I'll do *everything* to[3] *escape*.   7. At the *end* of two weeks at the university, Jack dropped his courses.   8. Paul and Anne-Marie see each other *every* day.   9. She is hurt[4] because they put her at the *end* of the table.   10. *Everyone* knows that.   11. That teacher is remarkable; he knows absolutely *everything*.   12. Is *everyone* there?   13. (*vous*) I don't know how you can *escape* his anger. 14. I heard *everything*.

[1] than to be = que d'être   [2] pris   [3] pour   [4] vexée

Verb Review

Review the verbs **être** and **aller** according to the outline on page 253.

Personal Pronouns

Interview par Jacques Chancel de Maurice Genevoix, alors doyen de l'Académie française, à propos de son livre *Un jour.*

Un écrivain âgé considère la vie et la mort

JACQUES CHANCEL—Maurice Genevoix, *je* suis frappé dans votre dernier livre par une nouvelle approche de la vie mais aussi de la mort que *vous* voulez rendre en quelque sorte acceptable. Est-ce que, à quatre-vingt-cinq ans, *vous* avez peur de votre âge?

5   MAURICE GENEVOIX—Non, *je* n'*en* ai pas peur, pas du tout, mais *j*'ai voulu, à la fin d'une carrière, livrer[1] sur *moi* un témoignage qui soit le moins possible contestable. Les critiques, *eux,* sont des types épatants, lucides, pénétrants, mais *on* n'est pas toujours de leur avis. Tandis que si *je* laisse de *moi* une certaine image, si *elle* ne *me* satisfait pas, mais si

10   c'est *moi* qui l'ai donnée, *je* sais à[2] qui *m'en* prendre et *je* n'ai qu'à *me* dire: «Tant pis pour *toi».* *J*'ai donc éprouvé le besoin de laisser de *moi* une certaine image et *j*'ai voulu que de mon livre, *Un jour,* émane une sorte d'éclairage qui se répandrait sur l'ensemble de mon oeuvre, qui *en* révélerait les thèmes d'inspiration les plus authentiques.

15   J. C.—*Vous y* avez réussi. Votre oeuvre, c'est votre vie . . .

M. G.—C'est en tout cas un témoignage que *je* laisse. *Vous* savez très bien qu'*il* n'y a pas un écrivain, pas un artiste qui ne souhaite *se* prolonger. Une oeuvre, c'est un moyen de protester contre la mort physique.

---

[1] livrer . . . contestable *give as reliable as possible an account of myself*   [2] à qui m'en prendre *whom to blame*

J. C.—Le moyen d'éloigner la mort, de l'écarter?

20   M. G.—Non. De laisser après *soi* quelque chose. *Je* crois qu'on s'*en* désintéresse après la mort. Même si *on* est croyant, *on* n'assiste pas au spectacle qui continue.

J. C.—*Vous* voudriez donc laisser une trace. N'est-ce pas un peu d'orgueil?

25   M. G.—C'est une réaction de vivant, c'est tout. Ce besoin de perpétuer, de durer au-delà de l'instant est commun à tous les hommes. La preuve: quand une situation devient critique ou difficile, presque chaque homme concerné veut *la* fixer par écrit, pour laisser quelque chose derrière lui. *Il* veut *la* fixer pour que le souvenir *en*[3] demeure après nous. Voyez

30   pendant la guerre sur laquelle *j*'ai aussi laissé un témoignage; tous les biffins[4], même les moins cultivés, avaient un petit carnet de route où *ils* notaient au jour le jour leurs impressions. Si *vous* explicitez et si ça tourne à l'obsession, *vous* arrivez à l'homme de lettres, à l'écrivain.

J. C.—Pourquoi ce titre: *Un jour?*

35   M. G.—Parce que *j*'ai mis en épigraphe à ce roman une phrase tirée de *L'Adolescent* de Dostoïevski. Un prince dit à quelqu'un: «Qu'est-ce que c'est, selon *vous,* la vraie vie?» Et son interlocuteur[5] *lui* répond: «*Je* ne *le* sais pas plus que *vous,* Prince, mais *j*'imagine que c'est quelque chose de tout à fait simple, de tout à fait ordinaire, si simple, si ordinaire que

40   depuis des milliers d'années, les gens passent[6] à côté sans *le* remarquer et sans *le* reconnaître!»

J'ai voulu, en racontant un jour où *il*[7] ne se passe rien, montrer dans mon livre tout[8] ce à côté de quoi nos semblables passent sans *le* remarquer et sans *le* reconnaître: une odeur, un beau crépuscule, n'importe

45   quoi! Et *j*'ai essayé d'*y* montrer que la vie était une chose merveilleuse . . .

D'après Jacques Chancel. Reporter perspicace de la radio et de la télévision, il a depuis de nombreuse années un programme très suivi d'interviews de toutes sortes de personnalités françaises. (*Radioscopie,* Vol. 4. Robert Laffont 1976)

---

[3] *of it* [4] *foot-soldiers (colloquial)* [5] *the person to whom he was speaking* [6] passe à côté . . . reconnaître *go by without noticing it and without recognizing it* [7] il ne se passe rien *nothing happens* [8] tout . . . sans *everything that our fellow men pass by without . . .*

A pronoun is a word that takes the place of a noun. The subject pronouns are: *I, you, he, she, it, we* and *they;* the object pronouns are: *me, you, him, her, it, us* and *them.*

I.   Object Pronouns and Their Uses

1. What are the direct object pronouns?

Jean **me** voit.   Louise **nous** appelle.
Jacques **la** vend.   Mes amis **vous** connaissent.
Je **l'**achète.   Nous **les** trouverons.

The direct object pronouns are:

me	*me*	**nous**	*us*
te	*you*	**vous**	*you*
le { *him, it*		**les**	*them*
la { *her, it*			

NOTE: When the forms **me, te, se, le,** or **la** precede a verb beginning with a vowel or a mute **h,** they elide, becoming **m', t', s',** or **l'.**

2. What are the indirect object pronouns?

Gilbert **me** montre sa voiture.   Brigitte **nous** téléphonera.
Anne **lui** explique la leçon.   Gérard **vous** indiquera la route.
Jacques **te** parlera demain.   Vous **leur** obéirez.

The indirect object pronouns are:

me	*to me*	**nous**	*to us*
te	*to you*	**vous**	*to you*
lui { *to him*		**leur**	*to them*
{ *to her*			

The reflexive pronoun **se** may be either a direct or indirect object and means: *(to) himself, herself, itself, themselves, oneself.* As a reciprocal pronoun **se** means *(to) each other.*

A. Remplacez les tirets par le pronom qui convient au sens.

1. Qu'est-ce que Paul vous a fait? Cessez de _____ tourmenter.
2. Quand il arrivera, dites _____ de venir _____ voir.   3. Jean est heureux que vous _____ ayez promis ce voyage.   4. Entrez donc, je suis seul et vous ne _____ dérangez pas.   5. Regardez bien ces gens, car vous ne _____ reverrez plus.   6. Ils sont partis avant que j'aie pu _____ parler.   7. J'aurais voulu _____ demander où ils allaient.

B. Traduisez en français.

1. *(tu)* Do you like spring? Yes, I prefer it to the other seasons.
2. *(vous)* My boys have arrived. I will ask them if they know your children and if they saw them on the way.   3. We'll tell them to[1] write him at once.   4. *(vous)* I will give you that magazine.

[1] de

3. **When is *y* used as the place pronoun** *there,* **and when is the adverb** *là* **used?**

—Allez-vous à Paris? —J'**y** vais demain.
—Je vais en classe. —**Y** serez-vous à neuf heures?
—Où est Georges? —Il est **là,** derrière vous.

The pronoun **y** is used to express *there* when the place has been previously mentioned. The adverb **là** points out *where,* usually when the place has not been previously mentioned.

4. **When is *en* used as a pronoun object instead of *le, la,* and *les*?**

Il voit **sa soeur** souvent.	*He sees* his sister *often.*
Il **la** voit souvent.	*He sees* her *often.*
Il achète **des fleurs** dans la rue.	*He buys* some flowers *in the street.*
Il **en** achète dans la rue.	*He buys* some *in the street.*
Il a trouvé **trois amis** au café.	*He found* three friends *in the café.*
Il **en** a trouvé trois au café.	*He found three* of them *in the café.*

The pronoun **en** replaces a noun object when that object is indefinite in nature. A noun object is indefinite when it is modified by a partitive construction, by a numeral, by adverbs of quantity, etc.

For practical purposes, one can say that **en** is used whenever in the English sentence the pronoun object is rendered by *some* or by *of them.*

C. Remplacez les tirets par *le, la, les, y,* ou *en,* selon le cas.

1. —Comment trouvez-vous sa maison? —Je _____ trouve superbe.   **2.** —Voyez-vous des taxis dans la rue? —Oui, nous _____ voyons.   **3.** —Combien d'enfants ont-ils? —Ils _____ont cinq.   **4.** —Il est parti pour Bordeaux. —Qu'est-ce qu'il va _____ faire?   **5.** —Combien de courses avez-vous à faire? —Nous _____ avons beaucoup.   **6.** —Georges a-t-il un but dans la vie?—Oui, il _____ a même plusieurs.   **7.** —Vous me dites que vous allez en France. _____ allez-vous bientôt?   **8.** —Connaissez-vous cette femme? —Oui, et je _____ plains.

D. Traduisez en français.

1. I have many friends and I see them every week.   **2.** (*vous*) I would like to spend a few days in the country. Do you want to go there with me?   **3.** (*tu*) Do you want some tea? Yes, I'll take some.   **4.** When will he arrive in Paris? He has already arrived there.   **5.** (*vous*) How many brothers do you have? I have two[1].   **6.** Are there many students in that class? Yes, there are many[2].   7. The telephone book is there, under the desk.

[1] In French, one must say *two of them*.   [2] In French, one must say *many of them*.

II.   Position of Object Pronouns

5. Where do object pronouns come in relation to the verb?

Je **le** donne à Jean.   Je ne **la** vois pas.   Donnez-**le** à Marc.
Il **en** a trouvé.   Ne **me le** dites pas.   Allez-**y.**

Pronoun objects come immediately before the verb except in the affirmative imperative, in which case they follow the verb and are appended to it by a hyphen.

6. Where do object pronouns come when the sentence contains an auxiliary verb followed by an infinitive?

Jacques veut **vous** voir.   Qui peut **me le** dire?
Vous devez **en** chercher.   Nous commencerons à **le** faire.
Qui a refusé de **lui** parler?   Ils vont **y** aller.

When there is a pronoun object in a sentence that has a verb followed by an infinitive, the pronoun object normally precedes the infinitive. This is because, in most cases, it is the infinitive that governs the pronoun object.

NOTE: When the auxiliary verb governs a pronoun object, that pronoun object precedes it. Ex.: Je **l'**ai laissé partir. **Vous** a-t-il vu sortir?

7. Where do *y* and *en* come in relation to other pronoun objects?

Je **lui en** ai donné.   Donnez-**lui-en.**   Il **y en** a dans le
couloir.
Il **vous en** a montré.   Montrez-**m'en** trois.   Donnez-**leur-en.**

The pronouns **y** and **en** follow all other object pronouns and **y** always precedes **en.**

8. What is the order of pronoun objects other than *y* and *en*?

Georges **me le** montre.   Montrez-**le-moi.**
Ils **nous les** expliquent.   Expliquez-**les-nous.**

When there are two object pronouns other than **y** or **en,** the *l*-form comes nearest the verb.

Je **le lui** indique.   Indiquez-**la-leur.**

When there are two *l*-forms, they come in alphabetical order, that is **le, la,** and **les** always precede **lui** and **leur.**

E. Remplacez les expressions en italique par des pronoms compléments.

1. —Expliquera-t-il aux élèves la théorie de l'évolution? —Non, il
n'expliquera pas *aux élèves la théorie de l'évolution.* **2.** —Portez
ce paquet à mon cousin. —Je porterai *ce paquet à votre cousin* quand
j'aurai le temps. **3.** —Êtes-vous allé voir ce film? —Oui, je suis
allé voir *ce film.* **4.** —Voulez-vous montrer vos tableaux à notre
ami? —Oui, je veux bien montrer *mes tableaux à notre ami.*
5. —Prêtez-moi les notes de votre cours. —Je vous rendrai *les notes*
la semaine prochaine. **6.** —Donnez ce dossier au directeur. —Je
donnerai *ce dossier au directeur.* **7.** —Est-ce qu'il a annoncé son
mariage à ses parents? —Oui, il a annoncé *son mariage à ses parents.*
8. —Puis-je demander des renseignements à cet agent? —Oui, bien
sûr, vous pouvez demander *des renseignements à cet agent.*
9. —Ne voulez-vous pas raconter votre accident à ces journalistes?
—Non, je ne veux pas raconter *cet accident aux journalistes.*
10. —Voulez-vous m'acheter un journal? —Oui, je vous achèterai
un *journal.* **11.** Les enfants aiment les jouets à Noël, mais il ne
faut pas donner *aux enfants* trop *de jouets.*

F. Traduisez en français.

1. (*tu*) Here are some oranges. If you see your brother, give him
some. **2.** (*vous*) Your first French[1] class must[2] have been
interesting. Describe it to us. **3.** (*tu*) I have seven books. I will
bring them to you tomorrow. **4.** (*vous*) Where are your magazines?
Show them to him at once. **5.** (*vous*) Did you hear the news[3]? Do
not tell it to them. **6.** She spoke of it to him. **7.** (*tu*) Those
rules are not difficult. The teacher will explain them to you
tomorrow. **8.** (*vous*) You have grapefruit[4]? Send me some this
afternoon. **9.** (*vous*) Do you have that article? Do you want to
read it to me? **10.** (*vous*) Give it to us tomorrow. **11.** (*tu*) Do
you know[5] any good jokes? Tell us some.

[1] **classe de français** [2] **a dû être** [3] Use the singular form. [4] The French word for
grapefruit is plural as used here. [5] Use a form of **connaître**.

III. Disjunctive Pronouns

9. What are the disjunctive pronouns?

moi	*me*		**nous**	*us*
toi	*you*		**vous**	*you*
lui	*him*		**eux**	*them (m.)*
elle	*her*		**elles**	*them (f.)*
		soi	*oneself*	

10. What are the seven most common uses of the disjunctive pronouns?

The disjunctive pronoun is always used in an emphatic position.

   (a) Nous sommes allés en France avec **eux.**

The disjunctive pronoun is used after prepositions.

   (b) Jean et **lui** sont partis ce matin.
       Eux et **moi** avons l'intention de la voir.
       Vous les avez vus les deux, Maurice et **lui?**

The disjunctive pronoun is used as a part of a compound subject or object.

   (c) **Moi,** je vais y aller.
       Lui, il n'en sait rien
       Eux seuls peuvent le faire.

The disjunctive pronoun is used to emphasize the subject of the sentence or when the subject is separated from the verb.

   (d) Mes frères sont plus grands   Je suis aussi intelligent qu'**eux.**
       que **moi.**
       Vous parlez mieux que **lui.**   Vous êtes aussi riche qu'**elle.**

The disjunctive pronoun is used after **que** meaning *as* or *than* in comparisons.

   (e) C'est **moi.**   C'est **lui.**   C'est $\Big\}$ **eux.**
                                           Ce sont

The disjunctive is used after **ce** + a form of the verb **être.**

   (f) —Qui est là? —**Lui.**   —Qui partira le premier? —**Toi.**

The disjunctive is used alone, in answer to questions.

   (g) **moi**-même   **lui**-même   **eux**-mêmes   **soi**-même

The disjunctive is used when compounded with **-même** (*self*).

11. When is *soi* ordinarily used as a disjunctive?

Là, on ne pense qu'à **soi.**   Il est si bon de rester chez **soi.**
Chacun travaille pour **soi.**   Il ne faut pas être trop content
                                       de **soi.**

La télévision en **soi** n'est pas   Ça va de **soi.**
   mauvaise.

The disjunctive **soi** is most often used after a preposition in a sentence where an indefinite subject such as **on** or **chacun** or one introduced by an impersonal expression is its antecedent and in the fixed expressions **en soi** and **de soi.**

G. Remplacez le mot anglais par le pronom disjoint convenable.

1. Je crois qu'ils finiront par se marier, (*she*) et Pierre.   2. Regardez ce que cet enfant a fabriqué (*himself*).   3. Pierre va aller avec (*me*) au bureau.   4. (*As for me*), maintenant, je m'en moque[1].   5. Ah! qu'on est bien chez (*oneself*[2]).   6. —Les voilà. —Qui? —(*They*). 7. Tu es ingrat après tout ce qu'ils ont fait pour (*you*).   8. Chacun parle pour (*himself*).   9. (*You*), tu as toujours eu de la chance! 10. Vous pouvez continuer sans (*me*).   11. C'est (*he*) qui m'a raconté votre aventure.   12. Qui a cassé le vase? —Ce n'est pas (*I*).   13. Est-ce qu'elle est aussi amusante que (*he*)?   14. Dans un moment de danger, pense-t-on à (*oneself*)?

[1] In this sense, the expression means: *I don't care.*   [2] Franch tends not to use the -**même** form unless it is absolutely needed for clarity.

H. Traduisez en français.

1. (*vous*) Would you like to work for him?   2. His friend and he can go to the movies this evening.   3. I found out[1] this news[2] through them.   4. (*tu*) You must do your exercises yourself. 5. They[3] are the ones who are happy[4] at his return.   6. (*vous*) You have a better car than he.   7. Who will go to that meeting? She and I.   8. He is much more patient than they.

[1] Use a form of **apprendre**.   [2] Use the singular noun.   [3]lit: *It is they who*   [4]contents **de**

12. What pronoun construction replaces *de* + <u>noun</u>?

(a) when the noun is a person

<table>
<tr><td>Je parle de ma sœur.</td><td>Je parle d'elle.</td></tr>
<tr><td>Il se souvient de son grand-
père.</td><td>Il se souvient de lui.</td></tr>
<tr><td>J'ai besoin d'amis.</td><td>J'en ai besoin.</td></tr>
</table>

In general, one may say that **de** + NOUN (person) is replaced by **de** + DISJUNCTIVE PRONOUN. However, **en** sometimes replaces this construction, especially when the person in question is indefinite.

(b) when the noun is a thing

<table>
<tr><td>Je parle de mon travail.</td><td>J'en parle.</td></tr>
<tr><td>Il se souvient de ses voyages.</td><td>Il s'en souvient.</td></tr>
<tr><td>Ils ont besoin d'argent.</td><td>Ils en ont besoin.</td></tr>
</table>

The construction **de** + NOUN (thing) is regularly replaced by **en.**

13. What pronoun construction replaces *à* + <u>noun</u>?

(a) when the noun is a person after verbs that take an indirect object

Jacques a raconté son aventure **à l'agent.**	Jacques **lui** a raconté son aventure.
Vous ressemblez **à vos frères.**	Vous **leur** ressemblez.
Ils obéissent **à leur mère.**	Ils **lui** obéissent.

When **à** + NOUN (person) follows a non-reflexive verb which takes an indirect object, the construction is replaced by the indirect object pronouns. In French, in addition to the common verbs such as **dire, raconter, demander,** etc., a number of other verbs such as **obéir à, ressembler à,** and **plaire à** take an indirect object.

(b) When the noun is a person after reflexive verbs and after certain non-reflexive verbs that are followed by **à** but do not take an indirect object

Je m'intéresse **à cet enfant.**	Je m'intéresse **à lui.**
Nous pensons **à Marie.**	Nous pensons **à elle.**
Faites attention **à l'agent.**	Faites attention **à lui.**

When **à** + NOUN (person) follows any reflexive verb and certain other verbs, the most common of which are **penser à** and **faire attention à,** the construction is replaced by **à** + DISJUNCTIVE PRONOUN.

(c) when the noun is a thing

Je réponds **à la lettre.**	J'**y** réponds.
Nous pensons **à nos problèmes.**	Nous **y** pensons.
Qui s'intéresse **aux langues?**	Qui s'**y** intéresse?

When **à** + NOUN (thing) follows a verb, it is generally replaced by **y.**

I. Remplacez l'expression en italique par le pronom convenable.

1. La police s'est emparée *de ces terroristes.*   2. Nous ressemblons *à nos parents.*   3. Je me chargerai *de ce problème.*   4. Croyez-vous *à cette histoire?*   5. Essayez de ne plus penser *à ces imbéciles.*
6. Je m'intéresse beaucoup *à la politique.*   7. A-t-on besoin *d'argent* pour s'amuser?   8. Ne vous adressez pas *à cet homme.*
9. Il a dit *à sa mère* ce qu'il voulait.   10. Obéissez *aux agents.*
11. Nous avons parlé *de vos camarades.*   12. Vous souvenez-vous *de ce monsieur?*   13. Je me souviens bien *de sa voiture.*   14. Ne vous fiez pas *à ces statistiques.*   15. Faites attention *au signal.*
16. Faites attention *à ces gens.*

J. Traduisez en français.

1. *(tu)* Why don't you ever speak of him?   2. *(vous)* She is rather strange, but you will get accustomed to her.   3. *(vous)* You are

very kind to take an interest in us.   **4.** I received their letter and I have already answered it.   **5.** When the teacher asked me a personal question yesterday, I didn't answer him.   **6.** His father is easy-going, but it is necessary to obey him.   **7.** I have a lot of work, but I'm not thinking of it right now.   **8.** (*tu*) It's Maurice. Were you thinking of him?

Exercices d'ensemble

K. Les pronoms compléments entre parenthèses sont en ordre alphabétique. Parfois l'ordre est juste, parfois faux. Changez l'ordre quand c'est nécessaire.

1. Voilà les renseignements que j'ai obtenus. Donnez (les, lui).
2. Vous avez acheté un nouveau jeu vidéo. Montrez (le, moi).   **3.** Je ne sais pas où est cette rue. L'agent (le, me) dira.   **4.** Ce crime est révoltant. Ne (le, nous) racontez pas.   **5.** J'aimerais savoir où ils sont allés. Je (le, leur) demanderai demain.   **6.** Nous aurons besoin de ces deux documents. Paul (les, nous) rapportera la semaine prochaine.   **7.** Ils connaissent le règlement. Je ne (le, leur) répéterai pas.   **8.** Ce paquet est trop lourd. Il est impossible de (le, lui) envoyer par la poste.   **9.** Vous avez appris son secret. Dites (le, nous).   **10.** Vous avez vu mes timbres. Si vous en faites collection, vous n'avez pas besoin de (les, me) rendre.   **11.** Voilà les disques que j'ai promis à Claude. Il (en, lui) faut six pour sa soirée.

L. Remplacez les tirets par le pronom qui convient au sens.

1. Nicole a acheté un cadeau pour _____ hier et elle me l'a offert ce matin.   **2.** Marie est fâchée contre son mari et elle refuse de _____ parler.   **3.** Cet acte aura de graves conséquences; il faut _____ penser.   **4.** —Avez-vous un cendrier? —Bien sûr, j'_____ ai plusieurs.   **5.** —Vous intéressez-vous à l'art moderne? —Oui, nous nous _____ intéressons beaucoup.   **6.** Ce sont des ingrats. Tâchez de ne plus penser à _____.   **7.** L'agent vous fait signe de vous arrêter. Vous feriez bien de _____ obéir.   **8.** Ma femme voudrait aller à l'opéra. Mais _____ , je ne tiens pas à _____ aller.   **9.** Tu as reçu une lettre importante l'autre jour. Il faut _____ répondre tout de suite.   **10.** Avez-vous besoin de papier à lettre? Je viens d'_____ acheter.   **11.** Vous connaissez Marc et Christophe? C'est _____ qui sont dans la pièce à côté.

M. Traduisez en français.

1. (*vous*) These books are too heavy. Don't take[1] them to them.
2. (*vous*) Tell them what happened to you.   **3.** Who will get[2] the first prize? I.   **4.** (*tu*) Do you like tea? Yes, I prefer it to coffee.
5. (*vous*) You have only one car; we have two.   **6.** (*tu*) Can you

do this problem yourself? 7. Helen is my best friend. I speak of her with pleasure. 8. They[3] are the ones who gave us this picture. 9. Are there many pupils in this class? Yes, there are many. 10. *(tu)* Do you remember them?

[1] Use a form of apporter. [2] Use a form of avoir. [3] Lit: *It is they*

N. Traduisez en français.

1. They too[1] can leave now. **2.** His brother is not as ambitious as he. **3.** *(tu)* Do you want to go to Europe with me? **4.** Since they are late, let's leave without them. **5.** *(vous)* Are you going to France, or are you coming back from there? **6.** *(vous)* You and I agree on this point. **7.** *(vous)* You like exotic countries, but do you go there from time to time? **8.** *(vous)* They want to know the truth; tell it to them. **9.** They should[2] be there, but I do not see them. **10.** *He* can do that, not I.

[1] Put *too* in this place in the sentence. [2] Use a form of **devoir**.

Problem Words

16. expect

(a) How to say *expect a person* or *a material thing*

J'attends ma femme demain.	I expect *my wife tomorrow.*
Nous **attendons** une augmentation le mois prochain.	We expect *a raise next month.*

The non-reflexive **attendre** may mean *expect* when it is followed by a direct object that is either *a person* or *a material thing*.

(b) How to say *expect an event* or *some other immaterial thing*

Nous nous attendons à une belle surprise.	We are expecting *a great surprise.*
Je ne m'attendais pas à vous voir.	I did not expect *to see you.*

The reflexive **s'attendre à** is often the equivalent of *to expect* followed by an event or some other immaterial thing.

(c) How to say *expect that* + CLAUSE

Jacques **s'attend à ce que nous venions.**	*Jack* expects us to come.

The expression **s'attendre à ce que** + SUBJUNCTIVE is the equivalent of *expect that* + CLAUSE.

(d) When *expect to = intend to*

Nous **comptons** le voir cet après-midi.	*We* expect to *see him this afternoon.*
J'ai l'intention de lire cet article.	*I* expect to *read that article.*

When *expect to = intend to*, French may express it by **compter** + INFINITIVE or **avoir l'intention de** + INFINITIVE.

(e) How to say: *What do you expect? What do you expect me to . . . ?*

Que voulez-vous, il est si jeune!	What do you expect, *he is so young!*
Où veut-il que j'aille?	Where does he expect *me to go?*

When *expect* is used to ask a question with a shrug of the shoulders and implies inevitability, the French often use a form of **vouloir** as in the above examples.

17. fail

(1) How to say *to fail to do something.*

Il **ne s'est pas arrêté** au feu rouge.	*He* failed to stop *at the red light.*

The French have no special way of expressing *to fail to do something.* They simply use the negative form of the main verb.

(b) How to say *not to fail to do something*

Ne manquez pas de nous **écrire** dès votre arrivée.	Don't fail to write *us when you arrive.*

To express *not to fail to do something,* use the negative of **manquer de** + INFINITIVE.

Notice that the affirmative of **manquer de** has another meaning, as for example: **J'ai manqué de tomber** = *I almost fell.*

(c) How to say *fail an examination* or *a course*

Jean-Pierre **a échoué à** son examen de biologie.	
Jean-Pierre **n'a pas réussi à** son examen de biologie.	*Jean-Pierre* failed *his biology test.*
Jean-Pierre **a raté** son examen de biologie.	

The English *to fail an examination* is **échouer à un examen** or, familiarly, **rater un examen;** and *fail a course* is **échouer à un cours.** But one can also say **ne pas réussir** or **ne pas être reçu à un examen.**

(d) How to say *to fail someone in a course*

Ce professeur **colle** rarement **ses élèves.**	*That teacher rarely* fails his pupils.

To express the English *to fail someone,* the expression **coller quel-qu'un** is used colloquially. More formal but not so common are: **refuser quelqu'un, ne pas recevoir quelqu'un,** and **faire échouer quel-qu'un.**

CAUTION: DO NOT say «échouer quelqu'un». Say either **refuser quel-qu'un, faire échouer quelqu'un,** or **coller quelqu'un.**

18. feel

(a) When to use **sentir que**

Georges **a senti qu**'il valait mieux partir.	*George* felt that *it was better to leave.*

The English *to feel that* + CLAUSE = **sentir que** + CLAUSE.

(b) When to use **se sentir**

Je **me sens** vraiment mal.	*I really* feel *bad.*
Vous **sentez-vous** un peu mieux?	Do *you* feel *a little better?*
Je **me sens** bien.	*I* feel *well.*

Forms of **se sentir** are used to express *feel* when it refers to the state of one's health; this verb is used with the adverbs **bien, mal, mieux,** etc. The verb **se trouver** is also used to express *feel.* Ex.: Si ça continue, je vais **me trouver** mal.

CAUTION: The verb **sentir** sometimes means *to smell.* Do not confuse: **Il se sent bien.** (*He feels good.*) with: **Ça sent bon.** (*That smells good.*)

(c) How to express *How do you feel?*

Comment **allez**-vous? ⎫ Comment **ça va?** ⎬	*How are you? How do you feel?*
Je **vais** bien, merci.	*I'm well, thank you.*

To ask a person how he feels in English, we normally say: *How are you?* although we sometimes say: *How do you feel?* To ask how a person is, French normally uses the verb **aller.** The familiar impersonal «Comment ça va?» and «Ça va?» are also very common.

19. get

(a) When *get = obtain*

J'ai pu **obtenir** un exemplaire de ce livre.	*I was able to* get *a copy of that book.*
Où est-ce que je peux **me pro-curer** un ordinateur?	*Where can I* get *a computer?*
Où **as**-tu **trouvé** cette machine à écrire?	*Where* did *you* get *that type-writer?*

When *get* = *obtain,* it may be expressed by **obtenir** or **se procurer** and in certain contexts by **trouver.**

(b) When *get* = *receive*

Avez-vous **reçu** ma lettre ce matin?	Did *you* get *my letter this morning?*

The verb **recevoir** is used to express *get* in the sense of *receive.*

Louis **a eu** une augmentation de salaire.	Louis got *a raise in pay.*
Philippe **a eu** une bonne note.	*Philip* got *a good grade.*

The compound past and simple past of **avoir** are often used in the sense of *got.*

(c) When *get* = *go and get*

Veux-tu **chercher** le journal?	*Will you* get *the paper?*
Allez chercher le courrier.	Get *the mail.*

When *get* = *go and get,* it may be expressed by **chercher** or **aller chercher.**

(d) When *get* = *catch* (a disease)

Jean a dû **attraper** la rougeole à l'école.	*John must have* gotten *the measles at school.*

The verb **attraper** + *disease* is used to mean *get a disease.*

(e) When *get* = *become*

Anne **se fatigue** facilement.	*Anne* gets tired *easily.*
Raymond **a** beaucoup **maigri** cette année.	*Raymond* got *very* thin *this year.*

Some reflexive verbs and also certain non-reflexive verbs carry with them the sense of *get* + ADJECTIVE in all tenses, some only in past tenses.

Tout à coup **il a fait** très **froid.**	*Suddenly* it got *very* cold.
J'**ai eu** très **sommeil** après le dîner.	*I* got *very* sleepy *after dinner.*

The compound past and the simple past of idiomatic expressions with **avoir** and **faire** are often used to express *get.*

Elle **est devenue** furieuse.	*She* got *furious.*

Normally, **devenir** + ADJECTIVE is used in the sense of *get* only when there is no verb equivalent to express that idea.

O. Remplacez les mots anglais par leur équivalent français.

1. Arrêtez-vous de tourner en rond, je vais (*feel*) mal.   **2.** Comment fait-on pour (*get*) un passeport?   **3.** (*vous*) Que (*do you expect*) qu'il fasse contre tous ces gens?   **4.** Je (*won't fail*) lui transmettre votre

message. **5.** On (*gets*) facilement des rhumes dans l'autobus.
6. Georges a l'air très fatigué; est-ce qu'il (*feels*) bien? **7.** Je ne
sais pas pourquoi il (*failed to come*). **8.** Je (*expected*) un mot
d'excuse de sa part. **9.** Dans ce milieu mondain Jules (*feels*) mal à
l'aise. **10.** Si Jean-Paul (*fails*) son examen, il sera obligé de suivre
des cours de vacances. **11.** Je (*expect*) faire le voyage de Paris à
Marseille en six heures. **12.** Eric était sûr de lui, mais les
examinateurs le (*failed*). **13.** Ma femme voudrait bien (*get*) cette
recette. **14.** Voudriez-vous (*get*) cette revue pour moi à la
bibliothèque? **15.** Ma propriétaire (*is getting*) complètement
sourde.

P. Traduisez en français. Attention aux mots en italique.

1. I *got* good results with that machine. **2.** (*tu*) Do you want me
to open the window? You'll *feel better*. **3.** (*vous*) Don't *fail* to
telephone me tomorrow before noon. **4.** (*vous*) What do you
expect her to do for him now? **5.** The most intelligent pupils can
fail an examination. **6.** I *got* an immediate reply to my letter.
7. If Monique *feels* tired, she should go to see the doctor. **8.** Alain
failed to hand in his work. **9.** I did not *expect* to go to Brussels
before next week. **10.** (*tu*) George, I left my purse in the car. Will
you *get* it, please? **11.** Frances *expects* a letter from Paul. **12.** I
did not *expect* to be invited to the Dubois. **13.** (*tu*) What did you
get for Christmas? **14.** Odette *gets* angry when people don't do
everything she wishes. **15.** It *got* so warm that we were able to
go out without a coat.

Verb Review

Review the verbs **boire** and **connaître** according to the outline on page
253.

6

Past Tenses in Narration

1. What sort of actions are expressed by the verbs in boldface type in the following passage? What is the normal function of the compound past?

Il **s'est** alors **levé** après avoir bu un verre de vin. Il **a repoussé** les assiettes et le peu de boudin[1] froid que nous avions laissé. Il **a** soigneusement **essuyé** la toile cirée de la table. Il **a pris** dans un tiroir de sa table de nuit une feuille de papier[2] quadrillé, une enveloppe jaune, un petit
5 porte-plume de bois rouge et un encrier carré d'encre violette. Quand il m'**a dit** le nom de la femme, j'**ai vu** que c'était une Mauresque[3]. J'**ai fait** la lettre. Je l'**ai écrite** un peu au hasard, mais je **me suis appliqué** à contenter Raymond parce que je n'avais pas de raison de ne pas le contenter. Puis j'**ai lu** la lettre à haute voix. Il m'**a demandé** de la relire.
10 Il **a été** tout à fait content.

Camus: *L'Étranger*

The COMPOUND PAST expresses a series of successive actions in conversation or in an informal narrative. Each successive action serves to forward the plot of the narrative.

The COMPOUND PAST also expresses a change of mental state. Thus, the last sentence in the above passage: **Il a été tout à fait content** means: *He was* (in the sense of *became*) *quite satisfied.*

---

[1] *black pudding*   [2] *paper ruled in squares*   [3] *Moorish woman*

2. What sort of actions are expressed by the italicized verbs in the following passage? What are the various functions of the imperfect?

    . . . Il m'a dit: «Je *savais* bien que tu *connaissais* la vie». Je ne me suis pas aperçu d'abord qu'il me *tutoyait*. C'est seulement quand il m'a déclaré: «Maintenant, tu es un vrai copain», que cela m'a frappé. Il a répété sa phrase et j'ai dit: «Oui». Cela m'*était* égal d'être son copain et il *avait*
5 vraiment l'air d'en avoir envie. Il a cacheté la lettre et nous avons fini le vin. Puis nous sommes restés un moment à fumer sans rien dire. Au dehors, tout *était* calme, et nous avons entendu le glissement d'une auto qui *passait*. J'ai dit: «Il est tard». Raymond le *pensait* aussi. Il a remarqué que le temps *passait* vite, et, dans un sens, c'*était* vrai. J'*avais* sommeil,
10 mais j'*avais* de la peine à me lever.

      Camus: *L'Étranger*

    The IMPERFECT describes a state or action which was going on when some other action took place. The imperfect often sets a background for the principal actions. Actions in the imperfect do not take place successively; they have no beginning or end in reference to the time of the main action. They simply go on.

    Let us consider the various types of imperfects in the above passage.

(a) Cela m'*était* égal d'être son copain et il *avait* vraiment l'air d'en avoir envie . . . Au dehors, tout *était* calme . . . C'*était* vrai. J'*avais* sommeil, mais j'*avais* de la peine à me lever.

    The IMPERFECT is used in past descriptions. Each of these verbs describes a state of being in the past. Note that these states have neither beginning nor end, nor are they successive actions which forward a narrative.

(b) Je ne **me suis** pas **aperçu** d'abord qu'il me *tutoyait* . . . Nous **avons entendu** le glissement d'une auto qui *passait* . . . Il **a remarqué** que le temps *passait* vite.

    The IMPERFECT often describes what was going on when it was interrupted by some other action.

    As a rule of thumb, we can say that most past actions in which the verb has an *-ing* ending in English are expressed by the imperfect in French.

    The action of each of the italicized verbs in the above passage was going on when it was interrupted by the action of the verbs in boldface type.

(c) «Je *savais* bien que tu *connaissais* la vie». . . . Raymond le *pensait* aussi.

The IMPERFECT is used to indicate a mental state in the past, for there is no beginning nor end to this state as far as the immediate actions are concerned.

Each of the above italicized verbs expresses a mental state.

3. The imperfect has still another important common function. What is the function of the imperfects in italics in the following passage?

À huit heures la cloche *annonçait* le souper. Après le souper, dans les beaux jours, on *s'asseyait* sur le perron. Mon père, armé de son fusil, *tirait* les chouettes[1] qui *sortaient* des crénaux[2] à l'entrée de la nuit. Ma mère, Lucile et moi, nous *regardions* le ciel, les bois, les derniers rayons
5   du soleil, les premières étoiles. À dix heures, on *rentrait* et l'on *se couchait*.

Les soirées d'automne et d'hiver *étaient* d'une autre nature. Le souper fini et les quatre convives revenus de la table à la cheminée, ma mère *se jetait,* en soupirant, sur un vieux lit de jour de siamoise[3] flambée; on
10   *mettait* devant elle un guéridon[4] avec une bougie[5]. Je *m'asseyais* auprès du feu avec Lucile; les domestiques *enlevaient* le couvert et *se retiraient*. Mon père *commençait* alors une promenade qui ne *cessait* qu'à l'heure de son coucher. Il *était* vêtu d'une robe de ratine[6] blanche, ou plutôt d'une espèce de manteau que je n'ai vu qu'à lui. Sa tête, demi-chauve,
15   *était* couverte d'un grand bonnet blanc qui *se tenait* tout droit. Lorsqu'en se promenant il *s'éloignait* du foyer, la vaste salle *était* si peu éclairée par une seule bougie qu'on ne le *voyait* plus; on l'*entendait* seulement encore marcher dans les ténèbres, puis il *revenait* lentement vers la lumière et *émergeait* peu à peu de l'obscurité comme un spectre,
20   avec sa robe blanche, son bonnet blanc, sa figure longue et pâle . . .

Chateaubriand: *Mémoires d'outre-tombe*

Habitual or repeated past actions are expressed by the IMPERFECT. In English, such actions are usually expressed by $\left.\begin{array}{l} used\ to \\ would \end{array}\right\}$ + VERB.

4. How can an English-speaking person avoid overusing the French imperfect?

English-speaking students tend to use the French imperfect where the French would use the compound past (**passé composé**). Before expressing an action or state in the imperfect, ask yourself some questions to test whether this is the proper tense.

---

[1] *owls*   [2] *indentures in the wall*   [3] *bright colored Siamese cotton*   [4] *round table*
[5] *candle*   [6] *woolen cloth*

Use of the COMPOUND PAST (**passé composé**)

(a) Does the action advance the narrative even in the slightest degree? In that case, use the compound past rather than the imperfect.
(b) Is the action limited in time in any way? In that case, use the compound past rather than the imperfect. Even if the action takes place over twenty years or twenty centuries, if the time is limited, do not use the imperfect.
(c) Does the action state a past fact, one which does not set a background? Then use the compound past rather than the imperfect.

NOTE: The fact that the action is continued has nothing to do with whether it is imperfect or **passé composé.** All actions continue for some time— some much longer than others—but the mere fact that they continue is no criterion for the choice of tense.

Use of the IMPERFECT (**imparfait**)

(a) Does the action merely form a background for the plot by describing a state? Then use the imperfect.
(b) Is it a question of a continuing action which is interrrupted by another action? In this case, put the continuing action in the imperfect.
(c) Is it a question of a past action expressed in English by $\left.\begin{array}{c} was \\ were \end{array}\right\}$ + the -*ing* form of the verb? Then use the imperfect.
(d) Is it a customary action, repeated regularly, which would be expressed in English by $\left.\begin{array}{c} would \\ used\ to \end{array}\right\}$ + verb? Then use the imperfect.
(e) Is it a question of a state of mind rather than a change of state of mind? Then use the imperfect.

There are a few other less common uses of the imperfect, but these are the principal ones.

5. What is the basic difference between actions expressed by the *passé composé* and those expressed by the imperfect?

C'*était* le 31 décembre. Je *me trouvais* seul chez moi ce soir-là. Je *lisais* dans mon bureau. Un peu avant minuit j'**ai entendu** des gens qui *chantaient* dans la rue. Ils **ont vu** de la lumière et **ont frappé** à ma fenêtre. Je ne les *connaissais* pas, mais je leur **ai ouvert** la porte. Ils *étaient* drôles, et nous **avons fêté** le Nouvel an ensemble.

Graphically, the imperfect may be represented by a straight line which indicates the flow of time. Actions above this line are going on while something else takes place. The **passé composé** (and the **passé simple**) may be represented by points in time (X) indicating the interrupting actions which take place successively.

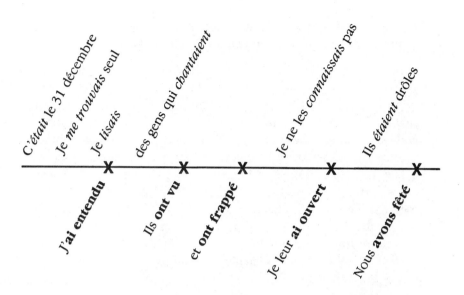

A. Remplacez l'infinitif par la forme convenable du passé composé ou de l'imparfait, selon le cas. Expliquez oralement chaque emploi de l'imparfait.

Il (faire) froid hier soir et nous n'(avoir) rien de spécial à faire. Je (vouloir) rester chez moi, mais Philippe (préférer) sortir. Nous (décider) d'aller voir Bernard, un de nos amis qui avait partagé notre appartement l'année dernière. Donc, nous y (aller), espérant le trouver chez lui. Nous
5   (quitter) la maison à huit heures du soir; quand nous (arriver) dans la rue, il (faire) déjà sombre et il (neiger). Nous (prendre) ma voiture et nous (rouler) pendant une demi-heure. Bernard (habiter) maintenant une jolie maison de la banlieue. Quand il nous (ouvrir) la porte, nous (entendre) des gens qui (parler). Nous ne (savoir) pas qui (être) là et nous ne (vouloir)
10 pas déranger notre ami. Mais il nous (dire) d'entrer.

Philippe (s'excuser) de ne pas l'avoir prévenu, disant que notre téléphone ne (marcher) pas. Nous (enlever) nos manteaux et nous (entrer) dans la salle de séjour. Il y (avoir) là plusieurs personnes que nous (connaître) et qui (parler) avec animation. Nous (être) en pleine conversation
15 sur le best-seller de la semaine quand la sœur de notre hôte (proposer) de nous montrer des diapositives de leurs vacances. Il (falloir) dire que oui et pendant une heure nous (regarder) les projections. Ensuite on nous (servir) une bonne collation. Nous (rester) chez Bernard deux heures. À onze heures nous (rentrer) chez nous, ayant passé après tout une agréable
20 soirée.

B. Traduisez en français en employant le passé composé et l'imparfait. Expliquez oralement chaque emploi de l'imparfait.

A curious thing happened[1] to me the other day. I was[2] taking a walk in the country with my dog. I was[3] walking along a road when I saw a man who wore an old coat. He was about[4] forty years old. When he caught[5] sight of me, he became afraid and began to run. That surprised
5 me, and I decided to follow him. We walked rapidly[6] for[7] five minutes. Finally, he slowed[8] down and I overtook him. I asked him why he was acting like that. He told me that I resembled a policeman[9] he knew and said: "I was afraid[10] when I saw you." The man spoke with an accent. I learned that he was a foreigner and that he didn't know English well.
10 He told me that he often used[2] to go walking in the country, where he would pick up fruit[11] and would eat at the farmer's[12]. We chatted a bit, and I tried to reassure him. Finally, we shook hands, and then we continued[13] on our way.

[1] Use a form of **arriver.**   [2] Use a form of **se promener.**   [3] Use a form of **marcher.** [4] **environ**   [5] Use a form of **apercevoir.**   [6] **à grands pas**   [7] **pendant**   [8] *slow down* = **ralentir**   [9] **un policier**   [10] This means that he became frightened. Use a form of **avoir peur.**   [11] **des fruits**   [12] *farmer* = **le fermier**   [13] Use a form of **continuer notre route.**

6. When is the simple past used?

Le tigre

Une femme *lavait* son linge dans une fontaine, à cent pas de la maison; elle *avait* avec elle un enfant de quatorze à quinze mois.

Elle **manqua** de savon, **retourna** chez elle pour en chercher, et, jugeant inutile d'emmener son enfant, le **laissa** jouer sur le gazon, près
5 de la fontaine.

Pendant qu'elle *cherchait* son savon, elle **jeta** par la fenêtre ouverte les yeux sur la fontaine pour s'assurer si l'enfant ne *s'aventurait* pas au bord de l'eau; mais sa terreur **fut** grande lorsqu'elle **vit** un tigre sortir de la forêt, traverser le chemin, aller droit à l'enfant et poser sur lui sa
10 large patte.

Elle **resta** immobile, haletante, pâle, presque morte.

Mais sans doute l'enfant **prit** l'animal féroce pour un gros chien; il lui **empoigna** les oreilles avec ses petites mains et **commença** de[1] jouer avec lui.
15 Le tigre ne **fut** pas en[2] reste; c'*était* un tigre d'un caractère jovial, il **joua** lui-même avec l'enfant.

Ce jeu effroyable **dura** dix minutes, puis le tigre, laissant l'enfant, **retraversa** la route et **rentra** dans le bois.

La mère **s'élança, courut** tout éperdue à l'enfant, et le **trouva** riant
20   et sans une égratignure.

Alexandre Dumas: *Le Caucase*

[1] Most often one finds **commencer à** + INFINITIVE, but sometimes **commencer de** + INFINITIVE is found in literary style.   [2] *backward, reticent*

The SIMPLE PAST is normally used in written French to express a series of successive actions in a literary narrative. It also sometimes states a past fact.

The SIMPLE PAST is a written tense, not used in speaking except in very formal lectures or orations. It is used in formal literary writing rather than in letters.

The SIMPLE PAST has the advantage over the COMPOUND PAST of being a single form and thus producing a smoother effect.

Notice the exact use of the simple past (**passé simple**) in the following sentences taken from the above passage:

Elle **manqua** de savon.
Mais sa terreur **fut** grande lorsqu'elle **vit** un tigre sortir de la forêt.
Elle **resta** immobile, haletante, pâle, presque morte.
Le tigre ne **fut** pas en reste; c'était un tigre d'un caractère jovial.
Ce jeu effroyable **dura** dix minutes.

The uses of the imperfect are the same, whether the passage is written in the **passé simple** or the **passé composé**.

C. Remplacez les infinitifs entre parenthèses par la forme convenable du passé composé ou de l'imparfait.
(Use the compound past for successive actions unless your instructor tells you to use the simple past for such actions.)

Monsieur Grinci (être) toujours de mauvaise humeur. Pour un rien il (crier), il (gronder) et il (faire) peur à tous ceux qui l'(approcher). Il (avoir) un domestique, Jean, qui (être) bien malheureux. Mais Jean (être) aussi intelligent et (savoir) bien qu'il (falloir) obéir à son maître s'il (vouloir)
5   garder sa place.

Un jour, Monsieur Grinci (rentrer) chez lui en colère et (se préparer) à dîner. La table (être) mise près d'une fenêtre qui (donner) sur la cour. Tout (être) joliment arrangé et il y (avoir) même un vase de fleurs au milieu.

10   Pendant que Jean (être) à la cuisine, Monsieur Grinci (goûter) la soupe et la (trouver) trop chaude. Il (se mettre) encore plus en colère et la (jeter) dans la cour par la fenêtre ouverte.

Ce jour-là, Jean (être) plus calme qu'à l'ordinaire. Quand il (voir) cela, il (penser) que son maître (mériter) une leçon. Il (aller) vers la table,

15 (prendre) l'assiette de son maître et la (jeter) dans la cour. Puis, il (prendre) les services, les verres et les fleurs et (jeter) le tout par la fenêtre.

Cela (mettre) monsieur Grinci hors de lui et il (ordonner) à Jean de lui dire ce qu'il (faire).

Jean lui (répondre) tranquillement: «Monsieur, quand je vous (voir)

20 jeter la soupe par la fenêtre, je (penser) que vous (vouloir) dîner dans la cour et c'est pour cela que je (jeter) tout le reste».

Monsieur Grinci (comprendre) cette leçon. Il (sourire) quand même et, depuis ce jour, s'il ne (changer) pas de caractère, du moins il (maîtriser) ses colères.

D. Traduisez en français, en employant le passé composé et l'imparfait où il y a lieu.
(Use the compound past for successive actions unless your instructor tells you to use formal literary style. In that case, use the simple past for such actions.)

Balzac, the great French writer of the nineteenth century, had the habit of working late into the night. Most of the time he did not take the trouble to lock the door of his house.

One night as Balzac was sleeping, a thief entered the house and opened

5 the door of the room of the writer. The latter seemed to be sleeping soundly. The thief, reassured, went to Balzac's desk and began to rummage around in the drawers. Suddenly, he heard[1] a loud laugh. He turned around[2] and caught[3] sight of the writer, who was laughing heartily. The thief became frightened[4], but he was not able to keep from asking Balzac

10 what was making him laugh. The latter answered him that it[5] amused him a great deal to see that a thief was coming in the night without light to look in a desk for money which he[6] had never been able to find even in[7] plain daylight.

[1] Use a form of entendre rire très fort.   [2] Use a form of se retourner.   [3] Use a form of apercevoir.   [4] Use a form of avoir peur.   [5] ça   [6] lui   [7] en plein jour

Exercice d'ensemble

E. Dans l'exercice suivant l'imparfait et le passé composé de la plupart des verbes sont donnés entre parenthèses. Choisissez la forme qui vous paraît la meilleure. En quelques cas les deux formes peuvent être employées.

Mon père (était, a été) comptable dans un petit bureau d'assurances où il n'y (avait, a eu) que cinq employés. C'est lui qui (restait, est resté) de garde de midi à une heure et demie car les bureaux et magasins (ne fermaient pas, n'ont pas fermé) à midi.

5   Il m' (arrivait, est arrivé) souvent d'aller voir mon père, surtout, je l'avoue, pour lui réclamer un peu d'argent. Je (le trouvais, l'ai trouvé) là, installé devant son travail. Nulle part ailleurs je ne (le voyais, l'ai vu) si serein. On (le sentait, l'a senti) heureux d'avoir le poids du bureau sur ses épaules, comme d'avoir ce bureau pour lui seul.

10   —Assieds-toi, fils, je suis à toi dans deux minutes.

Et un peu plus tard il (me demandait, m'a demandé) sans amertume, comme sans ironie: «Combien?»

Il (aimait, a aimé) le matin partir pour son bureau et y rester. (C'était, Ç'a été) lui qui en (possédait, a possédé) la clé et il en (était, a été) fier.

15   (Je retrouvais, J'ai retrouvé) cette fierté, ce plaisir de travailler, même à une tâche assez ingrate, chez mon grand-père, qui (travaillait, a travaillé) encore à soixante-quinze ans.

Si j'y pense aujourd'hui, c'est qu'on lit ou qu'on entend partout que le travail est une malédiction. Moi, aussi, pendant toute ma vie, j'(avais,

20   ai eu) quotidiennement mes heures de solitude dans mon bureau aux rideaux fermés, devant ma machine à écrire que j'(astiquais, ai astiqué) avec soin et que (je huilais, j'ai huilé) avant chaque roman. Certes, (c'était, ça a été) dur de garder à la fois la ligne des personnages et le rythme du récit. Je (m'usais, me suis usé) à ce travail que je (ne quittais, n'ai quitté)

25   que le jour de mes soixante-dix ans. Il n'empêche que cela constitue un des meilleurs souvenirs de ma vie.

D'après Georges Simenon, auteur d'excellents romans, policiers surtout, créateur du célèbre Inspecteur Maigret. (*De la Cave au Grenier,* Presses de la Cité, 1977)

Problem Words

20. go

(a) How to say *I'm going, I went,* etc.

—Il paraît qu'il y a un bon film au Rex. Tu **y es allé?**	*"It seems that there's a good film at the Rex.* Did you go?"
—Oui, **j'y suis allé** hier soir.	*"Yes,* I went *last night."*
—Moi, **j'irai** demain.	"I'll go *tomorrow."*

In English, we often say: "Are you going?" "Yes, I'm going." French rarely uses the verb **aller** without indicating a place to which one is going, and if the place has already been mentioned, it then uses the adverb **y** to refer to it.

But **y** is not used with the forms of the future and conditional of **aller,** because then two *i*-sounds would come together.

CAUTION: In French sentences such as the English "I'm going," and "Did you go?", do not use the verb **aller** without indicating the place to which or without using the adverb **y.**

(b) How to express certain combinations of *go* + PREPOSITION and *go* + ADVERB

go back	**retourner**	*go out*	**sortir**
go back home	**rentrer**	*go through*	**traverser**
go by	**passer**	*go toward*	**se diriger vers**
go down	**descendre**	*go up,*	**monter**
go in	**entrer**	*go with*	**accompagner**

The English verb *go* is used with certain prepositions and adverbs in special ways, and such combinations are expressed by separate verbs in French.

(c) When *go to = attend*

Avez-vous **assisté à la** confé-rence?	Did *you* go to the *lecture?*
Non, j'**ai assisté au** match de basketball.	*No, I* went to the *basketball game.*
En France il n'est pas obliga-toire d'**assister aux** cours de la faculté tous les jours.	*In France you don't have to go to university classes every day.*

The verb **assister** means *go to* when *go to* is equivalent to *be present at* or *attend.* However, **assister à** may be used only with certain places and specific occasions and not with all places. For instance, *"I go to the university"* is rendered in French by: «Je **vais** à l'université.»

The verb «assister» could not be used with **université.** Therefore, be careful when using **assister à.** In general, one can safely use **aller à** to express the idea of *being present at.*

21. happen

(a) When to use **se passer**

Qu'est-ce qui **s'est passé?**	*What* happened?
Il **s'est passé** beaucoup de choses.	*Many things* happened.
Dites-moi ce qui **s'est passé** chez les Monnier.	*Tell me what* happened *at the Monniers.*

When *happen = take place,* when there is no personal indirect object, and when the subject is impersonal and somewhat indefinite, **se passer** may be used to express *to happen.*

CAUTION: When there is a definite subject, avoid using «se passer» for *happen.*

CAUTION: When something *happens to someone,* DO NOT use «se passer» for *happen.* See Section (b).

(b) When to use **arriver**

Qu'est-ce qui **est arrivé?**	*What* happened?
Dites-moi ce qui **est arrivé** chez vous.	*Tell me what* happened *at your home.*
Qu'est-ce qui **est arrivé à Simone?**	*What* happened to Simone?
Quand est-ce que **cet accident est arrivé?**	*When* did that accident happen?

Whenever *happen* may be expressed by **se passer,** it may also be expressed by **arriver.** But, in addition, **arriver** may be used when there is a personal indirect object (something *happens to someone*) and when the subject is neither impersonal nor indefinite.

(c) How to say that someone *happened to do something*

J'**étais** là **par hasard.**	*I* happened to be *there.*
Nous **avons rencontré** Jean dans la rue **tout à fait par hasard.**	*We* happened to meet *John on the street.*

When *happen to* + VERB means *happen by chance,* French often uses **par hasard** or **tout à fait par hasard** with the verb.

(d) When *happen = it happens that . . .* (or *someone happens to . . .*)

Il se trouvait que j'habitais dans le même immeuble que Monsieur Martin.	*I* happened to *live in the same building as Mr. Martin.*
Il se trouve justement que Monsieur et Madame Drouet doivent venir ce soir.	It (just) happens that *Mr. and Mrs. Drouet are to come over this evening.*

When a sentence with *happen* can be begun *It happens that . . .* , the French often express this idea by placing the proper tense of: **Il se trouve que . . .** or **Il se trouve justement que . . .** before the main part of the sentence.

(e) How to say *How does it happen that . . .*

Comment se fait-il que vous $\begin{cases} \text{avez} \\ \text{ayez} \end{cases}$ acheté une nouvelle voiture?	How does it happen that *you brought a new car?*
Comment se fait-il que Marc $\begin{cases} \text{est} \\ \text{soit} \end{cases}$ absent?	How does it happen that *Mark is absent?*

How does it happen that . . . ? is expressed by **Comment se fait-il que . . . ?,** which is sometimes followed by the indicative, sometimes by the subjunctive.

22. hear

(a) How to say *to hear* (someone or something)

J'**ai entendu** un bruit en bas.   *I heard a noise downstairs.*

To hear (someone or something) is expressed by the verb **entendre.** Here there is no problem, for English and French usage are the same.

(b) How to say *to hear of* (someone or something)

Avez-vous **entendu parler de** cette invention?   *Have* you *heard of* that invention?

In French *to hear of* must be expressed by **entendre parler de.**

(c) How to say *to hear from* (someone)

Nous **avons** $\begin{cases} \textbf{eu} \\ \textbf{reçu} \end{cases}$ des nouvelles de notre fils ce matin.   *We* heard from *our son this morning.*

French expresses *to hear from* by **avoir** (or **recevoir**) **des nouvelles de.**

(d) How to say *to hear that* . . .

Nous **avons entendu dire que** le premier ministre va démissionner.   *We* heard that *the prime minister is going to resign.*

In French *to hear that* must be expressed by **entendre dire que.**

CAUTION: DO NOT use «entendre de» for *to to hear of* nor «entendre que» for *to hear that.*

F. Remplacez les mots anglais par leur équivalent français.

1. Je (*heard*) de cette affaire, mais il y a déjà longtemps.   2. Je me demande ce qui (*happened*) pendant mon absence.   3. Georgette refuse absolument de (*go*) à un match de boxe.   4. Est-ce que ce sont les cloches de la cathédrale que nous (*hear*)?   5. La chose (*happened*) comme je l'avais prévu.   6. J'aime bien (*hear*) tomber la pluie.   7. Vous les (*hear*) rire?   8. Je voudrais bien savoir ce qui (*is happening*).   9. C'est ennuyeux de (*hear*) la radio du voisin tous les soirs.   10. Il (*are happening*)[1] des choses bizarres dans la maison d'en face.   11. Je (*hear*) sortir les employés. Est-ce qu'il est déjà cinq heures?   12. Daniel (*heard from*) ses cousins hier.

[1] In French this verb agrees with Il.

G. Traduisez en français. Attention aux mots en italique.

1. (*vous*) Did you *hear* that we will have another meeting Thursday?
2. (*tu*) There will be a football game Saturday. Do you want to *go?*

3. (*tu*) How does it *happen* that you left[1] New York?   4. (*vous*) Did you *hear* from your mother-in-law recently?   5. (*vous*) To what lycée did you *go?*   6. (*tu*) Did you *hear* of Raoul's marriage? 7. Bernard broke his leg. How did that *happen?*   8. (*vous*) If you don't *go* to the concert, I won't *go* either.   9. (*vous*) We *heard* that you *were going* to Greece this summer.   10. I *happened* to see the Benoîts[2] at the florist's.   11. It was raining, but I *went* all the same.   12. (*vous*) Come[3] to dinner; we *happen* to have a nice[4] roast duck.   13. (*tu*) If you *happen* to receive a letter from Nicolas, telephone me right away.   14. How does it *happen* that the children are not in[5] school today?   15. (*tu*) There will be a parade tomorrow. Can you *go?*

[1] Use a form of **quitter**.   [2] French family names do not take -s in the plural.   [3] French says: *come to dine.*   [4] beau   [5] *in school* = à l'école

Verb Review

Review the verbs **courir** and **craindre** according to the outline on page 253.

CHAPTER
7

Possessives

Un ingénieur, Richard, a découvert une grotte dans le domaine d'un château. Il a des raisons de croire qu'un trésor y est caché. On l'a autorisé à faire des fouilles. Ce jour il emmène avec lui une jeune femme, Fanny.

Le souterrain

—Ce souterrain est très intéressant, dit Richard, en ressortant *son* visage sali. Il y a une pente à droite. Mais il faudrait que je puisse passer *les* épaules, elles sont trop larges. *Les vôtres* sont plus étroites. Voulez-vous essayer?

5 Devant l'obstacle Fanny hésitait. Elle pouvait imaginer *sa* photo en première page d'un journal . . . mais quand il s'agit de passer *la* tête dans un trou, cela devient très difficile. Elle s'approcha cependant, pencha *la* tête vers le trou noir et étroit.

—Mais Richard, ce n'est pas possible! dit-elle. Le trou est trop petit!

10 Il se mit à rire.

—Il faut mettre *la* tête de côté, voyons. Ma[1] tête, qui est plus grosse que *la vôtre,* y passe[2] bien . . .

Elle s'allongea sur *le* flanc[3], introduisit *la* tête dans la fente rocheuse. Elle vit une petite caverne qui s'élargissait un peu au-dessus de *sa*[4] tête

15 et dans laquelle, accroupie[5], elle eût[6] pu tenir tout entière.

Elle ressortit *la* tête avec un grand soulagement[7].

—Il faudrait tourner la lampe pour que je voie, dit-elle.

Quelle joie d'être enfin à l'air libre! Richard *lui* essuya *le* front avec un grand mouchoir qu'il tira de *sa* poche.

20 —Alors? Vous avez vu quelque chose?

---

[1] For this use of the possessive adjective with a part of the body, see page 87, §5 (c).
[2] **passe bien** *does go in indeed.* In this case, bien simply intensifies the meaning of the verb. [3] *side* [4] For this use of the possessive adjective with a part of the body, see page 87, §5 (a). [5] *squatting* [6] **eût pu tenir tout entière** *could have gotten in completely* [7] *relief*

—Ça a l'air de descendre, mais c'est trop noir.

—Il faut que vous[8] entriez vos[9] épaules. En vous tenant sur le côté, vous pourriez arriver à y entrer tout entière.

Tout entière! Tout entière dans ce trou? Et[10] si elle n'arrivait pas à en
25 ressortir?

—Oh non, ce n'est pas possible, dit-elle en frissonnant.

Il[11] se méprit sur son objection.

—Mais si. Tenez, remettez-vous de côté, je vais vous pousser. Vous[12] effacerez bien la poitrine et le[13] tour est joué.

30 Tout cela était affreux et pas du tout romanesque. Cependant, serrant *les* dents, Fanny s'allongea à nouveau. Il la saisit fermement par le milieu *du* corps et l'introduisit dans la fente. Elle y était jusqu'à mi-corps maintenant, paralysée de terreur; elle[14] avait eu beau gonfler *sa* poitrine, l'habileté de Richard avait[15] eu raison de cet obstacle. Elle était là, *les*
35 bras collés au corps, dans la demi-obscurité. Elle en était sûre à présent; elle[16] allait y rester, rester prisonnière dans ce trou, étouffer, *sa* poitrine prise entre deux parois de pierre humide.

Elle se mit soudain à hurler et il réussit, non sans écorchures[17], à l'extraire de l'ouverture.

40 —Mais qu'est-ce qu'il y a? dit-il.

Elle avoua honteusement, cherchant par un réflexe instinctif *son* épaule pour s'y cacher:

—J'ai si peur . . .

—Peur de quoi?

45 —Peur du trou.

—Mais pourquoi? Pourquoi?

C'était trop fort. De toutes *ses* forces, elle gifla cette[18] joue ronde de bébé.

Il était si comique, dans *sa* stupéfaction naïve, *les*[19] yeux arrondis, *la*[20]
50 bouche entrouverte, qu'elle éclata de rire. Et au bout de quelques instants, il rit aussi.

D'après Françoise Mallet-Joris. D'origine belge, membre de l'Académie Goncourt, elle est une des nombreuses et des plus remarquables femmes-écrivains d'aujourd'hui. («Le Souterrain», dans *Cordelia,* Julliard, 1956)

---

[8] vous entriez vos épaules *you get your shoulders in*   [9] In this case, les could also have been used.   [10] si elle n'arrivait pas à en ressortir?   *suppose she didn't manage to get out again?*   [11] Il se méprit sur son objection.   *He misunderstood her objection.*   [12] Vous effacerez bien la poitrine *You must take in (i.e. shrink) your chest*   [13] le tour est joué   *that's it!*   [14] elle avait eu beau gonfler *in spite of the fact that she had expanded*   [15] avait eu raison de   *had overcome*   [16] elle allait y rester   *she was going to have to stay there (and also) she would die there*   [17] *scratches*   [18] cette joue ronde de bébé   *his (that) baby face*   [19] les yeux arrondis   *with his eyes wide-open*   [20] la bouche entrouverte   *with his mouth half-open*

A possessive is a word that shows possession. English has possessive adjectives: *my, your, his, her, its, our, their,* and possessive pronouns: *mine, yours, his, hers, its, ours,* and *theirs.*

I.   Possessive Adjectives

1. What are the French possessive adjectives?

Singular		Plural		Singular		Plural	
Masculine	Feminine			Masculine	Feminine		
mon	ma	mes	*my*	notre	notre	nos	*our*
ton	ta	tes	*your*	votre	votre	vos	*your*
son	sa	ses	*his* *her,* *its*	leur	leur	leurs	*their*

2. How and with what do the French possessive adjectives agree?

J'ai perdu **mon** portefeuille et **ma** montre.

I've lost my *billfold and* my *watch.*

Jacques est allé voir **son** cousin chez **sa** tante.

Jack went to see his *cousin at* his *aunt's.*

Elle a mis **son** courrier et **sa** revue sur la table.

She put her *mail and* her *magazine on the table.*

The French possessive adjectives agree in gender and number with the thing possessed. They do not agree with the possessor.

In English, the possessive adjectives agree with the possessor, not with the thing possessed.

3. When are *mon, ton,* and *son* used for *ma, ta,* and *sa?*

Son auto est belle.

His car is beautiful.

Mon ancienne maison était plus commode que celle-ci.

My former house was more convenient than this one.

The forms **mon, ton,** and **son** are used to modify feminine singular nouns when the word immediately following these forms, whether a noun or an adjective, begins with a vowel sound.

4. How is the French usage in respect to the possessive adjective different from the English in a sentence such as the following:

Son père et sa mère sont partis ce matin.

Her father and mother left this morning.

In English, the same possessive adjective may refer to two or more connected nouns, whereas in French, the proper possessive adjective must be used before each noun.

A. Remplacez les mots anglais par l'adjectif français convenable.[1]

1. (*My*) parents et (*my*) oncle sont partis pour le Canada.   2. (*His*) livre est en bien mauvais état.   3. Je n'ai pas beaucoup aimé (*their*) remarque à (*your,* s.) sujet.   4. As-tu passé (*your*) examen? 5. Que pensez-vous de (*my*) tableaux?   6. (*Our*) existence est ce que nous la faisons.   7. (*Your,* p.) références sont bonnes, mais (*your*) expérience est insuffisante.   8. Avez-vous vu (*their*) nouveaux chapeaux?   9. Il veut me vendre (*his*) voiture, mais elle marche mal.   10. Elle m'a montré (*her*) maison et (*her*) jardin. 11. (*Her*) adresse est inconnue.

[1] In this exercise, s. = singular, p. = plural.

B. Traduisez en français.

1. (*vous*) My parents would like to invite you to our party[1].   2. (*tu*) Do we take my car or your motorcycle?   3. (*vous*) Do you know whether her brother and sister speak German?   4. (*tu*) Did you notice how[2] his voice has changed?   5. (*vous*) Would you do everything for your country?   6. My grandchildren are my greatest joy.   7. I hope that her son and daughter will have her good looks and intelligence.

[1] soirée   [2] comme

II. Possessive Adjectives with Nouns

(PARTS OF THE BODY)

5. How, in general, does French express possession with nouns denoting parts of the body?

Marie a baissé **les** yeux.	*Marie lowered* her *eyes.*
Nous avons mal à **la** gorge.	*Our throats are sore.*
Il dort toujours **la** bouche ouverte.	*He always sleeps with his mouth open.*

In French, the definite article is often used with nouns denoting parts of the body, where English would use the possessive adjective. However, French normally employs the possessive adjective with parts of the body: (a) if ambiguity would result from the use of the article; (b) usually if the part of the body is modified; (c) if the part of the body is the subject of the sentence.

The exact usage of the article with parts of the body is so complicated that at this stage we shall present only a few of the most frequently used constructions. (§§6–10)

6. How is possession indicated in French when the subject of the sentence performs an action <u>with</u> a part of his body?

Marie lève **la** main.   *Marie raises* her *hand.*
Jean tourne **la** tête.   *John turns* his *head.*

When the subject of the sentence performs an action <u>with</u> a part of his body, in French that part of the body is modified by the definite article. English would use the possessive adjective in such a sentence.

SUBJECT + VERB + DEFINITE ARTICLE + NOUN (part of body)

C. Traduisez en français.

1. (*vous*) Raise your hand.   2. Jack closed his eyes.   3. (*vous*) Be careful! Don't move[1] your arm.   4. She opened her mouth but didn't say anything.   5. The teacher shrugged his shoulders.

[1] Use a form of **bouger.**

7. How is possession indicated in French when the subject of the sentence performs an action <u>on</u> some part of his body?

Marie **se** lave **la** figure.   *Marie washes* her *face.*
Je **me** suis cassé **la** jambe.   *I broke* my *leg.*
Jean, tu **t**'es brossé **les** dents ce   *John, did you brush* your *teeth*
   matin?   *this morning?*

When the subject of the sentence performs an action <u>on</u> a part of his body, in French that part of the body is modified by the definite article where English would use the possessive adjective, and a reflexive pronoun is placed before the verb.

SUBJECT + REFLEXIVE PRONOUN + VERB + DEFINITE ARTICLE + NOUN (part of body)

NOTE: This reflexive pronoun is an indirect object.

D. Traduisez en français.

1. I rub my back every morning.   2. John broke his arm.
3. They brushed their hair.   4. I cut my finger yesterday.   5. (*tu*) Wash your face.

8. How Is possession expressed In French when the subject of the sentence performs an action on a part of someone else's body?

Marie **lui** lave **la** figure.	*Marie washes* his *face.*
L'infirmière **me** frotte **le** dos tous les matins.	*The nurse rubs* my *back every morning.*

When the subject of the sentence performs an action on <u>someone else's</u> body, that part of the body is modified by the definite article, and an indirect object pronoun is placed before the verb. English would use only a possessive adjective in such a sentence.

```
┌─────────────────────────────────────────────────────────────┐
│           INDIRECT                                            │
│                       DEFINITE                                │
│  SUBJECT + OBJECT   + VERB +          + NOUN (part of body)  │
│                       ARTICLE                                 │
│           PRONOUN                                             │
└─────────────────────────────────────────────────────────────┘
```

NOTE: Compare the above with what happens when a noun showing possession modifies the part of the body in the English sentence:

Marie lave **la figure de Jean.**	*Marie washes* John's face.
L'infirmière frotte **le dos du malade.**	*The nurse rubs* the patient's back.

E. Traduisez en français.

1. I rub his back every morning.   2. Michael twisted her arm.
3. (*vous*) Wash her face.   4. He shook my hand.   5. We cut their hair.

9. When a part of the body Is the subject of an English sentence, how does French express possession?

Il a les cheveux bruns.	His hair is *dark.*
J'ai mal **à la gorge.**	My throat is *sore.*

Whenever possible, the French avoid having a part of the body as the subject of the sentence. Generally, they use the verb **avoir** with the part of the body as the object of the sentence. The part of the body is often modified by the definite article.

F. Traduisez en français.

1. Your eyes are blue.   2. Her skin is soft.   3. My head aches.
4. My feet are sore.   5. (*tu*) Do your eyes hurt?   6. His finger hurts.

10. How does French express the attitude or state of being of a part of the body?

Il est entré **la tête baissée.**	*He entered with* his head down.
Bernard aime lire **les pieds sur le bureau.**	*Bernard likes to read with* his feet on the desk.

French expresses attitude or manner of a part of the body simply by modifying the part of the body by the definite article. English often uses the preposition *with* in such cases.

G. Traduisez en français.

1. He eats with his elbows on the table.   2. The little boy stood in front of the teacher with his hands in his[1] pockets.   3. Marie was sitting there with her face in her arms.   4. Her husband, with his hand in[2] the air, tried to stop a taxi.   5. Micheline was watching[3] me with her eyes almost closed.   6. The dog went off with his tail between his legs[4].

[1] Use the article. French sometimes but not always uses the article with a piece of clothing where English uses the possessive adjective.   [2] en l'air   [3] Use a form of **observer**.   [4] In French, the legs of an animal are expressed by **pattes** rather than **jambes**.

III.   Possessive Pronouns

11. What are the French possessive pronouns?

Singular		Plural		
Masculine	Feminine	Masculine	Feminine	
le mien	la mienne	les miens	les miennes	*mine*
le tien	la tienne	les tiens	les tiennes	*yours*
le sien	la sienne	les siens	les siennes	*his, hers*
le nôtre	la nôtre	les nôtres	les nôtres	*ours*
le vôtre	la vôtre	les vôtres	les vôtres	*yours*
le leur	la leur	les leurs	les leurs	*theirs*

12. How do the possessive pronouns agree? How are they used?

Vos leçons sont faciles; **les miennes** sont plus difficiles.

Your lessons are easy; mine *are more difficult.*

Elle expliquera cela à son père; je l'expliquerai **au mien.**

She will explain it to her father; I will explain it to mine.

Possessive pronouns, like possessive adjectives, agree in gender and number with the object possessed rather than the possessor. Possessive pronouns regularly take the place of nouns modified by a possessive adjective. Notice that the possessive pronouns contract with **à** and **de.**

H. Remplacez les pronoms possessifs anglais par l'équivalent français[1].

1. Il aime sa maison; j'aime (*mine*).   2. Je me souviens de mon premier bal; elles se souviennent de (*theirs, s.*).   3. Quelles aventures! Je ris encore quand je pense à (*his, p.*).   4. Je m'occupe

de mes affaires, occupe toi de (*yours*).   **5.** J'aime bien son studio, mais je préfère (*ours*, s.).   **6.** Est-ce votre chien? Non, c'est (*his*). **7.** Sa robe est beaucoup moins jolie que (*yours*, s.).   **8.** Si vous trouvez nos enfants mal élevés, vous devriez voir (*theirs*, p.).   **9.** Ma voiture ne marche pas; nous prendrons (*theirs*, s.).

[1] In this exercise, s. = singular, p. = plural.

13. What are three ways of showing possession in a sentence such as, *"This book is mine"?*

Ce livre **est à moi.**
Ce livre **m'appartient.**   This book is mine.
Ce livre **est le mien.**

The most common way of expressing possession after **être** is by **à** + DISJUNCTIVE PRONOUN. When the possessive pronoun is used instead, the idea of the possessor is stressed. Possession is also often expressed by using an indirect object with a form of the verb **appartenir.**

Exercices d'ensemble

I.   Traduisez en français.

1. (*vous*) Do your duty, and I'll do mine.   **2.** (*vous*) Why are you shrugging your shoulders?   **3.** When will they finish their exercises?   **4.** All the pupils raised their hands[1] to answer the question.   **5.** (*tu*) Give her your arm; that will please[2] her.   **6.** She always has a headache.   **7.** (*vous*) If that coat is yours, leave it here. **8.** He broke his arm.   **9.** (*vous*) Listen to him talk about his trip. **10.** (*tu*) If your feet hurt, rest.   **11.** (*vous*) I remember your sister and his.   **12.** (*tu*) I have something for you; close your eyes. **13.** She broke her leg for the third time.   **14.** (*vous*) I do not want to see your snapshots now.

[1] French uses the singular here.   [2] Use a form of faire plaisir à.

J.   Traduisez en français.

1. It is not proper to[1] sit with your legs crossed.   **2.** (*tu*) Is this new[2] car yours?   **3.** This dictionary is mine; I need it.   **4.** (*vous*) You are going to hurt him if you twist his arm.   **5.** (*tu*) It is perhaps your opinion, but not mine.   **6.** (*vous*) Put down your hand. **7.** It is his wife who cuts his hair.   **8.** What is there in this desk? I don't know; the desk isn't mine.   **9.** (*vous*) I have never seen a[3] diamond as beautiful as yours.   **10.** Her hairdresser will wash her hair tomorrow.   **11.** (*tu*) If you haven't any ballpoint pen, use[4] mine.   **12.** (*vous*) Do you have a sore throat?

[1] d'être assis   [2] Use a form of **neuf.**   [3] de   [4] Use the proper form of **se servir de.**

Problem Words

23. intend

The word *intend* may be expressed in several ways. Often, but not always, these expressions may be used synonymously.

Jacques **pense** partir demain matin.	*Jack* intends to *leave tomorrow morning.*
J'**ai l'intention de** lire l'article du professeur Dugard.	*I* intend to *read Professor Dugard's article.*
La secrétaire **compte** prendre ses vacances en juillet.	*The secretary* intends *to take her vacation in July.*

The word *intend* may be expressed by **penser** + INFINITIVE, **compter** + INFINITIVE, and **avoir l'intention de** + INFINITIVE.

24. introduce

How to say *introduce someone to someone*

Voulez-vous me **présenter** à Madame Leduc?	*Will you* introduce *me to Mrs. Leduc?*
Françoise m'**a présenté** à Isabelle.	*Frances* introduced *me to Isabelle.*
Qui vous **a présenté** à Michel?	*Who* introduced *you to Michael?*

The English *introduce a person* is expressed in French by **présenter.**

CAUTION: DO NOT use the French verb «introduire» with the meaning of *introduce a person*. The verb **introduire** sometimes expresses the English *introduce* in less common connotations; also, it often means *insert*.

25. a knock

How to say *a knock at the door*

On a frappé à la porte.	There was a knock *at the door.*
Avez-vous entendu frapper à la porte?	Did you hear a knock *at the door?*

French has no expression that corresponds to the English *a knock at the door*. Instead, it uses the verbal expression **frapper à la porte,** and *to hear a knock at the door* is **entendre frapper à la porte.**

CAUTION: DO NOT try to use a French noun to express the English noun *knock*.

26. know

(a) When *know = be acquainted with*

—**Connaissez**-vous Geneviève Leroy?	*"Do you know Genevieve Leroy?"*
—Oui, je la **connais** depuis longtemps.	*"Yes, I have known her for a long time."*

The verb **connaître** is always used to indicate *knowing a person*.

(b) When *know = be familiar with something*

Les jeunes **connaissent** bien les œuvres de Camus.	*Young people* know (are well acquainted with) *the works of Camus.*
Je **connais** Paris, mais je ne **connais** pas Marseille.	*I* know *Paris, but I don't* know *Marseilles.*

The verb **connaître** is used to indicate familiarity with works, places, etc.

(c) When *know = meet, get acquainted with*

Où **avez**-vous **connu** votre mari?	*Where did you* meet *your husband?* *Where did you* get acquainted with *your husband?* *Where did you* get to know *your husband?*

In the compound past and simple past, **connaître** sometimes means *to meet* in the sense of *to get to know* or *to get acquainted with*.

(d) When *know = know from memory*

Savez-vous les mois de l'année en français?	*Do you* know *the months of the year in French?*

Use **savoir** when *know = know from memory*.

(e) When *know = know from study*

Cet élève **sait** toujours sa leçon.	*That pupil always* knows *his lesson.*

Use **savoir** when *know = know from study*.

(f) When *know = be aware of*

Je **sais** où Pierre a mis son calculateur.	*I* know *where Peter put his calculator.*

Use **savoir** when *know = be aware of*.

(g) How to say *to know how to*

Est-ce que Suzanne **sait** faire la cuisine?	*Does Suzanne* know how to *cook?*

The verb **savoir** + INFINITIVE often means *to know how to.*

K. Remplacez les mots entre parenthèses par leur équivalent français.

1. Les Beaulieu (*intend to*) faire construire une nouvelle maison de campagne.   **2.** Tout le monde (*knows*) l'histoire de la femme du docteur.   **3.** Veux-tu me (*introduce*) à la jeune fille qui est assise là-bas?   **4.** Je (*don't know how to*) jouer d'un instrument, mais j'aime beaucoup la musique.   **5.** Je (*know*) parfaitement bien tout ce que vous avez dit.   **6.** J'habite ici depuis très longtemps; je (*know*) les plus petites rues de la ville.   **7.** Il (*intended to*) partir hier, mais il a manqué l'avion.   **8.** Vous (*know*) le russe; pouvez-vous m'aider à faire cette traduction?   **9.** (*Do you know how to*) conduire?

L. Traduisez en français. Attention aux mots en italique.

1. There was a *knock* at the door about midnight.   **2.** Raymond *knows* a great many very important people.   **3.** (*vous*) What do you *intend* to do this weekend?   **4.** Someone already *introduced* me to Mrs. Martel, but she probably doesn't remember me.   **5.** (*tu*) What[1]! You don't *know how to* swim?   **6.** Does Paul *intend* to spend his vacation in Corsica?   **7.** (*vous*) Do you *know* what happened to Mark?   **8.** (*tu*) Where did you *get to know* that artist?

[1] Comment

Verb Review

Review the verbs **croire** and **devoir** according to the outline on page 253.

CHAPTER
8

Participiples

Pages blanches

Nous étions d'une famille de saltimbanques[1] vénitiens[2] qui *avait émigré* en Russie à l'époque où Pierre le Grand ouvrait ce pays aux lumières de l'Occident. Mon grand-père Renato Zaga *était arrivé* de Venise avec[3] pour tout bien un singe savant, quelques saintes reliques, un costume
5 d'Arlequin[4] et cinq de ces masses creuses qu'utilisent encore aujourd'hui les jongleurs[5]. Il *avait dû* quitter Venise précipitamment, *fuyant* les foudres[6] de l'Inquisition. En effet, vers quarante-cinq ans, *ayant connu* une carrière fort honorable de comédien et de jongleur, il se mit à prédire l'avenir, ce qui eut pour lui de bien fâcheuses conséquences. Quand il
10 *se fut mis* à annoncer des événements désastreux qui se produisirent vraiment, il en fut *tenu* responsable par les dirigeants de la République, soucieux d'offrir au bon peuple un bouc[7] émissaire. Mon grand-père, *sachant* ce qui l'*aurait attendu en restant* à Venise, échappa à une triste fin en *se sauvant* par une belle nuit de lune.

15 Je ne me lassais pas d'interroger mon père sur la vie et les exploits de mon illustre aïeul. *Avait*-il *passé* tout son temps *à amuser* le monde? *Avait*-il *continué* à prédire le futur? Les événements continuaient-ils à se réaliser tels qu'il les *avaient annoncés?* Sur ce point mon père était formel[8]. Renato Zaga fuyait la vérité comme la peste. Il *avait compris*
20 que le plus grand don qu'un artiste *désirant* s'attirer les bonnes grâces du public pouvait faire à ce dernier, c'était un peu d'illusion, un peu d'espoir et non la vérité.

Mon père me raconta un jour que mon aïeul, Renato, sentant à l'âge de quatre-vingt-six ans, qu'il allait falloir quitter ce monde, fit venir auprès

---

[1] *entertainers in a traveling show*   [2] *from Venice*   [3] avec pour tout bien *with nothing more than*   [4] *Harlequin (a comic actor)*   [5] *jugglers*   [6] *dangers (lit., bolts of lightning)*   [7] bouc émissaire *scapegoat*   [8] *explicit*

25 de lui ses fils et leur communiqua alors «les deux secrets profonds et bienheureux de toutes choses», ainsi qu'il *s'était exprimé* avec ce fort accent italien dont nous ne *nous sommes* jamais *débarrassés.* Mon père se tut, comme *regrettant* d'en avoir trop dit . . . Je ne voulais pas le presser. Mais je ne pouvais *rester* ainsi *à attendre* et ma[9] jeune impatience
30 prit le dessus.

—Quel était le premier secret?

Mon père sortit de sa rêverie.

—C'est un livre, dit-il. Un très beau livre, et s'il ne contient à l'intérieur que quelques feuillets blancs, chacune de ces pages vides et *enivrantes*
35 nous enseigne une admirable leçon et nous donne la clé de la vérité la plus profonde. Les pages blanches signifient que rien n'*a* encore *été dit,* que rien n'est *perdu,* que tout *reste* encore *à créer* et *à accomplir.* Elles sont pleines d'espoir. Elles enseignent la confiance dans l'avenir.

J'étais terriblement *déçu.*
40 —C'est tout? Il n'y a pas quelques mots magiques qu'il suffirait de prononcer pour que tous nos vœux soient *exaucés*[10]? . . .

Je n'étais pas content du tout. Ce n'est pas ainsi que j'imaginais le secret «profond et bienheureux de toutes choses». Ce fameux[11] Livre ne me semblait même pas capable de me révéler la formule qui m'aurait
45 permis de faire marcher, danser et jouer avec moi le bonhomme de neige que j'*avais bâti* dans la cour et qui me désolait par son immobilité lourde et son air bêta[12].

Mon père, *sentant* que j'étais bien trop jeune pour tirer profit de la sagesse *souriante* et ironique du grand-père Renato, m'offrit le lende-
50 main un magnifique traîneau avec des clochettes plus gaies encore que celles de notre troïka, me *faisant* bien vite oublier ce Livre, lequel n'*étant* point *écrit,* nous fait à chaque page de si merveilleuses promesses . . .

D'après Romain Gary, d'origine russe, diplomate et l'un des grands romanciers contemporains. (*Les Enchanteurs,* Gallimard, 1973)

---

[9]*ma jeune impatience prit le dessus I couldn't refrain from asking him (lit., my youthful impatience got the better of me)* [10] *fulfilled* [11] *much talked of* [12] *stupid (in an indulgent way)*

A participle has properties of both a verb and an adjective. English and French have a present and a past participle.

VERB	PRESENT PARTICIPLE	PAST PARTICIPLE
(*speak*) parler	(*speaking*) **parlant**	(*spoken*) **parlé**
(*finish*) finir	(*finishing*) **finissant**	(*finished*) **fini**
(*lose*) perdre	(*losing*) **perdant**	(*lost*) **perdu**
(*drink*) boire	(*drinking*) **buvant**	(*drunk*) **bu**

Syntactically, the past participle offers almost no problems in spoken French and only the problem of agreement in written French.

The present participle is somewhat more complex, since French often expresses an English present participle by some construction other than the French present participle.

I. The Past Participle

1. With what auxiliaries are French verbs conjugated in the compound tenses?

1. most verbs	Nous **avons donné** un livre à l'élève.
	Robert **a vu** un film intéressant.
	Les étudiants **avaient** beaucoup **travaillé.**

2. intransitive verbs of motion	Vous **êtes venu** trop tard.
	Nous **sommes arrivés** vers trois heures.
	J'**étais parti** quand mon ami est arrivé chez moi.

3. reflexive verbs	La voiture **s'est arrêtée** devant notre porte.
	Nous **nous sommes échappés** par la fenêtre.
	Je ne **m'étais** pas **rasé** ce matin-là.

Most verbs are conjugated with the auxiliary **avoir.** Ordinarily, intransitive verbs of motion are conjugated with **être.** All reflexive verbs are conjugated with **être.**

A. Remplacez les tirets par l'auxiliaire convenable pour former le passé composé.

1. Qui _____ ouvert la porte pour laisser rentrer le chat? **2.** Pourquoi vous _____ -vous caché quand je _____ arrivé? **3.** Le président _____ reçu le nouvel ambassadeur aujourd'hui. **4.** Cette pièce était ennuyeuse; je _____ parti après le premier acte. **5.** Le chauffeur s' _____ arrêté brusquement pour éviter un accident. **6.** _____ -vous monté sur la Tour de Pise? **7.** À Paris nous nous _____ promenés le long de la Seine. **8.** Il était trois heures du matin quand Jacques _____ rentré. **9.** Ils ont une belle pelouse et ils _____ interdit aux enfants de jouer dessus.

B. Traduisez en français en faisant bien attention à l'auxiliaire des verbes au passé composé.

1. (*vous*) I recommend this hotel to you—we stayed there a month. **2.** I was so tired that I did not wake up early enough to go to[1] class. **3.** I have finished my exercises and now I can go out.   **4.** (*tu*) You'll be sick; you were warm, and you drank some ice water. **5.** Henry did not remember[2] his date with Pierrette.   **6.** After his retirement, he went back to[3] his little village.   **7.** (*vous*) What have you learned up to now[4]?   **8.** Many children were[5] born during the last war.   **9.** The little boys sat down in[6] the first row at the movies.

[1] en   [2] Use a form of **se souvenir de.**   [3] **dans**   [4] ici   [5] What tense will this verb be in? What will be the tense of the auxiliary?   [6] *in the* = **au**

2. **When and how does the past participle of a verb conjugated with *avoir* agree?**

Le père a **mené** ses enfants au cirque.	(No agreement. Why?)
Il **les** a **menés** au cirque.	(Agreement. Why?)
Les enfants qu'il a **menés** au cirque sont les siens.	(Agreement. Why?)
Quels enfants a-t-il **menés** au cirque?	(Agreement. Why?)

The past participle of a verb conjugated with **avoir** is invariable unless a direct object precedes the verb. The past participle of a verb conjugated with **avoir** agrees with the preceding direct object in gender and number.

3. **Does the past participle of a verb conjugated with *avoir* agree with a preceding *en*?**

Nous avons **mené** des enfants au cirque.	(No agreement. Why?)
Nous **en** avons **mené** au cirque.	(No agreement. Why?)

The past participle of a verb conjugated with **avoir** does not ordinarily agree with a preceding **en.**

C. Remplacez l'infinitif par la forme convenable du participe passé.

1. Où sont ces belles photos que vous avez (prendre)?   **2.** Nous avons (entendre) une bonne chanteuse.   **3.** —Avez-vous (voir) ma femme? —Oui, je l'ai (voir) il y a un instant.   **4.** Qui est la personne que vous avez (saluer)?   **5.** Quelles fleurs avez-vous (choisir)?

6. —Où sont les gâteaux? En avez-vous (acheter)?   7. —Je n'en ai pas (voir) sur le buffet.

D. Traduisez en français.

1. (*tu*) You have told me an interesting story.   2. (*vous*) Where is the person that you introduced to me just now?   3. (*vous*) What beautiful gifts you bought!   4. (*vous*) I didn't receive your letter. When did you send it?   5. I like his book. Has he written others[1]?
6. (*tu*) You want some stamps? I bought some yesterday.

[1] d'autres

4. Which common intransitive verbs of motion are conjugated with *être*? When, how, and with what does the past participle of an intransitive verb of motion conjuged with *être* agree?

Jacqueline était déjà **revenue** quand **nous** sommes **partis.**	(Agreement. Why?)
Mes camarades sont **morts** pendant la guerre.	(Agreement. Why?)
Ils sont **allés** à Paris pour les fêtes de Noël.	(Agreement. Why?)

The common intransitive verbs of motion conjugated with **être** are: **aller, arriver, descendre, devenir, entrer, monter, mourir, naître, partir, passer, rentrer, rester, retourner, revenir, sortir, tomber,** and **venir.**

The past participle of an intransitive verb of motion conjugated with **être** always agrees in gender and number with the subject of its clause.

NOTE 1: The verbs **descendre, monter, passer, rentrer,** and **sortir** are usually intransitive, that is, they do not ordinarily take a direct object. But these verbs sometimes do take a direct object. In that case, they become transitive and are conjugated with **avoir,** and the meaning is different.

USED INTRANSITIVELY	USED TRANSITIVELY
Elle **est descendue** au sous-sol.	Elle **a descendu** la chaise au sous-sol.
Nous **sommes montés** tout de suite.	Nous lui **avons monté** le petit déjeuner.
Ils **sont passés** par la porte.	Ils **ont passé** l'examen hier.
Denise **est rentrée** tard.	Denise **a rentré** la voiture dans le garage.
Es-tu **sorti** ce matin?	**As**-tu **sorti** le chien ce matin?

NOTE 2: Verbs of motion such as **courir, marcher, nager,** and **voler** show the *type* of motion and are conjugated with **avoir.** Ex.: Jean **a couru** pendant une heure autour du parc. J'**ai marché** des heures dans le musée. Georgette **a nagé** dans la grande piscine. L'avion **a volé** à 30.000 mètres.

5. **In matters of agreement, is the pronoun *vous* considered singular or plural?**

Vous êtes sorti(e)(s) hier,   (Agreement. Why?)
  n'est-ce pas?

The pronoun **vous** may be singular or plural, masculine or feminine. The past participle of a verb agrees according to whether **vous** refers to one or more than one person, and whether these persons are masculine or feminine. When **vous** refers to both masculine and feminine nouns the masculine plural agreement is used.

E. Remplacez l'infinitif par la forme convenable du participe passé.

1. Les élèves étaient déjà (partir) quand leur professeur est (arriver).
2. Marie est (sortir) sans se retourner.   3. Nous sommes (tomber) dans un piège.   4. Mes chers amis, vous êtes (arriver) trop tôt.
5. Pourquoi ne sont-ils pas (venir)?   6. Êtes-vous déjà (monter) sur la Tour Eiffel, Jacqueline?

F. Traduisez en français.

1. He had said that he would come back, and he came back.
2. (*vous*) Did you come[1] back home to[2] rest?   3. Our friends became important men.   4. Those who stayed all[3] died.
5. (*vous*) When did your sisters arrive?

[1] *come back home* = rentrer   [2] either **pour** or no preposition at all   [3] Put this word between the auxiliary and the past participle.

6. **When and how does the past participle of a reflexive or reciprocal verb agree?**

A reflexive verb is one in which the reflexive object refers back to the subject of the sentence. Ex.: *I* see *myself* in the mirror. *She* washes *herself*.

A reciprocal verb is one whose reciprocal object has the connotation of *each other*. Ex.: *They* see *each other* every week. *We* spoke to *each other* yesterday.

In French, reflexive and reciprocal verbs have the same pronominal forms and follow the same rules for agreement.

French reflexive objects may be:

(a) direct objects

Elle **s**'est coupée.   *She cut* herself.
Ils **se** sont lavés.   *They washed* themselves.

(b) indirect objects

Elles **se** sont parlé.	*They spoke* to each other.
Elle **s**'est coupé le doigt.	*She cut her finger* (lit: *She cut the finger* to herself).

(c) inherent objects

Some reflexive pronouns are neither direct nor indirect in function but simply an integral part of the verb. We may call the verbs with which they are used INHERENTLY REFLEXIVE VERBS.

Elle **s**'est souvenue de son rendez-vous.	*She remembered her appointment.*
Nous **nous** sommes échappés.	*We escaped.*
Elles **se** sont doutées de ce qui se passait.	*They suspected what was happening.*

Let us now examine the agreement of such verbs.

Votre femme et la mienne **se sont vues** hier.	(Agreement. Why?)
Nous **nous sommes levés** à dix heures.	(Agreement. Why?)
Janine **s'est souvenue** de ton adresse.	(Agreement. Why?)
Nos amis **se sont parlé** longtemps.	(No agreement. Why?)
Les enfants **se sont lavé** les mains.	(No agreement. Why?)

The past participle of a reflexive or reciprocal verb agrees with the reflexive object unless it is an indirect object. In that case, the past participle remains invariable. In other words, the past participle of a reflexive verb agrees with the reflexive object when it is direct or inherent but not when it is indirect.

G. Écrivez la forme convenable du participe passé.

1. Nous nous sommes (lever) à six heures, nous avons bien déjeuné, puis nous nous sommes (dire) au revoir.   **2.** Lucile s'est (habiller) mais elle ne s'est pas (brosser) les cheveux.   **3.** Ces enfants se sont-ils (laver) les oreilles comme il faut?   **4.** Ils se sont (raconter) leurs souvenirs pendant des heures.   **5.** Elle s'est beaucoup (amuser) à ce bal.   **6.** Nous nous sommes (apercevoir) qu'il était tard.   **7.** Sylvie s'est (marier) il y a deux mois.   **8.** Vous[1] êtes-vous

---

[1]lit.: *Did you render account to yourself of your error?* What is the function of the reflexive pronoun in this sentence?

(rendre) compte de votre erreur, Irène? 9. Comment vous êtes-vous (faire) mal, vous deux? 10. Nous nous sommes (revoir) avec plaisir.

H. Traduisez en français.

1. We met each other on[1] the street and we spoke to each other.
2. They rushed into the store. 3. Why didn't they write to each other? 4. She cut her finger yesterday. 5. Finally we all[2] found[3] each other again. 6. We were mistaken. 7. They blamed each other for the accident. 8. They related their adventures to each other. 9. (*vous*) You made fun of me, both[4] of you.

[1] dans [2] Place directly after the auxiliary. [3] *find again* = retrouver [4] vous deux

II. The Present Participle

7. How is the present participle formed?

First Person Plural Present	PRESENT PARTICIPLE	First Person Plural Present	PRESENT PARTICIPLE
donn**ons**	donn**ant**	dorm**ons**	dorm**ant**
finiss**ons**	finiss**ant**	lis**ons**	lis**ant**
perd**ons**	perd**ant**	pren**ons**	pren**ant**
buv**ons**	buv**ant**	voy**ons**	voy**ant**

The present participle is formed by adding **-ant** to the stem of the verb, which is derived by taking away the **-ons** from the first person plural present.

8. What three verbs have irregular present participles?

être **étant** avoir **ayant** savoir **sachant**

The verbs **être, avoir,** and **savoir** have irregular present participles.

9. What is the nature of the present participle?

Voyant la porte ouverte, je suis entré.	Seeing *the open door, I entered.*
Beaucoup de gens, **profitant** de leur week-end, étaient à la plage.	*Many people were at the beach, taking advantage of their weekend.*

The present participle is a verbal adjective, that is, it partakes both of the nature of an adjective and of a verb. As an adjective, it modifies some noun or pronoun in the sentence; as a verb, it indicates action or state of being and may be followed by whatever types of constructions other forms of the same verb are followed.

10. When and with what does the present participle agree?

Les Michaud ont de la chance d'avoir des enfants si **obéissants.**

The Michauds are lucky to have such obedient *children.*

When the **-ant** form of the verb is used entirely as an adjective, it agrees in gender and number with the noun it modifies.

In that case, it has none of the functions of a verb, that is, it does not indicate action or state of being, and it cannot govern an object or be followed by constructions that could follow it when used as a verb.

Les enfants, **obéissant** à leurs parents, sont allés se coucher.

The children, obeying *their parents, went to bed.*

When the **-ant** word is used as a present participle, it is invariable. As a present participle, the **-ant** word is an adjective in that it is identified with some noun or pronoun in the sentence, and it is a verb in that it tells what someone is or is doing and may be followed by whatever types of constructions other forms of the same verb are followed.

11. The present participle is sometimes used without *en,* at other times with *en* or *tout en.* To what does it refer when used without *en?* when used with *en?*

De bonne heure ce matin il a rencontré **Marie sortant*** de la bibliothèque.

Early this morning he met Marie leaving *the library.*

De bonne heure ce matin **il** a rencontré Marie **en sortant** de la bibliothèque.

Early this morning he met Marie on leaving *the library.*

When the present participle is used without **en,** it generally refers to the nearest noun or pronoun. When it is used with **en** or with **tout en,** its action regularly refers to the subject of the sentence.

12. How does the use of *en* or *tout en* with the present participle influence its relation to the action of the main verb in respect to time?

Disant ces mots, le pasteur **s'est levé.**

Saying *these words, the pastor arose.*

En sortant de la poste, notre facteur **a glissé** sur le verglas.

On leaving *the post office, our mailman* slipped *on the ice.*

Tout en parlant, le docteur **a remis** son manteau.

While he was talking, *the doctor* put on *his overcoat.*

Tout en étant sévère, le professeur **aimait** beaucoup ses élèves.

Although he was *strict, the teacher* was *very* fond *of his pupils.*

* More common than sortant in this sentence would be **qui sortait.** The use of a qui clause to express the English present participle is very common in French. See page 105, §14.

When the present participle is used without **en,** its action is usually followed by another action. When it is used with **en,** the two actions are somewhat more simultaneous, and when it is used with **tout en,** the simultaneous nature of the action is emphasized still more.

Notice that **en** + PRESENT PARTICIPLE is expressed in English by *in, on, by,* and *while* + PRESENT PARTICIPLE and sometimes by *while, when,* or *as* + CLAUSE. The expression **tout en** + PRESENT PARTICIPLE is expressed in a variety of ways in English: *while* or *still* + PRESENT PARTICIPLE, *all the while* + CLAUSE, *even though* + CLAUSE, etc.

I.   Dans le devoir suivant, le mot entre parenthèses se termine en **-ant.** Il peut être un adjectif pur ou un participe présent. Faites l'accord du mot entre parenthèses où il y a lieu.

1. Nous avons passé une journée (fatigant) à l'exposition. 2. (Fatiguant) tout le monde, Jeanne a recommencé son histoire. 3. Il y a dans la pièce des scènes (étonnant).   4. (Étonnant) ses amies, Madame Delom a déchiré toutes les lettres.   5. Nous avons trouvé les pauvres enfants (tremblant) de peur.   6. Le malade mangeait encore avec peine, la main (tremblant).   7. Nicole, (courant) vers la porte, a renversé la lampe.   8. Les Bérard ont l'eau (courant) dans leur ferme.

J.   Traduisez en français les phrases suivantes. La traduction française de chaque phrase comporte un participe présent—seul, avec *en* ou avec *tout en.*

1. Closing her[1] eyes, Genevieve listened attentively to the music. 2. The painter hurt himself by falling from the ladder.   3. Even though he was sick, George used to read a great deal.   4. Opening the door with care[2], Bernard looked into the room.   5. On seeing that Mr. Lambert was busy, we left at once.   6. I saw Frederick while coming back from the office.   7. All the while that I was listening to him, I was thinking of something else.   8. (*vous*) On arriving in Paris, go to see the Jamois.

[1] Not the possessive adjective in French.   [2] prudence

13. How does French express the English present participle when it stresses the idea of *in the act of?*

Marc était **en train de lire** le journal.	*Mark*	was reading was busy read- ing was in the act of reading	*the newspaper.*

When the English present participle stresses the idea of *in the act of,* French often uses **en train de** + INFINITIVE. This may also be expressed in English by *be busy doing something.*

14. How is the English present participle expressed after French verbs of perception, such as *voir, entendre, sentir,* etc.?

Nous avons vu Claire $\begin{cases} \textbf{ouvrir} \text{ la lettre.} \\ \textbf{qui ouvrait} \text{ la lettre.} \\ \textbf{en train d'ouvrir} \text{ la lettre.} \end{cases}$ *We saw Clara* opening *the letter.*

Je les entends $\begin{cases} \textbf{se préparer.} \\ \textbf{qui se préparent.} \\ \textbf{en train de se préparer.} \end{cases}$ *I hear them* getting ready.

After verbs of perception, the English present participle is usually expressed in French by either an INFINITIVE, a **qui** clause, or by **en train de** + INFINITIVE. The **qui** clause and the **en train de** + INFINITIVE constructions are also used after forms of the verb **trouver.**

15. When is the English present participle expressed by *à* + INFINITIVE in French?

Nous avons passé trois heures **à jouer** aux cartes.
   We spent three hours playing *cards.*

Paul est resté au moins dix minutes **à lire** l'affiche.
   Paul stood at least ten minutes reading *the announcement.*

L'enfant s'est amusé **à découper** des images.
   The child amused himself cutting out *pictures.*

The English present participle is not always expressed by a French present participle. English present participles and gerunds are expressed in a variety of ways in French. We give only a few of the most common of these.

When the English present participle expresses manner of passing time, French often uses **à** + INFINITIVE.

Especially after forms of the verb **passer** (*to spend time*), this construction must be used rather than a present participle.

K. Traduisez en français.

1. We spent two hours watching television.   2. We saw them getting[1] on the bus.   3. (*vous*) Will you spend the evening playing cards?   4. John was busy fixing his car when I came back.   5. (*tu*) Don't spend so much time reading detective stories.   6. (*vous*) Don't bother me now—I'm busy working.   7. I heard Jean playing the[2] violin.   8. We amused ourselves doing crossword puzzles. 9. I found Philip looking for his keys.   10. They see the children going to[3] school every morning.

[1] *get on* = monter dans   [2] du   [3] à l'

Exercices d'ensemble

L. Choisissez la forme convenable du participe passé.

1. Combien de tableaux avez-vous (vendu, vendus)?   2. J'en ai (vendu, vendus) trois.   3. Quels tableaux avez-vous (vendu, vendus)?   4. Les touristes japonais nous ont (demandé, demandés) où était le Musée de l'Industrie et nous leur avons (indiqué, indiqués) le chemin le plus court.   5. Simone et Monique se sont (cherché, cherchées) en vain aux Galeries Lafayette.   6. Nous nous sommes (aperçu, aperçus) que quelque chose n'allait pas.   7. Ces deux écrivains se sont (écrit, écrits) souvent; ils nous ont (laissé, laissés) une belle correspondance mais ils ne se sont jamais (rencontré, rencontrés).   8. Nous nous[1] sommes (rendu, rendus) compte qu'il serait impossible de passer plus d'un jour à Venise.   9. Mes amis se sont (demandé, demandés) ce qui allait se passer après ce scandale.   10. Est-ce que vous et Roland vous êtes (servi, servis) de la scie électrique que nous vous avons (prêté, prêtée)?

[1] *realized (lit., we rendered account to ourselves)*

M. Choisissez la forme convenable.

1. Ça m'a amusé de les entendre (parlant, parler) de leurs aventures au Mexique.   2. Les autres sont restés (discutant, à discuter, en discutant) les élections.   3. Nous étions (en train de fermer, fermant, fermants) le magasin quand nous avons entendu une explosion.   4. L'enfant s'est amusé (découpant, en train de découper, à découper) des images dans le livre.   5. Paul s'est endormi (en train de lire, en lisant, à lire) le journal.   6. J'ai découvert l'élève (lançant, qui lançait, à lancer) des boulettes de papier.   7. Robert a la mauvaise habitude de toujours lire (en mangeant, en train de manger).   8. J'ai passé une heure (à parcourir, en parcourant, parcourant) ce livre.   9. Voilà Bernard (sortant, qui sort, en sortant) de la pharmacie.   10. Madeleine (voyant, voyante) que tout était fini est partie (pleurant, en pleurant, qui pleurait).   11. Nous sommes restés un bon moment (nous demandant, en nous demandant, à nous demander) ce que nous allions faire après leur départ.

Problem Words

27. lack

(a) How *to lack* may be expressed by **manquer de**

Cet agent **manque de** tact.   *That policeman* lacks *tact.*

One of the most common ways of expressing *to lack* is: SUBJECT + **manquer de** + *what is lacking. What is lacking* is an indefinite noun, and it therefore follows **de** without a definite article.

(b) How *lack* may be expressed by the impersonal **il manque . . .**

Il lui manque de la farine pour faire son gâteau.   She lacks *flour to make her cake.*

When using the impersonal **Il manque . . .** to begin the sentence, *what is lacking* is a partitive and the person who *lacks* is the indirect object.

(c) How **manquer** is used when *what is lacking* is the SUBJECT

La volonté lui manque pour réussir.   He lacks the will *to succeed.*

When *what is lacking* is the SUBJECT of the sentence, it is modified by the definite article and the person who lacks is the indirect object.

28. last night

(a) When *last night = last evening*

Hier soir nous sommes allés au théâtre.   Last night *we went to the theater.*

When *last night = last evening,* the French say **hier soir.**

(b) When *last night* is *late in the night*

Il a fait très chaud **cette nuit.**   *It was very hot* last night.
Cette nuit je n'ai pas pu dormir.   Last night *I couldn't sleep.*
On a volé la banque **la nuit dernière.**   *The bank was robbed* last night.

When *last night* refers to something that happened later than the preceding evening, the French use the expression **cette nuit.** Also possible, but less common, is **la nuit dernière.**

29. late

(a) When *late = not early*

Il est **tard;** il faut partir.   *It is* late; *we must leave.*

When *late* means *not early,* use **tard.**

(b) When *late = not on time*

Il vaut mieux être en avance qu'**en retard.**   *It is better to be early than* late.

When *late* means *not on time,* use **en retard.**

30. leave

(a) How to say *to leave someone or something somewhere* (always with a direct object)

Nous **avons laissé Jean à la bibliothèque.**	*We* left John at the library.
Où avez-vous **laissé** votre **serviette?**	Where did *you* leave *your* towel?

The verb **laisser** is used when it is a question of *leaving someone or something somewhere.*

(b) How to say *to leave someone or something* (always with a direct object)

J'ai quitté mes amis à deux heures.	*I* left my friends *at two o'clock.*
Nous **avons quitté la maison** de bonne heure.	*We* left the house *early.*

The verb **quitter** is used when it is a question of *leaving someone or something.*

(c) How to say *to leave* (not usually followed by a place)

Je **m'en vais.**	*I'*m leaving.
Marianne **s'en ira** demain.	*Marianne* will leave *tomorrow.*

The verb **s'en aller** means *leave* in the sense of *go away, go off.* It is not usually followed by a place.

(d) How to say *to leave* (for more than just a moment)

Nous **sommes partis** hier soir.	*We* left *last night.*

The verb **partir** is sometimes used to mean *leave* or *go away without indicating a place.*

Quand **partirez**-vous **de New York?**	*When* will *you* leave New York?

When **partir** indicates *leaving a place,* it must be followed by **de.**

Jacques **est parti en Espagne.**	*Jack* left for Spain.
Michel **est parti pour la Grèce.**	*Michael* left for Greece.

The idea of *leaving for* + PLACE (proper noun) is expressed by **partir pour** or **partir** + PREPOSITION OF PLACE required by the proper noun. Purists prefer **partir pour.**

In general, **partir** means *to leave* in the sense of leaving for a trip or leaving a place for a certain length of time.

(e) When *leave* = *go out*

Sortez par la porte de derrière.	Leave (go out) *by the back door.*
Le patron vient de **sortir.** Revenez dans une heure.	*The boss has just* left. *Come back in an hour.*

The verb **sortir** means *leave* in the sense of *go out.* It often implies leaving for a short time as contrasted with **partir,** which implies leaving for a somewhat longer time and not merely temporarily.

Qui **est sorti du bureau** tout à l'heure?	*Who* left the office *just now?*
Les gens **sont sortis du restaurant** en riant.	*The people* left the restaurant *laughing.*
Rentrez tout de suite **en sortant du cinéma.**	*Come back home right away* after (leaving) the movies.

To indicate *leaving a place,* use **sortir de** + *place.*

(f) Other uses of **sortir** = *go out*

Êtes-vous **sorti** ce matin?	Did *you* go out *this morning?*

When **sortir** is used with no indication of from what place or with whom, it often means *going out of the place* where one habitually is at a given time.

Marc **sort avec** Françoise.	*Mark* is going out with *Frances.*

To indicate *going out with* in the sense of "keeping company with," use **sortir avec.**

N. Remplacez les mots anglais par leur équivalent français.

1. Bernard a une décapotable et toutes les jeunes filles veulent (*go out*) avec lui.   **2.** Avez-vous vu ce clair de lune sur le lac (*last night*)?   **3.** Je regrette d'être (*late*); j'ai été pris dans un embouteillage.   **4.** Par ce temps, je refuse de (*leave*) la maison.   **5.** Excusez-moi de vous presser, mais je ne voudrais pas que vous soyez (*late*).   **6.** Si les Couve ne sont pas là, nous (*will leave*) notre carte de visite.   **7.** Il y a eu un formidable incendie (*last night*) vers deux heures du matin.   **8.** Il est (*late*); rentrons.   **9.** Les oiseaux (*are leaving*); c'est la fin de la belle saison.   **10.** Les chiens n'ont pas arrêté d'aboyer (*last night*).   **11.** Si vous (*leave*), plusieurs de nos collègues (*will leave*) aussi.   **12.** Comment vous arrangez-vous pour être toujours (*late*)?   **13.** (*Let's leave*) nos manteaux au vestiaire; nous serons plus à l'aise.   **14.** Avant de (*leave*) le bureau, fermez bien la porte et les fenêtres.

O. Traduisez en français. Attention aux mots en italique.

1. (*vous*) Take the book that I *left* on my desk.   **2.** The men didn't *lack* courage, but they were not able to gain ground.   **3.** There was a good film on[1] television at nine *last* night. **4.** (*vous*) If you arrive too *late*, we won't be able to have dinner together. **5.** (*tu*) Why didn't you come *last* night, Colette? **6.** (*vous*) Your plants *lack* sunlight. **7.** I *left* the children at the movies. **8.** Gilbert *left last* night at eight o'clock. **9.** Roger always goes to bed *late*. **10.** Oliver doesn't *lack* ideas. **11.** (*tu*) Don't *leave* without saying good-bye. **12.** (*vous*) Don't fail to *leave* your address. **13.** The travelers *left* at[2] dawn. **14.** (*vous*) I hope you will not arrive *late*, because the bus *will leave* at one o'clock sharp.

[1] à la [2] à l'

Verb Review

Review the verbs **dire** and **écrire** according to the outline on page 253.

CHAPTER
9

Demonstratives

Le tableau soluble

Tout jeune, mon ami Jérôme Bastide aimait peindre les nuages et *ces* saules qui se reflètent si joliment dans les rivières. «J'aimais déjà, disait-il, *ce* qui bouge, *ce* qui avance». *Il* était fils du boulanger de notre village. *Celui-ci* ne prit pas *cette* vocation au sérieux. Il lui donna le choix de
5 travailler avec lui ou de s'en aller. *C*'est ainsi que Bastide arriva à Paris. De quoi vivait-il? *Il* est impossible de le dire mais nous savons qu'il allait chaque jour au musée du Louvre pour y copier les chefs-d'œuvre. Une nuit d'hiver il tenta d'incendier le musée et il brûla la Joconde[1]. «Les peintres d'aujourd'hui, expliqua-t-il au juge, répètent sans fin *ce* que
10 d'autres ont déjà dit. Faisons[2] table rase du passé, non pas en essayant d'oublier *ce* passé, mais en le supprimant».

Enfermé dans un asile, il se montra calme, docile, poli et jouit bientôt d'un régime de faveur. Il occupait une mansarde et obtint le droit d'aller en ville. Le jour anniversaire de l'incendie du Louvre, il sortit et revint
15 «chez lui» avec des toiles blanches, une palette et des tubes de couleur. La nouvelle circula aussitôt: *ce* fou, qui[3] ne l'était plus, s'était mis à peindre. Doué de génie, il peignit une Joconde aussi parfaite que l'original. L'ayant détruite autrefois, il n'avait pu résister au plaisir de la revoir. *Ce* tableau fut placé dans un lieu sûr. Il se mit ensuite à peindre des
20 toiles d'une vérité frappante. *C*'est ainsi que *cet* homme, qui avait su reproduire le plus beau sourire[4] du monde, peignit «Médor[5]», un simple chat[6] de gouttière. Or, *il* est difficile de le croire, mais *c*'est un fait, *ce* chat ronronnait quand on mettait le tableau près d'un radiateur. Sitôt que les journaux eurent diffusé la nouvelle, un collectionneur américain
25 offrit d'acheter «Médor» à dix mille dollars. *Ce* fut ensuite «La jeune fille

---

[1] *the Gioconda,* also known as the *Mona Lisa*   [2] Faisons table rase du passé   *Let's do away with the past*   [3] *who was no longer mad*   [4] that is, the famous smile of the *Mona Lisa*   [5] *«Médor»* is usually a dog's name   [6] chat de gouttière *alley cat*

au piano» qui jouait du Chopin pendant la nuit. Il y en eut bien d'autres . . .

A sa mort, on trouva dans sa chambre un portrait de lui-même si admirable que le musée du Louvre, lui ayant pardonné, l'acheta. Beaucoup
30   regrettèrent que Bastide ait abjuré[7] ses erreurs passées. *Ceci,* disaient les critiques, est un renoncement à ses théories. *C'*était sans doute dû à l'âge.

L'autoportrait fut donc pendu au Louvre. Le lendemain, un surveillant remarqua que la toile se couvrait d'une légère vapeur. «Il faut la vernir», dit le conservateur. On s'aperçut alors que la signature de Bastide n'était
35   plus visible. Qu'est-*ce* que *cela* signifiait? Le matin suivant, une des mains avait disparu. Dans la soirée *ce* fut les bras. Quand les experts et tous *ceux* qui pouvaient se dire compétents sur le sujet arrivèrent, ils purent constater que, durant la nuit, Bastide avait perdu son nez. Et puis ses oreilles, ses cheveux, son veston . . . *C'*était clair: le tableau se[8] défaisait,
40   s'effaçait, dans le sens inverse de sa création. *C'*est pourquoi la signature et la main furent les premiers atteints. *Ce* phénomène s'était produit à l'heure précise où Bastide était entré au musée du Louvre.

J'ai oublié de rapporter qu'il m'avait dit un jour: «Les statues des hommes célèbres devraient être faites d'un aggloméré de sucre et de sel.
45   Un jour de pluie, le ciel nous en débarrasserait».

Je suis certain qu'il[9] méditait depuis longtemps «le tableau soluble». *Celui* qui avait brûlé la Joconde pensait nous laisser son chef-d'oeuvre en peignant une toile qui redeviendrait blanche.

D'après Claude Spaak, auteur belge de pièces de théâtre et de contes fantastiques comme *celui-ci.* («De l'infini au zéro», dans *Le pays des miroirs,* Julliard, 1962)

---

[7] *renounced*   [8] *was disappearing*   [9] il méditait depuis longtemps «le tableau soluble»   *he had been considering (the possibility of) the dissolvable painting for a long time*

A demonstrative is a word that points out. The English demonstratives are *this, that, these,* and *those.*

A demonstrative may modify a noun; in that case, it is a demonstrative adjective. Ex.: *this* book, *that* table, *those* people.

A demonstrative may take the place of a noun; in that case, it is a demonstrative pronoun. Ex.: This book is red, *that one* is green. Don't do *that.*

In French, it is important to know whether the DEMONSTRATIVE is an ADJECTIVE or a PRONOUN. If it is a pronoun, it is necessary to know which type of demonstrative pronoun it is since there are three types of demonstrative pronouns.

I. The Demonstrative Adjective

1. What are the demonstrative adjectives and how do they agree?

MASCULINE

Ce livre est bleu.
Ces livres sont bleus.

Cet arbre est vieux.
Ces arbres sont vieux.

FEMININE

Cette ville est grande.
Ces villes sont grandes.

The demonstrative adjectives are:

		Singular	Plural
Masculine	**ce**	used before masculine noun or adjective beginning with a consonant*	**ces**
	cet	used before masculine noun or adjective beginning with vowel sound	**ces**
Feminine	**cette**	used before all feminine nouns and adjectives	**ces**

2. When and how do the French distinguish between *this* and *that*?

Ce professeur est excellent.
Ce professeur-**ci** est plus âgé que **ce** professeur-**là**.
À **ce** moment-**là** il n'y avait pas beaucoup de travail.

That *teacher is excellent.*
This *teacher is older than* that *teacher.*
At that *time there was not much work.*

In French there is one demonstrative adjective with several forms (**ce, cette,** etc.); in English there are two demonstrative adjectives (*this, that*).

French does not usually distinguish between *this* and *that* unless a contrast is desired. In other words, **ce** points out more definitely than **le,** but it does not make a contrast between *this* and *that.*

When two objects are mentioned and a contrast is desired, each of the nouns contrasted is preceded by a form of the demonstrative adjec-

---

* That is, all consonants except mute **h.**

tive, and the first noun is followed by **-ci** (to indicate *this*), the second noun is followed by **-là** (to indicate *that*). A hyphen connects **-ci** and **-là** to their nouns.

In certain time expressions referring to the past, **-là** is regularly appended to the noun modified by the demonstrative without there being any corresponding expression with **-ci.**

A. Remplacez les tirets par un adjectif démonstratif, en mettant *-ci* ou *-là* après le nom où[1] il y a lieu.

1. Que pensez-vous de _____ nouvelle élève?   2. J'aime bien voir _____ comédiens à la télévision.   3. _____ arbre a plus de deux cents ans.   4. Prenez _____ verre; _____ verre est pour moi.   5. À _____ époque il n'y avait pas d'automobiles. 6. Ne prenez pas _____ lettre; elle est très importante. 7. Combien coûtent _____ roses rouges?   8. _____ journaux de sport ne sont pas très intéressants.   9. _____ oiseau semble triste dans sa cage.   10. Je dois partir _____ soir pour Paris. 11. _____ élèves font trop de bruit.   12. Avez-vous besoin de _____ dictionnaire aujourd'hui?   13. Vous ferez _____ exercices mais pas _____ exercices.   14. D'où vient _____ lumière?

[1] where it is necessary.

B. Traduisez en français. Soulignez les démonstratifs.

1. Who is that gentleman?   2. (*vous*) Do you like that music? 3. At that time[1] I was only four years old.   4. (*tu*) When did you do these exercises?   5. This car is really better than that car. 6. At that time[2] there was no one in the street.   7. (*vous*) Have you read those short stories?   8. That child is a real prodigy. 9. At that time[3] I was doing the housework.   10. (*vous*) Do you know if that hotel is comfortable?   11. (*tu*) Give me this stamp and I'll give you that stamp.

[1] époque   [2] heure   [3] moment

II. The Indefinite Demonstrative Pronouns

3. What are the indefinite demonstrative pronouns? When are they used? When is *ça* used for *cela*?

Lisez **ceci**, ne lisez pas **cela**.	*Read* this, *don't read* that.
Avez-vous vu **cela**?	*Did you see* that?
Ne fais pas **ça**.	*Don't do* that.

The indefinite demonstrative pronouns are **ceci, cela,** and **ça.** They refer to something without gender or number, such as an idea, or they point out something indefinite. The pronoun **ça** is a shortened and familiar form of **cela,** common in spoken style but to be avoided in elegant written style.

The indefinite demonstrative pronouns are not normally used in good French before a form of **être.** Before a form of **être,** the demonstrative pronoun **ce** is used instead of **ça.** For example, not «Ça sera facile», but rather **Ce sera facile.**

III.   The Definite Demonstrative Pronouns

4. What are the definite demonstrative pronouns?

The definite demonstrative pronouns are:

	Singular	Plural
Masculine	**celui**	**ceux**
Feminine	**celle**	**celles**

5. How are the definite demonstrative pronouns used?

Ces livres-ci sont meilleurs que **ceux-là.**

These books are better than those.

The definite demonstrative pronouns often refer to a noun already mentioned which has number and gender. They then agree with this noun in gender and number.

Celui qui travaille gagne de l'argent.

He (The one) *who works earns money.*

Ceux qui veulent peuvent partir.

Those (The ones) *who wish can leave.*

The definite demonstrative pronouns + **qui** are also used to express the English *he who, she who, the one who,* etc. In this case, the gender and number of the definite demonstrative depends on its meaning.

6. By what must the definite demonstrative pronouns be followed?

Ceux qui sont en retard sont obligés de rester après la classe.

Those who *are late are obliged to stay after class.*

J'aime mieux mes chiens que **ceux du** voisin.

I like my dogs better than the neighbor's (those of *my neighbor*).

Choisissez les fleurs que vous préférez. **Celles-ci** sont plus fraîches que **celles-là.**

Choose the flowers you prefer. These are fresher than those.

The definite demonstrative pronouns are always followed by **-ci, -là,** by a relative pronoun, or by a preposition. They cannot be followed by **-ci** or **-là** if they are followed by either a relative pronoun or a preposition.

7. How are *the former* **and** *the latter* **expressed in French?**

Connaissez-vous ces deux dames? **Celle-ci** est anglaise; **celle-là** est polonaise.	*Do you know these two ladies? The former is Polish, the latter English.*
Le chiens et les chats sont des animaux domestiques; quand ils sont contents, **ceux-ci** ronronnent, tandis que **ceux-là** remuent la queue.	*Dogs and cats are domestic animals;* the former *wag their tails when they are pleased,* while the latter *purr.*

In English, in referring to two persons or things just mentioned, we use *the former* and *the latter*. In French, *the former* is expressed by **celui-là, celle-là, ceux-là,** and **celles-là,** whereas *the latter* is expressed by **celui-ci, celle-ci, ceux-ci, celles-ci.** The **celui-ci** forms (*the latter*) precede the **celui-là** forms (*the former*). Therefore, to render a sentence with *the former* and *the latter* in French, the word order must be changed so that *the latter* precedes *the former*.

Je cherche des renseignements sur Jean Dubois et Pierre Petit. **Ce dernier** habite à Chartres.	*I am looking for information concerning John Dubois and Peter Petit. The latter lives in Chartres.*

In sentences where only *the latter* is used, a form of **ce dernier** may also be used. However, a form of **celui-ci** is quite correct in such cases.

C. Remplacez les mots entre parenthèses par le pronom démonstratif convenable. Mettez *-ci* ou *-là* s'il y a lieu.

1. (*This*) doit rester strictement entre nous.   **2.** —Laquelle de ces dames est Madame Delatour? —(*The one*) qui porte une robe bleue. **3.** Si je découvre (*the one*) qui a fait cela, gare à lui!   **4.** Je l'avais dit, (*that*) devait arriver.   **5.** Le Rhône et la Garonne prennent leur source hors de France; (*the latter*) se jette dans l'Atlantique, (*the former*) dans la Méditerranée.   **6.** Ils sont partis; (*that*) me fait beaucoup de peine.   **7.** Savez-vous ce que veut dire (*this*)? **8.** J'envie (*those*) qui peuvent aller passer l'été en France.   **9.** Si votre voiture ne marche pas, pourquoi ne prenez-vous pas (*your brother's*)?   **10.** Il y a beaucoup de robes dans le magasin, mais il faut te décider. Veux-tu (*these*) ou (*those*)?

D. Traduisez en français. Soulignez les démonstratifs.

1. (*vous*) That belongs to me; don't take it.   **2.** (*tu*) If you don't like that, leave it.   **3.** This gift is not the one that I had hoped for.

4. This interests me a great deal. 5. That author wrote plays and novels. The former[1] are entertaining,, whereas the latter are boring. 6. Those who are not satisfied can go[2] and see the manager. 7. (*vous*) I know those girls. Go out with this one but not with that one. 8. My ideas are sometimes different from my partner's[3]. 9. (*vous*) Don't think of[4] that anymore. 10. I like these two lamps, especially this one.

[1] In French, *the latter* (referring to novels) precedes *the former* (referring to plays). [2] In the sense of "going to complain," *go and see* = s'adresser à. [3] French says *from those of my partner* [4] What preposition does French use with penser in this sense?

IV.   The Demonstrative Pronoun *ce*

When used as a demonstrative pronoun, **ce** is invariable and is usually the subject of some form of the verb **être**. It has several distinct uses. In one of its functions, we call it the *indefinite* **ce**, in another the *introductory* **ce**.

NOTE 1: A third function, sometimes called the *pleonastic* **ce**, will not be taken up here. Ex.: La guerre, **c'**est la ruine. Ce que Roger fait, **c'**est son affaire.

NOTE 2: The demonstrative pronoun **ce** is also used in the combinations **ce qui, ce que,** and **ce dont.** This use of **ce** will be taken up in the chapter on relative pronouns. See page 128.

THE INDEFINITE ce

8. How is the English *it* expressed in French when it refers back to an idea without gender or number?

Elle nage bien. **C'**est difficile.	*She swims well. It's difficult.*
—Venez avec moi. —**C'**est impossible.	*"Come with me." "It's impossible."*
Il lit vite. **C'**est facile à voir.	*He reads rapidly. It's easy to see.*
Ils vont partir. **C'**est bon à savoir.	*They are going to leave. It's good to know.*

The *indefinite* **ce** refers back to an aforementioned idea. Since an idea has neither gender nor number, the indefinite and neuter **ce** is used to refer to such an idea. English uses *it* to refer back to an idea.

When the indefinite **ce** + a form of **être** has its meaning completed by an infinitive, the preposition **à** normally connects the infinitive to what precedes.

$$\text{idea} \rightarrow \textbf{ce} + \begin{array}{c}\text{form} \\ \text{of} \\ \textbf{être}\end{array} + \text{ADJECTIVE} + \textbf{à} + \text{INFINITIVE}$$

9. When, on the other hand, is the English *it* expressed by the impersonal *il*?

Il est difficile de bien chanter.	It *is difficult to sing well.*
Il est impossible de partir avec vous.	It *is impossible to leave with you.*
Il est facile de lire vite.	It *is easy to read rapidly.*

When one would begin an English sentence with an *it* which does not refer to any previous idea, in French such a sentence is often introduced by the impersonal **il** followed by a form of **être** and an adjective. This construction is usually followed by **de** + INFINITIVE.

$$\boxed{\textbf{Il} + \begin{array}{c}\text{form}\\ \text{of}\\ \textbf{être}\end{array} + \text{ADJECTIVE} + \textbf{de} + \text{INFINITIVE}}$$

In conversational style, the French often replace the impersonal **il** by **ce**, so that **Il est difficile de bien chanter** often becomes **C'est difficile de bien chanter.** The latter is, however, less elegant.

E. Remplacez les tirets par *ce* ou *il*.

1. Jean n'est pas encore arrivé. _____ est ennuyeux.   2. Où tout cela nous mène-t-il? _____ est triste à penser.   3. _____ est impossible de retourner chez elle maintenant.   4. Voilà ce que je vous ai promis. _____ est joli, n'est-ce pas?   5. _____ est plus facile de critiquer que de créer.   6. Savez-vous taper à la machine? _____ est tellement utile.

F. Traduisez en français.

1. (*tu*) Is your father angry? It's evident.   2. It's easy to make mistakes.   3. (*vous*) What you have written surprises me, but it's interesting.   4. It is pleasant to travel.   5. It is useful to learn a foreign language.   6. Lawrence knows what he is doing. It's true. 7. John won't come back any more. It is difficult to believe.

THE INTRODUCTORY ce

10. When is the introductory *ce* used?

Qui est ce garçon? **C'est mon fils.**	*Who is that boy?* He's my son.
Qui est là? **C'est lui.**	*Who is there?* It's he.
Qui sont ces personnes? **Ce sont mes nièces.**	*Who are those people?* They *are* my nieces.
C'est Pasteur qui a découvert un vaccin contre la rage.	It *is* Pasteur *who discovered a vaccine for rabies.*

The *introductory* **ce** is used before a form of the verb **être** when what follows **être** could be the subject of the sentence. After **être,** normally a pronoun, a proper name, or a modified noun could be the subject of the sentence.

In such cases, the introductory **ce** is expressed in English sometimes by *it,* sometimes by *he, she,* or *they.*

NOTE: In sentences like **C'est le plus beau des mois,** the introductory **ce** is also used when a superlative form of the adjective follows a form of **être.**

11. When, on the other hand, are the subject pronouns *il, elle, ils,* and *elles* used as the subject of the verb *être?*

Où est Marie? **Elle** est en classe.	*Where is Marie?* She *is in class.*
Voyez-vous souvent Gilbert? **Il** est très intelligent.	*Do you often see Gilbert?* He *is very intelligent.*
Nous parlons de vos enfants. Sont-**ils** là?	*We are speaking of your children.* Are they *there?*

Whenever what follows a form of the verb **être** could not be the subject of the sentence, a third person subject pronoun must be used instead of the introductory **ce.** That is, whenever an adverb, an adjective, or a phrase follows **être,** it is NOT possible to use the introductory **ce.**

12. When is the personal pronoun and when is the introductory *ce* used with names of professions, nationalities, religions, etc., when they follow a form of *être?*

Il est **médecin.**	**C'est un médecin.**
Elle est **protestante.**	**C'est une protestante fervente.**
Ils sont **français.**	**Ce** sont **des Français distingués.**

When the unmodified name of a profession, nationality, religion, or any like noun is used after the verb **être,** it is considered an adjective rather than a noun. In such cases, **il, elle, ils,** or **elles** are used before the form of **être.** But if such a noun is modified, it is then considered as a noun, and since it can thus be the subject of the sentence, the form of the verb **être** is preceded by the introductory **ce.**

G. Remplacez les tirets par l'équivalent français du mot indiqué en anglais.

1. —Où est Jacques? —(*He*) est en France.   2. Voilà Solange. (*She*) est professeur.   3. Connaissez-vous M. Dupont? (*He*) est un célèbre écrivain.   4. Est-(*she*) catholique ou protestante?   5. Ne demandez pas cela à Jacques. (*He*) n'est pas riche.   6. —Que fait son père? —(*He*) est médecin.   7. —Où est votre frère maintenant? —(*He*) est à l'armée.   8. (*It*) sont eux qui m'ont ramené à la maison.

9. —De quelle nationalité sont ces gens? —(*They*) sont allemands.
10. (*They*) sont des célibataires endurcis, mais (*they*) semblent contents de leur sort.

H. Traduisez en français.

1. Who is this man? He is Mr. Lefranc.   2. I like this snapshot a great deal. It is very beautiful.   3. (*vous*) Look at these children; they are so cute.   4. Who took his dictionary? It wasn't[1] I.   5. I remember him; he is a teacher, isn't he?   6. Is he French or American?   7. Who is this girl? She is my sister-in-law.   8. (*vous*) Do you know Madame Dumont? She is our lawyer's second wife.

[1] Use present in French.

I. Remplacez les mots anglais pas l'équivalent français. Choisissez un des mots: *ce, il, elle, ils, elles.*

1. Voyez-vous cette femme au chapeau rouge? (*She*) est la sœur d'Henri.   2. Je connais Pierre et sa femme; (*they*) sont des catholiques pratiquants.   3. J'aime beaucoup cet écrivain. (*He*) est mon préféré.   4. —Qui est là? —(*It*) est moi, Françoise.   5. Je n'ai pas fait ce que j'aurais dû, (*it*) est vrai.   6. Parlez plus fort, s'il vous plaît; voilà, (*it*) est mieux.   7. Je voudrais voir votre professeur. Est- (*he*) ici?   8. Qui a dit ces mensonges sur moi? Est-(*it*) Brigitte?   9. Venez tout de suite, (*it*) est très important.   10. Voyez-vous ce monsieur? Qui est- (*he*)[1]?

[1] Since qui is a pronoun, how must *he* be expressed here?

Exercices d'ensemble

J. Remplacez les mots anglais par l'équivalent français.

1. Pardonne-nous nos offenses comme nous pardonnons à (*those*) qui nous ont offensés.   2. (*It*) est un petit arbre qui a donné tous (*those*) beaux fruits.   3. Je vous présenterai mon ami. (*He*) est ingénieur.   4. Ne recommencez pas à m'ennuyer avec (*that*).
5. (*He*) est un ancien prince russe.   6. (*This*) homme de science dit qu'il pourrait créer un être humain. (*It*) est extraordinaire.   7. Je me suis trompé de route. (*It*) est évident.   8. Connaissez-vous (*those*) jeunes gens? (*They*) sont très amusants.   9. Quant à Florence, (*she*) est fâchée de n'avoir pas été invitée.   10. Je connais plusieurs Belges. (*They*) sont tous catholiques.   11. (*It*) est une triste histoire.
12. Je retrouverai (*the one*) qui m'a joué (*that*) tour.   13. (*She*) est japonaise.   14. (*The one*) que je cherche n'est pas encore arrivé.

K. Remplacez les tirets par *c'est, il est, elle est,* ou *ils sont,* selon le cas.

1. _____ important de faire cette réparation immédiatement.
2. Je me souviens assez bien de lui. _____ un ancien camarade de classe.   3. _____ est difficile de comprendre ce qu'il a essayé de nous expliquer hier.   4. _____ un très gros industriel.   5. — Avez-vous confiance en votre docteur? —Oui, _____ un excellent médecin.   6. —Où est ma serviette? —_____ là, sur la table. Vous ne la voyez pas?   7. _____ clair que cette fois vous avez raison.
8. —Apportera-t-il son stéréo? —_____ probable.
9. _____une belle idée, une idée de bienfaiteur.   10. _____ toujours bon de vous revoir. Revenez bientôt.   11. _____ malade, mais il est venu quand même.   12. Allez voir mes cousins si vous avez le temps. _____ très rigolos.

L. Traduisez en français.

1. I like that song a great deal.   2. (*tu*) The ones who told you that lied.   3. (*vous*) You do not need two ballpoint pens; lend me that one.   4. I want to speak to those who couldn't come yesterday.   5. I have already seen this man somewhere, but where?
6. (*vous*) Take[1] her those flowers.   7. The ones I prefer are the pink carnations.   8. (*tu*) Don't say that; it's not polite.

[1] Use a form of **apporter.**

Problem Words

31. little

(a) When to use **peu**

Jeannot lit **peu,** il préfère s'amuser.	*Johnnie reads* little, *he prefers to have a good time.*
J'ai **peu** d'argent.	*I* do not *have* very much *money.*

When **peu** is used alone, that is, unaccompanied by **un,** it means *little, only a little, not very much.*

(b) When to use **un peu**

Si tu as **un peu** d'argent, mets-le de côté.	*If you have* a little *money, save it.*

Note that **un peu** means *a little* or *some.*

32. live

(a) When to use **habiter**

Nos amis **habitent** $\begin{cases} \text{à Genève.} \\ \text{Genève.} \end{cases}$ *Our friends live in Geneva.*

To indicate where one lives, the French commonly use the verb **habiter,** which may be followed either directly by the place or by the French equivalent of *in + place.* It is somewhat synonymous with the English *inhabit,* but it is much more common.

The verb **demeurer,** formerly very frequently used for *live* in the above sense, has now been almost entirely replaced by **habiter.**

(b) When to use **vivre**

Monsieur Seydoux **vit** de ses revenus.	*Mr. Seydoux* lives *from his income.*
Il est mort comme il **a vécu.**	*He died as he* lived.
Monsieur Rochebois **vivait** entièrement pour sa famille.	*Mr. Rochebois* lived *entirely for his family.*

The verb **vivre** means *live* in a larger and more general sense and is sometimes synonymous with *exist.* It is occasionally used in the sense of **habiter,** but the learner should avoid using it in this sense.

33. long

(a) How to say *as long as*

Tant que je serai là, il n'y aura rien à craindre.   As long as I am *there, there will be nothing to fear.*

The time expression *as long as* is rendered in French by **tant que** and is followed by the FUTURE whenever futurity is implied.

(b) How to say *how long*

Combien de temps avez-vous travaillé pour lui?	How long *have you worked for him?*
Pendant combien de temps êtes-vous resté en France?	How long *did you stay in France?*

The English *how long,* meaning *how much time,* may be expressed in French by **combien de temps** or **pendant combien de temps.**

Depuis quand êtes-vous ici?	How long *have you been here?*
Depuis combien de temps attends-tu?	How long *have you been waiting?*

The expressions **depuis quand** and **depuis combien de temps** are often used with the PRESENT where English uses *how long* + PRESENT PERFECT PROGRESSIVE to express the same idea.

(c) How to say *for a long time*

Nous avons parlé **longtemps** de ton avenir.	*We spoke about your future* for a long time.
Il y a **longtemps** que je connais les Jourdan.	*I have known the Jourdans* for a long time.

The English *a long time* is expressed in French by the adverb **longtemps.**

(d) How to say *at length*

Nous avons parlé **longuement** de ton avenir.	*We spoke* at length *of your future.*

The English *at length* is expressed in French by the adverb **longuement,** when *at length* = *in detail.*

34. make

How to say *make someone* + ADJECTIVE

Vous **me rendez très heureux** en disant cela.	*You* make me very happy *in saying that.*

The French equivalent of *to make someone* + ADJECTIVE is **rendre quelqu'un** + ADJECTIVE.

CAUTION: DO NOT use the construction «faire quelqu'un» + adjective. French uses **rendre** in such situations.

M. Remplacez les mots anglais par leur équivalent français.

1. Je ne conduis pas depuis (*a long time*), mais je suis très prudente. **2.** Inutile de se faire trop de soucis; il faut (*live*) au jour le jour. **3.** Henriette écrit (*little*), mais elle nous téléphone souvent. **4.** Votre présence (*made*) la soirée très agréable. **5.** J'ai (*at length*) réfléchi à ce que vous m'avez dit. **6.** Monsieur et Madame Renaud ont une belle auto, mais ils (*live*) dans une très vieille maison. **7.** Il faut faire (*a little*) de gymnastique tous les matins. **8.** J'observe vos progrès depuis (*a long time*) sans rien dire.

N. Traduisez en français. Attention aux mots en italique.

1. (*tu*) I know your friend Daniel *a little.* **2.** I *lived* in a large city for twenty years. **3.** (*vous*) If you remain here too *long,* you will forget your native language. **4.** (*vous*) Don't smoke so much, it[1] will *make* you sick. **5.** (*vous*) You really give me *little* time to[2] do that. **6.** People *live* a great deal *longer* today than formerly. **7.** The mayor spoke *at length* concerning the traffic problems.

8. Mr. Mollet no longer reads the newspaper; it[1] *makes* him nervous. **9.** Those young people went out for[3] *a long time* together before getting married.   **10.** (*tu*) Wait *a little*.

[1] ça   [2] pour   [3] Omit in translation.

Verb Review

Review the verbs **envoyer** and **faire** according to the outline on page 253.

CHAPTER 10

Relatives

Manifestation au lycée de Lausanne

En ce temps-là eut lieu une manifestation *qui* fit parler tout le pays et donna une célébrité définitive à M. Grapp, le directeur du lycée.

Tout avait commencé au cours de la cérémonie des «Promotions» *qui* marque le passage de centaines de garçons et de filles du collège secon-
5 daire au lycée. Un élève, Pierre Müller, *qui* devait réciter un poème à cette occasion, en profita pour critiquer le système scolaire, accuser les programmes[1], se moquer des professeurs—parmi *lesquels* j'étais—et engager ses camarades à se révolter. Ce fut un scandale épouvantable *auquel* personne ne s'était[2] attendu. Mais le jour même *où* cela arriva, M.
10 Grapp et l'administration prirent une décision spectaculaire: l'orateur contestataire fut suspendu pour six mois. Ce fut le prétexte à toutes sortes d'événements *que* les groupes de gauche provoquaient sans cesse: défilés avec pancartes, réunions sur les petites places autour du lycée, tracts quotidiens. «Réintégrez[3] Pierre Müller», criait sur la grande place une
15 foule colorée[4] et joyeuse à *laquelle* se mêlaient de nombreux clochards[5] et des curieux. Les jeunes gens débouchaient[6] de la rue de l'Université en cortèges désordonnés *où* l'on dansait, *où* l'on chantait. Les filles avaient dans les cheveux des fleurs *qu'*elles avaient cueillies dans les parcs publics. Rien ne manquait, c'était une vraie fête. Je regardais les specta-
20 cles avec un intense plaisir.

Cependant, trois jours après, comme j'arrivais au lycée à huit heures, je sortis de ma voiture et je sentis qu'il se passait quelque chose. Un type *dont* la figure ne m'était pas inconnue se cacha derrière un mur en m'apercevant. Des pancartes étaient entassées contre une porte. Je ne
25 pouvais imaginer *ce que* la matinée allait me révéler et l'effet fatal *qu'*elle devait exercer sur ma vie. C'était la manifestation.

---

[1] *courses of study*   [2] *had expected*   [3] Réintégrez Pierre Müller *Let Pierre Müller back in*   [4] *colorful*   [5] *tramps*   [6] *came out*

Des centaines de jeunes gens arrivent soudain en courant, en riant, en criant des slogans. Au moment *où* un mégaphone appelle les lycéens à réagir contre la décision du Directeur, des groupes se préparent à envahir
30 le bâtiment de l'administration. Tout à coup le[7] silence se fait, chacun demeure pétrifié: devant la porte est apparu M. Grapp, massif, immense, le crâne luisant, le[8] nez chaussé de ses terribles lunettes noires. Il[9] incarne la force concentrée et contemple l'adversaire. Mais *ce qui* stupéfie l'assistance[10], c'est qu'il tient à la main un long fouet, bouclé comme un
35 serpent prêt à mordre, monstruosité[11] sortie du fond des âges. Quand le mégaphone *qui* s'était tu[12] recommence ses exhortations, la foule des manifestants reprend sa marche vers la porte principale où l'attend M. Grapp. Alors celui-ci avance, lève le fouet, le fait siffler, attaque les pro-testataires. *Ce qui* les fait céder, ils le diront plus tard, ce n'est pas le
40 respect ni même la peur mais l'étonnement, la panique *qu'*inspire le spectacle de ce colosse armé de son fouet. Car il avance toujours en poussant des cris inarticulés, le fouet siffle toujours. Le groupe entier se sauve, M. Grapp court de l'un à l'autre, frappe les fuyards[13], arrive enfin à la grande porte *dont* il ferme la grille. La cour est vide. M. Grapp est
45 maître du terrain.

D'après Jacques Chessex, éminent essayiste, critique et romancier suisse. (*L'Ogre,* Grasset 1973)

---

[7] le silence se fait *everything became quiet*   [8] le nez chaussé de ses terribles lunettes noires *with his terrible black glasses on his nose*   [9] Il incarne *He represented*   [10] *crowd*   [11] monstruosité sortie du fond des âges *a monstrosity dating from prehistoric times*   [12] tu *is the past participle of* taire   [13] *fleeing students*

A relative pronoun is one that connects a dependent to an independent clause. The relative pronoun is part of the dependent clause, performs a function in that clause, and usually begins the dependent clause. The English relative pronouns are *who, whom, whose, which, that,* and *what.* Ex.: The student *who* wrote that essay is a genius.

The relative pronoun normally refers back to some noun in the independent clause. This noun is called the antecedent of the pronoun. In the above example, the antecedent of *who* is "student."

I corrected the <u>exercise</u> **that** John wrote.

independent clause	=	I corrected the exercise
		This is an independent clause because it makes sense by itself.

dependent clause	=	that John wrote
		This is a dependent clause because it is incomplete; it depends on the preceding clause.
relative pronoun	=	that
		that connects the dependent to the independent clause and is the direct object of the dependent clause.
antecedent	=	exercise
		This is the word to which **that** refers.

Sometimes, however, the relative pronoun is indefinite. In that case, there is no antecedent in the English sentence. Ex.: My father does not know *what* I am doing.

1. What relative pronoun is used as the subject of its clause?

C'est le professeur **qui** parle. — *It is the teacher* who *is talking.*
C'est une voiture **qui** coûte très cher. — *It is a car* which *costs a great deal.*

The relative pronoun **qui** is used as the subject of its clause, whether it refers to a person or a thing.

2. What relative pronoun is used as the object of its clause?

Je voudrais voir les malades **que** vous avez amenés. — *I should like to see the sick persons* whom *you brought.*
Montrez-moi la bague **que** vous voulez. — *Show me the ring* that *you want.*

The relative pronoun **que** is used as the object of its clause, whether it refers to a person or a thing.

The object relative pronoun may be omitted in English but not in French. Ex.: *Is the book you bought interesting?* Est-ce que le livre **que** vous avez acheté est intéressant?

3. Which two relative pronouns are used after prepositions?

Où habitent les amis avec
{ **qui**
{ **lesquels** vous parlez français?
— *Where do the friends with* whom *you speak French live?*

Montrez-moi la clé avec **laquelle** vous avez ouvert ma porte. — *Show me the key with* which *you opened my door.*

After a preposition, either **qui** or a form of **lequel** may be used to refer to persons; a form of **lequel** is used to refer to things.

The forms of **lequel** are: **lequel, laquelle, lesquels, lesquelles.**

4. How is the relative pronoun *what* expressed in French?

(a) Subject

Ce qui est sur la table est à moi.	What *is on the table is mine.*
Il ne faut pas faire **ce qui** est défendu.	*You mustn't do* what *is forbidden.*

The English *what* is expressed by **ce qui** when it is the subject of its clause.

(b) Object

Ce que vous écrivez est intéressant.	What *you are writing is interesting.*
Savez-vous **ce que** Jean a dit?	*Do you know* what *John said?*

The English *what* is expressed by **ce que** when it is the object of its clause.

(c) After a preposition

Je ne comprends pas **de quoi** vous parlez.	*I don't understand* what *you are talking* about.

The English *what* is expressed by **quoi** when it is used after a preposition.

NOTE: When this construction begins a sentence, one finds **Ce** + PREPOSITION + **quoi.** Ex.: **Ce à quoi** je pense ne vous regarde pas. (What *I am thinking* about *is none of your business.*) The **ce** + PREPOSITION + **quoi** combination may often also be used in the interior of a sentence, but just when is beyond the scope of this text.

The relative **quoi,** used after a preposition, is sometimes an indefinite that is expressed in English by *which.*

Maurice a fini ses devoirs, **après quoi** il est sorti.	*Maurice finished his exercises,* after which *he went out.*

5. How is *everything that* expressed in French?

Avez-vous lu **tout ce qui** est dans votre bibliothèque?	*Have you read* everything that *is in your library?*
Dites-moi **tout ce que** vous faites.	*Tell me* everything that *you are doing.*

The English *everything that* is expressed in French by
(a) **tout ce qui** when it is the subject of its clause;
(b) **tout ce que** when it is the object of its clause.

6. How can the relative pronouns be presented in graphic tabular form?

Function	Persons	Things	*what*
Subject	**qui**	**qui**	**ce qui**
Object	**que**	**que**	**ce que**
After preposition	**qui** **lequel***	**lequel***	**quoi****

A. Remplacez le mot anglais par le mot français.

1. (*What*) vous dites est vrai.   **2.** Les conseils (*that*) vous m'avez donnés sont excellents.   **3.** Les choses (*which*) semblent compliquées sont souvent bien simples.   **4.** L'acte dans (*which*) elle était le mieux était le dernier.   **5.** Il voudrait savoir à (*what*) vous vous intéressez.   **6.** (*What*) se passe aujourd'hui est terrible! **7.** Le professeur (*who*) va parler vient de France.   **8.** L'ami sur (*whom*) je comptais n'est pas venu.   **9.** L'homme (*whom*) la police vient d'arrêter est un espion.   **10.** C'est Jeanne avec (*whom*) je suis sorti dimanche.   **11.** (*What*) je vais chanter maintenant est très connu.   **12.** Moi (*who*) vous parle, j'ai passé par là.   **13.** Les roses (*which*) vous m'avez données sont superbes.

B. Traduisez en français.

1. (*vous*) The dress[1] you are wearing is very pretty.   **2.** The carpenter to whom I spoke is very nice.   **3.** (*vous*) My father, who is a businessman, will come to see you.   **4.** What we are studying is very useful.   **5.** (*tu*) The friend whom you invited is charming. **6.** (*vous*) I do not understand what you are speaking of.   **7.** The road by which he came is very bad.   **8.** (*tu*) Show me everything that you have in your drawer.   **9.** (*vous*) Tell me of[2] what you are thinking.   **10.** The parents gave the children some cookies, after which they left.   **11.** (*vous*) What is on the table is yours, but everything that is on the desk is mine.

[1] The relative pronoun is missing in English but must be expressed in French. See page 127, §2.   [2] Not «de».

7. How is *de* + RELATIVE normally expressed in French?

Le livre **dont** vous parlez est connu.	*The book* of which *you are speaking is well known.*

The form **dont** normally replaces **de** + RELATIVE.

---

*i.e., lequel, laquelle, lesquels, or lesquelles, according to the gender of the antecedent.
**Sometimes ce + PREPOSITION + quoi is required.

NOTE: When a preposition or a prepositional phrase comes between the antecedent and the relative, then **de** + RELATIVE are used instead of **dont**. The
relative **dont** must follow its antecedent immediately and therefore must
stand first in its clause. Ex.: C'est *un livre* au milieu **duquel** il y a de jolies
illustrations.

Also, *from which* (meaning *whence*) is usually expressed by **d'où** rather than
dont. Ex.: Je n'ai jamais visité la ville **d'où** il vient.

8. Sentences with the relative pronoun *dont* present certain problems
of word order. What is a practical way of determining the word order
of such sentences?

Voici le docteur Galand

dont le fils est mon meilleur
ami.

Here is Dr. Galand
$\begin{cases} \text{whose } \textit{son is my best friend.} \\ \text{of whom } \textit{the son is my best} \\ \textit{friend.} \end{cases}$

Note that in French, when **dont** is identified with the subject of its
clause, the subject is modified by the definite article.

Montrez-moi le livre

dont vous connaissez l'auteur.

Show me the book
$\begin{cases} \text{whose } \textit{author you know.} \\ \text{of which } \textit{you know the au-} \\ \textit{thor.} \end{cases}$

Note that when **dont** is identified with the object of its clause, that
object is in quite a different position than it is in the corresponding
English clause.

The word order of a French clause introduced by **dont** is:

> **dont** + SUBJECT + VERB + rest of sentence

In order to arrive at the French word order in **dont**-clauses, instead
of using *whose* in the English sentence, substitute *of whom* or *of which*.
The rest of the English sentence will then fall into exactly the same word
order that the French clause normally has.

C. Traduisez en français.

1. That is a decision of which he will repent.   2. Jack is a young
man whose parents are very strict.   3. (*vous*) We know the lady
whose husband you saw in Paris.   4. I finally found the book the
title of which I had forgotten.   5. I recommend the doctor whose
office[1] is on the first[2] floor.   6. He has trouble[3] with the neighbors
whose dogs bark so much.   7. (*vous*) The family whose address
you sent me has moved.   8. That actress, whose talent I admire
so much, lives in Sweden now.   9. The friend whose children
George adopted died ten years ago.

[1] Not «bureau».   [2] Not «premier étage».   [3] The plural form of ennui, histoire, or difficulté.

9. How is the relative *when* expressed in French?

Au moment **où** nous sommes arrivés ils étaient tous à table.	*At the time* when *we arrived, they were all at the table.*
Je vous dirai cela le jour **où** vous vous marierez.	*I'll tell you that the day* when *you get married.*

The ordinary French word for *when* is **quand.** But when the English word *when* modifies a preceding noun—usually a time expression—it is normally expressed by **où** in French.

The relative **où** also means *where* and indicates place, but this **où** constitutes no problem to the English-speaking student. Ex.: J'ai visité la ville **où** ce poète a vécu.

D. Traduisez en français.

1. (*vous*) Show me the house where Balzac was born. 2. (*tu*) Do you remember the day when we saw each other for the first time? 3. I'll leave the moment[1] he arrives[2]. 4. (*tu*) I did not feel well the evening when you came to see me. 5. (*vous*) Have you forgotten the winter when it was so cold? 6. I prefer the months when there is sun.

[1] French uses **au moment** followed by a relative pronoun. [2] What tense? See page 44, §6.

Exercices d'ensemble

E. Remplacez le mot anglais par son équivalent français.

1. Pouvez-vous me prêter les livres (*which I need*)? 2. Connaissez-vous la femme (*who*) vient de passer? 3. Il est parti; c'est le mois (*when*) il prend ses vacances. 4. Où est la montre (*which*) je vous ai achetée? 5. Racontez-nous seulement (*what*) est important. 6. Je me demande avec (*what*) ils ont pu faire cela. 7. Les élèves (*of which*) vous vous plaignez ne travaillent pas assez. 8. La sonnerie (*that*) vous entendez marque la fin de la classe. 9. Il fait (*everything that*) il veut. 10. Je vous prêterai ma voiture le jour (*when*) vous aurez du travail. 11. Elle vous promettra tout (*that*) vous voulez. 12. L'homme (*who*) doit venir me voir ce matin est russe. 13. C'est un ami pour (*whom*) je ferais n'importe quoi. 14. Puisque vous le pouvez, prenez donc (*what*) est devant vous. 15. Je ne sais pas exactement à (*what*) il pense. 16. Le train dans (*which*) je me trouvais a eu un accident.

F. Remplacez les tirets par le pronom relatif convenable.

1. L'homme pour _____ je travaille est très exigeant. 2. Les amis _____ nous ont invités ce week-end ont un gros bateau à

moteur.   3. Le pharmacien ne peut pas lire _____ le médecin a écrit.   4. Elle veut épouser ce jeune homme _____ l'oncle est millionnaire.   5. J'aimerais savoir à _____ vous pensez maintenant.   6. _____ se passe dans ces pays d'Amérique du Sud est inquiétant.   7. La chaise sur _____ il s'est assis s'est cassée et nous avons tous bien ri.   8. Dis-moi _____ te rend si songeur. 9. Où sont les livres _____ j'ai mentionné les titres hier?

G. Traduisez en français.

1. (*vous*) The person you are making fun of is one of my friends. 2. I remember the summer when we went to Europe for the first time.   3. (*vous*) What you say concerning[1] them does not surprise me.   4. (*tu*) He is very pale. You must ask him what he is suffering from.   5. She left the[2] moment I entered.   6. The dress with which she had[3] so much success came from Paris.   7. I can't stand the noise the neighbors[4] are making.   8. I like people who are optimistic.   9. Those who criticize his style should try to understand him.   10. What we are thinking of[5] is not important.

[1] à leur sujet   [2] The French say the equivalent of the English *at the moment when.*   [3] Use the passé composé.   [4] Place this subject after the verb.   [5] Not **de.**

Problem Words

35. marry

(a) How to say *to get married*

Michelle **s'est mariée** au mois de juin.	*Michelle* got married *in the month of June.*

French expresses *to get married* by **se marier.**

(b) How to say *to marry someone*

Robert **s'est marié avec la fille du patron.**	*Robert* married the boss's daughter.
Isabelle devrait **épouser un homme riche.**	*Isabelle should* marry a rich man.

French expresses *to marry someone* by either **se marier avec quelqu'un** or **épouser quelqu'un.**

(c) How to say *to marry someone to someone*

Les Moreau **vont marier leur fille à** l'aîné des Duparc.	*The Moreaus* are going to marry their daughter to *the oldest Duparc boy.*

French expresses *to marry someone to someone* by **marier quelqu'un à** + PERSON.

36. miss

(a) When *miss = feel the absence of*

Nous **regrettons** notre ancienne maison.	*We miss our former house.*

The verb **regretter** may be used in the sense of *miss;* in that case, the subject of the English and French sentences is the same.

Ma voiture **me manque** beaucoup ici.	I miss *my car a great deal here.*

The verb **manquer** may also be used in the sense of *miss,* but in that case, the object missed becomes the subject of the French sentence.

(b) When *miss = fail to reach*

Gérard **a manqué** l'autobus; il va encore être en retard.	*Gerard* missed *the bus; he is going to be late again.*
Pourquoi **avez**-vous **manqué** la classe?	*Why did you* miss (cut) *class?*
J'**ai raté** le train!	I missed *the train!*

French uses the verb **manquer** to express the idea of missing a means of transportation or of missing a gathering of some kind. With this sense, the subject of **manquer** is the person and the object of the sentence is the thing missed. Note that **manquer la classe** means *to cut class.* The verb **rater** is also used familiarly to express the idea of missing a means of transportation or a gathering.

37. more

(a) How to say *more and more*

Je m'intéresse **de plus en plus** à la politique.	*I am becoming* more and more *interested in politics.*
Je suis **de plus en plus** étonné.	*I am* more and more *surprised.*

The English *more and more* + ADJECTIVE is expressed by **de plus en plus** modifying an adjective, an adverb, or a verb.

NOTE: The formula *more and more* is really an intensive comparative, so that it also includes the English comparatives in *-er:*

Georges devient **de plus en plus** grand.	*George is getting tall*er *and tall*er*.

(b) How to say *the more . . . the more . . .*

Plus je connais Marianne, **plus** j'apprécie ses qualités.	The more *I know Marianne,* the more *I appreciate her good qualities.*
Plus Georges est riche, **plus** il veut d'argent.	The richer *George is,* the more *money he wants.*

French expresses *the more . . . the more* by **plus** + CLAUSE, followed by **plus** + CLAUSE.

CAUTION: DO NOT express *the more . . . the more* by «le plus . . . le plus». The correct formula is **plus . . . , plus . . . .**

NOTE: The formula *the more . . . the more* is a type of comparative, so that it also includes the English comparatives in *-er,* as in the sentence:

Les gens croient que **plus** on est riche, **plus** on est heureux.	*People think that* the *rich*er *one is,* the *happi*er *one is.*

38. next

(a) When *next* is expressed by **prochain**

Nous irons voir vos amis en France l'été **prochain.**	*We'll go to see your friends in France* next *summer.*
Est-ce que Toulon est le **prochain** arrêt?	*Is Toulon the* next *stop?*

The ordinary French word for *next* is **prochain.** In general, it can be used, except when one could substitute *following* for *next* in the English sentence without changing the meaning of the sentence.

(b) When *next* is expressed by **suivant**

J'ai expliqué à Robert pourquoi nous étions retournés en Suisse l'été **suivant.**	*I explained to Robert why we had returned to Switzerland the* next (= following) *summer.*
*Regardez la page **suivante.***	*Look at the* next (= following) *page.*

Whenever *next = following* and when *following* can be substituted for *next* without changing the meaning of the sentence, French uses **suivant.**

CAUTION: DO NOT use «prochain» for *next* when *next = following*. This is a very common error.

(c) How to say *the next day*

Le lendemain **Le jour suivant** **Le jour après**	nos invités sont partis.	The next day *our guests left.*

The next day may be expressed by **le lendemain, le jour suivant,** or **le jour après.**

CAUTION: DO NOT say «le jour prochain» for *the next day.*

(d) How to say *the next morning (afternoon, evening,* etc.)

Le lendemain matin	il a plu	The next morning *it rained*
Le matin suivant	sans arrêt.	*continually.*
Le matin après		

The adverb **lendemain** is used with times of day to express the English *next.*

H. Remplacez les mots anglais par leur équivalent français.

1. On ne demande plus beaucoup aujourd'hui l'avis de ses parents pour (*get married*). **2.** Allons bon! nous (*missed*) le train de sept heures quarante-cinq. **3.** (*The more*) ça change, (*the more*) c'est la même chose. **4.** Je serai à New York à minuit, et je m'envolerai pour Paris (*the next night*). **5.** On dit que cet acteur va (*marry*) une ancienne camarade d'enfance. **6.** Quand je voyage, je (*miss*) le confort de ma maison. **7.** Je suis (*more and more*) étonné par ton indifférence. **8.** Madame Drouet passera (*next week*) chez nous, et elle ira chez vous (*the next week*). **9.** Paul (*got married*) beaucoup trop jeune. **10.** J'ai passé mon baccalauréat et (*the next year*) j'ai fait mon service militaire. **11.** Suivez mon conseil: (*marry*) une jeune fille de votre condition.

I. Traduisez en français. Attention aux mots en italique.

1. (*vous*) Why don't you *marry* Albertine? **2.** Robert will spend *next* year in Italy. **3.** *The more* I know Paris, *the more* I like it. **4.** Do the children *miss* the television set? **5.** Mr. Martel would like to *marry* his daughter to a doctor. **6.** (*vous*) If you *miss* your bus[1], you will have to wait until tomorrow morning. **7.** That child is becoming *more and more* unbearable. **8.** Edmond went to bed late and the *next* morning he didn't hear his alarm clock. **9.** (*tu*) I *miss* you a great deal these days. **10.** If they arrive at midnight, they will certainly not leave[2] again the *next* day. **11.** Michael and Colette met at Nice and will *get married* in Paris. **12.** I arrived in London on[3] June 7 and the *next* week I went to Brussels. **13.** *The older* one is, *the harder* it is to get around.

[1] In French, a city bus is **un autobus**, whereas an interurban bus is **un autocar**. [2] *leave again* = **repartir** [3] For ways of expressing French dates, see page 159.

Verb Review

Review the verbs **falloir** and **lire** according to the outline on page 253.

CHAPTER 11

The Subjunctive

L'auteur, venu aux États-Unis avec un groupe d'intellectuels français, donne à son retour ses impressions sur les villes américaines.

Villes d'Amérique

Pour apprendre à vivre dans les villes américaines, à les aimer comme les Américains les aiment, il a fallu que je *survole*[1] d'immenses déserts[2] de l'Ouest et du Sud. En Europe, nos cités se touchent, elles sont situées dans des campagnes humaines dont chaque mètre carré est travaillé[3]. Et
5 puis, très loin de nous, de l'autre côté des mers, nous savons vaguement qu'il y a le désert, un mythe. Ce mythe, pour l'Américain, est une réalité quotidienne. Entre la Nouvelle-Orléans et San Francisco, nous avons volé pendant des heures au-dessus d'une terre rouge et sèche. Tout à coup une ville surgissait et puis, de nouveau, la terre rouge, la savane, le Grand
10 Canyon, les neiges des Rocky Mountains.

Au bout de quelques jours, j'ai compris qu'une ville américaine était, à l'origine, un campement dans le désert. Des gens qui venaient de loin, attirés par une mine, un gisement[4] de pétrole, un terrain fertile, arrivaient un beau jour et s'installaient au plus vite, dans une clairière[5], au bord
15 d'un fleuve. Pour que la vie *puisse* s'organiser, on construisait les organes essentiels, banque, mairie, église et puis, par centaines, des maisons de bois à un étage. La route, s'il y en avait une, servait d'épine[6] dorsale, et puis, perpendiculairement à la route, on traçait des rues, comme des vertèbres. Il serait difficile de compter les villes américaines qui ont[7]
20 ainsi la raie au milieu.

Rien n'a changé depuis le temps des caravanes vers l'Ouest; on fonde

---

[1] *fly over*   [2] *wildernesses*   [3] *utilized*   [4] gisement de pétrole *oil field*   [5] *clearing*
[6] épine dorsale *spinal column*   [7] ont ainsi la raie au milieu *thus have their hair parted in the middle*

chaque année des villes aux États-Unis et il semble que cela se *fasse* selon les mêmes procédés.

Dans ces villes qui[8] vont vite, qui ne sont pas construites pour vieillir,
25 qui progressent en encerclant les îlots[9] de résistance qu'elles ne peuvent pas détruire, le passé ne se manifeste pas, comme chez nous, par des «monuments», mais par des «résidus»[10], que l'on n'a pas pris le temps de démolir, et par des terrains[11] vagues qui servent du moins de parcs à autos.
30 Je voudrais que le touriste européen *soit* prévenu: il a tort de visiter les villes américaines comme il visite Paris ou Venise, car elles ne sont pas faites pour cela. En Europe, une rue est intermédiaire entre la grande route et le centre de la ville. Elle est de[12] plain-pied avec les cafés, comme le prouve l'usage de la «terrasse»[13] aux beaux jours. Aussi change-t-elle
35 d'aspect sans cesse car la foule qui la peuple se renouvelle toujours, quel que *soit* le moment de la journée. La rue américaine, elle, est un tronçon[14] de grand'route. Elle s'étend parfois sur plusieurs kilomètres. Elle n'invite pas à la promenade; elle n'a pas de secrets. C'est une ligne droite, sans mystère. D'ailleurs les distances sont si grandes qu'on ne se déplace
40 presque jamais à pied.
Pourtant on se met rapidement à aimer les villes d'Amérique. Quoi-qu'elles *aient* des ressemblances, on apprend vite qu'il est possible de les distinguer. Et puis on finit par aimer ce qu'elles ont en commun: cet air de provisoire. C'est dommage qu'on *étouffe* un peu dans nos villes[15]
45 closes, que nos rues *viennent*[16] buter contre des murs, contre des mai-sons. En Amérique, ces longues rues droites sans obstacle conduisent[17] le regard jusqu'en dehors de la ville. Où que vous *soyez,* vous voyez au bout de chacune d'elles la montagne ou les champs ou la mer . . . Parce que leurs boulevards sont des routes, elles[18] n'oppressent pas, elles n'en-
50 ferment jamais. Vous sentez, du premier coup d'œil, que votre contact avec elles est provisoire; ou bien vous les quitterez ou bien elles chan-geront autour de vous.
Gardons-nous[19] d'exagérer; nous avons connu les dimanches de la province américaine, plus[20] étouffants que partout ailleurs . . . Mais ces

---

[8] qui vont vite *which develop rapidly*   [9] îlots de résistance *pockets of resistance*
[10] *remains (i.e., what is left)*   [11] terrains vagues *vacant lots*   [12] de plain-pied *on the same level as*   [13] *refers to the terrace of French cafés*   [14] tronçon de grand'route *part of the main highway*   [15] villes closes *fenced-in cities*   [16] viennent buter *come to an end*   [17] conduisent le regard *allow you, indeed invite you, to see*
[18] elles n'oppressent pas, elles n'enferment jamais *they don't stifle anyone, they never confine anyone*   [19] Gardons-nous d'exagérer *Let's make sure not to exaggerate*
[20] plus étouffants que partout ailleurs *more oppressive than anywhere else*

55 villes légères, si semblables encore aux campements du Far West, montrent l'autre face des États-Unis: leur liberté. Chacun est libre ici, non de critiquer ou de réformer les mœurs, mais de les fuir, de s'en aller dans le désert ou dans une autre ville. Les villes sont ouvertes. Ouvertes sur le monde, ouvertes sur l'avenir . . .

D'après Jean-Paul Sartre, célèbre philosophe de l'existentialisme, dramaturge, romancier, essayiste, un des écrivains les plus importants de sa génération. («Villes d'Amérique» dans *Situations III,* Gallimard, 1949)

In connection with the subjunctive, we must consider four important questions:

(a) What is the basic function of the subjunctive as compared with that of the indicative?

(b) Under what specific circumstances is the subjunctive used in French, and how do those uses fit into the basic concept of the function of the subjunctive?

(c) When is the present subjunctive used and when is the past subjunctive used; in other words, what is the concept of time in the subjunctive tenses?

(d) When must the infinitive be used instead of the subjunctive, even though the nature of the main clause seems to indicate a subjunctive in the subordinate clause?

1. What is the essential difference between the indicative and the subjunctive mode when they deal with facts?

INDICATIVE	SUBJUNCTIVE
Jean **est** à la maison.	**Nous sommes contents** que Jean **soit** à la maison.
John is *at home.*	We are glad *that John is at home.*
Pierre ne **sait** pas la leçon.	**Je regrette** que Pierre ne **sache** pas la leçon.
Peter does *not* know *the lesson.*	I regret *that Peter* does *not* know *the lesson.*
Les enfants **ont perdu** leur ballon.	**C'est dommage** que les enfants **aient perdu** leur ballon.
The children lost *their ball.*	It is too bad *that the children* lost *their ball.*

The INDICATIVE states an objective fact. It is concerned with the fact as a fact.

The SUBJUNCTIVE sometimes deals with facts, but in such cases it deals with them not objectively, but from the point of view of the speaker of the main clause. It indicates the subjective attitude of the speaker in the main clause toward the action in the subordinate clause.

2. **What other types of state or action does the subjunctive deal with? Compare it with the indicative in this respect.**

INDICATIVE	SUBJUNCTIVE
Vous **faites** votre travail.	**Je voudrais** que vous **fassiez** votre travail.
You do *your work.*	I wish *that you* would do *your work.*
Monsieur Texier **viendra** demain.	**Il est possible** que Monsieur Texier **vienne** demain.
Mr. Texier will come *tomorrow.*	It is possible *that Mr. Texier* will come *tomorrow.*
Nous **sommes arrivés** trop tard.	**Roger avait peur** que nous **soyons arrivés** trop tard.
We arrived *too late.*	Roger was afraid *that we* arrived *too late.*

The INDICATIVE states an objective fact, whether in the present, past, or future.

The SUBJUNCTIVE often deals with hypothetical actions; that is, actions that have not occurred and may never occur. It often states the attitude of the subject in the main clause toward such hypothetical actions.

3. **Which types of verbs in the main clause are followed by the subjunctive in the subordinate clause, and why?**

Nous **craignons** qu'il **pleuve** toute la journée.	*We* fear *that it* will rain *all day long.*
Roland **a suggéré** que nous **soyons** au stade une heure à l'avance.	*Roland* suggested *that we* be *at the stadium an hour ahead of time.*
Je **suis content** que vous **sachiez** ce qui s'est vraiment passé.	I am glad *that you* know *what really happened.*
Le docteur Bertrand **préférerait** que sa fille **fasse** sa médecine à Paris.	*Dr. Bertrand* would prefer to have *his daughter* study *medicine in Paris.*

Verbs of wishing, preferring, suggesting, etc., and verbs and expressions of emotion, such as fearing, being glad, being sorry, etc., all of which indicate the attitude of the subject of the main clause toward either a fact or a hypothetical action, are followed by the subjunctive in the subordinate clause, that is, in the clause introduced by **que.**

NOTE 1: In affirmative statements, the verb **espérer** is always followed by the indicative. Ex.: J'**espère** que nos invités **viendront.** In interrogative sentences, it is usually followed by the indicative but may be followed by the subjunctive. In negative statements, it is followed by the subjunctive.

NOTE 2: Verbs of advising, commanding, permitting, preventing, requesting, etc., may be followed by a subjunctive clause, but they are usually followed by **de** + INFINITIVE.

USUAL CONSTRUCTION	POSSIBLE CONSTRUCTION
L'avocat **a conseillé** à son client **d'être** moins exigeant.	L'avocat **a conseillé** que son client **soit** moins exigeant.
L'inspecteur vous **permettra de téléphoner** à votre femme.	L'inspecteur **permettra** que vous **téléphoniez** à votre femme.
Nous les **avons empêchés d'aller** plus loin.	Nous **avons empêché** qu'ils **aillent** plus loin.

A. Choisissez la forme convenable du verbe et expliquez oralement pourquoi vous avez choisi la forme indicative ou subjonctive.

1. Nous préférons que vous (restez, restiez) ici; ce serait plus prudent. 2. Comment pouvez-vous permettre que vos voisins (font, fassent) tant de bruit à cette heure? 3. J'ai peur que tu ne me (comprends, comprennes) pas. 4. Vous savez que Brigitte ne (viendra, vienne) pas. 5. La radio dit qu'il (pleuvra, pleuve) demain. 6. Nous sommes contents que vous (avez, ayez) de bonnes nouvelles de votre famille. 7. Nous regrettons que Gilbert (n'est, ne soit) pas avec nous; nous aurions pu jouer au bridge. 8. Je vois que vous (êtes, soyez) pressé. Avez-vous encore une minute? 9. Qu'est-ce qu'il y a? J'espère que vous (n'êtes, ne soyez) pas malade.

B. Mettez les infinitifs entre parenthèses au subjonctif ou à l'indicatif, selon le cas.

1. Je suggère que vous (rentrer) immédiatement. 2. Ils savent que nous (être) à cet hôtel depuis deux jours. 3. Vous devez être bien content que votre belle-mère (être) si agréable. 4. Vos créanciers ont entendu dire que vous (aller) déménager le plus tôt possible. 5. Je m'étonne que vous (avoir) tant à faire maintenant que vous êtes à la retraite. 6. Nous espérons que vous (pouvoir) faire votre voyage au Canada cet été.

4. Certain constructions with the English verb *want* are handled differently in French. How does French express a sentence such as *George wants me to do everything?*

Georges **veut que je fasse** tout moi-même.	*George* wants me to do *everything myself.*
Je **veux que tu partes** tout de suite.	*I* want you to leave *at once.*

An English sentence consisting of a form of *want* + OBJECT + INFINITIVE is expressed in French by a form of **vouloir** + **que** + SUBJUNCTIVE.

C. Traduisez en français.

1. We want the baby to sleep for an hour.   2. I wanted Colette to learn her lesson.   3. (*tu*) Who wants you to be the judge?   4. I wanted Albert to return[1] my books.

[1] Use a form of **rendre**.

5. When is the present subjunctive used in French? When is the past subjunctive used? What is the concept of time in the subjunctive?

Je suis content que Maurice **puisse** le faire maintenant.	*I am glad that Maurice* can *do it now.*
Je suis content que Maurice **puisse** le faire demain.	*I am glad that Maurice* will be able *to do it tomorrow.*
Je suis content que Maurice **ait pu** le faire hier.	*I am glad that Maurice* could *do it yesterday.*

The only two tenses of the subjunctive used in conversational French are the present and the past. The PRESENT SUBJUNCTIVE is used if the action of the subordinate clause takes place <u>at the same time</u> as the action of the main clause or <u>after</u> the action of the main clause. The PAST SUBJUNCTIVE is used if the action of the subordinate clause took place <u>before</u> the action of the main clause. In other words, time in the subjunctive is relative to time in the main clause.

The past subjunctive (**passé du subjonctif**) is a compound tense corresponding to the compound past in the indicative. Ex. (COMPOUND PAST OF INDICATIVE): j'**ai vu**, tu **as parlé**, il **est parti**; (PAST SUBJUNCTIVE): ... que j'**aie vu**, ... que tu **aies parlé**, ... qu'il **soit parti**, etc.

D. Remplacez les infinitifs entre parenthèses par le présent ou le passé du subjonctif, selon le cas.

1. Je suis content que tu (venir) à notre réunion demain.   2. Je suis content que tu (venir) à notre réunion hier.   3. Est-ce que ton père regrette que tu (partir) en Australie l'année prochaine?   4. Est-ce que ton père regrette que tu (partir) en Australie l'année dernière? 5. Nous avons peur que Georges (perdre) son argent quand il est sorti avec ce type.   6. Nous avons peur que George (perdre) son argent s'il sort avec ce type.   7. Philippe s'étonne que nous (se lever) de si bonne heure avant-hier.   8. Philippe s'étonne que nous (se lever) de si bonne heure demain.   9. Je suggère que vous (téléphoner) tout de suite.   10. Nous regrettons que vous ne (pouvoir) pas venir demain soir.   11. Avez-vous peur que Gilbert (faire) des bêtises quand il sortira avec Gisèle?   12. Je m'étonne que vous n'(avoir) pas de nouvelles de Serge récemment.

6. When must the infinitive be used instead of a *que*-clause with the subjunctive even after constructions which seem to require a subjunctive?

SUBJUNCTIVE	INFINITIVE
Avez-**vous** peur **que Marcel fasse cela?** *Are* you *afraid* that Marcel will do it?	Avez-**vous** peur **de faire cela?** *Are* you *afraid* that you will do it?
Anne-Marie veut **que vous le sachiez.** Anne-Marie *wants* you to know it.	**Anne-Marie** veut **le savoir.** Anne-Marie *wishes* that she might know it.
Je suis content **que vous ayez gagné.** I *am glad* that you won.	**Je** suis content **d'avoir gagné.** I *am glad* that I won.
Nous regrettons **que vous soyez parti si tôt.** We *are sorry* that you left so soon.	**Nous** regrettons **d'être partis si tôt.** We *are sorry* that we left so soon.

When the subject of a subordinate clause requiring the subjunctive would be the same as the subject of the main clause, the INFINITIVE is normally required instead of **que** with the SUBJUNCTIVE.

NOTE 1: Both **ne** and **pas** precede a present infinitive. Ex.: J'ai peur de **ne pas arriver** à l'heure.

NOTE 2: Both **ne** and **pas** usually precede the auxiliary of a past infinitive. Ex.: J'ai peur de **ne pas avoir vu** le vrai responsable. Nous regrettons de **ne pas être partis** de bonne heure ce matin.

Verbs of wishing are followed directly by the infinitive without a preposition; verbs of emotion require **de** before an infinitive.

E. Écrivez les phrases suivantes en mettant à la forme convenable les mots entre parenthèses.

1. (*tu*) Raymond est content (*that you will finish*) ce travail demain.
2. Raymond est content (*that he will finish*) ce travail demain.
3. N'êtes-vous pas heureux (*that we will spend*) l'année prochaine en Europe? 4. N'êtes-vous pas heureux (*that you will spend*) l'année prochaine en Europe? 5. (*vous*) Nous sommes contents (*that you went*) en ville. 6. Nous sommes contents (*that we went*) en ville. 7. Je suis étonné (*that I found*) ma montre. 8. Je suis étonné (*that Philip found*) sa montre. 9. Je crains (*that John does not know*) ce que tu veux. 10. Je crains (*that I do not know*) ce que tu veux. 11. Robert regrette (*that he does not understand*) l'italien. 12. Robert regrette (*that we do not understand*) l'italien.

13. Est-ce qu'Alain est content (*that he has retired*)?   14. Je m'étonne (*that Martha isn't*) ici.   15. Denise préfère (*that her children know*) la vérité.   16. Nous sommes contents (*that we did not go*) à cette conférence.   17. Je regrette (*that I arrived*) trop tard.

7. When is the indicative and when is the subjunctive used after impersonal expressions?

INDICATIVE

Il est certain que Louis **est** intelligent.
  It is certain *that Louis* is *intelligent*.

Il est évident que vous **savez** votre leçon.
  It is obvious *that you* know *your lesson.*

Il est exact que Monsieur et Madame Minard **vont** en France cet été.
  It is true *that Mr. and Mrs. Minard* are going *to France this summer.*

SUBJUNCTIVE

Il est possible que Louis **soit** intelligent.
  It is possible *that Louis* is *intelligent.*

Il est important que vous **sachiez** votre leçon.
  It is important *that you* know *your lesson.*

Il est naturel que Monsieur et Madame Minard **aillent** en France cet été.
  It is natural *that Mr. and Mrs. Minard* should go *to France this summer.*

Impersonal expressions that insist on a fact or on the certainty of a fact are followed by the INDICATIVE.

Impersonal expressions where not the fact but the attitude or opinion of the speaker toward a hypothetical state or action is given are followed by the SUBJUNCTIVE.

Among the impersonal expressions followed by the INDICATIVE are:		Among the impersonal expressions followed by the SUBJUNCTIVE are:	
Il est certain	Il est bien	Il est possible	
Il est clair	Il est bon	Il est préférable	
Il est évident	Il est douteux	Il est peu probable	
Il est exact	Il est étonnant	Il est rare	
Il est probable	Il est étrange	Il est temps	
Il est sûr	Il est important	Il faut	
Il est vrai	Il est impossible	Il importe	
	Il est juste	Il se peut	
	Il est naturel	Il suffit	
	Il est nécessaire	Il vaut mieux	

F. Dans le devoir suivant, mettez les infinitifs indiqués entre parenthèses soit au présent soit au passé du subjonctif ou au temps convenable de l'indicatif. Justifiez oralement votre choix du temps et du mode.

1. Il est évident que vous (avoir) besoin de leçons. **2.** Il est étrange que Jacqueline ne nous (écrire) pas depuis son départ. **3.** Docteur, vaut-il mieux que vous lui (dire) la vérité? **4.** Il est possible que Monsieur Moreau (acheter) cette maison l'année dernière. **5.** Il est certain que l'accusé (être) coupable. **6.** —Vous paraissez si jeune! Il est impossible que vous (être) sa mère. **7.** Il est sûr qu'ils ne (revenir) pas la semaine dernière. **8.** Il serait bon que vous (se reposer) un peu. **9.** Il est possible que vous (connaître) cette affaire mieux que moi. **10.** Il est vrai que nous (avoir) peur de lui. **11.** —Mon garçon, il est grand temps que tu (prendre) tes responsabilités. **12.** Il suffit que son fils (dire) ce qu'il veut pour l'obtenir.

G. Traduisez en français. Justifiez oralement l'emploi du temps et du mode.

1. (*vous*) It is rare that your wife comes to see us. **2.** (*vous*) It is clear that you are mistaken. **3.** (*vous*) It[1] is important for you[1] not to speak of this story. **4.** It is probable that the treaty will be signed this week. **5.** (*tu*) It is good that you have already finished your work. **6.** It is surprising that he is so hateful[2]. **7.** (*tu*) It[1] is necessary for me[1] to think[3] before answering you. **8.** It is time that the president act energetically. **9.** It is doubtful that they have found the money. **10.** (*tu*) It is natural that you should wish to have a good time. **11.** It is remarkable that man can go to[4] the moon. **12.** It is correct[5] that he has never read a single book. **13.** I[6] am surprised, but it is possible that I said that. **14.** (*vous*) It is evident that you do not work too much.

[1] Rearrange the wording before translating.   [2] méchant   [3] Use a form of réfléchir.
[4] dans or sur   [5] Not «correct»   [6] Ça m'étonne

8. What mode follows verbs of "thinking" and "believing" in French?

AFFIRMATIVE	NEGATIVE AND INTERROGATIVE
Je **crois** que vous **êtes** malade.	Je **ne crois pas** que vous $\left\{ \begin{array}{l} \textbf{êtes} \\ \textbf{soyez} \end{array} \right.$ malade.
Il **pense** que sa femme **partira**.	Il **ne pense pas** que sa femme $\left\{ \begin{array}{l} \textbf{partira.} \\ \textbf{parte.} \end{array} \right.$
Nous **croyons** que Paul **a lu** cela.	**Croyez-vous** que Paul $\left\{ \begin{array}{l} \textbf{a lu} \text{ cela?} \\ \textbf{ait lu} \text{ cela?} \end{array} \right.$
Moi, je **trouve** qu'il **a** bien **fait**.	**Trouvez-vous** qu'il $\left\{ \begin{array}{l} \textbf{a} \text{ bien } \textbf{fait?} \\ \textbf{ait} \text{ bien } \textbf{fait?} \end{array} \right.$

Affirmative forms of verbs of thinking and believing are ALWAYS followed by the indicative—NEVER by the subjunctive.

Negative and interrogative forms of verbs of thinking and believing may be followed by the subjunctive when there is considerable doubt on the part of the speaker, and when the speaker is grammatically precise in the use of the subjunctive. When the element of doubt is minor and especially when the idea in the subordinate clause is of a future nature, the indicative is normally used. This also applies to negative and interrogative forms of impersonal expressions, which are always followed by the indicative in the affirmative form.

Forms of the verb **douter** are normally followed by the subjunctive.

NOTE: It is true that the subjunctive after forms of the verb **douter** and after expressions such as **Je ne crois pas** indicates doubt. However, in the great majority of cases, the subjunctive is used to show attitudes other than those of doubt. For instance, the subjunctive after **Il faut que . . .** or **Je suis content que . . .** indicates not the slightest indication of doubt. Students should not try to justify the use of a given subjunctive by saying that it expresses doubt, except in cases where doubt actually exists.

H. Mettez les infinitifs à la forme convenable et expliquez oralement le temps et le mode que vous aurez choisis.

1. Je trouve que cette robe vous (aller) très bien.   2. Nous doutons que votre idée (valoir) grand-chose.   3. Je ne pense pas que nous (pouvoir) nous revoir.   4. Ils croient que leur fils (être) toujours un enfant.   5. Ne croyez-vous pas que vos amis (savoir) cela? 6. Je ne crois pas que Jean (venir) demain.   7. Je trouve qu'elle (conduire) bien.   8. Je crois que cet homme (connaître) bien son métier.   9. Nous ne pouvons pas croire que Philippe (venir) hier soir.

I. Traduisez en français.

1. He thinks we are foolish.   2. (*vous*) Do you think that he will do that?   3. I do not believe that he can get to the airport in time. 4. He believes that they are going to Paris.   5. (*tu*) Do you believe that they will invite us?   6. (*vous*) I don't think that you understand the problem.

9. What are the subordinate conjunctions that are always followed by the subjunctive in French, and what in the nature of their meaning causes them to be followed by a subjunctive rather than an indicative?

afin que }
pour que } *in order that, so that*

bien que }
quoique } *although*

pourvu que }
à condition que } *provided that*

à moins que *unless*

sans que *without*

avant que *before*

jusqu'à ce que *until*

Each of these expressions embodies a concept that is concerned either with a hypothetical action or with an attitude toward a real action:

(a) **afin que** and **pour que** indicate purpose, and the intended purpose is hypothetical, not yet real.

(b) **bien que** and **quoique** indicate concession on the part of the speaker toward what is either a reality or something that could be so and is therefore hypothetical.

(c) **pourvu que** and **à condition que** introduce a restrictive condition that is not a reality.

(d) **à moins que** and **sans que** also introduce a restrictive condition that is not a reality.

(e) **avant que** and **jusqu'à ce que** are conjunctions concerned with actions to take place at some time after the action of the main clause and which, in the mind of the speaker, depend on some other action taking place. Thus, they are restrictive to a certain extent.

10. Under what conditions are these conjunctions replaced by a corresponding preposition followed by an infinitive?

Je lui écrirai **pour qu'il sache** cela.
I *will write him* so that he may know *that.*

Je lui écrirai **pour savoir** cela.
I *will write him* so that I may know *that.*

Je conduirai vite **afin que vous arriviez** à l'heure.
I*'ll drive fast* so that you arrive *on time.*

Je conduirai vite **afin d'arriver** à l'heure.
I*'ll drive fast* { in order to arrive *on time.* / so that I may arrive *on time.* }

Je viendrai **à moins que Marc soit malade.**
I*'ll come* unless Mark is sick.

Je viendrai **à moins d'être malade.**
I*'ll come* unless I am sick.

Je partirai **avant que Georges apprenne** les résultats de l'examen.
I*'ll leave* before George learns *the results* of the examination.

Je partirai **avant d'apprendre** les résultats de l'examen.
I*'ll leave* before learning *the results* of the examination.

Je ferai cette affaire **sans que vous perdiez** un sou.
I *will carry this thing out* without your losing *a penny.*

Je ferai cette affaire **sans perdre** un sou.
I*'ll carry this thing out* without losing *a penny.*

When the subject of the subordinate clause introduced by conjunctions requiring the subjunctive in French would be the same as the subject of the main clause, French normally uses a preposition with an infinitive if such a construction exists.

The most common conjunctions with a prepositional counterpart are:

CONJUNCTION	PREPOSITION	
à moins que + subjunctive	**à moins de** + infinitive	*unless*
afin que + subjunctive	**afin de** + infinitive	*in order that (to)*
pour que + subjunctive	**pour** + infinitive	*so that*
avant que + subjunctive	**avant de** + infinitive	*before*
sans que + subjunctive	**sans** + infinitive	*without*

NOTE : In a few cases, such as in sentences with **bien que, quoique, pourvu que,** and **jusqu'à ce que,** it is impossible to replace a clause in the subjunctive by an infinitive construction even when the subject of the main clause and that of the dependent **que**-clause would be the same, since there is no prepositional construction that corresponds to the subordinate conjunctions. In these cases the subjunctive must be used even when the subject of the main clause and that of the dependent clause are the same. Ex.: Nous viendrons **bien que nous soyons** fatigués. Jean-Paul le fera **pourvu qu'il soit** libre.

However, in the case of **à moins que,** one finds both **à moins que** + SUBJECT OF MAIN CLAUSE and **à moins de** + INFINITIVE.

J. Écrivez les phrases suivantes en mettant à la forme convenable les mots entre parenthèses.

1. Je te conseille de finir (*before your father comes back*).   2. Il est dur d'oreille. Parlez-lui plus fort (*so that he hears you*).   3. J'ai pu quitter la salle (*without the lecturer noticing*[1] *it*).   4. Je passerai par le bureau (*before I come*) vous voir.   5. Daniel sera toujours pauvre (*unless his uncle should die*).   6. Elle refuse de parler (*although she knows*) toute l'histoire.   7. Il est parti (*without having done*) la moitié du travail.   8. J'ai envoyé cette lettre hier (*so that I might have*) une réponse demain.   9. Amuse-toi bien (*before it is too late*).

[1] Use a form of s'apercevoir de.

K. Traduisez en français les phrases suivantes. Attention au temps et au mode.

1. (*tu*) I'll go with you although I am very busy.   2. (*vous*) Do something so that they will go away sooner.   3. (*vous*) Do what you[1] please provided that you do not make any[2] noise.   4. She truly loves me, although she doesn't tell me so[3].   5. How[4] can we leave without their being angry?   6. They did everything[5] so that

[1] Either vous voulez or vous voudrez   [2] de   [3] le   [4] *How can we leave* = Comment partir   [5] Place between auxiliary and past participle.

their children might be happy.   7. I'll work until I understand these rules.

11. **Why do the sentences on the left use the indicative in the subordinate clause, while those on the right use the subjunctive?**

INDICATIVE	SUBJUNCTIVE
	(a) the antecedent is as yet unattained
J'ai un domestique **qui sait** tout faire.	Je cherche un domestique **qui sache** tout faire.
	(b) doubt is expressed as to the attainability of the antecedent
Vous avez un collègue **qui est** très au courant de ces choses.	Avez-vous un collègue **qui soit** très au courant de ces choses?
	(c) the antecedent is negative
Je connais quelqu'un **qui peut** vous accompagner.	Je ne connais personne **qui puisse** vous accompagner.
Il y a des professeurs **qui vont** en Europe tous les ans.	Il n'y a pas de professeur **qui aille** en Europe tous les ans.

The INDICATIVE is normally used in dependent relative clauses, since relative clauses normally state a fact.

The SUBJUNCTIVE is often used in relative clauses where there is some doubt or denial of the existence or attainability of the antecedent, but certain tenses of the indicative are also found in such clauses.

L. **Remplacez l'infinitif entre parenthèses par le temps convenable de l'indicatif ou du subjonctif, selon le cas.**

1. Avez-vous une amie qui (pouvoir) venir avec nous dimanche?
2. Il y a à la porte un homme qui (vouloir) vous voir.   **3.** Pouvez-vous m'indiquer un film qui (plaire) à tout le monde?   **4.** Il cherche quelqu'un qui (vouloir) bien acheter sa vieille maison.   **5.** Y a-t-il ici un étudiant qui (savoir) parler chinois?   **6.** Connaissez-vous une seule personne qui (être) capable de se sacrifier pour cela?   **7.** Nous cherchons un cadeau qui lui (faire) plaisir.   **8.** Je vous apporte un livre qui vous (intéresser).   **9.** Y a-t-il quelque chose que je (pouvoir) faire pour vous?

M. **Traduisez en français.**

1. (*vous*) We do not know anyone who is able to solve your problem.
2. He is looking for someone who can help him.   **3.** I know a girl who drives very well.   **4.** (*vous*) Can you tell me the name of a

student who knows how to type?   5. Is there a restaurant near here that is not too expensive?   6. (*tu*) Bring me a book that is not too long.   7. We are looking for an apartment that is near a shopping center.   8. I see no one I know.   9. There are many people who know how to speak several languages.   10. There is nothing that can save that child.

12. When and why is the subjunctive used in the following examples?

C'est **le plus beau musée** que je **connaisse.**
It is the most beautiful museum *that I* know.

Quel est **le plus grand édifice** qu'on **ait (a)** construit à Paris?
What is the largest building *that they* have built *in Paris?*

C'est **le seul homme** qui **puisse (peut)** faire cela.
He is the only man *who* can *do that.*

C'est **le plus long voyage** que nous **avons (ayons)** jamais fait.
It is the longest trip *that we* have *ever* taken.

In clauses whose antecedent is modified by a superlative or by adjectives such as **premier, dernier,** and **seul,** the verb may be in either the indicative or subjunctive. The INDICATIVE is used when the speaker wishes to state an objective fact. When there is an element of doubt or personal opinion or of subjective feeling, the SUBJUNCTIVE may be used.

N. Traduisez en français.

1. (*vous*) Who[1] is the most interesting author that you have read?   2. It is the first thing that he must do.   3. Here are the only friends that we were able to find.   4. Is France the only country where one is really free?   5. It's the last book that I am obliged to read for this course.   6. (*tu*) What is the most beautiful opera you ever heard?   7. Here is the only person who saw the accident.   8. (*vous*) Who is the best teacher you have had?

[1] Quel

13. How does French express the English indefinites *whoever, whatever, wherever, however,* **etc.? Why is the verb of French clauses introduced by such indefinites in the subjunctive?**

Qui que ce **soit**, il n'a pas le droit de fumer.
Whoever *he* { is, may be, } *he does not have the right to smoke.*

Quel que soit son métier, il faut qu'il fasse son service militaire.
Whatever *his trade* { is, may be, } *he must do his military service.*

Quoi qu'il en **soit,** vous devez revenir.
However *that* may be, *you must come back.*

Où que nous **soyons,** nous n'oublierons pas nos parents.

Wherever *we* $\begin{cases} \text{are,} \\ \text{may be,} \end{cases}$ *we will not forget our parents.*

Si riches qu'ils **soient,** ils ne sont pas heureux.

However rich *they* $\begin{cases} \text{are,} \\ \text{may be,} \end{cases}$ *they are not happy.*

Quelles que soient vos objections, il s'en ira.

Whatever *your objections* $\begin{cases} \text{are,} \\ \text{may be,} \end{cases}$ *he will go away.*

The common French indefinites that correspond to the English indefinites in *-ever* are:

qui que	*whoever*	**quoi que**	*whatever*
quel que	*whoever, whatever*	**si** + ADJECTIVE + **que**	*however* + ADJECTIVE

When a clause introduced by one of the above indefinites indicates concession, that is, admits that something is or may be the case, its verb is in the subjunctive. Clauses of this kind have a certain vagueness, which places them in the realm of the hypothetical subjunctive rather than in that of the factual indicative.

NOTE 1: The idea of concession is illustrated in the above examples. For instance, **Quel que soit son métier** concedes that he does or may have a trade. **Si riches qu'ils soient** admits that they are or may be rich.

NOTE 2: The **quel** of the expression **quel que** agrees with the noun it modifies in gender and number. Ex.: **Quelle que** soit <u>votre préférence</u> . . . (Whatever <u>your preference</u> *is/may be* . . .); **Quelles que** soient <u>ses raisons</u>. . . (Whatever <u>his reasons</u> *are/may be* . . .).

NOTE 3: The English *However* + ADJECTIVE is expressed in current spoken French by **Si** + ADJECTIVE. Ex.: **Si** <u>intéressant</u> que soit ce roman . . . (However <u>in-teresting</u> *this novel is/may be* . . .), **Si** <u>grands</u> que soient ces jeunes gens . . . (However <u>tall</u> *these young men are/may be* . . .).

O. Traduisez en français.

1. (*tu*) Whoever[1] he is, tell him to come to see me at once. 2. (*vous*) Whatever[2] your religion may be, you must help your neighbor[3]. 3. (*vous*) Whatever[2] your ideas are, keep them to[4] yourself. 4. Whatever he does, he will not be able to change the situation. 5. However[5] lazy they may be, they are obliged to work in order to live. 6. (*vous*) However that may be, you must come to class every day. 7. Wherever he goes, he makes[6] friends easily. 8. Whatever he does, fate is against him. 9. However[5] good[7] they may be, their mother is never satisfied[8].

[1] Either Qui que ce soit or Quel qu'il soit. [2] In such constructions, the Quel must agree with the noun that follows. [3] prochain [4] *to yourself* = pour vous [5] Use si + AD-JECTIVE. [6] Use a form of se faire. [7] sages [8] contente

Exercices d'ensemble

P. Remplacez les infinitifs entre parenthèses par la forme convenable de l'indicatif ou du subjonctif, ou bien gardez l'infinitif où il le faut.

1. Il est certain que ces gens ne (savoir) pas ce qu'ils font. **2.** Nous cherchons une maison qui (être) climatisée et qui (avoir) un grand jardin. **3.** Je pense que vous (travailler) mieux la semaine prochaine. **4.** Claire craint de (rentrer) seule chez elle la nuit. **5.** Monsieur Parrain regrette beaucoup que vous (refuser) son offre hier matin. **6.** Je vous prêterai cette somme pourvu que vous me (promettre) de me rembourser dans un an. **7.** Où que vous (aller), je vous suivrai. **8.** Nous nous étonnons de (voir) que le gouvernement ne fait rien pour ces gens. **9.** Demande l'auto à ton père avant qu'il (aller) se coucher. **10.** Anne-Lise a peur que son père la (mettre) en pension.

Q. Remplacez les infinitifs entre parenthèses par la forme convenable de l'indicatif ou du subjonctif, ou bien gardez l'infinitif où il le faut.

1. Je sais que vous (plaisanter) sur tout, mais ce n'est pas le moment. **2.** Réfléchissez donc avant de (répondre) n'importe quoi. **3.** C'est le plus grand acteur que nous (avoir) jamais vu. **4.** Il est naturel que les étudiants (vouloir) faire connaître leur point de vue. **5.** Nos parents sont désolés que vous (décider) de ne plus venir à nos réunions. **6.** Qui que vous (être), vous avez les mêmes droits que les autres. **7.** Il est possible que vous (avoir) une allergie quelconque. **8.** Il faut être bien naïf pour (croire) tout ce qu'il raconte. **9.** Il faut que nous (prendre) une décision une fois pour toutes.

R. Traduisez en français.

1. It is true that we are sometimes too demanding toward others[1]. **2.** (*vous*) Do you know someone who can repair my television right away? **3.** (*tu*) Madame Lesage is glad that you promised to come to her evening party. **4.** (*vous*) I don't find that you are making a great deal of progress. **5.** They questioned the suspect until he confessed his crime. **6.** (*tu*) I believe that this new novel will interest you, but I do not believe that you can read it in[2] two hours. **7.** The boss wants everyone to be at the office at eight o'clock. **8.** (*vous*) However busy you may be, give[3] some[4] time to your family. **9.** My lawyer wants his oldest daughter to be an[5] architect. **10.** (*tu*) It is evident that you are sick and it is important for you to go see the doctor.

---

[1] les autres   [2] en   [3] Use a form of **consacrer**.   [4] *some time* = quelques heures   [5] Omit in translation.

S. Traduisez en français.

1. Are they the only persons who can really save the country?
2. (*vous*) It is important for you not to say a word about[1] that affair.
3. Whatever her reasons are, she did not explain them.   4. I'll go to see him next week unless he writes me not[2] to come.   5. I believe that it will soon be necessary to buy a new air-conditioner.
6. (*tu*) I am giving you this ring so that you will remember me.
7. It is probable that we will not come back before Christmas.   8. I am glad that Michael has arrived, but I am sorry that I will not have time[3] to see him.   9. (*vous*) Think[4] before you speak.   10. The children are sorry that they were so nasty this afternoon.   11. His uncle will take him to Paris on the condition that he passes his examination.

---

[1] sur   [2] *not to* = de ne pas   [3] Supply definite article.   [4] Use a form of réfléchir.

Problem Words

39. notice

(a) When *to notice* is expressed by **remarquer**

Avez-vous **remarqué** ces deux personnes au premier rang?	Did *you* notice *those two people in the first row?*
J'**ai remarqué** tout de suite que tu n'avais pas reconnu Monsieur Lévêque.	I noticed *right away that you had not recognized Mr. Lévêque.*

The verb **remarquer** may be used for *notice* in almost any circumstance.

(b) When *to notice* is expressed by **apercevoir**

J'**ai aperçu** Elizabeth dans un taxi.	I noticed *Elizabeth in a taxi.*

The verb **apercevoir** means *notice* in the sense of *catch sight of.*

(c) When *notice* is expressed by **s'apercevoir**

Le conférencier ne **s'aperçoit** pas qu'on ne l'écoute plus.	*The lecturer doesn't* notice (= realize) *that people are no longer listening to him.*
Je **me suis aperçu** de son inquiétude.	*I* noticed (= realized) *his uneasiness.*

The verb **s'apercevoir** may be followed by **que** or by **de.** It is synonymous with *realize* or *be aware of.* When **s'apercevoir** is followed by **de,** the object of **de** is something intangible.

40. opportunity

(a) When *opportunity* = **l'occasion**

J'espère que nous aurons souvent **l'occasion** de nous revoir.

*I hope that we will often have
the opportunity to see each
other.*

When *opportunity* means a favorable conjunction of circumstances, it
is expressed by **l'occasion.**

(b) When *opportunity* = **la possibilité**

Ces étudiants n'ont pas encore
eu **la possibilité** d'aller en
France.

*Those students haven't yet had
the opportunity to go to
France.*

The English *opportunity* is expressed by **la possibilité** when *opportunity* means *possibility.*

CAUTION: DO NOT use the word «opportunité» for *opportunity.* The
word **opportunité** means *opportuneness* and is relatively uncommon.

41. paper

(a) When *paper* = *a piece of paper*

Jacques dit qu'il ne peut pas finir son devoir parce qu'il n'a
plus de **papier.**

*John says that he can't finish
his homework because he
doesn't have any more pa-
per.*

Votre livre est imprimé sur un
beau **papier.**

*Your book is printed on very
good paper.*

When *paper* means *material to write on* it is expressed by **le papier.**

(b) When *paper* = *newspaper*

Avez-vous lu **le journal** ce matin?

*Did you read the paper this
morning?*

When *paper* is used in the sense of *newspaper,* it is **le journal.**

CAUTION: DO NOT use «papier» for *newspaper.*

(c) When *paper* is *a classroom exercise*

Remettez vos **copies** à la fin de
l'heure.

*Hand in your papers at the end
of the hour.*

For *papers* to be handed in to the teacher one can say **les copies, les
devoirs,** or **les exercices.** The classroom expression: *Hand in your
papers* is: **Remettez vos copies** or **Donnez-moi vos copies.**

CAUTION: DO NOT use «papier» for *classroom exercise,* and do not say «Passez les papiers» for *Hand in your papers.* The classroom exercise is **la copie;** say **Remettez les copies** for *Hand in your papers.* *

(d) When *paper* is *a classroom report*

J'ai **un travail** à préparer.   *I have* a paper *to prepare.*

In French, there are various names for *classroom report,* such as **un travail, un compte rendu, une composition, une dissertation,** or **une étude**—but NOT «un papier».

42. people

(a) When *people* is expressed by **personnes**

Ses idées ont offensé plusieurs **personnes.**   *His ideas offended several* people.

When *people* means *a few persons,* French uses **personnes.**

(b) When *people* is expressed by **gens**

Il y a trop de **gens** sur la Côte d'Azur en été.   *There are too many* people *on the French Riviera in summer.*

Il y a des **gens** qui n'ont aucun scrupule.   *There are* people *who have no scruples.*

When *people* means *a considerable number of persons,* French often uses **les gens.**

(c) When *people* is expressed by **monde**

Il y avait beaucoup de **monde** au concert.   *There were many* people *at the concert.*

To state that there were *many people* at some function, French often uses **monde.** When used in this sense, **monde** cannot be modified by a relative clause.

(d) When *people* is expressed by **peuple**

Les Italiens sont **un peuple** très musicien.   *The Italians are* a *very musical* people.

The English *a people,* in the sense of *a nation,* is expressed by **le peuple.** Note that **le peuple** also sometimes means *the masses.*

CAUTION: DO NOT use «peuple» to express *people* except when it means *nation* or *the masses.*

(e) When *people* is expressed by **on**

Qu'est-ce qu'**on** dirait si on savait cela?   *What would* people *say if they knew that?*

* Either the definite article or the possessive adjective may be used in this sentence.

When *people* has the very indefinite sense of *people in general,* French uses the indefinite pronoun **on.**

T. Remplacez les mots anglais par leur équivalent français.

1. (*vous*) (*Notice*) que nous sommes presque du même avis.
2. (*People*) n'aime pas conduire quand il neige.   3. Venez me voir à la première (*opportunity*).   4. Étienne corrige des (*papers*) pour le professeur Grémillot.   5. Les Hongrois sont un' (*people*) très artiste.   6. Nous (*noticed*) un renard au bord de la route cette nuit.
7. Deux (*people*) sont venues pendant que vous étiez absent.   8. Ce (*paper*)-là a des tendances libérales.   9. J'aimerais vivre dans ce pays, mais je n'aurais pas la (*opportunity*) d'y travailler.   10. D'où vient tout ce (*people*)?   11. Ce (*paper*) n'est pas assez bon pour taper une thèse.   12. Tous ces (*people*) attendent[1] la sortie des artistes.   13. Il lui a fallu longtemps pour (*notice*) qu'on le volait.
14. (*People*) aime bien prendre des vacances l'été.

[1] are waiting for the artists to come out

U. Traduisez en français. Attention aux mots en italique.

1. Anne always writes on purple *paper.*   2. Several *people* came to see me this morning.   3. Irene *noticed* the new painting as soon as she entered the house.   4. A *people* should know its history.
5. I have never had the *opportunity* to visit Sweden.   6. I *noticed* too late that I had left my briefcase in the taxi.   7. One mustn't believe everything one sees in the *paper.*   8. I saw many *people* that I didn't know.   9. I *noticed* Guy at the theater last evening.
10. Would there be an *opportunity* to see the director?   11. Were there many *people* at the reception?   12. (*vous*) Don't forget to hand in your *papers.*   13. The teacher didn't *notice* that I was finishing my exercises in class.   14. (*vous*) Don't believe everything that *people* tell you.

Verb Review

Review the verbs **mettre** and **mourir** according to the outline on page 253.

CHAPTER
12

The Article

Brassens[1], *un* des chansonniers[2] *les* plus aimés des Français, lauréat du Grand prix de poésie de l'Académie française, est interviewé par une journaliste à la suite d'*un* sondage[3] où il est choisi comme *l'*homme *le* plus heureux dans *une* longue liste de personnalités proposées aux lecteurs.

Moi, *le* plus heureux des Français?

L'EXPRESS—*Un* sondage nous indique que pour 65%[4] des Français vous représentez *l'*homme heureux.

GEORGES BRASSENS—Ah! les idiots . . .

EXP—Sans doute parce que vous symbolisez à travers vos chansons
5 *une* forme de liberté à *la* limite de *l'*anarchie dans laquelle beaucoup de Français aiment à se reconnaître. Il y a *la* fidélité aux copains d'abord, à *la* bonne langue populaire et poétique ensuite. Vous êtes *un* peu libertin, *un* peu libertaire[5].

G. B.—Mon bonheur à moi, c'est de faire des chansons. *Le* bonheur,
10 c'est deux vers agréables à entendre. Si je n'étais pas célibataire, mes enfants auraient eu plus d'importance que mes chansons mais comme je n'en ai pas . . . J'écris des chansons depuis *l'*âge de 14 ans. J'essaie d'en faire *une* par semaine, en tout cas *une* par mois. En dehors de ça, je n'existe pas. J'aurais d'ailleurs été plus pleinement heureux si j'avais été
15 <u>musicien</u>*. *Les* vrais bonheurs physiques et psychiques que j'ai éprouvés, c'est en écoutant *une* nouvelle mélodie qui me touche. *La* musique me donne des frissons que je n'éprouve pas autrement . . . C'est *une*[6] espèce de truc qui me donne envie de pleurer[7] comme *un* veau, *une* vibration . . .
20 EXP—Y a-t-il *une* période de votre vie dont vous ayez *la* nostalgie?

G. B.—*Le* passé est *un* thème pour moi, je ne l'évoque que dans mes

---

[1] *Pronounce* [brasēs] [2] *writers and performers of popular songs and songs dealing with social and political satire* [3] *poll* [4]*% = pour cent* [5] *partisan of absolute and total freedom* *Underscored words are examples of THE NOUN ALONE not preceded by an article.* [6] *une espèce de truc a sort of thing* [7] *pleurer comme un veau   cry like a baby*

chansons, pas dans *la* vie. J'ai eu *une* enfance heureuse mais gâchée par *l*'école. Ma mère était sévère, elle exigeait de moi de bonnes notes. Ça m'embêtait de ne pas lui faire plaisir mais, <u>en égoïste</u>, je préférais lui
25   déplaire et ne rien faire!

EXP—Vos débuts ont été difficiles. *Le* confort, c'est nécessaire?

G. B.—Non. Quand j'étais dans *le* besoin, il se trouvait toujours quelqu'un pour me procurer *un* paquet de tabac ou de quoi manger *le* lendemain. J'étais plus heureux alors que *le* type que je suis aujourd'hui qui
30   s'achète *une* paire de chaussures. On ne se met pas à table *le* ventre plein.

EXP—*L*'amour est-il indispensable au bonheur?

G. B.—*L*'amour? Je ne sais pas bien ce que c'est. Je ne fais pas *la* différence entre *l*'amour que j'ai pour *une* femme et celui que j'ai pour mes
35   amis ou pour mes chats. J'ai *une* somme de sentiments à donner. A qui que ce soit que je les dispense, ils sortent du même coin, non?

EXP—Vous donnez *l*'impression d'être *un* homme libre.

G. B.—Quelle liberté? Pendant *les* 20 ans que j'ai eu des coliques[8] néphrétiques, je n'étais plus libre. À ce moment-là, j'aurais donné toutes
40   mes chansons pour cesser de souffrir. Je l'aurais regretté après . . . Mais j'étais borné par *la* maladie, donc, prisonnier. Si vous parlez de *la* liberté en pensant à *la* censure, il faut admettre que, sous *un* régime totalitaire, je serais <u>en[9] cabane</u>. Et que, dans cette démocratie fatiguée qui est *la* nôtre, je peux dire à peu près tout ce que je veux. Comme tout *le* monde,
45   d'ailleurs.

EXP—On vous a reproché de[10] ne pas vous engager . . .

G. B.—Mais c'est *un* engagement total que j'ai pris. Depuis *le* début, j'ai dans mes chansons *le* même comportement en face de *la* vie, en face de *l*'argent, en face de *la* réussite, en face des grands[11], en face des
50   humbles. Mais si on entend par là appartenir à *un* parti, je ne reconnais à aucun parti *le* droit de[12] m'avoir.

EXP—Peut-on mesurer *le* bonheur des gens?

G. B.—*La* notion que nous avons du bonheur est celle d'*une* midinette[13]. Il y a des gens qui sont heureux lorsque *la* sirène de *l*'usine
55   sonne, parce qu'ils vont sortir, cesser de bosser[14]. Pour *l*'ouvrier, qu'il soit payé au maximum ou au minimum de *l*'heure, c'est *une* plus grande joie, peut-être, *la* sirène qui sonne, que [15] pour moi de trouver *un* quatrain. <u>A vélo, en auto</u> ou <u>en métro</u> il va rentrer chez lui, trouver sa femme, ses enfants, sa télévision, sa pipe. Il est heureux, *le* type, si c'est son
60   bonheur. Pour lui, pour *les* autres, pour moi, ce n'est que *l*'accumulation

---

[8] *kidney pains*   [9] *in prison*   [10] de ne pas vous engager *for not getting involved*
[11] *rich and powerful*   [12] de m'avoir *claim me (as a member)*   [13] *working girl*
[14] *work*   [15] que pour moi de trouver un quatrain *than I do hitting on a good verse (lit., a verse of four lines)*

des petites joies qui rend *la* vie possible. Et puis on ne devrait jamais demander à quelqu'un s'il est heureux.

EXP—Et pourquoi?

G. B.—Parce que c'est indiscret.

D'après Georges Brassens. («Moi, le plus heureux des Français?» *l'Express,* 19 septembre 1977)

1. What are the forms of the definite and indefinite articles?

| | Definite | | Indefinite | |
	Singular	Plural	Singular	Plural
Masculine	**le**	**les**	**un**	**des**
Feminine	**la**	**les**	**une**	**des**

Before any singular noun or adjective beginning with a vowel or a mute **h, le** and **la** elide, that is, they become **l'.**

This elision must be made before a noun or adjective beginning with a vowel or mute **h.**

2. What is the most common use of the definite article in both French and English?

Les œufs sont dans **le** réfrigérateur.

The *eggs are in* the *refrigerator.*

Le papier et **les** crayons sont sur **la** table.

The *paper and pencils are on* the *table.*

The definite article is used to indicate a particular noun.

When there is more than one noun used with the definite article, the article must be repeated before each noun. English often uses the article before the first noun only.

3. How do English and French differ in their treatment of nouns used in a general sense?

Les pommes sont bonnes pour la santé.

Apples *are good for the health.*

J'aime beaucoup **les chiens.**

I like dogs *a great deal.*

La justice est une chose bien relative.

Justice *is a very relative thing.*

Le travail éloigne de nous trois grands maux: **l'ennui, le vice** et **le besoin.** (Voltaire)

Work *protects us from three great evils:* boredom, vice, *and* need.

In French the definite article is placed before nouns used in a general sense. This is not the case in English.

A great many nouns used in a general sense are abstract.

4. In French, how is the definite article used with the days of the week?

Lundi nous aurons un examen.	Monday *we'll have a test.*
Nous avons toujours un exa-men **le lundi.**	*We always have a test* Mondays.

Days of the week are used without the article when they refer to an occurrence that takes place once on a given day. The definite article is used with the singular form of the day of the week when the occurrence takes place regularly every week on a given day.

5. How is the article used with dates?

le lundi 30 avril   Monday, *April 30*

When both the day of the week and the date are given, the definite article is normally placed before the day of the week, but not before the day of the month. No comma separates the day of the week from the day of the month. Also found is **lundi,** 30 avril. In this case, a comma separates the day of the week from the day of the month.

le 30 avril 1984   *April* 30, *1984*

When the date alone is given, the article normally precedes the day of the month. No commas are used.

6. When is the article used with the seasons?

Le printemps est très beau.	Spring *is very beautiful.*
Nous en parlerons **l'été** pro-chain.	*We'll speak of it next* summer.
Au printemps nous avons beaucoup à faire.	In the spring *we have a great deal to do.*
Où irez-vous **en hiver?**	*Where will you go* in winter?

The article is used with names of seasons, except when they are pre-ceded by **en.** Note the expressions **au printemps, en été, en automne, en hiver.**

7. When is the article used with names of languages?

Le français est une langue fa-cile.	French *is an easy language.*
Comprenez-vous **l'allemand?**	*Do you understand* German?
Je ne parle pas **anglais.**	*I do not speak* English.
Marie parle bien **(le) russe.**	*Marie speaks* Russian *well.*
En italien on prononce toutes les lettres.	In Italian *all the letters are pro-nounced.*

The article is used with names of languages except when the language is preceded by **en** or when it follows a form of the verb **parler.**

When the language does not follow a form of the verb **parler** immediately, sometimes the article is used with the language, sometimes not.

All names of languages are masculine.

A. Traduisez en français.

(In each sentence of the English-to-French exercises of this lesson there is some word with which the definite article must be either used or omitted. Identify this word and connect it with one of the rules in the preceding sections. Explain orally why you use or omit the definite article.)

1. Summer is a very beautiful season.   2. It is necessary to be patient with children.   3. For the United States the Second World War began on December 7, 1941.   4. The flowers that I prefer are roses.   5. We celebrate our anniversary Tuesday, February 28.   6. I like to hear my friend Sergio Tonelli speak Italian.   7. He loves animals.   8. In spring all nature awakens.   9. It is difficult to know German well[1].   10. In English they use the word "sorry" a great deal.

[1] Place this adverb before *know.*

B. Traduisez en français.

1. Men are truly curious.   2. (*vous*) Do you like French coffee?   3. (*tu*) Are you free Saturday afternoon?   4. Many Frenchmen speak Spanish.   5. Sundays I always go to church.   6. There are interesting concerts in winter.   7. French is a beautiful language.   8. We never have any class on Saturday.   9. Undeveloped countries need help.

8. When is the article used with nouns in apposition?

Pasteur, **le grand savant français,** mourut en 1895.	*Pasteur,* the great French scientist, *died in 1895.*
Philippe, **le fils de notre voisin,** est parti à l'armée.	*Philip,* our neighbor's son, *has left for the army.*
Pierre Dupont, **étudiant en médecine,** habite à Paris.	*Pierre Dupont,* a medical student, *lives in Paris.*
Yvetot, **petite ville de Normandie,** se trouve entre Le Havre et Rouen.	*Yvetot,* a little Norman town, *lies between Le Havre and Rouen.*

In French, the definite article is normally used with nouns in apposition to state what the speaker considers a well-known fact. This is also English usage.

But in French the indefinite article is not often used with nouns in apposition. Whenever the noun in apposition furnishes additional and presumably unknown information, the noun in apposition tends to be used without any article.

9. What about the use of the article with a noun following the preposition *en*?

Jacques est un étudiant **en droit.**	*Jack is a* law *student.*
L'Europe est divisée **en pays.**	*Europe is divided* into countries.

Normally, no article follows the preposition **en.** Note, however, the following:

L'Arc de Triomphe fut construit **en l'honneur** des armées de Napoléon.	*The Arc de Triomphe was constructed* in honor *of Napoleon's armies.*
L'agent a tiré **en l'air.**	*The policeman fired a shot* into the air.
En l'absence du professeur les élèves ont fait beaucoup de bruit.	In the absence *of the teacher the pupils made a lot of noise.*

In certain set expressions, the most common of which are **en l'honneur, en l'air,** and **en l'absence,** the article is used after **en.**

10. Is the article used with given (first) names?

Marie est partie hier avec **le petit Claude** et son frère **Henri.**	*Mary left yesterday with* little Claude *and her brother* Henry.

The article is not normally used with first names. But it is used with first names modified by an adjective.

11. When speaking of someone, how is the article used with titles?

Hier, j'ai vu **le docteur Lemaître.**	*Yesterday, I saw* Dr. Lemaître.
Le capitaine Lebeau arrivera demain.	Captain Lebeau *will arrive tomorrow.*
Connaissez-vous **le professeur Dupré?**	*Do you know* Professor Dupré?
Le président Wilson est allé en Europe en 1919.	President Wilson *went to Europe in 1919.*

When speaking of a person, the definite article is used before titles indicating a profession.

Monsieur Lebrun habite 30, rue de Vaugirard.	Mr. Lebrun *lives at 30 Vaugirard Street.*
Où est **Madame Rivière?**	*Where is* Mrs. Rivière?
Jacques sort souvent avec **Mademoiselle Moreau.**	*Jack often goes out with* Miss Moreau.

But no article is used before **monsieur, madame,** or **mademoiselle** when they are followed by the person's name.

CAUTION: When **madame** and **mademoiselle** are used as common nouns, they must not be accompanied by an article. Do not say: «La mademoiselle qui passe là-bas est une avocate.» Say: «La **demoiselle** qui passe là-bas est une avocate.»

monsieur = **M.**   madame = **Mme** or **Mme**   mademoiselle = **Mlle** or **Mlle**

A period is used after the abbreviation for **monsieur,** but no period is used after the abbreviations for **madame** and **mademoiselle.**

12. How is the article used with titles when addressing a person?

Docteur, je ne me sens pas bien du tout.	Doctor, *I don't feel well at all.*
J'ai suivi vos conseils, **Dr. Perret.**	*I followed your advice,* Dr. Perret.

In addressing a doctor, no article is used either with or without the name of the doctor.

—Bonjour, **mon capitaine.**	*"Good morning,* captain."
—Je suis à vos ordres, **mon commandant.**	*"I am at your orders,* major."

In the military, when a soldier of lower rank or an officer speaks to an officer of higher rank, the possessive adjective is used before the title.

Bonsoir, **Monsieur.**	*Good evening,* Mr. Jones.
Bonjour, **Madame.**	*Good morning,* Mrs. Leroque.
Mademoiselle, j'espère que nous nous reverrons.	Miss Smith, *I hope that we'll see each other again.*

In French, a person is usually addressed as **Monsieur, Madame,** or **Mademoiselle,** and no last name is normally used when addressing a person, although the last name is sometimes heard in familiar speech.

Je n'ai pas encore lu ce livre, **monsieur.**	*I haven't yet read that book,* Professor Lemercier.

In addressing teachers in France, including professors, neither the title nor the name is used, but simply **monsieur, madame,** or **mademoiselle.**

Monsieur le Président, vous avez toujours raison.

Mr. President, *you are always right.*

Monsieur le professeur, voulez-vous nous donner votre opinion?

Professor Bruce, *will you give us your opinion?*

With certain titles, the formula **Monsieur le . . .** is sometimes used in address.

C. Traduisez en français.

1. He was speaking of Mr. Leduc, a publisher from Strasbourg. 2. There will be a big dinner in honor of Senator Amieux. 3. (*tu*) Have you invited beautiful Sylvia to the dance? 4. She knows Prince Louis very well[1]. 5. General Lacaze will inspect the troops tomorrow morning. 6. Pasteur, the great French scientist[2], was a very generous man. 7. They spent the night in prison. 8. In the absence of the manager, his assistant will make[3] the decisions. 9. Doctor, I don't know what[4] is the matter with me. 10. (*vous*) I'll do what you wish, colonel. 11. Miss Duneau, a mathematics professor at the university, has just written a new book. 12. We'll go to France by[5] plane. 13. She loves Roger and would like to marry him. 14. The best specialist in that field[6] is Dr. Petit. 15. (*vous*) I'll follow you, lieutenant.

[1] Where will these words come in relaton to the verb?   [2] Not «scientiste»   [3] Not a form of «faire»   [4] This is an idiom.   [5] en or par   [6] domaine

13. When is the article used before names of countries and continents?

La France est un grand pays.

France *is a large country.*

Je suis allé **en Angleterre.**

I went to England.

Il vient **de Grèce.**

He comes from Greece.

L'Europe et **l'Afrique** sont séparées par la Méditerranée.

Europe *and* Africa *are separated by the Mediterranean.*

Nous sommes arrivés **au Portugal.**

We arrived in Portugal.

Il vient **du Danemark.**

He comes from Denmark.

The article is normally used before names of countries and continents.

But the article is not used after **en** (which expresses *in* or *to* with feminine countries) nor after **de** (meaning *from*) when it precedes a feminine country.

NOTE: For the gender of countries, see page 213.

14. Is the article used with names of cities?

Il va à **Paris.**	*He is going to* Paris.
Avez-vous vu **Londres?**	*Have you seen* London?
La Nouvelle-Orléans est en Louisiane, **Le Havre** en France.	New Orleans *is in Louisiana,* Le Havre *in France.*

The article is not usually found with names of cities. However, a few cities, such as **La Haye** (*The Hague*), **La Nouvelle-Orléans, Le Havre, La Rochelle,** etc., have the article as part of the name.

15. When is the article used before names of streets and avenues?

Dites-moi où est **la rue Racine.**	*Tell me where* Racine Street *is.*
Le Boulevard Saint-Germain est très pittoresque.	Boulevard Saint-Germain *is very picturesque.*
Connaissez-vous **l'avenue des Champs-Élysées?**	*Do you know* Champs-Elysées Avenue?

The article is normally used before names of streets and avenues.

Nous sommes arrivés **Boulevard Saint-Michel.**	*We arrived at* St. Michel Boulevard.
On me trouvera **rue Royale.**	*They'll find me on* Royal Street.

When the prepositions *in* or *on* precede the street name in English, the French tend to omit the preposition and article. However, the preposition and the article may be used.

The French say:

dans la rue	*on the street*
dans ⎱ **l'avenue**	*on the avenue*
sur ⎰	
sur la place	*in the square*
sur le boulevard	*on the boulevard*

16. How is the English word *per* expressed in French with various types of units of measure?

(a) speed per hour

Le train roulait à cent soixante kilomètres **à l'heure.**	*The train was going at a hundred miles* per hour.

With expressions of *time indicating speed,* **à** + ARTICLE is used, and this is especially common with **à l'heure.**

(b) money per hour

Marie gagne cinq dollars **de l'heure.**	*Mary earns five dollars* per hour.

Money per hour is expressed by **de l'heure.**

(c) something accomplished per unit of time

Dans ce pays on travaille huit heures **par jour** et quarante heures **par semaine.**	*In this country they work eight hours* a day *and forty hours* per week.
Jacques gagne deux mille dollars **par mois.**	*Jack earns two thousand dollars* per month.

In general, French expresses *per* + UNIT OF TIME by **par** + UNIT OF TIME: **par jour, par semaine, par mois, par an.** No article is used after **par.**

(d) expressions of dry measure, weight, etc.

Les pommes de terre coûtent dix francs **la livre.**	*Potatoes cost ten francs* per pound.
Le sucre coûte quatre francs **le kilo.**	*Sugar costs four francs* per kilogram.

French expresses *per* with expressions of *dry measure, weight,* and so on, by placing the definite article before the expression.

17. What prepositions are used with expressions of means of locomotion, and when is the article used?

Nous sommes venus **en train** (*or* **par le train**), **en voiture, en avion** (*or* **par avion**),**à pied, à bicyclette.**	*We came* on *the train,* in *a car,* by *plane,* on *foot,* on *a bicycle.*

The prepositions used with means of locomotion must often be learned. In general, **dans** or **en** is used if one can enter the vehicle, **à** if one is on the vehicle. However for *on a motorcyle* the French say **en moto.**

18. What about the use of the article in stating the profession, nationality, or religion of the subject of the sentence?

M. Badin est **avocat.**	*Mr. Badin is* a lawyer.
Sa femme est **américaine.**	*His wife is* (an) American.
Mlle Bajard est **un excellent professeur.**	*Miss Bajard is* an excellent teacher.

After forms of the verb **être,** French designates profession, religion, nationality, etc., by an unmodified noun. English uses the noun modified by an indefinite article.

In French, if the name of the profession, nationality, or religion is modified, the indefinite article is used as in English.

D. Traduisez en français.

1. Mrs. Dallier is an interior decorator.   2. Did they arrive by train or on[1] a motorcycle?   3. Products imported from Japan are cheap.

4. In the United States people[2] work a great deal.   **5.** Mr. Perrier is Catholic.   **6.** First we arrived at Peace Street, where we found some very elegant stores.   **7.** In summer there are sometimes several storms per day.   **8.** It is dangerous to go[3] faster than eighty kilometers per hour.   **9.** *They* left on foot, *we* in a car.   **10.** His mother is a good doctor.

[1] en   [2] on   [3] Use a form of **rouler à plus de.**

E. Traduisez en français.

1. These toys come from Germany.   **2.** Formerly, there was a prison in the Place de la Bastille.   **3.** There are many lakes in Canada.   **4.** I caught a fish which I'll sell for a dollar a pound. **5.** Our neighbors came back from Poland yesterday.   **6.** She charges[1] ten dollars an hour, which[2] seems expensive.   **7.** My mother-in-law comes to see us twice a year.   **8.** I should like to go to Italy.   **9.** They left[3] for Portugal yesterday.   **10.** In Paris life has a special charm.   **11.** He earns $550 a week, but that will not last.

[1] Use a form of **prendre.**   [2] ce qui   [3] Use a form of **partir.**

Exercices d'ensemble

Remplacez les tirets des phrases dans les devoirs F, G et H par l'article défini ou indéfini où un article est nécessaire. Expliquez oralement votre choix.

F. **1.** Depuis quand apprends-tu _____ chimie?   **2.** Veux-tu aller _____ voiture ou _____ moto?   **3.** _____ dimanche est un jour de fête.   **4.** Je te verrai _____ mardi, _____ 2 février. **5.** Fait-il très froid en _____ hiver?   **6.** Bien que je préfère _____ français, je dois apprendre _____ russe.   **7.** Tout le monde cherche _____ bonheur.   **8.** Mme Lebeau, avocate à Bordeaux, fera un voyage en _____ Afrique du Nord.   **9.** En _____ absence de ses parents, Simone a reçu plusieurs amis.   **10.** J'ai vu _____ Mme Delaunay dans la rue ce matin.

G. **1.** Aimez-vous mieux _____ chats ou _____ chiens?   **2.** Parlez-vous _____ espagnol ou _____ portugais?   **3.** _____ vie n'est pas toujours agréable, mais elle est toujours supportable. **4.** Camus, _____ célèbre romancier, est mort dans un accident d'auto.   **5.** Christophe, _____ étudiant en _____ médecine depuis le mois d'octobre, passera ses vacances à _____ Québec. **6.** Connaissez-vous _____ Lieutenant Beauchamp?   **7.** Ma femme a _____ rendez-vous avec _____ Docteur Perrot à cinq heures. **8.** _____ Pologne et _____ Roumanie sont dans l'est de _____ Europe.   **9.** Nous avons marché le long de _____ rue de Seine. **10.** Comment dit-on «non» en _____ russe?

H. 1. Quand serez-vous de retour, _____ docteur? 2. Nous avons passé trois jours à _____ Montréal et deux jours à _____ Nouvelle-Orléans. 3. Il faut voir _____ Boulevard des Capucines et _____ avenue Matignon après six heures du soir. 4. Mlle Mandel est _____ psychiatre; elle a étudié pendant cinq ans à _____ Vienne. 5. Trouvez-vous que M. Cumin est _____ bon professeur? 6. _____ enfants peuvent être très gentils quand ils le veulent. 7. Marc va toujours au cinéma _____ samedi. 8. C'est aujourd'hui _____ 30 octobre. 9. Florence a commencé _____ école _____ automne dernier.

I. Remplacez les mots entre parenthèses par l'équivalent français. Faites attention à l'emploi de l'article et des prépositions.

1. Venez-vous (*from*) Danemark ou (*from*) Suède? 2. Nous avons passé quatre jours (*in*) Baton Rouge. 3. Je suis (*in*) Lyon pour le week-end mais je vais (*to*) Marseille demain. 4. Nous avons trouvé ce collier dans une bijouterie (*in*) rue de la Paix. 5. Il est défendu de faire plus de cent vingt kilomètres (*per*) heure sur cette route. 6. Vous verrez la statue (*in the*) place de la Sorbonne. 7. Combien gagnez-vous (*per*) heure? 8. Combien d'heures (*per*) jour travaillez-vous? 9. L'essence coûte cinq francs (*per*) litre. 10. Avez-vous voyagé (*by*) autobus, (*by*) train ou (*by*) avion?

Problem Words

43. piece

(a) How to say *piece* in general

Aimez-vous ce **morceau** de musique?   *Do you like this* piece *of music?*

The general word for *piece* is **le morceau.**

(b) Ways of saying *a piece of paper*

Donnez-moi **un bout de papier.**
Donnez-moi **un morceau de papier.**   *Give me* a piece of paper.
Donnez-moi **une feuille de papier.**

The word *piece* in *piece of paper* may be expressed by **morceau** or **feuille** (*sheet*) or **bout** (somewhat familiar).

The noun **bout** is also used with **fil** (*thread, wire*) and **ficelle** (*string*) to mean *piece*.

CAUTION: Do NOT use «la pièce» for *piece;* **la pièce** means *play* (to be acted) or *room.*

44. place

(a) When *place* is expressed by **endroit**

Le guide nous fera voir les **endroits** les plus curieux.

The guide will show us the most curious places.

Il y a bien des **endroits** où la vie est plus facile qu'ici.

There are many places where life is easier than here.

The common word for *place* is **l'endroit** (*m.*).

(b) When *place* is expressed by **lieu**

Il paraît qu'on revient toujours au **lieu** de son crime.

It seems that one always returns to the place of one's crime.

The word **le lieu** means *place* in the sense of *spot*. It is literary and not very common, but it is used specifically in certain instances and also in some compound expressions such as **le chef-lieu** (county seat). It is also used in the idiomatic expression **avoir lieu.** It is best to avoid using **lieu** in other cases.

(c) When *place* means *space*

Avez-vous **de la place** pour ma voiture dans votre garage?

Do you have a place for my car in your garage?

When *place* means *space*, French uses **la place.**

(d) When *place* means *a seat*

Montez vite dans le train si vous voulez **une place** près de la fenêtre.

Get on the train right away if you want a place near the window.

When *place* means *a seat*, often a paid accommodation, *place* is expressed by **la place.**

(e) When *place* means *a job*

Jean-Paul a une bonne
$\left\{ \begin{array}{l} \text{situation.} \\ \text{position.} \\ \text{place.} \end{array} \right.$

Jean-Paul has a good place (= job).

When the English word *place* means *job*, it may be expressed by **la situation, la position,** or **la place.**

CAUTION: DO NOT use «place» to express *place in general.* The ordinary word for *place* is **endroit.**

45. rather

(a) How to say *rather than*

Je voudrais une revue **plutôt qu'**un journal.	*I would like a magazine* rather than *a newspaper.*
Allez vous promener **plutôt que de** rester ici par ce beau temps.	*Go and take a walk* rather than *stay* here in this nice weather.

The expression *rather than* is often rendered in French by **plutôt que,** and when it precedes an infinitive, it may be rendered by **plutôt que de.**

(b) How to say *rather* + ADJECTIVE or ADVERB

Je suis **assez fatigué** ce soir après cette longue journée.	*I am* rather tired *this evening after this long day.*
Après un an d'étude vous parlerez **assez couramment.**	*After a year of study you will speak* rather fluently.

When the adverb *rather* modifies an adjective or another adverb, French uses **assez.**

(c) How to say *I would rather . . .*

Nous **aimerions mieux** rester à la maison ce soir.	*We* would rather *stay home this evening.*
Nous **préférerions** rester à la maison ce soir.	
J'**aimerais mieux** jouer au bridge qu'au poker.	*I* would rather *play bridge than poker.*
Je **préférerais** jouer au bridge **plutôt** qu'au poker.	

The English *would rather* + VERB may be expressed in French by the conditional of **aimer mieux** + INFINITIVE or of **préférer** + INFINITIVE. In comparisons, **plutôt** is required to complete the meaning of **préférer.**

46. reason

(a) How to say *the reason for*

Quelle est **la raison de** votre refus?	*What is* the reason for *your refusal?*

French expresses *the reason for* by **la raison de.**

(b) How to say *the reason that*

Philippe m'a expliqué **la rai-son pour laquelle** il n'a pas pu venir.	
Philippe m'a expliqué **pour quelle raison** il n'a pas pu venir.	*Philip explained to me* the reason that *he could not come.*
Philippe m'a expliqué **pour-quoi** il n'a pas pu venir.	

French expresses *the reason that* (colloquially *the reason why*) by **la raison pour laquelle** or **pour quelle raison** or simply by **pourquoi.**

CAUTION: DO NOT say «la raison pourquoi», which is incorrect even colloquially.

I. **Remplacez les mots anglais par leur équivalent français.**

1. Je ne peux pas être dans deux (*places*) à la fois.   2. Béatrice est (*rather*) découragée par tout ce qui s'est passé.   3. Je voudrais savoir (*the reason*) Monsieur Béraud a changé d'avis.   4. Allez en avant et gardez-nous une (*place*).   5. Il me faut un petit (*piece*) de cette étoffe.   6. Les enfants (*would rather*) passer leurs vacances à la mer qu'à la montagne.   7. Il n'y a pas assez de (*place*) pour deux dans ce bureau.   8. Le beau vase chinois s'est cassé en mille (*pieces*). 9. Juliette a laissé une lettre pour expliquer (*the reason for*) son départ.   10. On ira voir (*the place*) de l'accident.   11. Faisons quelque chose chez nous (*rather than*) d'aller au restaurant ce soir.

J. **Traduisez en français. Attention aux mots en italique.**

1. I know a *place* where we can work in peace.   2. Lucien works *rather* well, but he could do better.   3. (*vous*) Now you know the *reason* I came back.   4. The children don't have enough *place* to play.   5. What are those *pieces* of paper on the floor?   6. (*tu*) Johnnie, give your *place* to that lady.   7. I would *rather* leave this evening than tomorrow morning.   8. What is the *reason* for his absence?   9. (*vous*) Do you take one *piece* of sugar or two?   10. I decided that Jack should do that work *rather* than George.

Verb Review

Review the verbs **ouvrir** and **pouvoir** according to the outline on page 253.

CHAPTER
13

Indefinite Nouns

La maison

Il y a deux ans, dit-elle, quand je fus malade, je faisais toutes les nuits le même rêve. Je me promenais dans la campagne; j'apercevais de loin une maison blanche, basse et longue, qu'entourait un bosquet *de*[*] tilleuls[1]. À gauche de la maison, un pré bordé *de* peupliers rompait agré-
5 ablement la symétrie du décor, et la cime[2] de ces arbres, que l'on voyait de loin, se balançait au-dessus des tilleuls.

Dans mon rêve, j'étais attirée par cette maison et j'allais vers elle. Une barrière peinte en blanc fermait l'entrée. Ensuite on suivait une jolie allée bordée *d*'arbres sous lesquels je trouvais les fleurs du printemps: *des*
10 primevères[3], *des* pervenches[4], beaucoup *d*'anémones[5] qui se fanaient dès que je les cueillais. Devant la maison s'étendait une grande pelouse bien tondue[6], entourée *d*'une bande *de* fleurs violettes.

La maison, bâtie *de* pierres blanches, portait un toit *d*'ardoises[7]. Une porte *de* chêne[8] clair était au sommet d'un petit perron[9]. J'avais <u>envie</u>[**]
15 de visiter cette maison, mais personne ne répondait à mes appels. J'étais profondément désappointée, je sonnais, je criais, et enfin je me réveillais.

Tel était mon rêve et il se répéta, pendant *de* longs mois, avec une précision et une fidélité telles que je finissais par penser que j'avais cer- tainement, dans mon enfance, vu ce parc et ce château. Pourtant je ne
20 pouvais en retrouver le souvenir, et cette recherche devint pour moi une obsession si forte qu'un été, ayant appris à conduire une petite voiture, je décidai de passer mes vacances sur les routes de France, à la recherche de la maison de mon rêve.

Je ne vous raconterai pas mes voyages. J'explorai la Normandie, la
25 Touraine, *d*'autres provinces et ne trouvai rien. En octobre je rentrai à

---

[*] The italicized **de** and **des** indicate that an indefinite noun follows.   [1] *linden trees*
[2] *top*   [3] *primroses*   [4] *periwinkles*   [5] *windflowers*   [6] *cut, mown*   [7] *slate*   [8] *oak*
[9] *flight of stairs at the top of which is a landing*   [**] Underscored words are examples of THE NOUN ALONE not preceded by **de**.

Paris et, pendant tout l'hiver, je continuai à rêver de la maison blanche. Au printemps, je recommençai mes promenades aux environs de Paris. Je n'avais pas eu *de* chance mais je ne me décourageai pas. Un jour, comme je traversais une vallée voisine de l'Isle-Adam, je sentis tout d'un

30 coup un choc agréable, cette émotion curieuse que l'on reconnaît, après une longue absence, *des* personnes ou *des* lieux que l'on a aimés.

Bien que je ne fusse jamais venue dans cette région, je connaissais parfaitement le paysage qui s'étendait à ma droite, les cimes *de* peupliers qui dominaient la masse *de* tilleuls, le tapis *de* fleurs, la pelouse verte, le

35 petit perron, la porte *de* chêne clair . . . Je sus sans aucun doute que j'avais trouvé le château de mes rêves. Je sortis de ma voiture, montai rapidement les marches et sonnai.

J'avais très <u>peur</u> que personne ne répondît, mais, presque tout de suite, un domestique parut. C'était un homme au visage triste, fort vieux et

40 vêtu d'un veston noir. En me voyant, il parut très surpris et me regarda avec <u>attention</u>, sans parler.

—Je vais, lui dis-je, vous demander une faveur un peu étrange. Je ne connais pas les propriétaires de cette maison, mais je serais heureuse s'ils pouvaient m'autoriser à la visiter.

45 —Le château est à louer, Madame, dit-il, comme[10] à regret, et je suis ici pour le faire visiter.

—À louer? dis-je. Quelle chance! Comment les propriétaires eux-mêmes n'habitent-ils pas une maison si belle?

—Les propriétaires l'habitaient, Madame. Ils l'ont quittée depuis que

50 la maison est hantée.

—Hantée? dis-je. Voilà qui ne m'arrêtera guère. Je ne savais pas que, dans les provinces françaises, on croyait encore aux revenants[11].

—Je n'y croirais pas, Madame, dit-il sérieusement, si je n'avais moi-même si souvent rencontré dans le parc, la nuit, le[12] fantôme qui a mis

55 mes maîtres en fuite.

—Quelle histoire! dis-je en essayant de sourire.

—Une histoire, dit le vieillard d'un air *de* reproche, dont vous au moins, Madame, ne devriez pas rire, puisque ce fantôme, c'était vous.

D'après André Maurois, membre de l'Académie française, auteur très connu pour ses écrits sur la civilisation anglo-saxonne et ses biographies de grandes figures littéraires et politiques. («La Maison», dans *Toujours l'inattendu arrive*, Éditions de la Maison française, 1943)

---

[10] **comme à regret** *as if he regretted saying it*   [11] **ghosts**   [12]**le fantôme qui a mis mes maîtres en fuite** *the ghost that caused my masters to flee*

1. A noun may be definite, general, or indefinite. How is an indefinite noun expressed in English and in French?

Il y a **du papier** sur mon bureau.

There is (some) paper *on my desk.*

Vous trouverez **des cartes postales** dans le tiroir.

You will find (some) postcards *in the drawer.*

Avez-vous **des enfants?**

Have you any children?

In English, a noun is made indefinite either by the use of <u>the noun alone</u> or by the use of *some* or *any* with the noun.

In French, a noun is usually made indefinite by the partitive construction.

NOTE: In both French and English, a noun modified by the indefinite article is also indefinite. Ex.: **un livre** (*a book*), **une pomme** (*an apple*).

2. What are the partitive articles?

	Singular	Plural
Masculine	**du**	**des**
Feminine	**de la**	**des**
Masculine or feminine	**de l'**	**des**

If the word following the partitive singular begins with a vowel or a mute **h,** the form **de l'** must be used.

The partitive construction is, in effect, **de** + DEFINITE ARTICLE, but as a partitive it has lost its original meaning of *of the.*

3. What is the partitive construction?

Vous trouverez **du beurre** et **de la crème** au supermarché.

You will find butter *and* cream *in the supermarket.*

Y a-t-il **des chevaux** dans la ferme?

Are there any horses *on the farm?*

The partitive construction indicates that an indefinite quantity of a given noun (part of all there is) exists in the sentence at hand.

In French, a noun is made indefinite by the partitive construction except in certain cases, when <u>the noun alone</u> indicates indefiniteness. The fact that there are times when <u>the noun alone</u> rather than the partitive is used complicates the problem.

4. When an indefinite noun is modified by a preceding adjective, how is the partitive construction modified?

(a)   when the noun is singular

Nous avons entendu **de la belle musique.**	We *heard* some beautiful music.
Avez-vous **du bon vin?**	Do you *have* any good wine?

When an adjective precedes an indefinite singular noun, the partitive construction is normally used.

(b)   when the noun is plural

Nous avons vu **de jolies fleurs** dans le bois.	We *saw* some pretty flowers *in the woods.*
Il y a **de magnifiques châteaux** dans ce pays.	*There are* some magnificent castles *in that country.*

When a preceding adjective modifies a plural indefinite noun, **de** takes the place of the partitive construction. One normally finds **de** + ADJECTIVE + PLURAL NOUN.

5. When does one find *des* + adjective + plural noun?

Ils ont vu **des jeunes gens** sur le boulevard.	*They saw* some young men *on the boulevard.*
Y a-t-il **des jeunes filles** dans cette pension?	*Are there* any girls *in that boarding house?*
Voulez-vous **des petits pois?**	Do you *want* any peas?

When ADJECTIVE + NOUN constitute a unit, so that the adjective has lost its identity as an adjective, the construction is treated like a single word, and as a single word it is modified by the partitive article **des** with the plural noun.

A. Remplacez les tirets par l'article partitif ou par *de.* Expliquez oralement votre choix.

1. Il y a _____ arbres tout le long de la Seine.   2. Les étudiants vont au café passer _____ bons moments avec leurs camarades. 3. Avez-vous entendu _____ bon jazz hier soir?   4. Les femmes aiment acheter _____ nouvelles robes.   5. Avez-vous trouvé _____ petits pois dans ce magasin?   6. Il y a _____ excellents romans dans votre bibliothèque.   7. Ce fermier vient nous vendre _____ pommes de terre et _____ maïs.   8. Il n'est pas très intelligent, mais il a _____ bonne volonté.

B. Traduisez en français. Expliquez oralement chaque article partitif et chaque *de.*

1. (*vous*) I saw some cats and dogs in your garden.   2. There were some girls in the group who did not know how to speak French.

3. One finds good milk in Denmark.   4. Is there any ice in the refrigerator?   **5.** We drank some good cider in Normandy. 6. (*tu*) Were there any young men[1] on your boat?   7. There were numerous tourists on the beach.   8. They spent long hours in[2] the library.

---

[1] The plural of **jeune homme** is NOT «jeunes hommes».   [2] **à la**

6. Is an indefinite noun always modified by a partitive article?

J'ai **faim.**	*I'm* hungry. (lit., *I have* hunger.)
Jacques a travaillé avec **soin.**	*Jack worked with* care (*carefully*).
Nous sommes arrivés sans **argent.**	*We arrived without* money.
La maison est pleine de **poussière.**	*The house is full of* dust.

There are several cases in which an indefinite noun is not modified by a partitive but rather in which the noun stands alone.

We shall now examine each of these cases—and their exceptions.

7. When is the noun alone used in idiomatic sentences with *avoir*?

Marie **a soif.**	*Mary* is thirsty. (lit., *Mary* has thirst.)
J'**ai mal** à la gorge.	*I* have a sore throat. (lit., *I have* hurt *in the throat.*)

Certain set expressions made up of a form of **avoir** + the noun alone came into the language before there was any partitive article. Many of these expressions still exist.

8. When is the preposition *avec* used with the noun alone?

Pierre a accepté cette offre avec **hésitation.**	*Peter accepted that offer with* hesitation (i.e., hesitatingly, *in a hesitating manner*).
Sa femme l'a reçu avec **joie.**	*His wife received him with* joy (joyfully).

The preposition **avec** is used with abstract nouns alone when the resulting prepositional phrase indicates manner. Often this phrase can be expressed by an adverb in English.

9. When is the noun alone used with *sans* and *ni . . . ni . . .*?

Paul est parti sans **livres.**	*Paul left without* books.
Nous n'avons ni **crayons** ni **papier.**	*We have neither* pencils *nor* paper.

The noun alone follows **sans** and **ni . . . ni . . .** when it is an indefinite noun.

C. Traduisez en français. Expliquez oralement chaque omission de l'article partitif devant un nom indéfini.

1. The poor child is hungry.   2. Without friends life is not pleasant.   3. They fought with courage, but they lost.   4. Was he able to fix the faucet without tools?   5. What are we going to do? There are neither chairs nor tables here.   6. He claims that he has a headache.   7. We left their house without regret.   8. (*vous*) What are you afraid of?   9. (*vous*) If you are right, I must be wrong. 10. (*tu*) We need your dictionary.   11. (*tu*) Did you go out without a hat?   12. (*vous*) Are you sleepy? You are yawning all[1] the time. 13. (*tu*) "Will you help me move?" "With pleasure."   14. They are ashamed of their mistakes.   15. He is a lawyer; he speaks with ease.   16. I am cold and I have a sore throat.

[1] Use **sans** with the noun **arrêt** (*m.*).

10. How is an indefinite noun expressed when it is immediately preceded by the preposition *de*?

J'ai beaucoup **de travail.**	*I have a lot* of work.
Jacques n'a pas **de chance.**	*Jack doesn't have* any luck.
Ne me privez pas **de ciga-rettes.**	*Don't deprive me* of cigarettes.
Elle porte une robe **de soie.**	*She is wearing a silk* dress.

Whenever the preposition **de** precedes an indefinite noun for any reason whatever, the noun follows **de** immediately, without any partitive article.

We will now examine the cases in which **de** most often precedes an indefinite noun.

11. What construction follows adverbs of quantity?

Nous avons **beaucoup de livres.**	*We have* many books.
Avez-vous **assez d'argent?**	*Have you* enough money?
Il y a **trop de voitures** dans la rue.	*There are* too many cars *in the street.*

Adverbs of quantity are followed by **de** because of the nature of their meaning (*much of, enough of, too much of, more of,* etc.). The <u>noun alone</u> follows **de.**

NOTE 1: However, the adverb of quantity **bien** (meaning *many*) is followed by the partitive **des** before a plural indefinite noun. Ex.: Il a **bien des** ennuis. (He has *many* troubles.) **Bien des** fois nous restons à la maison. (*Many* times we stay home.)

The adverb **bien** is simply an intensifier; it does not affect the partitive article of the construction that follows it.

NOTE 2: **La plupart des** (*the majority of*) is followed by a definite noun and the plural form of the verb. Ex.: **La plupart des** romans sont intéressants. Here, **des** = **de** + **les** means *of the* and is not a partitive.

The only singular construction with **la plupart** is **la plupart du temps.** Otherwise, say: **la plus grande partie.** Ex.: **la plus grande partie de l'été,** etc.

12. **What construction follows the negative *pas* when it indicates negative quantity?**

Je n'ai **pas de temps** à perdre.	*I don't have* any time *to lose.*
Nous ne voyons **pas de bateaux.**	*We see* no boats.

When **pas** indicates negative quantity, it is followed by **de,** as are other adverbs of quantity. Then **pas** is translated into English as *not . . . any* or *no.*

NOTE: Therefore, in most cases **pas** is followed by **de** rather than the partitive article. By analogy, **de** also follows other negatives used quantitatively. Ex.: Il **n'a jamais d'argent.** (*He* never *has* any *money.*)

13. **When is *pas* followed by the partitive article?**

Ce n'est **pas du beurre.**	*That isn't* butter.
Ce ne sont **pas des soldats.**	*Those aren't* soldiers.

When **pas** is used as an absolute negative and indicates type or quality, **pas** is followed by the partitive article before the noun, and in that case is translated into English as *not.* This construction is most often found in sentences such as: **Ce n'est pas . . .** and **Ce ne sont pas . . . .**

14. **How is the indefinite noun expressed after verbs and adjectives regularly followed by *de*?**

Les enfants seront **privés de dessert.**	*The children will be* deprived of dessert.
Leur maison est **entourée d'agents.**	*Their house is* surrounded by policemen.
Il y a encore trop de gens qui **manquent de pain.**	*There are still too many people who* lack bread.
Le pays **manque de ressources.**	*The country* lacks resources.
Il **a rempli** le sac **de billets** de mille francs.	*He* filled *the bag* with *thousand-franc* bank notes.
J'ai besoin de timbres.	*I* need stamps.

Whenever a verb, adjective, or special construction is followed by **de,** the indefinite noun alone follows **de.**

15. How are English adjectives or phrases indicating material expressed in French?

une maison **de bois**	*a* wooden *house*
un chapeau **de paille**	*a* straw *hat*

Where English uses an adjective or a phrase of "material," French uses an adjectival phrase consisting of **de** + NOUN.

NOTE: Sometimes **en** is used to indicate material. One can say: **une maison de pierre** or **une maison en pierre.** But distinguish between **un sac d'argent** (*a bag of money,* or, *a bag of silver*) and **un sac en argent** (*a silver bag,* i.e., a bag made of silver).

D. Remplacez les tirets par l'article partitif ou par *de.* Expliquez oralement votre choix.

1. J'aimerais avoir un bon pull-over _____ laine.   2. Ces arbres ne sont pas _____ orangers, ce sont des pommiers.   3. Bien _____ étrangers viennent visiter l'Amérique.   4. Ses parents lui laissent trop _____ liberté pour son âge.   5. Donnez-moi une tasse _____ thé avec _____ citron, s'il vous plaît.   6. Ils ont plus _____ ressources que vous.   7. Nous ne mangeons pas _____ viande le soir.   8. Nous avons tous besoin _____ affection pour vivre.   9. Il y a bien _____ gens qui seraient heureux d'aller en France avec vous.   10. Cet arbre est plein _____ oiseaux tous les soirs.   11. Ce ne sont pas _____ maisons, ce sont des taudis.   12. Je me passerai _____ café parce qu'il m'empêche de dormir.

E. Traduisez en français. Expliquez oralement chaque emploi de l'article partitif ou du *de.*

1. We'll give them a silver tray for their wedding.   2. These men aren't spies.   3. Many[1] times I regretted my indifference.
4. They are students, and they have few distractions.   5. The room was full of people.   6. He bought a new silk shirt to go to Florida.
7. Those aren't mountains; they are hills.   8. That house is very quiet; one doesn't hear any noise there.   9. Today they use[2] machines for all sorts of things.   10. They always watch television and do not read any books.   11. He has good[3] qualities, but he lacks initiative.   12. We know few people in our building[4].
13. They sent him a package[5] filled with toys.   14. The majority of people like to travel.

[1] Use bien.   [2] Use a form of se servir de.   [3] *good qualities* = qualités   [4] Use immeuble.
[5] Use colis.

Exercices d'ensemble

F. Remplacez les tirets par *de* ou par l'article partitif dans les phrases où il faut avoir l'un ou l'autre.

1. Invitez _____ gens amusants à dîner.   **2.** Ce ne sont pas _____ Japonais, ce sont _____ Chinois.   **3.** Il faut apprendre le plus tôt possible à se débrouiller sans _____ argent.   **4.** Si vous voulez faire plaisir à votre femme, achetez-lui un manteau de fourrure. **5.** Vous avez _____ courage pour parler si franchement.   **6.** À l'université on ne veut pas _____ professeurs sans _____ doctorat.   **7.** Il y a bien _____ gens qui aimeraient avoir sa place. **8.** Nous avons passé _____ longues heures à Notre-Dame.   **9.** Il y a beaucoup _____ choses intéressantes à voir quand on voyage. **10.** Nous manquons _____ sucre.   **11.** Je connais _____ jeunes gens qui sont vraiment formidables.   **12.** Certains auteurs écrivent avec _____ facilité, mais moi, j'écris avec _____ peine. **13.** Allez donc dans ce café; on y sert _____ bon vin.

G. Traduisez en français.

1. One sees a lot of men without hats.   **2.** In that house there are some valuable pictures.   **3.** (*vous*) I learned with regret that you will no longer be with us next year.   **4.** There are elegant[1] hotels in all the large cities.   **5.** (*tu*) If you need money, you have only to tell me[2].   **6.** The majority of the pilots are strong men. **7.** There are still some poor areas where there are no schools. **8.** (*vous*) If you have neither pencil nor paper, you can return home. **9.** These aren't amateurs; they are true artists.   **10.** I have just bought a beautiful leather suitcase for my trip.   **11.** There is enough room in the car for everyone.

[1] First write the sentence with **élegant** following its noun; then write it with **élegant** preceding its noun.   [2] French often says *"tell me it."*

Problem Words

47. return

(a) When *return = give back*

Guy ne m'**a** pas encore **rendu** mon magnétophone.	*Guy* has *not yet* returned *my tape recorder to me.*

The verb **rendre** means *to return* in the sense of *give back.*

(b) When *return = come back*

Revenez le plus tôt pos- Return ⎫
   sible.   Come back ⎬ *as soon as possible.*

The verb **revenir** means *return* in the sense of *come back.*

(c) When *return = go back*

Je ne **retournerai** pas *I will not* ⎰ return ⎱ *to Paris at once.*
   tout de suite à Paris.   ⎱ go back ⎰

The verb **retourner** means *return* in the sense of *go back.*

CAUTION: DO NOT use «retourner» when you mean *return* in the sense of *come back* or *give back.* The verb **retourner** does not have the all-inclusive meaning of the English *return.*

(d) When *return = return home*

Tu   devrais   parler   à *You should speak to George; he*
   Georges; il **est rentré** à   returned
   trois heures du matin.   came back home ⎬ *at three in the*
                  morning. ⎰

The verb **rentrer** means *return* in the sense of *to return home.*

48. room

(a) How to express *room* without indicating the type of room

Combien de **pièces** y a-t-il dans *How many* rooms *are there in*
   ce château?   *that castle?*

The general word for *room* is **la pièce.**

(b) When *room = bedroom*

Est-ce que Madame Renaud loue *Does Mrs. Renaud rent* rooms?
   des **chambres?**

The word **chambre** indicates a *bedroom.*

(c) When a *room* is used for meetings

Nous   avons   besoin   d'une *We need a large* room *for our*
   grande **salle** pour notre pro-   *next meeting.*
   chaine réunion.

The word **salle** indicates a room used for meetings.

(d) When *room = space*

Il n'y a pas beaucoup de **place** *There isn't much* room *in your*
   dans ta voiture.   *car.*

When *room* = *space,* the French use **place.**

Note that **le salon** is the formal living room, but the room where the family lives is **la salle de séjour,** also called **le séjour.**

49. save

(a) When *save* means *to save from destruction*

Marius m'**a sauvé** la vie.	*Marius* saved *my life.*
L'inondation a tout emporté; on n'a rien pu **sauver.**	*The flood took everything; we couldn't* save *anything.*

The verb **sauver** indicates *saving a person or a thing from destruction.* It is most often used to refer to saving persons.

(b) When *save* means *to keep*

Nous **avons gardé** quelques fruits pour vos amis.	*We* saved *some fruit for your friends.*

The verb **garder** means *save* in the sense of *to keep.*

(c) How to say *save money*

Jean **a fait des économies** pour s'acheter une moto.	*John* has been saving up *in order to buy himself a motorcycle.*
J'ai donné une tirelire aux enfants pour les encourager à **économiser.**	*I gave a piggy bank to the children to encourage them to* save.
Économisez votre argent au lieu de le dépenser inutilement.	Save *your money instead of spending it uselessly.*

The expression **faire des économies** is often used to mean *to save money* in the sense of *to save up;* the verb **économiser** is used with or without an object to mean *to save money.*

(d) When *save* is expressed by **mettre de côté**

Je **mettrai** mes notes **de côté,** elles pourront vous être utiles plus tard.	*I will* save *my notes; they can be useful to you later.*
Les Berger **ont mis** assez **de côté** pour se faire construire une belle maison.	*The Bergers* saved *enough to have a nice house constructed for themselves.*

The expression **mettre de côté** means *save* in the sense of *put aside* something for later use, whether it be money or something else.

50. sit

(a) How to say that *someone is sitting* = *seated*

La dame **assise** devant moi avait une coiffure si haute que je ne pouvais rien voir.

The lady $\begin{cases} \text{sitting} \\ \text{seated} \end{cases}$ *in front of me had such a high hairdo that I couldn't see anything.*

When **assis** is used as a pure adjective, it means *sitting* or *seated.*

Tout le monde **est assis**; on peut commencer.

Everyone is $\begin{cases} \text{sitting down;} \\ \text{seated;} \end{cases}$ *we can begin.*

When **assis** follows the verb **être,** it is also an adjective. When *is sitting* (or its equivalent in other tenses) expresses a state rather than an action, it must be expressed by a form of **être assis.**

CAUTION: DO NOT express *is sitting* by the verb «s'asseoir»; rather, use a form of **être assis.**

(b) How to say that *someone is sitting down*

Après avoir chanté l'hymne national, tout le monde **s'est assis.**

After singing the national anthem, everyone sat down.

When *sit down* indicates an action rather than a state, a form of the verb **s'asseoir** must be used.

Note the difference between:

Elle **est assise.**   *She* is sitting (= is seated).
Elle **s'est assise.**   *She* sat down.

H. Remplacez les mots anglais par leur équivalent français.

1. Est-ce que le voisin nous (*returned*) notre échelle?   **2.** Les enfants sont trop grands; il leur faut une (*room*) à chacun.   **3.** Il y a bien des façons de (*save*).   **4.** Ouf! Quelle journée! Je suis content de (*sit down*).   **5.** Cela vaut toujours la peine de (*save*).   **6.** Le maire devrait faire construire une plus grande (*room*) pour les fêtes. **7.** Attendez-moi; je (*will return*) dans un instant.   **8.** On a pu (*save*) tous les papiers importants de l'incendie.   **9.** On est content de se remettre au travail en (*returning*) de vacances.   **10.** Inutile d'acheter ce buffet; il n'y aurait pas de (*room*) dans la salle à manger. **11.** Même dans les moments les plus durs, je (*saved*) de l'argent. **12.** Les Ponsard ont acheté une maison de dix (*rooms*) dans la banlieue.   **13.** Les Arnoux (*will not return*) à l'Hôtel Terminus, parce qu'il est devenu trop cher.   **14.** Lucie a fait un grand nettoyage; elle ne (*saved*) que quelques objets.   **15.** L'étudiant qui (*is sitting*) au cinquième rang s'endort toujours pendant le cours.

I. Traduisez en français. Attention aux mots en italique.

1. (*tu*) If you didn't smoke, you would *save* a great deal of money.
2. How can that family live in those two *rooms?*   3. Guy will *return* to Japan next year.   4. Marie-Claire bought some pretty green curtains for her *room.*   5. I *save* all the stamps I receive from abroad for Regis.   6. Juliette *sat down* on the sofa and listened to the music.   7. (*vous*) *Save up* for your old age.   8. In what *room* will the tournament be held?   9. (*tu*) *Return* home early this evening, since we are going out.   10. I like houses with a lot of *room.*   11. My old grandmother *was sitting* in her armchair near the window.   12. Their dog *saved* a child's life.   13. (*vous*) I am willing to lend you that book if you promise to *return* it to me.
14. When Roland receives his check, he always *saves* ten percent of it.   15. (*vous*) I didn't know that you had already *returned.*

Verb Review

Review the verbs **prendre** and **rire** according to the outline on page 253.

14

The Passive Voice and the Causative Construction

Une jeune fille de dix-sept ans, Cécile, très proche de son père, passe avec lui et des amis des vacances heureuses sur la Méditerranée. Le père, un veuf, a invité Anne Larsen, une ancienne amie de la famille, femme séduisante et autoritaire. Elle jette le trouble dans les relations entre le père qui lui fait la cour et Cécile qui veut se débarrasser d'elle et qui ne peut plus maintenant compter que sur elle-même dans la vie.

Émancipation

Mon père avait loué sur la Méditerranée une grande villa blanche, iso-lée, ravissante. Les premiers jours furent éblouissants[1]. Nous passions des heures sur la plage, prenant peu à peu une couleur saine et dorée. Dès l'aube, j'*étais plongée* dans l'eau, une eau fraîche et transparente où
5   je m'enfouissais[2], où je m'épuisais en des mouvements désordonnés pour me laver de toutes les poussières de Paris. Je m'allongeais dans le sable, en prenais une poignée[3] dans ma main, le laissais s'enfuir de mes doigts en un jet jaunâtre et doux; je me disais qu'il s'enfuyait comme le temps, que c'était une idée facile et qu'il était agréable d'avoir des idées faciles.
10   C'était l'été . . . Et puis Anne Larsen arriva . . .

---

[1] *fascinating, dazzling*   [2] *buried myself*   [3] *handful*

J'avais loupé[4] mon baccalauréat en juin. Anne disait qu'il fallait absolument que je le passe en octobre. Elle voulait me *faire travailler,* ces
vacances, ces vacances qui pourraient me faire tant de bien, et par ces
chaleurs! . . . J'eus[5] beau faire, c'était une femme[6] de tête. J'aurais voulu
15 *être appuyée* par mon père, mais il ne répondait à mes regards désespérés
que par de petits sourires gênés. Je *fus* donc *obligée* d'ouvrir quelquefois,
distraitement, mes livres de philosophie . . .

Un jour, cependant, où je somnolais[7] sur la plage, après le bain du
matin, mon père s'assit auprès de moi et me regarda. Je sentais son regard
20 peser sur moi. J'allais me lever et lui proposer d'aller dans l'eau, avec un
air faussement[8] enjoué, quand il posa sa main sur ma tête et éleva la voix
d'un ton lamentable:

—Anne, venez voir cette sauterelle[9], elle est toute maigre. Si le travail
lui fait cet effet-là, il faut qu'elle s'arrête.

25 Anne s'approchait. Elle s'assit près de nous et murmura:

—C'est vrai que ça[10] ne lui réussit pas. D'ailleurs, il lui suffirait de
travailler vraiment au lieu de tourner[11] en rond dans sa chambre.

Je m'étais retournée, je les regardais. Comment savait-elle que je ne
travaillais pas? Peut-être même avait-elle deviné mes pensées meurtrières[12]
30 à son égard. Je *fus prise* d'une peur subite à cette idée.

—Je ne tourne pas en rond dans ma chambre, protestai-je.

—Est-ce ton ami Cyril qui te manque? demanda mon père.

—Non!

C'était un peu faux. Mais il est vrai que je n'avais pas eu le temps de
35 penser à Cyril. Et il n'était pas question de le *faire revenir.*

—Tu ne te portes pas bien, dit mon père sévèrement. Anne, vous la
voyez? On dirait un poulet qu'on aurait vidé et qu'on *ferait rôtir* au
soleil.

—Ma petite Cécile, dit Anne, faites un effort. Travaillez un peu et
40 mangez beaucoup. Cet examen est important . . .

—Je[13] me fous de mon examen, criai-je, vous comprenez, je m'en fous!

Je la regardai désespérément, bien[14] en face, pour qu'elle comprît que
c'était plus grave qu'un examen. Il fallait qu'elle me dise: «Alors, qu'est-
ce que c'est?», qu'elle me harcèle[15] de questions, qu'elle me force à tout
45 lui raconter. Et là, elle me convaincrait, elle déciderait ce qu'elle voudrait,
mais ainsi je ne *serais* plus *infestée* de ces sentiments acides et dépri-
mants. Ma détresse devait pourtant *se voir* sur mon visage, *s'entendre*

---

[4] *failed*   [5] J'eus beau faire *In spite of anything I could do*   [6] une femme de tête *a
strong-willed woman*   [7] *was dozing*   [8] faussement enjoué *seemingly jovial*
[9] *grasshopper*   [10] ça ne lui réussit pas *that doesn't agree with her*   [11] tourner en
rond *walk around*   [12] *murderous*   [13] Je me fous de *I don't give a damn about*
[14] bien en face *straight in the eye*   [15] pester, *harass*

dans mes paroles. Elle me regardait attentivement, je voyais le bleu de ses yeux assombris par l'attention, le reproche. Et je compris que jamais
50 elle ne penserait à me questionner, à me délivrer parce qu'elle estimait que cela ne *se faisait* pas . . .

Je me rejetai sur le sable avec violence, j'appuyai ma joue sur la douceur chaude de la plage, je tremblai un peu. La main d'Anne, tranquille et sûre, *se posa* sur ma nuque un moment.

55 —Ne vous compliquez pas la vie, dit-elle. Vous qui étiez si contente, vous[16] qui n'avez pas de tête, vous devenez cérébrale[17] et triste. Ce[18] n'est pas un personnage pour vous . . . Venez déjeuner . . .

Mon père s'était éloigné; il n'*était* pas *fait* pour ce genre de discussions; dans le chemin, il me prit la main et la garda. C'était une main
60 dure et réconfortante: elle[19] m'avait mouchée à mon premier chagrin d'amour, elle avait tenu la mienne dans les moments de tranquillité et de bonheur parfait, elle l'avait serrée furtivement dans les moments de complicité et de fou-rire[20]. Cette main sur le volant, ou sur les clés, le soir, cherchant vainement la serrure, cette main sur l'épaule d'une femme
65 ou sur des cigarettes, cette main ne pouvait plus rien pour moi. Je la serrai très fort. Se tournant vers moi, il me sourit.

D'après Françoise Sagan. Depuis *Bonjour tristesse* écrit à vingt ans, elle connaît un grand succès avec des œuvres sensibles et élégantes, écrites dans la meilleure manière traditionnelle. (*Bonjour tristesse*, René Julliard, 1954)

---

[16] vous qui n'avez pas de tête *you who are not an intellectual*   [17] *intellectual*
[18] Ce n'est pas un personnage pour vous *That's out of character for you*
[19] elle m'avait mouchée *it (the hand) had consoled me (lit., had blown my nose)*
[20] *uncontrolled laughter*

I. The Passive Voice

When the subject of the sentence acts, we say that the sentence is in the ACTIVE VOICE. When the subject of the sentence is acted upon, we say that the sentence is in the PASSIVE VOICE.

ACTIVE VOICE	PASSIVE VOICE
John found *the money.*	*The money* was found *by John.*
The teacher will correct *that examination.*	*That examination* will be corrected *by the teacher.*

In the two examples above, note:

(a) The subject of the sentence in the active voice (*John, teacher*) becomes the object of the preposition *by* and is called the "agent" of the sentence in the passive voice.

(b) The object of the sentence in the active voice (*money, examination*) becomes the subject of the sentence in the passive voice.

(c) The verb of the sentence in the passive voice is in the same tense as the verb of the sentence in the active voice.

(d) The verb of the sentence in the passive voice is made up of a form of the auxiliary *to be* + THE PAST PARTICIPLE of the verb in the active voice.

1. How is the passive voice formed in French?

Cet escroc **sera mis** en prison.	*The swindler* will be put *in prison.*
Les enfants **étaient** toujours **récompensés** pour leurs bonnes notes.	*The children* were *always* rewarded *for their good marks.*
La maison **a été vendue** hier.	*The house* was sold *yesterday.*

In French, the passive voice is made up of:

> a form of auxiliary verb **être** + PAST PARTICIPLE

2. How and with what does the past participle of a verb in the passive voice agree?

(See examples in §1.)

The past participle of a verb in the passive voice agrees in gender and number with the subject of the sentence.

3. By what preposition is the agent usually introduced in French?

Cet article sera certainement lu **par tout le monde.**	*That article will certainly be read* by everyone.
Ce roman a été écrit **par un Russe.**	*That novel was written* by a Russian.
Cette maison a été détruite **par l'incendie.**	*This house was destroyed* by the fire.

In French, **par** usually introduces the phrases indicating the agent.

The agent is the person or the thing by which the action of a sentence in the passive voice is caused or performed.

4. When is *de* used to introduce the phrase indicating the agent?

Elle était aimée **de tous.**	*She was loved* by all.
Le Président était suivi **de plu-sieurs ministres.**	*The President was followed* by several ministers.
Il sera accompagné **de deux secrétaires.**	*He will be accompanied* by two secretaries.
La maison était entourée **d'un jardin.**	*The house was surrounded* by a garden.

The preposition **de** is less strong than **par.** It usually follows verbs that indicate a state, a mental action, or an habitual action, where the role of the agent is less dynamic.

Also, certain verbs are normally followed by **de,** as, for example, **entourer de, couvrir de, remplir de,** etc.

5. If a verb can be followed by both *par* and *de*, what determines whether *par* or *de* should introduce the phrase indicating the agent?

Les verres ont été de nouveau remplis **par** le garçon.	Les verres étaient remplis **de** vin.
L'enfant qui allait tomber a été saisi **par** son frère.	L'enfant était saisi **de** peur.
Irène était très aimée **par** son fiancé.	Irène était aimée **de** ses amis.

One can almost always use **par** to introduce a phrase indicating the agent unless the past participle is habitually followed by **de.**

The preposition **par** is dynamic, the preposition **de** is weaker. When the role of the agent is forceful, **par** is likely to be used; when the role of the agent is less active, **de** is often found. The preposition **par** is likely to indicate an action that took place at one time; both **par** and **de** may indicate habitual actions.

A. Mettez les verbes de phrases suivantes à la voix passive en employant le temps indiqué.

1. (PASSÉ COMPOSÉ) Cette chambre (réserver) par Monsieur et Madame Amieux, mais ils ne peuvent pas venir.   **2.** (PRÉSENT DE L'INDICATIF) Les fleurs (récolter) pour en faire des parfums.   **3.** (PRÉSENT DU SUBJONCTIF)   J'aimerais que Charlotte (inviter) à votre soirée.   **4.** (FUTUR)   Les   manifestations   (interdire)   à   l'Université.   **5.** (IMPARFAIT) Ce restaurant (tenir) par les parents de Pierre.   **6.** (FUTUR) Si le coup réussit, ce peuple (gouverner) par des gens capables de tout.   **7.** (PASSÉ DU SUBJONCTIF) Je ne crois pas que ce poème (écrire) par Georges.   **8.** (IMPARFAIT) Les hommes les plus influents (inviter) chez le maire.   **9.** (PASSÉ COMPOSÉ) Le petit garçon du voisin (mordre) par son chien.   **10.** (FUTUR) Dépêchez-vous, sinon toutes les cerises (cueillir).

B. Traduisez en français.

1. I wonder why Mr. Lenoir is being watched by the police.
2. Considerable sums are being spent each year by the state.
3. The criminal was being defended by Maître Olivier.
4. Everything they had was lost in this fire.   5. The new ambassador was received by the President.

6. **How does French often avoid an English passive when there is no agent expressed in the English sentence?**

On a donné le prix au meilleur élève.	*The prize* was given *to the best pupil.*
On verra l'éclipse demain soir.	*The eclipse* will be seen *tomorrow evening.*

Although the passive is by no means uncommon in French, it is not used as frequently as in English. There are certain verbs with which it is never used, other verbs with which it is not used in certain tenses, still others where it could be used but sounds somewhat unnatural. Long experience in speaking French is necessary to develop a precise feeling for when a French sentence sounds natural in the passive and when it does not. But French has various other ways of expressing certain sentences that English puts into the passive.

To express an English passive in a sentence where there is no agent, French often uses the indefinite pronoun **on** + VERB IN ACTIVE VOICE.

C. Traduisez en français en évitant la voix passive.

1. Why was I awakened at six o'clock?   2. How is this sentence translated?   3. That was said at the beginning of the hour.   4. The prizes will be distributed to the winners Saturday morning.   5. The door was opened to allow[1] a little more air to come in.   6. Bridge will be played after the reception.   7. Christmas carols are always sung in the month of December.   8. That evening[2] the doors were locked at 8:30.   9. French is spoken in that store.   10. His name was[3] taken out of the telephone book.

[1] *allow to come in* = laisser entrer   [2] In time expressions referring to the past, how is *that* expressed?   [3] *take out* = enlever

7. **How does French often avoid an English passive when an agent is expressed in the English sentence?**

Un célèbre humoriste **a dit** cela.	*That* was said *by a famous humorist.*
Ceux qui l'ont vu n'**oublieront** pas cet incident.	*That incident* will not be forgotten *by those who saw it.*

French often uses the active voice to express an idea that English might express with a sentence in the passive voice. Some French verbs are not normally used in the passive voice.

D. Traduisez en français en évitant la voix passive.

1. That explosion was heard by several persons.   2. The boss would be liked by everyone if he were more patient.   3. All the money for the family was earned by the oldest brother.   4. This doctor had been criticized by several of his colleagues.   5. The problem was explained to the students by the teacher.   6. That talk will be given[1] by a well-known specialist.   7. The car was driven by a sixteen-year-old boy[2].   8. By whom was that man seen?

[1] Use a form of faire.   [2] The French say: *a boy of sixteen years.*

8. **How does French express an English passive sentence whose subject would be the indirect object in the active sentence?**

Le notaire montrera le testament **aux héritiers** jeudi.	The heirs will be shown *the will* by the notary *Thursday.*
On a permis à Suzanne de passer le week-end chez les Grillet.	Suzanne was allowed *to spend the weekend at the Grillets'.*

Consider the passive and active forms of the following English sentence:

PASSIVE: *I was given the book by a friend.*
ACTIVE: A friend *gave* the book *to me.*

The subject of the passive sentence is *I.* This *I* would become *to me* in the active sentence. Thus, the subject of the passive sentence is the indirect object of the active sentence. As you can see from the preceding examples, this is not the case in French.

The indirect object of the active form of a French sentence CANNOT become the subject of the passive form of that sentence. Instead, French expresses the sentence in the active voice only.

E. Traduisez en français.

1. We were forbidden to enter that room.   2. The workmen were promised a raise in[1] pay.   3. (*vous*) You will be given the necessary information by my secretary.   4. We were served coffee and sandwiches on the plane.   5. The delegates were told to come back the next day.   6. The defendant was asked by the lawyer where he had been that evening.   7. (*vous*) You will be sent some

[1] de

samples by the salesman[2] of that company[3].   **8.** We were shown some snapshots at the Arnauds'[4].   **9.** The children were allowed to go to the movies yesterday evening.

[2] **représentant**   [3] **maison**   [4] In French, proper names do not take an -s in the plural. The plural is indicated by the plural form of the definite article.

9. When is the English passive expressed by a French reflexive?

Ce produit **se vend** partout.   *That product* is sold *all over.*
Ça ne **se fait** pas ici.   *That* isn't done *here.*

The reflexive form of a French verb is often used to express an English passive when the sentence describes a general rather than a specific action.

Compare the following three sentences, each of which has a different meaning, although English uses approximately the same construction in each.

a. Ce livre **se vend** partout.   *That book* is sold *everywhere.*

Here, French uses the reflexive form of the verb to describe a general action.

b. Ce livre **est vendu.**   *That book* is sold.

Here, a form of **être** + PAST PARTICIPLE describes a state, so that **vendu** is an adjective, and the sentence is not in the passive voice at all.

c. Ce livre **a été vendu** hier.   *That book* was sold *yesterday.*

Here, **a été vendu** is a real passive, which describes one specific action.

10. In what other way is the reflexive form of a French verb used to express an English passive?

Mon ami **s'appelle** Jean Colin.   *My friend* is called *Jean Colin.*
Orléans **se trouve** au sud de   *Orléans* is located *to the south*
  Paris.   *of Paris.*

The reflexive forms of certain French verbs are used idiomatically where English uses the passive voice. Each verb of this type must be learned individually with its meaning.

F. Traduisez en français.

1. Everything is done automatically in that factory.   **2.** The Pyrenees are[1] situated between France and Spain.   **3.** That telephone is used[2] only in case of an[3] emergency.   **4.** Green[4] was

[1] Use a form of **trouver.**   [2] Use a form of **employer.**   [3] Omit in French.   [4] Supply the definite article.

worn a great deal last year.   **5.** That is said, but it[5] isn't written.
6. Hundreds[6] of novels are published each year.

[5] ça   [6] Here, *hundreds* is a noun.

II.   The Causative Construction

11. What is the causative construction? With what verb does French express it?

Le professeur **fera lire** les élèves.	*The teacher* will have *the pupils* read.
Notre voisin **a fait peindre** la maison.	*Our neighbor* had *the house* painted.

The causative construction expresses the idea of "having something done" or of "having someone do something"—of causing something to be done or of causing someone to do something.

NOTE: When the English infinitive follows a form of *have,* it is used without *to.* For example, in the sentence "The teacher will have the pupils read," *read* is an infinitive without *to.*

In English, this idea is expressed by *have* + INFINITIVE or *have* + PAST PARTICIPLE.

NOTE: When the infinitive follows a form of *have,* it is used without *to.*

In French, the causative is expressed by **faire** + INFINITIVE.

The causative always has at least one object and often it has two objects.

NOTE: Consider the sentence: **Le professeur fera lire les élèves.** In this sentence, **les élèves** is the object of the verb **fera,** and the subject of the infinitive **lire.**

Now consider the sentence: **Notre voisin a fait peindre la maison.** Here, **la maison** is the object of the verb **peindre.**

In a sentence with a causative construction, the object is sometimes governed by a form of **faire,** sometimes by the INFINITIVE following **faire.**

12. When the causative has only one object, what kind of object is it?

Nous **ferons écrire les enfants.**	*We'll have* the children write.
Ils **faisaient écrire des lettres.**	*They* used to have letters written.

When a causative has only one object, it is always a direct object—whether a person or a thing.

G. Traduisez en français.

1. The teacher doesn't have Roger[1] work because he was sick.
2. Our neighbors are having a garage[1] built. **3.** (*vous*) Why did you have your father-in-law[1] intervene? **4.** (*tu*) When will you have the television[1] repaired? **5.** We'll have those records[1] played later.

[1] In the causative construction in French, the noun object directly follows the infinitive.

13. When a causative construction has two objects—usually a person and a thing—what kind of objects are they?

Nous avons fait étudier **sa leçon à Lucie.**	*We had* Lucy *study* her lesson.
Je ferai ranger **ses affaires à Jean.**	*I'll have* John *put* his things *in order.*

When a causative construction has two objects, the thing is the direct object and the person the indirect object.

NOTE: Occasionally, a causative construction has two personal objects. In such cases, the person receiving the action is the direct object of the infinitive, and the person performing the action is the agent and is introduced by **par.**

Le président fera présenter **le conférencier par son collègue.**	*The president will have* his colleague *introduce* the speaker.

14. Sometimes the use of the indirect object for the person causes ambiguity. How may this ambiguity be avoided?

J'ai fait écrire une lettre **par mon frère.**	*I had* my brother *write a letter.*
Il fait lire ce roman **par tous ses amis.**	*He has* all his friends *read that novel.*

In cases where the use of **à** + PERSONAL OBJECT could result in ambiguity, it is not incorrect to use that construction for the causative, but such a sentence is often made clearer by using instead **par** + PERSONAL OBJECT.

NOTE: Equally correct is: **J'ai fait écrire une lettre à mon frère.** But this could mean either: "I had a letter written to my brother" or "I had my brother write a letter." Likewise, equally correct is: **Il fait lire ce roman à tous ses amis.** But this could mean either: "He has all his friends read that novel" or "He has that novel read to all his friends."

H. Traduisez en français.

1. We had his parents correct his mistakes. **2.** Mr. Géré had his wife pack[1] his suitcase. **3.** Businessmen have their secretaries[2]

[1] *pack a suitcase* = faire une valise   [2] Use the singular in French.

write their letters.   4. I will have the cleaning woman wash the windows.   5. That teacher has all his students copy the same poem.

15. When the causative construction governs a pronoun object, what is the position of the pronoun object?

Jacques **fera lire le testament de son oncle.**	Jacques **le fera lire.**
Nous **ferons réparer notre voiture** demain.	Nous **la ferons réparer** demain.
La ville **a fait abattre cette vieille maison au propriétaire.**	La ville **la lui a fait** abattre.
Mon père **m'a fait recommencer mes devoirs.**	Mon père **me les a fait recommencer.**

The pronoun objects of a causative construction normally precede the form of the verb **faire.** Pronouns come in their usual order.

NOTE: When the causative construction is in the affirmative imperative, pronoun objects follow the form of **faire.** Ex.: **Faites-le lire.**

16. When the verb *faire* is used in a compound tense, what about the agreement of its past participle with a preceding direct object?

Je **les ai fait** vendre.	*I* had them *sold.*
Où sont **les lettres que** nous **avons fait** copier?	*Where are* the letters *that we* had *copied?*

When the past participle of the verb **faire** is followed by an infinitive, the past participle of **faire** is always invariable. In other words, when it is used as part of the causative construction, the past participle of **faire** does not agree with its preceding direct object.

I.   Copiez les phrases françaises et traduisez en français les phrases anglaises. Attention à la position et à l'ordre des pronoms compléments.

(Use the French sentence of the exercise as a model in translating the following English sentence. Watch the position and order of pronoun objects and the agreement of the past participle.)

1. Avez-vous fait construire le garage cette année? (*Yes, I had it constructed this year.*)   2. Ferez-vous envoyer ce paquet par avion? (*Yes, I'll have it sent by plane.*)   3. Faisiez-vous travailler vos élèves pendant les week-ends? (*Yes, I used to have them work during the weekends.*)   4. M. Duchamp a-t-il fait couper ces beaux arbres? (*No, he didn't have them cut down.*)   5. Le médecin vous a-t-il fait prendre un nouveau remède? (*No, he didn't have me take any.*)

6. Claude vous a-t-il fait conduire sa voiture? (*Yes, he had me drive it.*)   7. Leur mère a-t-elle fait ranger leurs jouets aux enfants? (*Yes, she had them put them away.*)

Exercices d'ensemble

J. Répondez aux phrases suivantes en vous servant du nom donné après la question et en employant la forme passive.

MODÈLE: Qui a annoncé la nouvelle? M. Lemaître.
  La nouvelle a été annoncée par M. Lemaître.

1. Qui chantera l'hymne national? Mme Robin, de l'Opéra.   2. Qui vend ces terrains? Mon frère.   3. Qui a blessé cet homme? Le patron du café.   4. Qui a attaqué cette ville? Un groupe de rebelles.   5. Qui invitera les étudiants après la cérémonie? Le doyen.   6. Qui avait repeint cet appartement? Le propriétaire lui-même.   7. Qui explorait alors ces territoires? Les Français.   8. Qui a mené Lucie à la gare? Henri.   9. Qui a recommandé ce remède? Le docteur Cler.   10. Qui a écrit cette lettre? Mon avocat.

K. Les phrases suivantes indiquent que le sujet accomplit une action. Changez-les de sorte que le sujet fasse accomplir cette action.

1. Nos voisins peindront leur maison en rouge vif.   2. Suzanne a cueilli les plus belles fleurs pour son salon.   3. Jacques lavait sa voiture quand elle était vraiment sale.   4. Denise a fait une très jolie robe pour le mariage.   5. Je traduirai cette lettre.   6. Vous pouvez ouvrir le coffre-fort.   7. Il faudra tondre la pelouse aujourd'hui.   8. Nous enverrons le colis par exprès.

Problem Words

51. soon

(a) When *soon* is expressed by **bientôt**

Ma fille aura **bientôt** vingt ans.   *My daughter will* soon *be twenty years old.*

The common word for *soon* is **bientôt**. But **bientôt** is not usually modified.

(b) When *soon* is expressed by **tôt**

Ne venez pas si **tôt**.   *Don't come so* soon.
Vous avez parlé trop **tôt**.   *You spoke too* soon.
Il aurait fallu faire cela **plus tôt**.   *You should have done that* sooner.

To express *soon* modified by an adverb, use **tôt.** Also, **tôt** is used in the expression **tôt ou tard,** which means *sooner or later.*

(c) Expressions embodying *soon*

dès que (common) **aussitôt que** (mainly literary) }	*as soon as*
dès que possible **aussitôt que possible** **le plus tôt possible** **au plus tôt** }	*as soon as possible*

52. spend

(a) When it is a question of *spending money*

Vous **dépensez** beaucoup trop d'**argent** pour des choses superflues.

You spend *much too much* money *for* superfluous things.

The verb **dépenser** is used when it is a question of *spending money.*

(b) When it is a question of *spending time*

Nous **avons passé deux semaines** au Portugal.
J'**ai passé une heure** à écrire cette lettre.

We spent two weeks *in Portugal.*
I spent an hour *writing that letter.*

The verb **passer** is used when it is a question of *spending time.*

CAUTION: The verb **passer** must NOT be followed by the present participle to express the idea of spending a given amount of time doing something. French expresses this construction by **à** + INFINITIVE.

53. stop

(a) When *stop* may be expressed by **cesser**

Le bruit **a cessé.**
Tiens! Il **a cessé de neiger.**
Quand est-ce que les gens du dessus **cesseront de faire** tout ce bruit?

The noise stopped.
Look! It has stopped snowing.
When will the people upstairs stop making *all that noise?*

The verb **cesser** never takes a direct object. It is most often used with **de** + INFINITIVE, although it may be used as in the first example when a thing is the subject of the verb.

(b) When *stop* may be expressed by **arrêter**

Arrêtez donc **la voiture** un peu plus doucement.
Arrête donc **de prendre** tous ces médicaments!

Stop the car *a little more gently.*

Stop taking *all that medicine!*

The verb **arrêter** is usually followed by a direct object. It is sometimes followed by **de** + INFINITIVE.

(c) When *stop* may be expressed by **s'arrêter**

Nous **nous sommes arrêtés** pour admirer la vue.	*We* stopped *to admire the view.*
Je ne peux pas **m'arrêter** si près du carrefour.	*I can't* stop *so near the crossing.*
Il **s'est arrêté de parler.**	*He* stopped talking.

The reflexive form **s'arrêter** is used when no object follows. It is sometimes followed by **de** + INFINITIVE.

54. such

(a) How to say *such a* + NOUN

Avez-vous jamais entendu **une histoire pareille?**
Avez-vous jamais entendu **une histoire comme ça?**   ·*Have you ever heard* such a story?
Avez-vous jamais entendu **une telle histoire?**

The English *such a* + NOUN may be expressed by **un** + NOUN + **pareil,** by **un** + NOUN + **comme ça,** and by **un tel** + NOUN.

(b) How to say *such a* + ADJECTIVE

Je n'ai jamais entendu une histoire **aussi (tellement) drôle.**
Je n'ai jamais entendu une histoire **aussi drôle que ça.**   *I never heard* such a funny *story.*

The English *such a* + ADJECTIVE may be expressed by **aussi (or tellement)** + ADJECTIVE or **aussi** + ADJECTIVE + **que ça.**

L. Remplacez les mots anglais par leur équivalent français.

1. Pourquoi Nicolas est-il rentré (*sooner*) que toi?   **2.** (*tu*) Où (*will you spend*) les trois mois d'été?   **3.** Voulez-vous (*stop*) votre taxi au coin de la rue?   **4.** Si Marcel ne revient pas (*soon*), je m'en vais. **5.** J'ai dû (*stop*) plusieurs fois en route pour me reposer. **6.** Personne ne peut (*spend*) tant d'argent sans se ruiner.   **7.** (*As soon as*) vous recevrez sa lettre, prévenez-moi.   **8.** Je ne peux rien entendre; (*stop*) l'aspirateur, s'il te plaît.   **9.** Quand Thomas (*stops*) de travailler, c'est pour dormir.

M. Traduisez en français. Attention aux mots en italique.

1. (*vous*) You'll come to see me *soon,* won't you?   **2.** Ah, that Micheline! She never *stops* talking!   **3.** I never saw *such* a hard exercise! 4. *Stop* making that noise! 5. (*vous*) If you *spend* your money like that, you won't go[1] far. 6. (*vous*) Come *soon* enough to have[2] dinner with us. 7. (*tu*) If you need information, *stop* someone on[3] the street. 8. *Such a* person should be the mayor of the city. 9. I *stopped* to have[4] lunch at the Hôtel de la Poste. 10. We are invited to *spend* the evening at Dr.[5] Beaugendre's. 11. (*vous*) Come[6] and see me *as soon as possible.* 12. Won't it ever *stop* raining? 13. I have rarely heard *such a* boring lecture. 14. (*tu*) Have you ever seen *such a* monster?

[1] Use a form of **aller loin.** [2] *have dinner* = **dîner** [3] **dans** [4] *have lunch* = **déjeuner** [5] Use the article before such titles. [6] French uses **venir** + INFINITIVE.

Verb Review

Review the verbs **savoir** and **suivre** according to the outline on page 253.

CHAPTER
15

The verb *devoir*

Les grands-parents de la narratrice sont originaires du Québec. Un jour, le grand-père se représente les grandes plaines de l'Ouest et veut partir. La grand-mère résiste longtemps et cède enfin. «C'est presque toujours, dans une famille, le rêveur qui l'emporte», écrit Gabrielle Roy. De nombreux Québecois ont ainsi quitté leur province, autrefois, pour des plaines plus fertiles.

Souvenirs du Canada

De nouveau, l'année suivante, à l'automne, à l'époque des moissons qu'elle aimait tant, je partis avec ma mère pour notre visite annuelle à son frère.

Nous arrivâmes chez l'oncle Cléophas en[1] plein temps des battages.

5   Quelle activité régnait alors dans nos fermes du Manitoba! Douze à quinze hommes, loués pour la saison, logeaient à la ferme; quelques-uns *devaient* coucher dans de petites granges aménagées[2] en dortoirs, avec la porte toujours ouverte pour admettre l'air.

Ces gens, à la fois serviteurs, hôtes et amis, venaient de tous les coins
10   du Canada, je *devrais* dire du monde peut-être, car chose bien étonnante, des hommes de nationalité et de caractère les plus divers s'étaient assemblés dans nos terres lointaines pour récolter le blé: jeunes étudiants, vieux bougres[3] revenus de tout, voyageurs[4] de passage, conteurs[5] nés, émigrés de toutes sortes.

15   En cette maison perdue au milieu de la plaine, pendant les veillées[6], vibrait quelque chose de l'univers. Car jamais la fatigue de ces hommes ne *devait* les empêcher, le soir venu, de raconter un peu leur vie, de

---

[1]en plein temps des battages *in the middle of the threshing season*   [2] aménagées en dortoirs *arranged as dormitories*   [3] bougres revenus de tout *disillusioned fellows*
[4]voyageurs de passage *travelers passing through*   [5]conteurs nés *born storytellers*
[6] *evening social gatherings*

tâcher de se communiquer quelque chose d'unique en chacun d'eux et qui les rapprochait.

20   C'est de ces soirées de chants et d'histoires que date sans doute mon désir d'apprendre à bien raconter car j'avais saisi alors le poignant[7] et miraculeux pouvoir de ce don.

Maman, il est vrai, m'en avait toujours donné l'exemple, mais jamais comme en ces temps de forte stimulation où le passé revivait en elle avec 25   une force particulière . . .

Plus d'une fois, déjà quand j'étais enfant, elle m'avait raconté l'arrivée des grands-parents dans l'Ouest; elle m'avait redit comment, *ayant dû* quitter notre village, tous entassés dans le chariot[8] couvert, serrés les uns contre les autres, grand-mère ayant emporté quelques-uns de ses meu- 30   bles, son rouet[9] et d'innombrables ballots, ils s'en allaient à travers l'immense pays.

—La plaine alors, me disait-elle, paraissait encore plus immense qu'aujourd'hui, et le ciel aussi, plus immense; car il n'y avait pour ainsi dire pas de village le long de la piste et même très peu de maisons. En 35   apercevoir une, tout au loin, à une grande distance, était déjà toute une aventure. . . .

Ce soir-là, dans la grande salle de la ferme, j'écoutais ma mère et l'oncle Cléophas un peu à l'écart et occupés à se[10] remémorer grand-mère.

40   Un tout jeune homme réfugié dans un coin de la salle jouait doucement de l'harmonica. L'air un peu traînant formait un accompagnement discret aux paroles et peut-être les poussait-il quelque peu à la nostalgie.

—Te souviens-tu, Eveline, rappela mon oncle, de sa colère subite qu'elle nous fit le premier soir où en chariot vers notre destination, 45   n'ayant pas trouvé en route de maison pour nous loger, nous *avons dû* camper à[11] la belle étoile? Était-ce à cause du feu qui prenait[12] mal? Était-ce la peur de la plaine nue tout autour? Elle se dressa, nous traitant de bohémiens[13] et nous menaça: «Tiens, j'en ai assez de vous suivre, bande d'inconnus[14]! Allez[15] donc votre chemin; moi, j'irai le mien».

50   Maman souriait avec un peu de tristesse.

—Avant de quitter son village, elle n'avait sans doute pas entrevu toute l'ampleur du changement. C'est le soir dont tu parles qu'elle[16] *a dû* en saisir la portée.

—Mais nous traiter d'inconnus! Et d'ailleurs, *il fallait* partir, soutint

---

[7] *intense, gripping*   [8] chariot couvert *covered wagon*   [9] *spinning wheel*   [10]se remémorer *recall*   [11] à la belle étoile *in the open*   [12] qui prenait mal *which wouldn't start*   [13] *gypsies*   [14] *strangers*   [15] **Allez** votre chemin *You go your way*   [16] qu'elle a dû en saisir la portée *that she must have understood the significance of*

55 mon oncle. Là-bas, dans les collines, rappelle-toi, Eveline, ce n'était que cailloux, maigre terre . . .

—Sans doute, dit maman, mais elle y était attachée, et toi-même tu *dois* savoir à présent que l'on ne s'attache pas uniquement à ce qui nous est doux et facile.

60 —Qu'aurions-nous pu faire d'autre que ce que nous avons fait? reprit mon oncle. L'Ouest nous appelait. C'était l'univers alors. Du reste, il nous a donné raison.

D'après Gabrielle Roy, une des romancières les plus en vue d'un groupe brillant d'écrivains canadiens aussi estimés en France que dans leur pays d'origine. (*La Route d'Altamont,* Editions H. M. H. Montréal and Editions Flammarion, 1966)

The verb **devoir** constitutes a difficulty for an English-speaking person because no one English verb corresponds exactly to the French verb **devoir.** Each tense of **devoir** has its own translation, and in some tenses **devoir** may have several meanings, according to the context.

1. What meanings may *devoir* have in the present tense?

M. Guillot **doit** arriver demain.	*Mr. Guillot* is to *arrive tomorrow.*
Vous **devez** partir tout de suite.	*You* must (have to) *leave at once.*
Anne **doit** beaucoup aimer la musique.	*Anne* must *like* (probably *likes*) *music a great deal.*
Votre fils **doit** lire beaucoup.	*Your son* must *read* (has to *read*) (probably *reads*) *a great deal.*

In the present tense, **devoir** means either *is to* (*am to, are to*) or *must.* But *must* itself has two possible meanings: *has to* and *probably does.* In the second example above, *must* clearly means *have to.* The *must* of the third example clearly means *probably does.* But in the fourth example, there are two possibilities. "*Your son must read a great deal*" may mean: *Your son has to read a great deal,* or: *Your son probably reads a great deal.* When the two possible interpretations exist, the context decides.

A. Traduisez en anglais les phrases suivantes. Attention au verbe *devoir.* Si vous traduisez ce verbe par *must,* indiquez le sens de *must.*

1. Mon collègue *doit* me rendre mon livre demain, et je vous le passerai. **2.** Si vous *devez* leur écrire, faites-le tout de suite. **3.** Il *doit* y avoir des ours dans cette forêt.   **4.** On *doit* toujours faire de son mieux.   **5.** Le professeur *doit* nous expliquer ces règles cette semaine.   **6.** Vous *devez* avoir beaucoup d'argent.

2. What meanings may *devoir* have in the imperfect?

M. Guillot **devait** arriver ce matin.	*Mr. Guillot* was to *arrive this morning.*
Gilbert **devait** travailler plus dur pour se rattraper.	*Gilbert* had to *work harder to catch up.*
Ces gens-là **devaient** être très riches.	*Those people* must have *been* (probably *were*) *very rich.*
Votre fils **devait** lire beaucoup.	*Your son* used to have to *read* probably used to *read* } a *great deal.*

In the imperfect, **devoir** sometimes means *was to* (*were to*), sometimes *had to,* and sometimes *must have.* (Occasionally, the imperfect of **devoir** has other less common meanings.)

3. When does the imperfect of *devoir* mean *had to* and when *must have*?

Claude **devait** finir son travail avant de s'occuper de nous.	*Claude* had to *finish his work before turning his attention to us.*
Cet homme **devait** savoir plusieurs langues.	*That man* must have *known* (probably *knew*) *several languages.*

When the imperfect of **devoir** represents the past of the English *must = have to,* it is often translated by *had to.*

When the imperfect of **devoir** is the past of the English *must = probably does,* it is usually translated by *must have = probably did.*

When the imperfect of **devoir** is expressed by the English *must have,* it normally represents an habitual state or action. Even though *must have* looks like an English present perfect, it corresponds to the French imperfect of **devoir.** The best way to determine the proper translation is to rephrase the sentence, using the word *probably* + THE MAIN VERB.

B. Traduisez en anglais les phrases suivantes. Attention au verbe *devoir.*

1. Nous *devions* partir demain, mais c'est impossible.   **2.** Avant de sortir le soir, nous *devions* montrer à nos parents ce que nous avions fait.   **3.** Votre neveu *devait* être bien embarrassé chaque fois que vous racontiez cette histoire.   **4.** Quand Florence habitait chez nous, elle *devait* passer l'après-midi à garder les enfants. **5.** Les Lemaire *devaient* faire le tour du monde cet été, mais ils n'ont pas pu.

4. What two meanings may *devoir* have in the compound past?

J'**ai dû** travailler toute la nuit pour faire mes devoirs.	*I* had to *work the whole night to do my exercises.*
Guy **a dû** se faire mal en tombant.	*Guy* must have *hurt himself (probably hurt himself) when he fell.*
Leurs portes étaient fermées à clé; les voisins **ont dû** entrer par la fenêtre.	*Their doors were locked; the neighbors* must have }*entered through* probably } *the window.*

In the compound past, the verb **devoir** sometimes means *had to,* which is the past of *must = has to.* This is clearly the case in the first example above. It sometimes means *must have = probably did,* which is the past of *must = probably does.* This is clearly the case in the second example above. But in the third example, either possibility is present, and the context must decide.

When the imperfect of **devoir** means *must have,* it describes a customary state or action, whereas when the compound past of **devoir** means *must have,* it indicates a past action at one definite past time.

C. Traduisez en anglais les phrases suivantes. Attention au verbe *devoir.*

1. Si vous étiez chez les Lagarde, vous *avez dû* voir Pierre. 2. Personne ne parlait anglais ici; Agnès *a dû* aller en Angleterre pour l'apprendre.   3. Comme il n'y avait pas assez de place dans la voiture, nous *avons dû* laisser les enfants à la maison.   4. Julien n'est pas encore là; il *a dû* se tromper de route.

5. What does *devoir* mean in the conditional?

On annonce le froid; vous **devriez** mettre un manteau.	*They say it will be cold; you* should *put on an overcoat.*
Les Lepic **devraient** être plus patients avec leurs enfants.	*The Lepics ought to be more patient with their children.*

In the conditional, **devoir** means *should, ought to.*

6. What does *devoir* mean in the past conditional?

Les Aubry n'**auraient** pas **dû** acheter cette voiture.	*The Aubrys should* not *have bought that car.*
Vous **auriez dû** nous dire que vos parents seraient là.	*You* ought to have *told us that your parents would be there.*

In the past conditional, **devoir** means *should have, ought to have.*

D. Traduisez en anglais. Attention au verbe *devoir*.

1. Les Bréger *auraient dû* prendre l'avion pour venir ici.   **2.** Nous *devrions* leur dire de quoi il s'agit.   **3.** Georges, tu *devrais* aider ton frère à finir sa leçon.   **4.** Robert *aurait dû* faire cela quand je le lui ai demandé.   **5.** Ce film est très drôle; vos amis *devraient* aller le voir.

7. In what other ways does French express the idea of *must = has to?*

Il faut que vous vous couchiez plus tôt.	You must *go to bed earlier.*
Nous étions obligés de surveiller cet enfant tout le temps.	We used to have to *watch that child all the time.*

Note the following equivalents:

Je dois + INFINITIVE	**Il faut que je** + SUBJUNCTIVE	**Je suis obligé de** + INFINITIVE
Je devais + INFINITIVE	**Il fallait que je** + SUBJUNCTIVE	**J'étais obligé de** + INFINITIVE
J'ai dû + INFINITIVE	**Il a fallu que je** + SUBJUNCTIVE	**J'ai été obligé de** + INFINITIVE
Je devrai + INFINITIVE	**Il faudra que je** + SUBJUNCTIVE	**Je serai obligé de** + INFINITIVE

In the present, imperfect, compound past, and future, the appropriate tenses of *must = have to* may also be expressed by forms of **il faut que** + SUBJUNCTIVE and by forms of **être obligé de** + INFINITIVE.

The **il faut que** construction is somewhat stronger than **devoir.** When *must* is expressed by forms of **être obligé de,** it is about the equivalent of *to be obliged to.* Sometimes, but not always, any of the three forms may be used to express the same idea.

NOTE: In affirmative statements the verb **falloir** has two meanings: *must* and *be necessary.* For instance, **Il faut être là** and **Il faut que vous soyez là** means both *You must be* there and *It is necessary for you to be there.* But in negative statements, **falloir** means only *must not.* For instance, **Il ne faut pas être là** and **Il ne faut pas que vous soyez là** mean only *You must not be there.* They do not mean "It is not necessary that you be there."

E. Traduisez en français chaque phrase de trois façons différentes.

1. We used to have to work every day except Sunday. **2.** Yesterday I had to leave at five o'clock.   **3.** Our friends have to stay in Bordeaux this evening.   **4.** The Leclercs[1] will have to move next week.

[1] In French, the plural form of proper names does not take an *-s.*

Exercices d'ensemble

F. Remplacez par la forme convenable de ***devoir*** les mots anglais entre parenthèses.

1. Nous (*had to*) prendre l'autocar pour aller à Paris hier. 2. Même si cela vous ennuie, vous (*must*) leur faire cette visite. 3. Les acteurs (*must have been*) furieux chaque fois qu'ils lisaient les critiques de M. Lafont. 4. Georges (*has to*) finir cette affaire avant de partir. 5. Maurice est seul; nous (*should have*) l'inviter pour dimanche. 6. Je (*am to*) passer mon examen aujourd'hui. 7. Madame Gervaise est toute pâle, elle (*must*) être malade. 8. François (*must have*) perdre sa montre, il n'en porte plus. 9. Les Gaspard (*were to*) arriver ce matin; je me demande pourquoi ils ne sont pas là. 10. Vous (*should*) acheter une nouvelle voiture. 11. Le gardien (*had to*) nous ouvrir la porte chaque fois que nous arrivions tard dans la nuit.

G. Traduisez en français les phrases suivantes, en employant dans chaque phrase une forme du verbe ***devoir.***

1. (*vous*) You *should* always *knock* before entering a room[1]. 2. Mrs. Henriot was always very elegant; her husband *must have spent* a lot of money on[2] her. 3. The visitors *must* not *touch* the paintings. 4. We *had to hand in* our papers[3] yesterday morning. 5. Hubert *was to write* me every day, but I have received only one letter from him. 6. George doesn't have any money; he *must have spent* it last week. 7. Our neighbors have a new boat; they *must be* rich. 8. My friends are late; they *should have taken* a taxi. 9. We *are to eat* at grandmother's today. 10. When I was young, I *used to have to get up* at six in[4] the morning.

[1]pièce   [2]pour   [3]Not «papiers»   [4]du

Problem Words

55. take

(a) When *take is expressed by* **prendre**

Qui **a pris** la voiture? *Who took the car?*

The verb **prendre** is the most common way to express *take*. But it cannot be used indiscriminately to express *take*.

(b) When *take* is expressed by **porter** or **apporter**

Le chauffeur **a porté** nos valises au taxi. *The driver took our suitcases to the taxi.*

When *take* is the equivalent of *carry to,* it is usually expressed by **porter** or **apporter.**

(c) When *take* is expressed by **emporter**

N'**emporte** pas la télévision   *Don't* take the television *into*
dans ta chambre.   *your room.*

When *take* means *to carry something away,* it may be expressed by **emporter.**

(d) When *take* is expressed by **mener**

Nous **avons mené** nos invités   *We* took *our guests to the res-*
au restaurant.   *taurant.*

French has several ways of expressing *to take a person (somewhere).* When the verb **mener** is used, the destination must be indicated.

(e) When *take* is expressed by **emmener**

J'**emmène** Françoise ce soir.   *I* am taking *Frances* (with me)
                                     this evening.

J'**emmène** Françoise **au ci-**   *I* am taking *Frances* to the mov-
néma ce soir.   ies *this evening.*

The verb **emmener** means *to take someone away.* It may be used either with or without the destination.

NOTE: In certain cases, forms of the verb **amener** may also be used to express the idea of taking *a person or thing away,* but **amener** also has the meaning of *bringing a person or a thing.*

(f) How to say *to take time to . . .*

Le menuisier **a mis** cinq jours   *The carpenter* took *five days* to
à ⎫   do *that work.*
  ⎬**faire** ce travail.
pour⎭

The idiomatic **mettre** + period of time + **à** (or **pour**) + INFINITIVE expresses *to take (so much) time to do something.*

(g) How to say *to take an examination*

Nous **passons notre examen**   *We* take our test *at two o'clock.*
à deux heures.

The expression **passer un examen** means *to take an examination.*

NOTE: In present-day French, **passer un examen** is also often used to mean *to pass an examination.*

(h) How to say *to take a course*

Suivez-vous **des cours** inté-   Are *you* taking *interesting*
ressants?   courses?

The expression **suivre un cours** means *to take a course*. It is becoming more and more common to say **prendre un cours,** but it is best for the learner to avoid this expression.

(i) How to say *to take a magazine*

Je vais **m'abonner à** plusieurs revues.	*I am going* to take *several magazines.*
Je **suis abonné** au journal du matin.	*I take the morning paper.*

When *take = subscribe to,* French uses **s'abonner à** to indicate the action of subscribing or the state of being a subscriber, and **être abonné à** to indicate the state of being a subscriber.

(j) How to say *to take (away) from*

Ce jouet est dangereux. **Enlevez**-le **à** cet enfant.	*That toy is dangerous.* Take *it* away from *that child.*
À qui **as**-tu **pris** cet argent?	*Who(m) did you* take *that money* from?

When *to take from* has the clear implication of *to take away from,* **enlever** is usually found with an indirect object. Otherwise, **prendre** may be often used with an indirect object.

(k) How *take* is expressed by **faire** in some expressions

There are many idiomatic expressions with **faire** which English expresses with *to take,* such as:

faire une promenade	*take a walk*
faire un tour	*take a stroll*
faire un voyage	*take a trip*

56. teach

(a) When *teach* is expressed by **enseigner**

Qui **a enseigné votre classe** pendant votre absence?	*Who* taught your class *during your absence?*
Mademoiselle Bouillet **enseigne les mathématiques** au lycée.	*Miss Bouillet* teaches mathematics *in high school.*

The verb **enseigner** is used with a direct object to mean *teach.* The direct object may be the subject taught, but not normally the person taught. For instance, to express in French: *Mr. Duparc teaches John,* one would have to say something like: **Monsieur Duparc est le professeur de Jean.**

Qui **enseignera** le latin **à Philippe?**	*Who will* teach *Latin* to Philip?

The verb **enseigner** may also be used with a direct object indicating what is taught and an indirect object indicating who is taught.

(b) When *teach* may be expressed by **apprendre**

C'est un ami brésilien qui **nous a appris le portugais.**	*It is a Brazilian friend who* taught us Portuguese.
C'est un ami brésilien qui **a appris le portugais à Brigitte.**	*It is a Brazilian friend who* taught Brigitte Portuguese.

The basic meaning of **apprendre** is *learn.* But it means *teach* when it is followed by a direct object denoting the thing taught and an indirect object indicating the person taught.

Ma mère **a appris à ma sœur à jouer** du piano.	*My mother* taught my sister to play *the piano.*

The verb **apprendre** means *teach* when followed by a *personal indirect object* + **à** + INFINITIVE.

57. time

(a) When *time* is expressed by **le temps**

Je n'ai pas **le temps** de réparer la radio.	*I don't have* the time *to repair the radio.*
Combien de **temps** faut-il pour faire cela?	*How much* time *is needed to do that?*

The general word for *time is* **le temps.**

The following expressions are used with **temps:**

à temps	*in time (for)*
en même temps	*at the same time*
de temps en temps	*from time to time*

In certain contexts **le temps** means *weather.*

(b) When *time* is expressed by **la fois**

Robert a dû répéter son explication trois **fois.**	*Robert had to repeat his explanation three* times.
Chaque **fois** que tu viens il pleut.	*It rains each* time *you come.*

The word **fois** is somewhat synonymous with *occasion.* It is used with numerals as well as with other words that indicate quantity.

(c) When *time* is expressed by **heure**

Quelle **heure** est-il?	*What* time *is it?*
C'est **l'heure** du thé.	*It is tea* time.

The word **heure** is used to ask *what time it is* and sometimes to indicate the *time* of a given function. When it tells time in sentences such as **Il est cinq heures,** it is expressed by *o'clock* in English.

(d) When *time* is expressed by **le moment**

En ce moment nous apprenons le latin.	At this time *we are learning Latin.*
À ce moment-là j'étais en France.	At that time *I was in France.*

The word **moment** indicates *a point in time;* **en ce moment** means *now* or *at this time;* **à ce moment-là** means *then* or *at that time.*

(e) When *time* is expressed by **l'époque**

À cette époque-là nous n'avions pas le téléphone.	At that time *we didn't have a telephone.*

The word **époque** indicates a longer period of time than does **moment** and usually refers to a time that is farther in the past.

(f) How to express *have a good time*

Passez une bonne soirée.	Have a good time this evening.
Nous **avons fait un excellent séjour** en France cet été.	*We* had a very good time *in France this summer.*
Les enfants **se sont bien amusés** au cirque.	*The children* had a very good time *at the circus.*

The French have no word-for-word translation of the English expression *to have a good time.* The verb **s'amuser** is often used to express this idea, especially when referring to younger people, but, depending on the occasion, other expressions such as those found in the above examples are also used.

H. Remplacez les mots anglais par leur équivalent français.

1. Il faut (*take*) Pierrot à sa leçon de danse tous les jeudis. 2. Nous parlions justement de vous (*at the time*) où vous êtes entré. 3. Lucienne voudrait (*take*) une revue de mode de Paris. 4. Il ne faut jamais regretter le (*time*) passé. 5. Cette lettre est importante; je la (*will take*) moi-même à la poste. 6. Il faut réussir à ce concours pour (*teach*) dans un lycée. 7. Ce film est excellent; je l'ai vu trois (*times*). 8. En juin la plus grande partie des élèves (*take*) des examens. 9. Je crois que nous (*will have a good time*) chez les Barois. 10. Si tu veux me faire plaisir, (*take*) les enfants au jardin zoologique. 11. C'est Florence qui me (*taught*) à nager quand j'avais quatre ans. 12. Nous n'avons plus besoin de ces affaires; vous pouvez les (*take*) chez vous. 13. (*At the time*) où j'habitais Londres, les choses n'étaient pas faciles. 14. Il faut (*take*) les choses

un peu plus au sérieux, mon ami.   **15.** C'est toi qui a permis à Pierre de (*take*) l'auto?   **16.** À quelle (*time*) est le dernier métro? **17.** Jeannot (*takes*) un journal de sport.   **18.** Depuis son mariage, Lucie n'a plus le temps de (*take*) des cours.

I. **Traduisez en français. Attention aux mots en italique.**

1. Someone *has taken* the silverware.   **2.** (*vous*) If you don't have *time* to write, telephone me Sunday.   **3.** (*vous*) Will you *take* Mr. Galant to the laboratory?   **4.** (*vous*) At what *time* do you want to see me?   **5.** I wonder who *taught* Rose to cook.   **6.** I think I am going to *take* another magazine.   **7.** (*tu*) Did you have a good *time* last night?   **8.** (*tu*) Don't forget to *take* your suit to the cleaner's. **9.** Louise *teaches* art, and her sister *teaches* history.   **10.** Susan *is taking* some Spanish courses[1].   **11.** Claude can't *take* us; his car broke down.   **12.** Felix arrived just at the *time* when I was leaving. **13.** Did Peter pass the examination he *took* last week?   **14.** Every *time* he comes, Paul brings us something.   **15.** (*tu*) When are you going to *take* your vacation?   **16.** At the *time* of my grandparents there wasn't any television[2].   **17.** I *took* an hour to read that book.

[1] cours d'espagnol   [2] Use the definite article.

Verb Review

Review the verbs **tenir** and **valoir** according to the outline on page 253.

CHAPTER
16

Constructions with Prepositions

Pourquoi j'ai choisi d'écrire

Pourquoi ai-je choisi *d'*écrire? Lorsque j'étais enfant, je n'avais guère attaché d'importance à mes gribouillages[1]; mon véritable souci avait été *de* m'instruire; je me plaisais à rédiger mes compositions françaises, mais «ces demoiselles», mes professeurs, me reprochaient *d'*avoir un style
5 guindé[2]; je ne me sentais pas «douée[3]». Cependant, quand à quinze ans, une amie me demanda *d'*inscrire sur son album les prédilections, les projets qui étaient censés[4] définir ma personnalité, je n'hésitai pas. À la question: «Que voulez-vous faire plus tard?» je répondis d'un[5] trait: «Être un auteur célèbre». Touchant mon musicien favori, ma fleur préférée, je
10 m'étais inventé des goûts plus ou moins factices[6]. Mais sur ce point je n'hésitai pas: je convoitais[7] cet avenir à l'exclusion de tout autre. Il m'est facile *de* l'expliquer.

La première raison, c'est l'admiration que m'inspiraient les écrivains; mon père les mettait bien au-dessus des savants, des érudits, des profes-
15 seurs. J'étais convaincue moi aussi de leur suprématie; l'œuvre d'un spé-cialiste, même si son nom était largement connu, ne s'ouvrait qu'*à* un petit nombre; mais tout le monde lisait les livres: ils touchaient l'imagi-nation, le cœur; ils valaient à leur auteur la gloire la plus universelle. En[8] tant que femme, ces sommets me semblaient en outre plus faciles *à*
20 atteindre que les pénéplaines[9]; les plus célèbres de mes sœurs s'étaient illustrées dans la littérature.

Et puis j'avais toujours eu le[10] goût de la communication. Sur l'album

---

[1] *scribblings*   [2] *stilted*   [3]*gifted*   [4] *supposed*   [5] d'un trait   *without hesitating*
[6] *artificial*   [7] *set my heart on*   [8] en tant que   *as a*   [9] *slopes*   [10] le goût de   *a*
propensity, an inclination for

211

de mon amie, je citai comme divertissements favoris: la lecture et la conversation. J'étais loquace[11]. Tout ce qui me frappait au cours d'une
25 journée, j'essayais *de* le raconter. Je redoutais la nuit, l'oubli; c'était un déchirement[12] *d*'abandonner au silence ce que j'avais vu, senti, aimé. Émue par un clair de lune, je souhaitais avoir une plume, du papier et savoir m'en servir. J'aimais, à quinze ans, les correspondances, les journaux[13] intimes qui s'efforcent[14] *de* retenir le temps. J'avais compris
30 aussi que les romans, les nouvelles, les contes ne sont pas des objets étrangers à la vie mais qu'ils l'expriment à leur manière.

Si j'avais souhaité autrefois me faire institutrice, c'est que je rêvais *d*'être[15] ma propre cause et ma propre fin; je pensais à présent que la littérature me permettrait *de* réaliser ce vœu. Elle m'assurerait une im-
35 mortalité qui compenserait l'éternité perdue; il n'y avait plus de Dieu *pour* m'aimer, mais je[16] brûlerais dans des millions de cœurs. En écrivant une œuvre nourrie de mon histoire, je me créerais moi-même à neuf et je justifierais mon existence. En même temps, je servirais l'humanité: quel plus beau cadeau lui faire que des livres? Je m'intéressais à la fois *à*
40 moi et *aux* autres; ce projet conciliait tout; il flattait toutes les aspirations qui s'étaient développées en moi au cours de ces quinze années.

D'après Simone de Beauvoir. Professeur comme Sartre et comme lui philosophe existentialiste, elle est dramaturge, essayiste, romancière et elle a écrit une importante autobiographie. (*Mémoires d'une jeune fille rangée,* Gallimard, 1958)

---

[11] *talkative*   [12] *agony*   [13] journaux intimes   *diaries*   [14] s'efforcent de retenir le temps   *try to make time stand still*   [15] d'être ma propre cause et ma propre fin *that I was a law unto myself*   [16] je brûlerais dans des millions de cœurs   *I would shine like a beacon*

I.   Prepositions of Place

TO, IN, AT

In French, *in, at,* and *to* are all expressed by the same preposition before proper nouns used as place names. The preposition used depends on whether the place name is a city, a masculine country, or a feminine country or continent.

1. What preposition of place is used to express *in, at,* and *to* with cities?

Nous sommes **à** Paris.   *We are* in (at) *Paris*
Gérard va **à** Tours.   *Gerard is going* to *Tours.*

The preposition **à** is used before cities to express the English prepositions *in, at,* or *to.*

2. How can one determine the gender of countries in French?

la France   **la** Grèce   **la** Belgique   **la** Suisse   **la** Bolivie
la Chine

All countries ending in **-e** are feminine except **le Mexique.**

le Canada   **le** Japon   **le** Portugal   **le** Danemark   **le** Pérou

All countries not ending in **-e** are masculine.

NOTE: These rules hold usually with the well-known and well-established countries, but they do not always seem to apply to the so-called "emerging countries," where uniform usage has not yet been well determined. Likewise, **en** is used to express *in* or *to* with certain masculine countries beginning with a vowel, as, for instance **en** Israël.

3. What preposition of place is used to express *in* or *to* before feminine countries and continents?

Michel est **en** France.   *Michael is* in *France.*
Louise va **en** France.   *Louise is going* to *France.*
Maurice a passé deux ans **en**   *Maurice spent two years* in *Af-*
Afrique.   *rica.*

French uses **en** to express both *in* and *to* before feminine countries and continents.

4. What preposition of place is used to express *in* or *to* before masculine countries?

Charlotte est **au** Danemark.   *Charlotte is* in *Denmark.*
Gilbert va **au** Danemark.   *Gilbert is going* to *Denmark.*
Restez-vous longtemps **aux**   *Are you staying* in *the United*
États-Unis?   *States for a long time?*
Nous allons **aux** États-Unis l'an-   *We are going* to *the United*
née prochaine.   *States next year.*

French uses **à** + DEFINITE ARTICLE to express *in* or *to* before masculine countries.

NOTE 1: Although the same prepositions **à** and **en** are used to express both *in* and *to* with French place names, this does not ordinarily lead to ambiguity. **Je suis allé en France** clearly means *I went to France,* **Je suis allé au Canada** clearly means *I went to Canada.* **J'ai passé un an en France** clearly means *I spent a year in France,* **J'ai passé un an au Canada** clearly means *I spent a year in Canada.*

NOTE 2: In sentences with the verb **voyager,** however, a problem does exist. **J'ai voyagé en France cet été** means *I traveled in France this summer,* and not "I traveled to France this summer." To avoid ambiguity in express-ing the idea of traveling *to a place,* it is best to use the verb **aller.** Ex.: **Je suis allé en France cet été.**

NOTE 3: However, *in* or *to Cuba* is expressed by **à** alone. Ex.: Nous sommes allés **à Cuba** avant la révolution. Le sucre est une industrie très importante **à Cuba.**

NOTE 4: French makes certain states of the United States feminine by ending them in **-e.** Ex.: **la Californie, la Géorgie, la Floride.** With such states, *in* and *to* are therefore expressed by **en.** With other states, which are con-sidered masculine, **dans le** is most often used, although one sometimes finds **au.** Ex.: dans l'Ohio, dans le Texas, dans le Michigan.

5. **What preposition of place is used before modified countries, cities, and continents?**

   (a) if the modifying phrase or adjective is an integral part of the place name

Il habite **à** la Nouvelle-Orléans.	*He lives* in *New Orleans.*
Nous allons **en** Amérique du Sud.	*We are going* to *South Amer-ica.*
Le Maroc, l'Algérie et la Tunisie sont **en** Afrique de Nord.	*Morocco, Algeria, and Tunisia are* in *North Africa.*

   If the modifying phrase or adjective is an integral part of the place name, the same preposition would be used as if the place were not modified.

   (b) if the modifying phrase or adjective is not an integral part of the place name

Quelle université est située **dans la** Belgique flamande?	*What university is located* in the *Flemish part of Belgium?*
Nous avons passé des journées **dans le** vieux Paris.	*We spent days* in *old Paris.*

   When a place name is modified by an adjective or phrase that is not an integral part of the name, **dans** + DEFINITE ARTICLE is used to express *in* or *to.* But this construction is rather rare.

A. **Remplacez les tirets par la préposition convenable.**

   1. Beaucoup de catholiques vont _____ Rome pour voir le Vatican.
   2. Quand vous serez _____ Naples, allez donc voir les ruines de Pompéi.   3. Quand j'étais _____ Angleterre, j'aimais prendre le thé à quatre heures.   4. Puisque vous aimez les sports d'hiver, allez passer l'hiver _____ Colorado.   5. Nous avons renoncé à aller _____ Chine, c'est un trop long voyage.   6. Ces jeunes Français passeront un mois _____ États-Unis pour étudier la chimie.
   7. Quand vous serez _____ Danemark, vous verrez que presque tout le monde parle anglais.

B. Traduisez en français.

1. They want to spend their vacation in Madrid, but they do not know Spanish.   **2.** (*vous*) If you want to go to Canada, I advise you to take the train at eight in[1] the evening.   **3.** Many Americans go to Florida to spend the winter.   **4.** Our friends were[2] to come back, but they want to stay in Portugal in April.   **5.** A large number of American engineers work[3] in Mexico.   **6.** I took some very beautiful photographs on arriving in Japan and some[4] others while I was in China.   **7.** We did not stay in Russia long[5] enough to learn Russian.   **8.** This old man would now like to go back to Italy to see his relatives.

[1] du   [2] Use a form of **devoir**.   [3]This verb is in the plural.   [4] d'autres   [5]assez long-temps pour

FROM

6. How is *from* expressed with cities?

Je suis parti **de** Paris hier pour voir les environs.	*I left Paris yesterday to see the surrounding country.*

With cities, *from* is expressed by **de.**

7. How is *from* expressed with feminine countries and continents?

Nous sommes revenus **de** France la semaine dernière.	*We returned* from *France last week.*
Philippe partira-t-il **d'**Angleterre la semaine prochaine?	*Will Philip leave England next week?*

Before feminine countries and continents, *from* is expressed by **de.**

8. How is *from* expressed with masculine countries?

Nos cousins sont partis **du** Canada hier.	*Our cousins left Canada yesterday.*
Quand reviendrez-vous **du** Portugal?	*When will you come back* from *Portugal?*

Before masculine countries, *from* is expressed by **de** + DEFINITE ARTICLE (**du, de l', des**).

C. Remplacez les tirets par l'équivalent français de *from*.

1. Il part _____ Japon la semaine prochaine à cause de la situation politique.   **2.** À leur accent, je devine qu'ils viennent _____ Belgique.   **3.** Des avions partent tous les jours _____ Canada pour l'Europe.   **4.** Ces messieurs viennent _____ Lyon pour montrer leurs étoffes de soie.   **5.** Beaucoup de gens qui reviennent _____ Mexique sont contents de retrouver la cuisine américaine.   **6.** Les Russes ne peuvent pas toujours sortir librement _____

Russie.   7. Si vous allez _____ France en Angleterre, prenez donc
l'avion.

D. Traduisez en français.

1. I like to take the boat when I go from Japan to the United States.
2. It is sometimes difficult to say whether someone comes from the
United States or from England.   3. We are coming back from
Greece delighted[1] by the beauty of that country.   4. He is coming
back from Spain, where he spent the whole month of July.   5. (*tu*)
When you come back[2] from Portugal, we'll go to Wisconsin to spend
the summer.

[1] enchantés par   [2] Not the present tense.

II.   Verb + Preposition + Infinitive

9. What words does French use to join a verb to a following infinitive?

Je **voudrais aller** en France.	*I* should like to go *to France.*
Nous **avons commencé à lire.**	*We began* to read.
Les ouvriers **ont refusé de travailler.**	*The workmen* refused to work.

Some verbs are followed directly by an infinitive, some verbs require
à before an infinitive, some require **de** before an infinitive, a few require
still other prepositions.

10. How can one determine which construction to use before an infinitive?

Ils **viendront voir** leur nouveau petit-fils la semaine prochaine.	*They* will come to see *their new grandson next week.*
Nous **voulons régler** cette affaire le plus tôt possible.	*We* want to take care of *this matter as soon as possible.*

Verbs of motion (**aller, venir**) and the common verbs of wishing
(**vouloir, désirer**) are followed directly by the infinitive.

Le mari de Janine lui **a demandé de faire des économies.**	*Janine's husband* asked *her* to be saving.
Nous **avons regretté d'apprendre** son départ si précipité.	*We* were sorry to learn *of his very hasty departure.*

Verbs of telling, asking, ordering, advising, etc. (someone to do something)
and most verbs of emotion (**craindre, avoir peur, regretter,
s'étonner,** etc.) are followed by **de** before an infinitive.

But except for these, the preposition to be used after each verb before
an infinitive must be learned.

11. Which verbs require no preposition before an infinitive?

The following are the most common verbs that are followed directly by the infinitive:

aimer	*like*	falloir	*be necessary*
aimer mieux	*prefer*	laisser	*leave, allow, let*
aller	*go, be going*	oser	*dare*
compter	*intend*	pouvoir	*can, be able*
croire	*believe*	préférer	*prefer*
désirer	*desire, wish*	savoir	*know, know how*
devoir	*am to, must,*	sembler	*seem*
	should	venir	*come*
entendre	*hear*	voir	*see*
espérer	*hope*	vouloir	*want, wish*
faire	*do, make, have*		

12. Which verbs require *de* before an infinitive?

The following are the most common verbs that require **de** before an infinitive:

avoir peur de	*be afraid*	finir de	*finish*
cesser de	*cease*	ordonner de	*order*
craindre de	*fear*	oublier de	*forget*
décider de	*decide*	permettre de	*permit*
défendre de	*forbid*	prier de	*beg, ask, pray*
demander de	*ask*	promettre de	*promise*
se dépêcher de	*hurry*	refuser de	*refuse*
dire de	*tell*	regretter de	*regret*
écrire de	*write*	remercier de	*thank*
empêcher de	*prevent*	tâcher de	*try*
essayer de	*try*		

13. Which verbs require *à* before an infinitive?

The following are the most common verbs that require **à** before an infinitive:

aider à	*help*	enseigner à	*teach*
s'amuser à	*amuse oneself*	s'habituer à	*accustom*
apprendre à	*learn, teach*		*oneself*
arriver à	*succeed*	hésiter à	*hesitate*
avoir à	*have*	inviter à	*invite*
commencer à	*begin*	recommencer à	*begin again*
consentir à	*consent*	réussir à	*succeed*
continuer à	*continue*	songer à	*think,*
se décider à	*decide*		*dream*
demander à*	*ask*	tarder à	*delay in*

* The verb **demander** + AN INDIRECT OBJECT meaning *to ask to* requires **de** before an infinitive. Compare: Il demande **à** venir. Il demande à son ami **de** venir.

E. Remplacez les tirets par une préposition s'il[1] y a lieu.

1. —Allô chérie, j'ai invité le patron _____ dîner chez nous ce soir.   **2.** J'avais un oiseau en cage, mais je l'ai laissé _____ partir.
3. Dépêche-toi _____ finir ton travail pour qu'on puisse sortir.
4. Je n'aime pas qu'il s'amuse _____ faire des expériences de chimie dans la maison.   **5.** Dépêche-toi, ils peuvent _____ arriver d'un moment à l'autre.   **6.** Cessez _____ bavarder avec votre voisin, ou prenez la porte.   **7.** Il faut _____ vivre mieux que ça; je vais _____ essayer _____ gagner un peu plus d'argent.   **8.** Il vient d'avoir cinquante ans et il a décidé _____ se remarier.
9. Commencez _____ économiser de l'argent dès que possible.
10. J'aime mieux _____ sortir quand il pleut, l'air est plus pur.
11. Oseriez-vous _____ répéter ce que vous venez de dire?
12. Beaucoup de réfugiés refusent absolument _____ retourner dans leurs pays.

[1] *If one is necessary*

F. Remplacez les tirets par une préposition s'il y a lieu.

1. Il est malade, mais il continue _____ faire ses classes.   **2.** J'ai été un peu brusque, je crains _____ l'avoir vexé.   **3.** Faites un petit effort pour apprendre _____ parler correctement.   **4.** À partir de demain, je veux _____ travailler dix heures tous les jours.
5. Je regrette _____ ne pas être plus riche.   **6.** Il est bon de savoir _____ faire plusieurs métiers.   **7.** Bien des Américains espèrent _____ aller un jour en Europe.   **8.** J'ai cru qu'ils ne se décideraient jamais _____ partir.   **9.** Il faut s'habituer _____ vivre dans l'incertitude.   **10.** Si vous voulez un chat, nous cherchons _____ placer les nôtres.   **11.** S'il tarde _____ rentrer, sa femme imagine qu'il a eu un accident.   **12.** On doit _____ réfléchir avant de parler.

G. Traduisez en français. Attention aux prépositions.

1. His work prevents him from playing poker with his friends this evening.   **2.** I completely forgot to telephone him[1] today, and it's[2] too late now.   **3.** Several friends will help me paint my house.
4. (*vous*) Don't hesitate to interrupt me if you have a question.
5. As soon as one speaks of France, Anne begins[3] to dream.   **6.** He is stubborn; I didn't succeed in changing his opinion.   **7.** Few people like to write long letters.   **8.** (*tu*) If you want to see him, come quickly, because he is going to leave.   **9.** (*vous*) Look at that man; he seems to want to speak to us.

[1] Which type of object is this?   [2] Either **il est** or **c'est**, but with a slight difference in meaning.   [3] Use a form of **se mettre**.

III.   The *à* + *de* Verbs

14. How does French express the idea *to tell someone to do something?*

J'**ai dit à mon frère de** partir tout de suite.	*I told my brother to leave immediately.*
Michel **a promis à ses enfants de** leur apporter des jouets.	*Michael* promised his children to *bring them some toys.*

Certain verbs require **à** before a noun object and **de** before a following infinitive in French but not necessarily in English. These may be called the **à** + **de** verbs. Among these are:

conseiller à quelqu'un de	*advise someone to*	Je **conseille à Paul de** partir.
défendre à quelqu'un de	*forbid someone to*	Il **défend à Marie de** sortir.
demander à quelqu'un de	*ask someone to*	Elle **demande à sa mère de** venir.
dire à quelqu'un de	*tell someone to*	Je **dis à mon frère de** se taire.
écrire à quelqu'un de	*write some to*	Nous **écrivons à Guy de** rester.
ordonner à quelqu'un de	*order someone to*	Il **ordonne au soldat de** se lever.
permettre à quelqu'un de	*permit someone to*	Je **permets à Jean d'**entrer.
promettre à quelqu'un de	*promise someone to*	Elle **promet à Henri de** lui écrire.
téléphoner à quelqu'un de	*telephone someone to*	Il **téléphone à Claude de** revenir.

H. Traduisez en français.

1. (*vous*) Telephone your father to send you some money.
2. After that trouble[1], I advised Gerard to leave town[2].   3. (*vous*) If you want to marry my daughter, promise me to come to work here every day.   4. There are always people who want to forbid others[2] to do what they wish.   5. (*tu*) Ask your uncle to buy you a car, since he is rich.   6. (*vous*) If he comes, tell Mr. Fondeville to leave his address and I'll write him.   7. (*vous*) You are wrong to[3] permit your children to do everything[4] they wish.   8. (*vous*) I'll write my friends to come to get[5] you at the airport.

---

[1] histoire   [2] Use the definite article.   [3] de   [4] tout ce que   [5] chercher

IV.   Verb (+ Preposition) + Noun

15. How do the <u>verb</u> + <u>noun</u> constructions in French compare with those in English?

Nous **attendons** le train.	*We* are waiting for *the train.*
Je **suis entré dans** la maison.	*I* entered *the house.*
Il **pense à** ses examens.	*He* is thinking of *his examinations.*

While many VERB + NOUN constructions are the same in French and English, some verbs require a preposition before a noun in French but not in English, and others require a preposition before a noun in English but not in French. Still other verbs require one preposition in English, another in French.

16. What are some common verbs that require a direct object in French but a preposition before the object in English?

attendre	*wait for*	Paul **attend** son ami.
chercher	*look for*	Marie **cherche** son livre.
demander	*ask for*	Pierre **demande** cinq cents francs.
écouter	*listen to*	Nous **écoutons** la musique.
payer	*pay for*	Il **a payé** cet objet mille francs.
regarder	*look at*	Je **regarde** le plan de Paris.

The verbs listed above require a direct object in French.

17. What are some common verbs that require a preposition before the object in French, but a direct object in English?

approcher de	*approach*	Nous **approchons de** la rivière.
assister à	*attend*	Il **assiste à** la réunion.
changer de	*change*	Elle **a changé de** robe.
entrer dans	*enter*	Qui **entre dans** la salle?
échapper à	*escape*	Le soldat **a échappé à** la mort.
s'échapper de	*escape*	Le voleur **s'est échappé de** prison.
jouer à	*play*	Je **joue au** football, lui **aux** échecs.
jouer de	*play*	Elle **joue du** piano et **du** violon.
manquer de	*lack*	Je **manque de** renseignements.
se marier avec	*marry*	Denise **se marie avec** Jean-Pierre.
obéir à	*obey*	Paul **obéit à** son père.
plaire à	*please*	Yvonne **plaît à** tout le monde.
répondre à	*answer*	Je **réponds à** la lettre.
résister à	*resist*	Il **résiste à** la tentation.
ressembler à	*resemble*	Maurice **ressemble à** son frère.
se servir de	*use*	Ils **se servent de** la machine à écrire.
se souvenir de	*remember*	Je **me souviens de** cette affaire.

The verbs listed above require a preposition before the object in French.

NOTE: The verb **échapper à** means *to escape getting into something;* **s'échapper de** means *to escape from something one has gotten into.*

The construction **jouer à** means *to play a game;* the construction **jouer de** means *to play a musical instrument.*

18. **What are some common verbs that require one preposition in French and another in English?**

s'intéresser à	*be interested in*	Il **s'intéresse à** la musique.
s'occuper de	*busy oneself with*	Je **m'occupe de** la maison.
penser à	*think of*	Il **pense à** son travail.
penser de	*think of*	Que **pensez-vous de** cet homme?
remercier de	*thank for*	Il **a remercié** sa mère **de** son cadeau.
rire de	*laugh at*	Nous **rions de** sa réponse.
songer à	*think of*	Il **songe à** son voyage en France.

The verbs listed above require one preposition in French and another in English.

NOTE: The construction **penser à** means *to think of someone or something;* the construction **penser de** is most often used in questions *to ask one's opinion of someone or something.*

The verb **remercier** may also be followed by **pour** before a noun. Ex.: Il **a remercié** sa mère **pour** son cadeau.

I. Remplacez les expressions anglaises entre parenthèses par les équivalents français.

(Each sentence has a verb that entails the use or nonuse of a preposition. In certain sentences, it may be necessary to combine a preposition with the definite article.)

1. Je (*am looking for*) une bonne réponse à sa lettre, mais c'est difficile.   2. Certains élèves peuvent travailler en (*listening to*) la radio.   3. (*Look at*) bien le ciel et vous verrez peut-être des satellites.   4. Avec cette foule il sera impossible de (*approach*) la scène.   5. Victor (*escaped from*) la maison qui brûlait juste à temps. 6. Il faut de longues années d'étude pour (*play*) le violon en virtuose. 7. Trop de familles (*lack*) argent.   8. Chacun rêve de (*marry*[1]) la personne idéale.   9. Il y a des gens qui croient pouvoir (*escape*) la maladie.   10. Tout évolue et il est impossible de (*resist*) longtemps les changements.   11. (*Concern yourself with*[2]) vos affaires. 12. Il faut le (*thank for*) les fleurs qu'il m'a envoyées.   13. Ce n'est pas gentil de (*laugh at*) une personne qui tombe.   14. Il (*is waiting for*) son amie, mais je sais qu'elle ne viendra pas.

[1] Use a form of **se marier**.   [2] Use a form of **s'occuper**.

J. Traduisez en français. Attention aux prépositions.

1. (*vous*) Live in the present; do not think too much of the past.
2. I attended a fine concert last evening.   **3.** They change cars
every other year.   **4.** I have lost my key, and I can't get into the
house.   **5.** It is amusing to[1] play chess.   **6.** Teenagers often refuse
to obey their parents.   **7.** He is spending a fortune to please that
woman.   **8.** (*vous*) Do not wait to[2] answer those letters.   **9.** He
does not resemble his father at all[3].   **10.** Today one uses[4] knives
and forks[5] to[2] eat.   **11.** She doesn't like poetry; she is interested
in sports.   **12.** (*tu*) What do you think of the work of that painter?

[1] de   [2] pour   [3] Place directly after pas.   [4] Use a form of se servir.   [5] Repeat the
preposition before the second noun.

V.   The *It is* + Adjective + Infinitive
Constructions

19. What construction follows the impersonal *Il est* + adjective?

Il est impossible **de** partir aujourd'hui.	It is *impossible* to *leave today.*
Il serait difficile **de** lui donner cet argent.	It would be *hard* to *give him that money.*

The construction used with the impersonal **il est** + ADJECTIVE is:

> (impersonal) **il est** + ADJECTIVE + **de** + INFINITIVE (+ idea)

NOTE: In conversational French, this impersonal **il** may always be replaced by
ce, and the following construction is exactly the same as though the impersonal **il** were used.

20. What construction follows idea + *c'est* + adjective?

Est-ce que cet écrivain écrit vraiment bien? **C'est** difficile **à** dire.	*Does that author really write well?* It's *hard* to *say.*
Votre frère est-il bon élève? Non, et **c'est** impossible **à** comprendre.	*Is your brother a good student? No, and* it's *impossible* to *understand.*

When **c'est** + adjective refers to a preceding idea without gender or
number, the following construction is used:

> IDEA in preceding sentence + **c'est** + ADJECTIVE + **à** + INFINITIVE

K. Remplacez les tirets par *à* ou *de,* selon le cas.

1. —Les planètes sont-elles habitées? —Peut-être, mais c'est impossible _____ prouver.   2. Il est maintenant possible _____ aller dans la lune.   3. Il est agréable _____ prendre un petit cognac après un bon repas.   4. —Comment avez-vous fait pour apprendre à jouer si bien? —C'est difficile _____ expliquer.   5. Les candidats ont discuté pendant une heure. C'était intéressant _____ écouter.   6. Il n'est pas toujours facile _____ dire ce qui est bien et ce qui est mal.   7. Vous l'avez vraiment vu voler cette montre? C'est difficile _____ croire.

L. Traduisez en français.

1. It is interesting to see a football[1] game between two good teams.
2. Man is master of his destiny. It's easy to say.   3. It is necessary to write a great many letters, even if it is sometimes boring to do.
4. It is difficult to understand certain scientific theories.   5. It is amusing to observe people in the street.   6. Maurice wants to buy an airplane. It's impossible to believe.   7. I'm going to paint my house. It's easy to do.   8. It is restful to interrupt one's[2] work from time to time.   9. Mark is so stubborn that it is useless to try to convince him.   10. Jack says that he is capable of writing a novel. It is hard to imagine.   11. Mr. Laroque does not believe that his son was at my house last night, but it's easy to prove.   12. It is impossible to get[3] to the top of that mountain.

[1] *football game* = match de football   [2] Use a form of son.   [3] Use a form of arriver à.

VI. Verbal Constructions after Prepositions; Constructions with *pour*

Most English prepositions are followed by the present participle. One says *on arriving, in coming, by working, without leaving,* etc., but this is not usually the case in French.

21. What verbal construction usually follows a French preposition?

Ne partez pas **sans laisser**   *Don't go away* without leaving
    votre adresse.   *your address.*

All French prepositions except **en** are followed by the infinitive.

When we use the term infinitive, we mean SIMPLE INFINITIVE, for it is by far the most common infinitive to be used. But there is also a COMPOUND INFINITIVE, which is made up of the infinitive of **avoir** or **être** and the past participle of the main verb. The compound infinitive is also known as the PAST INFINITIVE.

SIMPLE INFINITIVE	COMPOUND INFINITIVE
parler	avoir parlé
finir	avoir fini
venir	être venu(e)(s)
se laver	s'être lavé(e)(s)

22. By what verbal construction is the preposition *en* followed?

En entrant dans le café, nous avons vu Robert et Marie.	On entering *the café, we saw Robert and Marie.*

The preposition **en** is followed by the present participle. (For a complete treatment of **en** + PRESENT PARTICIPLE, see pages 103–104.)

23. When is a French preposition followed by the compound infinitive?

Les voisins ont puni leur fils **pour avoir cassé** nos vitres.	*The neighbors punished their son* for breaking *our windowpanes.*

When the verbal action after a preposition clearly takes place before the action of the main verb of the sentence, the compound infinitive is used in order to preserve the time distinction.

24. What French construction is used to express the English *before* + verb + *-ing*?

Regardez à droite et à gauche **avant de traverser** la rue.	*Look left and right* before crossing *the street.*

French uses **avant de** + INFINITIVE for the English *before* + VERB + *-ing*.

25. What French construction is used to express the English *after* + verb + *-ing*?

Après avoir lu le journal, je me suis mis au travail.	After reading *the newspaper, I got down to work.*

French uses **après** + COMPOUND INFINITIVE to express the English *after* + VERB + *-ing*.

26. How does French express purpose?

Mon agent de change a acheté ce terrain **pour planter** des arbres fruitiers.	*My broker bought this land* to plant *some fruit trees.*

To express purpose, English uses $\begin{cases} to \\ in\ order\ to \end{cases}$ + VERB. French uses the preposition **pour** + THE INFINITIVE to indicate purpose.

27. When may the preposition *pour* **be omitted before the infinitive in purpose phrases?**

Jean **est venu** (pour) **travailler** avec Daniel aujourd'hui.

John came *(in order) to work with Daniel today.*

Nous **sommes allés** à la ferme (pour) **chercher** du lait.

We went *to the farm (in order) to get* some milk.

In purpose phrases, the preposition **pour** is usually omitted after forms of **aller** and **venir** and sometimes after other verbs of motion. When **pour** is used after forms of **aller** and **venir**, it emphasizes the idea of purpose much as *in order to* does in English. The preposition **pour** is also often used when several words separate the main verb and the infinitive.

28. How does French express the idea of enough . . . to **and** too much . . . to **or** too . . . to?

Louise chante **assez** bien **pour** faire partie du chœur.

Louise sings well enough to *be in the choir.*

Nous avons **trop** à faire **pour** partir maintenant.

We have too much to *do to leave now.*

Jacques est **trop** jeune **pour** rester dehors après neuf heures du soir.

Jack is too *young to* stay out *after nine o'clock at night.*

French expresses the idea of *enough . . . to* by **assez . . . pour** and of *too much . . . to* and *too . . . to* by **trop . . . pour.**

M. Remplacez l'infinitif entre parenthèses par la forme convenable du verbe, s'il y a lieu.

1. Pourquoi êtes-vous venu ici sans (téléphoner) d'avance? 2. Il faut aller au Maroc pour (acheter) un beau tapis. 3. Après (monter) dans ma chambre, j'ai réfléchi à ce qui venait de se passer. 4. En (parler) à l'agent, j'ai appris ce qui s'était passé. 5. Faites peser mes lettres avant de les (mettre) à la poste. 6. Nous avons commencé par (ouvrir) toutes les fenêtres. 7. Michel a répondu après (réfléchir)[1] un moment. 8. Au lieu de (se[1] plaindre), vendez donc votre voiture. 9. Je me suis intéressé à la science en (lire) la biographie des Curie. 10. Jean est encore parti sans (fermer) la porte. 11. On apprend mieux quelque chose en l'(expliquer) à d'autres.

[1] Even in the infinitive form, the reflexive object must agree in person with the subject of the sentence. In what person is the subject of an imperative sentence?

N. Traduisez en français.

1. Paul is too proud to admit his error. 2. Someone came to ask for some information[1] concerning[2] Jack. 3. We left after hearing

[1] Use the plural. [2] **sur**

the results of the election.   4. Robert is old[3] enough to have a motorcycle.   5. (*vous*) Did you come to our house only to talk business?   6. The children went to play at the neighbor's. 7. (*vous*) Before leaving for Paris, reserve a room in a good hotel. 8. (*tu*) You are intelligent enough to understand those things. 9. Paul went to get[4] some books at the library.   10. I am too tired to go out this evening.   11. (*vous*) Correct your mistakes before erasing the sentences.   12. (*tu*) At what time will you come to get[4] me?

[3] âgé   [4] chercher

Exercices d'ensemble

Dans les trois devoirs suivants, remplacez les tirets par la préposition convenable si une préposition est nécessaire. Quelques tirets doivent être remplacés par une préposition et l'article défini.

O. 1. Ecoutez-moi _____ vous fâcher.   2. Le Grand Bazar importe beaucoup de beaux objets _____ Canada.   3. Laure espère _____ être nommée vice-présidente de la compagnie cette année. 4. Jules est trop âgé _____ conduire un camion.   5. Chacun de nos enfants joue _____ la guitare.   6. Il faut que je téléphone _____ fleuriste _____ envoyer des roses à Madame Darmoy _____ la remercier _____ son dîner.   7. _____ Belgique on parle deux langues: le français et le flamand.   8. Nous ne savons pas qui a essayé _____ pénétrer chez nous pendant notre absence. 9. Je ne peux pas _____ régler cette affaire avant de partir. 10. Le patron a dit _____ Thomas _____ ne plus être en retard s'il veut _____ garder sa place.   11. Je pense _____ ma tante Julie. N'oublie pas _____ l'inviter pour Pâques cette année.

P. 1. Gilbert a décidé _____ abandonner sa profession et _____ apprendre la mécanique.   2. Il est impossible _____ travailler avec tout ce bruit.   3. Philippe sera en retard. Son sous-sol est plein d'eau et il doit _____ attendre _____ le plombier.   4. Des millions de gens dans le monde voudraient _____ vivre _____ États-Unis.   5. Monsieur Laroche a des ennuis parce qu'il refuse _____ payer une partie de ses impôts.   6. Tu as vu comme ce petit ressemble _____ son père?   7. Il faut de la patience _____ élever les enfants.   8. Le soleil brille presque toute l'année _____ Afrique du Nord.   9. C'est malheureux mais Paul ne s'intéresse _____ rien.   10. Presque tout le monde écoute _____ la radio en conduisant.   11. Les clients de Maître Gagnon ne veulent pas _____ suivre ses conseils. C'est difficile _____ comprendre.

Q. **1.** Ne sois pas si timide, invite Simone ou Monique _____ danser, elles seraient ravies. **2.** Christiane est assez grande _____ sortir avec qui elle veut. **3.** Roger s'est marié _____ Phyllis il y a un an et ils ont déjà un beau bébé. **4.** On peut s'étonner _____ voir le nombre de gens qui fréquentent toujours des restaurants aussi chers. **5.** _____ Texas il y a des ranches immenses et de vastes gisements de pétrole. **6.** _____ petit Gervais est revenu _____ Espagne enchanté par son voyage. **7.** Demande _____ ton frère _____ t'aider. **8.** Ce week-end nous aiderons les voisins _____ déménager. **9.** Cet élève est ennuyeux, il demande toujours _____ sortir. **10.** Ne manquez pas d'aller au carnaval si vous vous trouvez _____ Nouvelle-Orléans au Mardi-Gras. **11.** Nous préférons _____ prendre nos vacances en juin ou en septembre.

Problem Words

58. very much

Ways of expressing *very much* and *very many*

J'ai **énormément** à faire.
J'ai { **un tas** / **des tas** } de choses à faire.
J'ai **une quantité de choses** à faire.

⎫
⎬ *I have* very much *to do.*
⎭

Ces étudiants ont **énormé-ment de** livres à lire.
Ces étudiants ont **des tas de** livres à lire.
Ces étudiants ont **une quan-tité de** livres à lire.

⎫
⎬ *Those students have* very many *books to read.*
⎭

Depending on the exact sentence, *very much* and *very many* may be expressed by **énormément de, une quantité de, un tas de, des tas de**[1], and other similar expressions. In familiar speech, the French sometimes say **beaucoup** twice, so that one might hear: **J'ai beaucoup beaucoup à faire,** and **Ces étudiants ont beaucoup beaucoup de livres à lire.** This latter construction should be avoided in writing.

French often expresses *not very much* by **pas grand-chose.** This is somewhat colloquial. Ex.: Je n'ai **pas** fait **grand-chose** ce matin.

CAUTION: In French, **très** cannot modify **beaucoup.** Therefore, *very much* and *very many* cannot be expressed by «très beaucoup».

[1] The expressions **un tas de** and **des tas de** are colloquial.

59. visit

(a) How to say *to visit a person*

Hier je **suis allé voir Mon-**   *Yesterday I* visited Mr. Moreau.
sieur Moreau.

The most common way of saying *to visit a person* is **aller voir quel-**
qu'un.

Il faudra **faire une visite aux**   *We must* visit the neighbors.
voisins.

Another way of saying *to visit a person* is **faire une visite à quel-**
qu'un.

Nous **avons rendu visite à**   *We* visited (paid a visit to) Mrs.
Madame de Rosemont.   de Rosemont.

More formal and therefore less common is **rendre visite à quel-**
qu'un.

CAUTION: DO NOT use the verb «visiter» to express the idea of *visiting*
a person. The most common way of saying *to visit a person* is **aller**
voir une personne.

(b) How to say *to visit a place*

Avez-vous **visité le Louvre?**   *Did you* visit the Louvre?
Quand nous étions en Italie,   *When we were in Italy, we* vis-
nous **avons visité Naples.**   ited Naples.
Ne manquez pas de **visiter les**   *Don't fail* to visit the old sec-
vieux quartiers de Paris.   tions *of Paris.*

The verb **visiter** is used to express the idea of *visiting a place.*

60. while

(a) When to express *while* by **pendant que**

Attendez-moi dans la voiture   *Wait for me in the car* while *I*
pendant que je vais   *go and get the children.*
chercher les enfants.

When *while* means *during the time that*, it is expressed by **pendant**
que.

(b) When to express *while* by **tandis que**

Marc travaille bien, **tandis que**   *Mark works well,* while *Joseph*
Joseph ne fait pas grand-   *doesn't do much of anything.*
chose.

When *while* means *whereas,* it is expressed by **tandis que** (pronounced either [tãdikə] or [tãdiskə]).

Sometimes **tandis que** is also used in the sense of *during the time that,* but it is best for the learner to reserve **tandis que** for *while = whereas.*

61. wish

(a) How to *wish someone something*

Je vous **souhaite** un bon voyage.	*I* wish *you a good trip.*

The verb **souhaiter** is used to *wish someone something.*

(b) How **désirer** expresses *wish*

Pauline **désire** toujours avoir ce qu'ont les autres.	*Pauline always* wishes *to have what others have.*

The verb **désirer** means *wish* or *desire.* It may be used in the spoken language but is much less common than the verb **vouloir.**

(c) How to express *wish* by the conditional of **vouloir** and **aimer**

François $\begin{cases} \textbf{voudrait} \\ \textbf{aimerait} \end{cases}$ être très riche.	*Francis* wishes *that he were very rich.*

The conditional of **aimer** and **vouloir** is used with the INFINITIVE to express *wish* when the subject of the main and subordinate clauses are the same in the English sentence.

Nous $\begin{cases} \textbf{voudrions} \\ \textbf{aimerions} \end{cases}$ que Roger vienne avec nous.	*We* wish (*that*) *Roger would come with us.*

The conditional of **aimer** and **vouloir** + **que** + SUBJUNCTIVE is used to express wish when the subject of the main and subordinate clauses is different in both the English and French sentences.

R.   Remplacez les mots anglais par leur équivalent français.

1. Vincent est marié, mais il (*visits*) sa mère tous les jours.   **2.** Vous avez accepté sa proposition tout de suite (*while*) vous auriez dû discuter.   **3.** Le directeur (*wishes*) vous parler.   **4.** Il peut bien être fatigué, il a (*very much*) travaillé.   **5.** Nous (*visited*) plusieurs musées à Rome.   **6.** Je travaillerai au bureau (*while*) tu seras chez Martine.   **7.** Les Marcellin sont revenus de la mer; nous devrions (*visit them*).   **8.** Je (*wish*) que tu m'apprennes à jouer de la guitare. **9.** Il fait bon chez vous (*while*) il fait toujours froid chez nous. **10.** Si vous n'avez pas le temps de (*visit*) la ville, montez au moins sur la colline.   **11.** (*tu*) Jean a un examen aujourd'hui; (*wish*)-lui bonne chance.

S. **Traduisez en français. Attention aux mots en italique.**

1. (*vous*) If I have time, I will *visit* you Friday afternoon.   2. (*tu*) I *wish* you a[1] Happy New Year.   3. Louis learned Arabic *while* he was in Africa.   4. This morning I *visited* my former teacher.   5. I have always *wished* to travel.   6. I speak only one language, *while* Alexander speaks several.   7. (*vous*) Have you ever *visited* Athens? 8. I *wish* I could go to Portugal this year.   9. I would be glad to see Madeleine again; I like her *very much.*

[1] une bonne année

Verb Review

Review the verbs **venir** and **vivre** according to the outline on page 253.

17

Problem Prepositions

L'auteur a perdu son oncle Eugène, un modèle de vertu. Le jour de l'enterrement[1] un[2] envoi de librairie arrive contre[3] remboursement. Comme cette dernière dette est «sacrée», la famille la paie. Or le livre est polisson[4] et fait[5] scandale. Plus tard il apprend qu'un ami a perdu une vieille tante, la pauvre Jeanne, une ignorante. Le jour de l'enterrement un envoi de librairie arrive contre remboursement: une grammaire russe. On paie les 300 francs, la tante devient presque une héroïne posthume et sert d'exemple à tous.

L'auteur se met à la recherche du libraire qui envoie ces livres aux morts. Il découvre enfin son adresse le jour de l'enterrement du capitaine à la retraite Jean-Baptiste Plat, dont la famille a reçu à son nom le *Manuel du relieur*[6]. Il va le voir.

Contre remboursement

M. Beutre était dans sa librairie, un magasin fort petit, *d'*aspect minable[7]. C'était un petit homme *à*[8] barbiche qui m'invita à m'asseoir.

—Monsieur Beutre, lui dis-je sans prendre la peine de voiler mon émotion, je viens vous voir à propos d'un mystère que vous seul pouvez
5 éclaircir. Il y a *environ* deux ans, vous ne vous en souviendrez peut-être pas, vous avez envoyé à mon oncle, M. Eugène Bosserand, un volume . . .

—C'est fort possible *car* je me charge, pour quelques clients, de rechercher les ouvrages qui les intéressent.

10 —Vous avez également envoyé un volume à Mlle Jeanne Dufour. . . .
—Cela[9] n'est pas exclu.

---

[1] *funeral*　[2] un envoi de librairie *a package from a bookstore*　[3] contre remboursement *COD*　[4] *off-color*　[5] fait scandale　*causes a scandal*　[6] *bookbinder*　[7] *shabby*　[8] à barbiche　*with a goatee*　[9] Cela n'est pas exclu.　*That's quite possible.*

—Et, tout récemment, un ouvrage au capitaine Plat.

—En effet, celui-là, je m'en souviens.

—Eh bien! monsieur, ces trois personnes sont mortes.

15 —Mortes! Que me dites-vous là?

—La vérité, monsieur!

La décence aurait dû lui commander une expression d'étonnement navré[10]. Mais je ne lisais rien de[11] pareil sur son visage. *Jusque*-là, la tête penchée, il se contentait de[12] me regarder fixement.

20 —Mais il y a autre chose, monsieur: dans chacun des cas, le volume envoyé par vous est arrivé le[13] jour même de l'enterrement.

—Non? Comme c'est curieux!

—Oui, toutes les coïncidences sont possibles, je le sais. Ce qui me tracasse[14], ce qui me ronge[15], c'est ceci: chaque fois, le volume envoyé

25 ne[16] répondait en rien au caractère du défunt, à ses habitudes ou, du moins, à l'idée que nous[17] nous en faisions.

M. Beutre leva ses deux mains.

—Je ne suis pas responsable de ce que me commandent mes clients.

—Mais[18] précisément s'agit-il bien des volumes qu'ils vous ont com-

30 mandés? C'est cela que je veux savoir. N'avez-vous pas fait d'erreurs dans vos expéditions? Tout cela est tellement étrange. Je concevrais encore que le capitaine Plat vous ait commandé quelque ouvrage de stratégie ou même un traité de jardinage. Mais un manuel de reliure[19] alors que, *d'après* mes informations, il ne s'intéressait pas à cet art et qu'il ne lisait

35 pas deux livres par an? . . . Et Mlle Dufour? Mlle Dufour était une brave femme, mais une sotte, monsieur, dont l'univers intellectuel ne dépassait pas le mouron[20] de ses oiseaux. Et elle vous aurait commandé une grammaire russe du troisième[21] degré? Impossible! Et mon oncle enfin! Mon oncle était un modèle de vertu. Et vous lui avez envoyé un ouvrage

40 polisson. Oh! je sais, chacun a son secret, on est étonné parfois de ce qu'on découvre, les hommes se[22] plaisent à cacher leurs tares[23]. Oui, pour mon oncle, cela s'explique. Mais pourquoi le capitaine Plat eût-il dissimulé qu'il s'intéressât à la reliure? Quelle étrange pudeur[24] pouvait inciter Mlle Dufour à cacher qu'elle apprenait le russe? Dois-je croire que

45 rien n'est vrai, que nos jugements sont précaires[25]? . . . Pourtant la psychologie existe, monsieur . . .

M. Beutre eut l'air d'émerger enfin de son impassibilité.

---

[10] *distressed*   [11] In French an indefinite (in this case, **rien**) is always separated from the following adjectives (in this case, **pareil**) by **de**.   [12] **de me regarder fixement**   *to stare at me*   [13] **le jour même**   *the very day*   [14] *bothers*   [15] *torments*   [16] **ne répondait en rien**   *in no way corresponded*   [17] **nous nous en faisions**   *we had of him*
[18] **Mais précisément s'agit-il bien des volumes**   *But was it really those books*
[19] *bookbinding*   [20] *chickweed*   [21] **troisième degré**   *third level*   [22] **se plaisent à** *like to, be in the habit of*   [23] *vices*   [24] *modesty*   [25] *uncertain*

—Monsieur, me dit-il en me posant la main sur le bras, votre émotion me touche. Mais vous ne me dénoncerez pas?

50 —Promis.

—Puis-je vous croire et vous parler *en* ami?

—Oui, monsieur.

—La chose est simple. Il y a deux ans, dans une vente, j'ai acheté au[26] poids du papier chez un revendeur un lot de cinq cents kilos de volumes

55 parce que je croyais pouvoir les[27] écouler avec profit. *Après que* le lot a été inventorié[28], je me suis aperçu qu'il s'agissait d'ouvrages invendables. Que pouvais-je faire? Me résigner à cette perte[29] sèche? J'ai femme et enfants, monsieur. C'est alors que l'idée m'est venue de consulter les nécrologies[30] des journaux et d'envoyer mes volumes contre rembourse-

60 ment aux personnes dont j'apprenais ainsi le décès. La psychologie existe, m'avez-vous dit? C'est ce qui m'a touché, monsieur. Car mon procédé est fondé sur la psychologie. Où arrive mon envoi? Dans des maisons riches où un domestique indifférent ne dérange pas pour si peu ses patrons en[31] deuil et paie sans regarder. Dans des maisons pauvres

65 où on se[32] ferait scrupule de ne pas acquitter, *malgré* le prix, cette dernière dette du défunt. Le croiriez-vous? Il n'arrive pas deux fois *sur* dix que l'envoi soit refusé. Ah, il y a encore plus de braves gens qu'on ne le croit, monsieur. Certes, dans ces conditions, on[33] ne saurait demander que, chaque fois, l'ouvrage envoyé réponde aux desiderata[34] du client.

70 Mais quels desiderata au fond? Puisqu'ils sont morts . . . D'ailleurs, mon stock maintenant est *à peu près* épuisé[35]. Il ne me reste que quelques volumes. Tenez, je m'apprêtai précisément à envoyer un des derniers. Un ouvrage *sur* la Chine. Il n'est pas sans intérêt. Si vous le voulez, je vous donnerai volontiers la préférence. Non?

D'après Félicien Marceau. D'origine belge, il est l'auteur de contes, de romans et de pièces pleines d'observation profonde et de fantaisie. («Contre remboursement», dans *Les belles natures,* Gallimard, 1975)

---

[26] au poids *by weight* [27] les écouler *dispose of them* [28] *catalogued* [29] perte sèche *dead loss* [30] *obituaries* [31] en deuil *in mourning* [32] se ferait scrupule de *would have scruples about* [33] on ne saurait demander que *one could not expect that* [34] *possible interests* [35] *sold out*

I. English Words that are both Prepositions and Conjunctions

Certain English words, such as *after, as, before,* and *since* are sometimes used as prepositions to introduce a prepositional phrase, and sometimes as conjunctions to introduce a dependent clause, which has its own subject and verb. It is important to know when such English words are used as a preposition and when as a conjunction, for French often uses one word to express the English preposition and another to express the English conjunction.

Among the most common English words used both as a preposition and a conjunction are:

PREPOSITION   CONJUNCTION

1. after

après*

Nous sommes partis **après** l'annonce des résultats.

We left after *the announcement of the results.*

après que

Nous sommes partis **après que**
le directeur a annoncé les résultats.

We left after *the director an-
nounced the results.*

Après is used to express English *after* when a preposition, and **après que** when a conjunction.

2. as

comme

Comme mécanicien, il est excellent.

As a *mechanic, he is excellent.*

comme

Comme j'ai du travail à finir, je
ne peux pas aller chez vous.

As *I have work to finish, I cannot go to your house.*

Sometimes **comme** is used to express the English *as* both when a preposition and a conjunction.

The preposition **comme,** meaning *as,* is normally followed by the noun alone, without **un, une,** or **des** and is used in a phrase which has a general sense.

On the other hand, when **comme** is followed by **un, une,** or **des** plus a noun, it means *like* and is used in a phrase implying a comparison. Ex.: Il parle **comme** un professeur. (*He talks* like *a teacher.*) Il conduit **comme** un fou. (*He drives* like *a madman.*)

As a conjunction, **comme** means *as = because.*

en

Il s'est conduit **en** véritable ami.

He behaved as *a true friend.*

à mesure que

À mesure qu'il vieillissait, il
devenait moins sévère.

As *he got older, he became less
strict.*

---

* For après + VERBAL CONSTRUCTION, see page 224, §25.

The preposition **en** followed by the noun unmodified by **un, une,** or **des,** means *as* in the sense of *in the character of.*

The conjunction **à mesure que** means *as* = *in proportion as.*

3. because

à cause de	parce que
Je suis resté à la maison **à cause de** la pluie.	Je suis resté à la maison **parce qu**'il pleuvait.
I stayed home because of *the rain.*	*I stayed home* because *it was raining.*

The English preposition *because of* is expressed in French by **à cause de** and is followed by a noun or pronoun, whereas the English conjunction *because* is expressed in French by **parce que** and is followed by a clause.

4. before

avant	avant que
Nous sommes partis **avant** l'annonce des résultats.	Nous sommes partis **avant que** le directeur annonce les résultats.
We left before *the announcement of the results.*	*We left* before *the director announced the results.*

The conjunction **avant que** is always followed by the subjunctive, and both the present and past subjunctive are found with it. Thus, «Nous sommes partis **avant que** le directeur **ait annoncé** les résultats» is also correct.

5. but

sauf	mais
Tout le monde est parti **sauf** Suzanne.	Georges est parti, **mais** où est-il allé?
Everyone left but *Suzanne.*	*Georges left,* but *where did he go?*

The word *but* is usually a conjunction. However, it is occasionally used as a preposition, and then it is equivalent to the English *except.* The preposition *but* may be expressed in several ways*, the most common of which is probably **sauf.**

---

* For other ways, see page 242, §18.

6. for

pour	**car**
Nous avons fait cela **pour** vous.	Nous avons fait cela, **car** vous n'étiez pas ici.
We did that for *you.*	*We did that,* for *you were not here.*

The commonest way of expressing *for* as a preposition is **pour.** *

The conjunction *for* is always expressed by **car,** and its meaning is somewhat similar to that of *because.*

7. since

depuis	**depuis que**
Philippe est chez nous **depuis** jeudi.	Philippe est chez nous **depuis que** ses parents sont partis pour la Suisse.
Philip has been with us since *Thursday.*	*Philip has been with us* since *his parents left for Switzerland.*

When *since* indicates time, it is expressed by **depuis** as a preposition and by **depuis que** as a conjunction.

Note that the preposition **depuis** and its equivalents are usually followed by the present tense in French where English uses the present perfect tense.

puisque

Puisque vous partez pour la Suisse, Philippe peut venir chez nous.

Since *you are leaving for Switzerland, Philip can come to our house.*

When *since* = *because,* it is a conjunction and is expressed in French by **puisque.**

8. until

jusqu'à	**jusqu'à ce que**
Nous resterons ici **jusqu'à** dimanche.	Nous resterons ici **jusqu'à ce que** vous reveniez.
We'll stay here until *Sunday.*	*We'll stay here* until *you come back.*

* For other ways, see pages 242–43, §19.

In affirmative sentences, the English *until* is expressed by **jusqu'à** when used as a preposition; as a conjunction, French expresses *until* by **jusqu'à ce que,** and the verb of dependent clause is always in the subjunctive.

pas avant	**pas avant que**
Nous n'irons <u>pas</u> à Paris **avant** dimanche.	Nous n'irons <u>pas</u> à Paris **avant que** vous so<u>yez</u> rétabli.
We *will* <u>not</u> *go to Paris* until Sunday.	We *will* <u>not</u> *go to Paris* until *you are better.*

In negative sentences, the English *not until* (= *not before*) is expressed by **pas avant;** as a conjunction, French expresses *not until* (= *not before*) by **pas avant que,** and the verb of the dependent clause is always in the subjunctive.

CAUTION: DO NOT use **jusqu'à** or **jusqu'à ce que** to express *until* in a negative sentence.

A. Remplacez les mots anglais indiqués entre parenthèses par l'équivalent français.

1. Nous vous traiterons tout à fait (*as a*) camarade. 2. Marie a retrouvé toutes ses clés (*but*) celle de sa voiture. 3. Roland regrette de ne pas avoir connu Françoise (*before*) elle se marie. 4. Vous viendrez me voir (*after*) la classe. 5. Je m'ennuyais (*before*) votre arrivée. 6. Il ne faut pas renoncer à un projet (*because*) on a des difficultés. 7. (*Since*) nous sommes ici, il pleut tous les jours. 8. Cherchez (*until*) vous trouviez la solution de ce problème. 9. Ma colère montait (*as*) son avocat parlait.

B. Remplacez les mots anglais indiqués entre parenthèses par l'équivalent français.

1. Il ne faut pas négliger votre famille (*because of*) vos affaires. 2. Je vous dirai mon opinion (*after*) vous aurez vu ce dossier. 3. (*Since*) votre séjour en Égypte, vous n'êtes plus le même. 4. Je voulais vous voir, (*but*) je n'ai pas pu. 5. (*Before*) son accident, il faisait toutes sortes de sports. 6. (*Since*) vous êtes debout, voulez-vous m'apporter le dictionnaire? 7. Cet argent leur permettra de vivre (*until*) la fin du mois. 8. Tu ne peux pas trouver mieux (*as a*) ami. 10. Ne partez pas (*until*) je revienne.

C. Traduisez en français.

1. The children will come[1] home immediately after the movies. 2. I visited every country in Europe but Spain. 3. Juliette was becoming[2] more and more worried as time went by. 4. (*vous*)

[1] *come home* = rentrer   [2] *become worried* = s'inquiéter

Mr. Forestier will give you a good job after you have done[3] your military service. 5. We'll not go out this evening because of the snow. 6. Since my operation, I am[4] much better. 7. Almost everyone left before Mr. Ponsard's lecture. 8. Mark and Irene danced until six o'clock in[5] the morning.

[3] What tense does French use here?   [4] *be much better* = aller beaucoup mieux   [5] du

D. Traduisez en français.

1. As a minister, Mr. Boyer was remarkable. 2. Anne cannot come until five o'clock. 3. Peter has many shortcomings, but he is very nice. 4. (*tu*) All that happened because you were careless. 5. As we have little time, we'll take an[1] airplane. 6. (*vous*) Since you like the theater, why don't you go there more often? 7. (*vous*) The director would like to speak to you before you hand[2] in your resignation. 8. The astronaut was received in his native city as a hero.

[1] Use the definite article.   [2] *hand in* = donner

II. Other English Prepositions that Pose Problems in French

Certain English prepositions pose problems in French (1) because they may also be used as another part of speech, in which case they are expressed by two different words according to their function; (2) because some English prepositions have several connotations, each of which is expressed in a special way in French.

The words presented in this section are all used as prepositions some of the time. Sometimes it seems sufficient to give just the French equivalent, at times examples best show the differences, other times an explanation of usage appears clearest.

9. about

(a) *concerning* = **de, sur, au sujet de, à propos de**

Nous parlions **de** votre nouvelle maison de campagne.
We were speaking about your new country house.

Paul nous a écrit plusieurs lettres **sur** son voyage.
Paul wrote us several letters about his trip.

Qu'est-ce que vous avez à dire **au sujet de** votre conduite?
What do you have to say about your behavior?

Personne n'a rien dit **à propos de** mon absence.
No one said anything about my absence.

When *about* means *concerning,* it is a preposition and is sometimes expressed by **de** (especially after forms of **parler**), sometimes by **sur,** and sometimes by **au sujet de** or **à propos de.** At times, but not always, several of these words could express *about* in the same sentence.

(b) *approximately* = **environ, vers, à peu près, -aine** (appended to a cardinal numeral)

J'ai vu **environ** dix apparte-ments.	*I saw* about *ten apartments.*
Michel est arrivé **vers** six heures.	*Michael came at* about *six o'clock.*
Il est **environ** dix heures.	*It is* about *ten o'clock.*
C'est **à peu près** ce que j'ai dit.	*That's* about *what I said.*
Il s'est passé une **vingtaine** d'années.	About *twenty years went by.*

The word **environ** modifies a numeral. The preposition **vers** is usually found in sentences with the time of day except when the verb of such sentences is a form of **être.** In that case, *about* is expressed by **environ.** When the suffix **-aine** is appended to a cardinal numeral, it indicates an approximation. The expression **à peu près** may be used for **environ,** but it may also modify words other than numerals.

(c) *be about to* = **être sur le point de**

Nous étions **sur le point de** partir.	*We were* about *to leave.*

10. above

En général les avions volent **au-dessus des** nuages.	*Airplanes generally fly* above *the clouds.*

The preposition *above,* meaning *over, in,* or *to a higher place,* is expressed in French by **au-dessus de.**

11. according to

Selon **Suivant** }Voltaire, il faut culti- **D'après** ver son jardin.	*According to Voltaire, one must cultivate one's garden.*

The English preposition *according to* is expressed by **selon, suivant,** and **d'après,*** which are normally interchangeable.

---

* See §13 below for another use of **d'après.**

12. across

Marc a couru après son chien **à travers** les champs.	*Mark ran after his dog* across *the fields.*
Je l'ai vu **traverser** la place **en courant.**	*I saw him* run across *the square.*
Je l'aurais salué, mais il était **de l'autre côté** de la rue.	*I would have greeted him, but he was* across *the street.*
Nous **avons traversé** le pont.	*We* went across *the bridge.*

The preposition *across* is often expressed by **à travers.** But when *across* means *on the other side of,* the French say **de l'autre côté de,** and to *run across* is **traverser en courant.** The idea of *to go across* is often expressed by using the verb **traverser.**

13. after

On l'**a appelé** Victor **d'après** son parrain.	*They* named *him Victor* after *his godfather.*

The preposition *after* is usually **après,** but *to name after* is **appeler d'après.**

14. along

Il est agréable de se promener **le long de** la Seine.	*It is pleasant to walk* along *the Seine.*
Il y a des voitures stationnées tout **le long de** la rue.	*There are cars parked all* along *the street.*
Il **a suivi le chemin** jusqu'au pont.	*He* went along the road *up to the bridge.*

The preposition *along* is usually expressed by **le long de.** But *to go along the road* is **suivre le chemin (la route)** and *to go along the street* is **suivre la rue.**

E. Remplacez le mot anglais indiqué entre parenthèses par l'équivalent français.

1. Georges fume (*about*) deux paquets de cigarettes par jour.
2. Claude et Sophie se promènent (*along*) la rivière.   3. Avez-vous vu ce qui se passe (*across*) la frontière?   4. Hier, j'ai entendu parler (*about*) votre voyage.   5. C'est (*about*) la même chose.
6. (*According to*) le traité, il n'y a aura plus de douane entre ces pays.   7. Il y avait des fleurs tout (*along*) le sentier.   8. J'ai entendu une conférence (*about*) l'énergie atomique.   9. Ils se sont revus (*at about*) six heures et demie.   10. (*After*) qui avez-vous appelé votre fils Christian?   11. (*According to*) les experts, on ne peut pas construire un pont à cet endroit.   12. Donnez-moi (*about twenty*) francs.   13. Qu'est-ce que c'est que ce fil (*above*) le pont?

14. Il ne faut pas vous inquiéter (*about*) vos enfants.
15. (*According to*) les journaux, on trouvera bientôt le coupable.
16. Je n'aime pas avoir des gens bruyants dans l'appartement (*above*) moi.   17. Je voudrais vous demander des renseignements (*about*) les hôtels à Paris.   18. Il est (*about*) trois heures du matin.

F. Traduisez en français.

1. According to his father, Francis doesn't work enough.   2. It is about five o'clock now, but Mr. Dupont locked the door at about four thirty.   3. We went along the road up to the white house.
4. After the lecture, we went home.   5. Have you heard about George's accident?   6. Our friends traveled across the whole country on a motorcycle.   7. There were about two hundred people in the library.   8. We had some good discussions about modern music.   9. We called my daughter Rose after her grandmother.

G. Traduisez en français.

1. The little boy ran across the street.   2. Louise spoke to the class about her trip to Mexico.   3. According to Mr. Parrain, they are going to build a new city hall.   4. Our friends were about to telephone us when we arrived.   5. My friend lives across the street.
6. The sun was directly above us.   7. There are about thirty girls in the dormitory.   8. It's about all I have to do.   9. Professor Martin wrote me about my examination.

15. at

With nouns, *at* is usually expressed by **à** or **dans.**
The preposition *at* with place names is taken up on pages 212–14.
With the connotation of *at the home of, at the place of business of,* or *in the country of, at* is often expressed by **chez.** Note the uses of **chez** in the following sentences.

Nous irons passer la soirée **chez les Moreau.**	*We'll go to spend the evening* at the Moreaus.
Chez nous* on dîne à six heures du soir.	In our country *we eat at six in the evening.*
N'oublie pas de passer **chez le boulanger** à ton retour.	*Don't forget to go* to the bakery *on your return.*
On retrouve cette même idée **chez tous les grands écrivains.**	*One finds this same idea* in the works of all the great writers.

* In this sentence, chez nous may also mean *at our house.*

16. before

Il y a un écran **devant** la classe.   *There is a screen* before *the class.*

Venez **avant** huit heures. }   *Come* before *eight o'clock.*
Nous avons **déjà** fait ça. }
Nous avons fait ça **avant.** }   *We did that* before.

The preposition *before* is expressed by **devant** when it indicates place and means *in front of,* and by **avant** when it indicates *time.* As an adverb, *before* may be expressed by **déjà, avant,** and **auparavant.**

17. down

Ils **sont* descendus** tout de suite.   *They* came down *at once.*

Nous **avons* descendu** la rue.   *We* went down *the street.*

The English *down* is often part of the French verb **descendre,** which may mean *to come down* or *to go down.* The English *to go down the street* is expressed in French by **descendre la rue.**

18. except

Tout le monde m'a félicité   *Everyone congratulated me* except *Mr. Picard.*
  sauf }
  à part } M. Picard.
  excepté }

The English *except* may be expressed by **sauf, à part,** and **excepté.**

19. for (time)

Nos amis sont chez nous **depuis** quinze jours.   *Our friends have been with us* for *two weeks.*

When an action begins in the past and is still going on in the present, French uses **depuis** with the present to express *for.***

Nos amis sont restés chez nous **(pendant)** quinze jours.   *Our friends stayed at our house* (for) *two weeks.*

A completed action describing a certain duration of time uses **pendant** with the compound past, where English uses *for.* This **pendant** may be omitted, just as *for* may be omitted in the English sentence.

Ces jeunes gens voyageront en Afrique **pendant** quinze jours.   *These young men will travel in Africa* for *two weeks.*

---

* Intransitive verbs of motion are usually conjugated with **être,** but when a verb of motion governs a direct object, it becomes transitive and is then conjugated with **avoir.**
** For other ways of expressing this idea, see page 43.

In the future *for* is usually expressed by **pendant.**

J'irai à Paris **pour** quinze jours. *I'll go to Paris* for *two weeks.*
Pour combien de temps par- *For how long will you be gone?*
tirez-vous?

However, with verbs of motion and the verb **être** the future is often used with **pour** to express duration of time.

20. in

(a) The preposition *in* with place names is taken up on pages 212–14.

(b) *in* + A COMMON NOUN

Nos amis sont **au** restaurant. *Our friends are* in *the restaurant.*

Jacques est **dans** sa chambre. *Jack is* in *his room.*

The usual word for *in* is **dans,** but **à** + DEFINITE ARTICLE is often used to express *in the.*

(c) *in* + **matin, après-midi, soir**

Ne faites pas de bruit **le soir** *Don't make any noise* in the
après dix heures. evening *after ten o'clock.*

For *in the morning, in the afternoon,* and *in the evening* French says **le matin, l'après-midi,** and **le soir** without the preposition **dans.**

(d) *in* to express time required to do something

Monsieur Goulet travaille très *Mr. Goulet works very fast; he*
vite; il pourrait réparer votre *could fix your television set*
télévision **en une heure.** in an hour.

To indicate the length of time required to do something, French uses **en** to express the English *in.*

(e) *in* to express time at which an action can begin

Je n'ai pas le temps maintenant, *I don't have time now, but I*
mais je pourrais réparer votre *could fix your television set*
télévision **dans trois jours.** in (meaning "after") three
days.

To indicate the moment at which an action can begin, French uses **dans** to express the English *in.*

(f) *in* used to introduce a phrase of manner

Madame Renard parle **d'une** *Mrs. Renard speaks* in a very
voix très douce. soft voice.

Phrases of manner are often introduced by the preposition **de.**

(g) *—o'clock in the—*

Je me suis réveillé **à deux heures du matin.**	*I woke up* at two o'clock in the morning.

In expressions such as **deux heures du matin, trois heures de l'après-midi** and **huit heures du soir,** the English *in the* is expressed in French by **de** + DEFINITE ARTICLE.

H. Remplacez les mot anglais indiqués entre parenthèses par leur équivalent français.

1. Paul fait tout bien (*except*) ses leçons de musique.   **2.** Vous êtes fou de dépenser votre argent (*in*) une façon aussi extravagante. **3.** Couchez-vous de bonne heure (*in the evening*).   **4.** Jean a passé le week-end (*at*) les Biéville.   **5.** (*For*) dix jours on ne savait pas où ils étaient.   **6.** Je viens de parler à Nicole; elle était (*in*) mauvaise humeur.   **7.** Le petit a dormi jusqu'à quatre heures (*in the afternoon*).   **8.** Nous partirons (*for*) huit jours.   **9.** (*In*) Molière il y a toujours des choses amusantes.   **10.** Marc a fait ses devoirs (*in*) vingt minutes.   **11.** Nous regardons la télévision (*for*) deux heures. **12.** Dépêchez-vous, le train part (*in*) une demi-heure.   **13.** Cela ne se passe pas comme ça (*at*) les Italiens.   **14.** Son mari lui a répondu (*in*) un ton ferme.   **15.** (*For*) combien de temps partirez-vous à Londres?

I. Traduisez en français.

1. Those boys have been playing here for an hour.   **2.** My alarm clock rang at six o'clock in the morning.   **3.** I will go to England for three days.   **4.** (*vous*) Your little boy went down the street a little while ago.   **5.** (*vous*) Do you want to see me at your home or in your office?   **6.** I saw Mr. Lebrun at the barber's.   **7.** I'll begin that work in a half hour.   **8.** We get up early in the morning. **9.** I slept a great deal during my illness.   **10.** Everyone came except Michael.   **11.** In Balzac one finds extraordinary characters[1]. **12.** I can finish that book in an hour.   **13.** One is always well received at their home.   **14.** We read that before.

[1] Not «caractères». See page 38.

21. in spite of

Malgré le mauvais temps, je vais sortir ce soir.	In spite of *the bad weather, I'm going out this evening.*

The English *in spite of* is expressed in French by **malgré.**

22. instead of

Au lieu d'un cadeau, j'ai donné de l'argent à Jacques.	Instead of *a gift, I gave Jack some money.*

The English *instead of* is expressed in French by **au lieu de,** which may be followed by a noun, a pronoun, or an infinitive.

23. out of

(a) *out of* = **hors de**

Votre ami est **hors de** danger maintenant.

Your friend is out of *danger now.*

The commonest equivalent of *out of* is **hors de.**

(b) *out of* = *without*

Vous êtes toujours **sans** argent.

You are always out of *money.*

When *out of* means *without,* it is expressed by **sans.**

(c) *out of* between numerals (one *out of* three)

Un étudiant **sur** cinq a déjà été en France.

One student out of *five has already been in France.*

When *out of* is used idiomatically between numerals in phrases such as *two out of three,* French expresses *out of* by **sur.**

(d) *go out of, come out of, fall out of*

Louis **est sorti de** la maison avec son chien.

Louis came out of the house with his dog.

Votre carte d'identité **est tombée de** votre portefeuille.

Your identification card has fallen out of your billfold.

The verbs *come out of* and *go out of* are expressed by **sortir de,** and *fall out of* is expressed by **tomber de.**

24. toward

Tout le monde s'est précipité **vers** la porte.

Everyone rushed toward the door.

Vers la fin de la journée, je me sens fatigué.

Toward *the end of the day I feel tired.*

The word *toward* is usually expressed by **vers,** whether it indicates motion or means *about* with an expression of time.

Il faut être loyal **envers** ses amis.

One must be loyal toward one's friends.

Quelle est son attitude **envers** ses parents?

What is his attitude toward his parents?

Used figuratively in referring to a person, *toward* is expressed by **envers.**

25. under

Le métro passe **sous** la Seine.

The subway goes under the Seine.

The most common way of expressing *under* is **sous.**

La famille Delorme habite **au-dessous de** nous.	*The Delorme family lives* under *us.*
Raymond a quinze employés **au-dessous de** lui.	*Raymond has fifteen employees* under *him.*

However, *under* and *underneath* are expressed by **au-dessous de** when used figuratively and when *under* does not mean *immediately under.*

26. up

Je **monte** cet escalier cinq fois par jour.	*I go up that stairway five times a day.*
En sortant de son bureau, Monsieur Clément **a remonté la rue.**	*On leaving his office, Mr. Clement went up the street.*

The English *up* is often part of the French verb. Two of the common expressions that express *up* are **monter,** meaning *to go up,* and **remonter la rue,** which means *to go up the street.*

27. with

(a) *with* = **avec**

Je vous ai vu **avec** une dame hier soir.	*I saw you* with *a lady yesterday evening.*

The common way of expressing *with* is **avec.**

(b) *with* = **de** after verb or adjective

Son bureau est toujours **couvert de** poussière.	*His desk is always* covered <u>with</u> *dust.*
Es-tu **content de** ta voiture?	*Are you* satisfied <u>with</u> *your car?*

Certain verbs and adjectives are regularly followed by **de** in French, and their English equivalents are followed by *with.*

(c) *with* = **chez**

Louise habite **chez** sa tante.	*Louise lives* with *her aunt.*
Chez Verlaine, la qualité musicale des mots est très importante.	*With Verlaine, the musical quality of the words is very important.*

When *with* means *at the house of* or *in the case of* + A PERSON, French generally uses **chez.**

(d) *with* in phrases of manner = **de**

Françoise regardait sa montre **d'un air anxieux.**	*Frances was looking at her watch* with an anxious air.

French phrases of manner are introduced by **de.** Sometimes this **de** is expressed in English by *with,* sometimes by *in.*

(e) *with* in phrases of characteristic = **à** + ARTICLE

Cette brune **aux yeux bleus** a beaucoup de charme.

That brunette with blue eyes *has a great deal of charm.*

French uses **à** + DEFINITE ARTICLE to indicate a characteristic of a person. English uses the preposition *with* in the same way.

(f) *with* to express attitude or manner of a part of the body = DEFINITE ARTICLE

Louis dort toujours **les bras sous les couvertures.**

Louis always sleeps with his arms under the blankets.

English uses *with* to express attitude or manner of a part of the body, whereas French uses the DEFINITE ARTICLE without a preposition.

J. Remplacez par l'équivalent français les mots anglais entre parenthèses.

1. Restez à la maison (*instead of*) vous fatiguer.   **2.** Je suis allé en classe (*in spite of*) la neige.   **3.** Connaissez-vous ce jeune homme (*with*) cheveux roux?   **4.** Les enfants (*under*) sept ans paient demi-place.   **5.** Cet homme est toujours (*out of*) travail.   **6.** Nous nous sommes dirigés (*toward*) le centre de la place.   **7.** Nous sommes très satisfaits (*with*) vos progrès.   **8.** Êtes-vous toujours indulgents (*toward*) vos amis?   **9.** Comment trouvez-vous la famille qui habite (*under*) vous?   **10.** Nous habitons (*at*) mes beaux-parents. **11.** Dans ce pays, deux personnes (*out of*) cinq savent une langue étrangère.   **12.** La terre était couverte (*with*) neige.   **13.** Aidez-moi à porter ce bureau (*toward*) la fenêtre.   **14.** Achetez une voiture (*instead of*) une moto.

K. Traduisez en français.

1. He was so surprised that he looked at me with his mouth open. **2.** Read instead of watching television.   **3.** Who is that girl with bare feet?   **4.** (*vous*) What is your attitude toward foreigners? **5.** (*vous*) Are you satisfied[1] with your new job?   **6.** (*tu*) What fell out of your pocket?   **7.** My son lives at his grandmother's. **8.** Toward the end of the play, everybody was laughing.   **9.** (*vous*) What do you have under your coat?   **10.** The room was filled with smoke.   **11.** (*tu*) Don't forget to go to the dentist's before going to the movies.   **12.** Our friends came to see us in spite of the bad weather.   **13.** One girl out of three gets married before the age of twenty[2].   **14.** Who just came out of the office?   **15.** (*vous*) I

---

[1] content   [2] Supply ans.

hope that your father is out of danger.   16. My brother-in-law has been out of work for a month.   17. When Mr. Saunier came out of the hotel, he went up the street.

Exercices d'ensemble

L. Remplacez les mots anglais entre parenthèses par l'équivalent français.

1. Nous ne pourrons pas finir votre livre (*until*) demain.   2. Nous ne pourrons pas finir votre livre (*until*) vous partiez.   3. La femme de ménage a nettoyé la maison hier (*but*) avec cette pluie tout est sale de nouveau.   4. La femme de ménage a tout nettoyé (*but*) la chambre des garçons.   5. Rentrez (*before it rains*).   6. Rentrez (*before midnight*).   7. (*As a doctor*) Georges n'est pas très compétent.   8. (*As it is snowing*), restons à la maison.   9. Je vous verrai (*after*) le concert.   10. Je vous verrai (*after*) vous aurez fini votre travail.

M. Remplacez les mots anglais entre parenthèses par l'équivalent français.

1. J'ai perdu la partie (*because*) je n'ai pas assez réfléchi.   2. J'ai perdu la partie (*because*) du bruit autour de nous.   3. Gérard restera en France (*until*) la fin du mois.   4. Gérard restera en France (*until*) il ait fini ses recherches.   5. Joseph a travaillé (*for*) il le fallait. 6. Joseph a travaillé (*for*) sa famille.   7. Frédéric est installé chez nous (*since* = *because*) ses frères sont revenus.   8. Frédéric est installé chez nous (*since*) hier soir.   9. Frédéric est installé chez nous (*since*) il a eu son accident.

Dans les devoirs N et O, sur les trois prépositions proposées, employez celle qui convient le mieux au sens de la phrase.

N. 1. (Malgré, Sauf, Suivant) les risques, les contrebandiers traversent toujours la frontière.   2. Le jeune homme (aux, avec des, des) cheveux longs vient toujours s'asseoir à la terrasse à dix heures. 3. Le Concorde vole de Paris à New York (dans, en, envers) deux heures.   4. De plus en plus, les gens veulent habiter (au-dessus de, hors de, le long de) la ville.   5. J'aime tout dans ce roman (après, sauf, selon) le dernier chapitre.   6. Où peut-on être mieux que (autour de, avec, chez) soi?   7. Solange s'habille toujours (à la, de, sans) façon extravagante.   8. Dans ce pays, cinq habitants (dans, hors de, sur) six ne savent ni lire ni écrire.   9. Pourquoi est-ce que le bateau se dirige (dans, envers, vers) cette île?

O. 1. Jeannot a dû faire un mauvais rêve et il est tombé (au-dessus de, dans le, du) lit.   2. Un drôle de bruit m'a réveillé à trois heures (dans le, du, le) matin.   3. Je ne pourrai jamais être à l'aéroport (avec, dans, en) deux heures.   4. Tu ne vas pas t'arrêter (avant, derrière, devant) chaque vitrine?   5. Essaie de ne pas tousser (depuis, devant, pendant) le concert.   6. Prenez donc l'avion (au lieu de, avec, vers) l'autobus.   7. Il faut faire son chemin avec courage et (avec, sans, vers des) illusions.   8. Votre attitude (envers, sur, vers) vos collègues me semble irréprochable.

Problem Words

62. would

(a) When *would* is used to express a condition

Je **partirais** tout de suite si j'avais le temps.   *I* would leave *immediately if I had time.*

The word *would* is often a part of the conclusion of an English conditional sentence. In this case, French puts the verb in the CONDITIONAL.

Que **ferais**-tu à ma place?   *What* would *you* do *in my place?*

Sometimes *would* is the auxiliary of the verb of an implied condition, that is, one in which the *if*-clause is missing but implied. The above sentence, for instance, means: *What would you do if you were I?* In an implied condition, French uses the CONDITIONAL of the verb of the sentence to express the English *would.*

(b) When *would* means *used to*

Je **partais** de bonne heure tous les matins.   *I* would (= used to) *leave early every morning.*

When *would* = *used to,* it indicates a customary past action, and in such cases the IMPERFECT of the verb must be used.

CAUTION: Whenever you find *would* in an English sentence that you wish to express in French, determine whether *would* is part of a condition or whether it is used to describe a customary action and is the equivalent of *used to.* If *would* is the equivalent of *used to,* use the imperfect rather than the conditional.

63. year

(a) When *year* is expressed by **année**

En quelle **année** êtes-vous né?	*In what* year *were you born?*
Cette **année**-là il a beaucoup neigé.	*That* year *it snowed a great deal.*
J'ai passé beaucoup d'**années** en France.	*I spent many* years *in France.*
Ma troisième **année** à l'université a été très amusante.	*My third* year *at the university was very entertaining.*

The most common word for *year* is **année.** It should be used except in the cases stated in (**b**).

(b) When *year* is expressed by **an**

Nous avons passé **trois ans** en France.	*We spent* three years *in France.*
Nous y retournons **tous les ans.**	*We go back there* every year.
Sans indiscrétion, combien gagnez-vous **par an?**	*If it isn't indiscreet to ask, how much do you earn* a year?

The word **an** is used for *year* when it is modified by a cardinal numeral, in the expressions **tous les ans** (*every year*) and **par an** (*per year*) and occasionally in other circumstances.

64. yes

(a) When *yes* is expressed by **oui**

—Êtes-vous arrivé hier?	*"Did you arrive yesterday?"*
—**Oui,** je suis arrivé hier.	*"Yes, I arrived yesterday."*

The usual word for *yes* is **oui;** it indicates the speaker's agreement with the previous statement or question.

(b) When *yes* is expressed by **si**

—**N'êtes**-vous **pas** arrivé hier?	*"Didn't you arrive yesterday?"*
—**Si,** je suis arrivé hier.	*"Yes, I arrived yesterday."*
—Guy **ne** comprend **pas** bien l'anglais.	*"Guy doesn't understand English well."*
—**Si,** il le comprend bien.	*"Yes, he does understand it well."*

After a negative statement or question, **si** is used for *yes.* It contradicts the preceding statement or question.

65. young men

How to express the plural of **jeune homme**

Il y avait **des jeunes gens** et des jeunes filles à cette réception.	*There were* some young men *and some young ladies at that reception.*
Lucile voudrait connaître **des jeunes gens** avec qui elle puisse sortir.	*Lucille would like to get acquainted with* some young men *with whom she could go out.*

The plural of **jeune homme** is **jeunes gens.** A frequent meaning of **jeunes gens** is therefore *young men.* The expression **les jeunes hommes** seldom occurs, and you should avoid using it.

Les **jeunes gens** s'amusent beaucoup pendant la traversée en bateau.	Young people *have a very good time during a boat trip.*

The term **jeunes gens** also means *young people.* The context must decide where **jeunes gens** means *young men* and where *young people.*

P. Remplacez les mots anglais par leur équivalent français.

1. Dans quelques (*years*) j'espère savoir plusieurs langues. **2.** Ces (*young men*) avec leurs cheveux longs ressemblent à des filles. **3.** Nos amis mexicains ne sont pas retournés dans leur pays depuis dix (*years*) **4.** —Pourquoi ne prenez-vous pas le train de cinq heures? —Parce que je (*would arrive*) au milieu de la nuit. **5.** —Je ne parle pas bien le français. —(*Yes*), vous le parlez fort bien. **6.** Agnès ne veut sortir qu'avec des (*young men*) de son âge. **7.** Le patron change de voiture (*every year*). **8.** Quand je préparais mes examens, je (*would get up*) à six heures du matin. **9.** —Voulez-vous m'accompagner chez les Bridoux?—(*Yes*), volontiers.

Q. Traduisez en français. Attention aux mots en italique.

1. I think I could go to France in[1] two *years.* **2** (*vous*) *Would* you lend me your car this weekend? **3.** Our cousins from Pontigny come to see us twice a *year.* **4.** (*tu*) "Do you like that music?" "*Yes,* very much." **5.** Robert and Roger are very serious *young men.* **6.** (*vous*) In[2] what *year* did you come to the United States? **7.** When we were young, we *would*[3] play tennis every Saturday. **8.** I found the first *year* of medicine the most difficult. **9.** (*tu*) "Haven't you seen Alain?" "*Yes,* he's coming."

[1] dans [2] en [3] faire du tennis

Verb Review

Review the verbs **voir** and **vouloir** according to the outline on page 253.

Verbs

The Organization of the French Verb

To be able to use the French verb adequately, you must know the forms of the present, imperfect, future and compound past of the indicative, the conditional, and the present and past subjunctive of each type of regular verb and of the common irregular verbs. To have a complete picture of the verb, you should also know the other compound tenses, the simple past, and the imperfect subjunctive of these verbs.

Regular verbs may be classified as follows:

1. **-er** verbs
2. **-ir** verbs which insert **-iss-** in the plural of the present, throughout the imperfect, and in the present subjunctive
3. **-ir** verbs which do not insert **-iss-** anywhere
4. **-re** verbs

In addition to these, you should know the forms of verbs in **-cevoir,** such as **recevoir,** verbs in **-aindre** and **-eindre,** such as **craindre** and **peindre,** verbs with past participles in **-ert,** such as **ouvrir,** and the following frequently used irregular verbs:

aller	**être**	**rire**
avoir	**faire**	**savoir**
boire	**falloir**	**suivre**
courir	**lire**	**tenir**
croire	**mettre**	**valoir**
devoir	**mourir**	**venir**
dire	**pouvoir**	**vivre**
écrire	**prendre**	**voir**
envoyer		**vouloir**

Once you know the forms of an irregular verb such as **prendre,** you can also handle its compounds, such as **apprendre** and **comprendre.**

Regular verbs are formed on the verb stem which is found by taking the infinitive ending from the infinitive:

INFINITIVE	STEM
1. **donn-er**	**donn-**
2. **fin-ir**	**fin-**
3. **dorm-ir**	**dorm-**
4. **perd-re**	**perd-**

Both types of **-ir** verbs have peculiarities.

Verbs of the type of **finir** insert an **-iss-** between the stem and the ending in the present participle, the plural forms of the present indicative, throughout the imperfect indicative, and in the present subjunctive.

Verbs of the type of **dormir** drop the last consonant of the stem before adding the endings in the singular of the present indicative.

Irregular verbs are formed on several stems.

In order to get a complete picture of the verb and thus facilitate learning it, it is helpful to know the five principal parts of the verb and also to know which tenses are formed from each of these principal parts.

Below are the five principal parts of the regular verbs and of some of the irregular verbs. The stems are in boldface type.

INFINITIVE	PRESENT PARTICIPLE	PAST PARTICIPLE	PRESENT (*singular*)	SIMPLE PAST (*singular*)
donner	**donn**ant	donné	je **donn**e	je **donn**ai
finir	**fin**issant	fini	je **fin**is	je **fin**is
dormir	**dorm**ant	dormi	je **dor**s	je **dorm**is
perdre	**perd**ant	perdu	je **perd**s	je **perd**is
recevoir	**recev**ant	reçu	je **reçoi**s	je **reçu**s
craindre	**craign**ant	craint	je **crain**s	je **craign**is
ouvrir	**ouvr**ant	ouvert	j'**ouvr**e	j'**ouvr**is
boire	**buv**ant	bu	je **boi**s	je **bu**s
écrire	**écriv**ant	écrit	j'**écri**s	j'**écriv**is
faire	**fai**sant	fait	je **fai**s	je **fi**s
venir	**ven**ant	venu	je **vien**s	je **vin**s

There follows a list of the five principal parts of the verb along with the tenses derived from each principal part:

INFINITIVE	PRESENT PARTICIPLE	PAST PARTICIPLE	PRESENT	SIMPLE PAST
future	plural of present	compound past	singular of present	simple past
conditional	imperfect indicative	pluperfect indicative		imperfect subjunctive
	present subjunctive	future perfect		
		past conditional		
		past anterior		
		«passé surcomposé»		
		past subjunctive		
		pluperfect subjunctive		

Here is the conjugation of the verb **boire** with the tenses arranged under the principal part from which each is derived.

INFINITIVE	PRESENT PARTICIPLE	PAST PARTICIPLE	PRESENT INDICATIVE	SIMPLE PAST
boire	**buvant**	**bu**	je **bois** tu bois il boit	je **bus** tu bus il but nous bûmes vous bûtes ils burent

FUTURE	PLURAL OF PRESENT INDICATIVE	COMPOUND PAST INDICATIVE		
je boirai	nous buvons	j'ai bu, etc.		
tu boiras	vous buvez			
il boira	ils boivent			
nous boirons		PLUPERFECT INDICATIVE		IMPERFECT SUBJUNCTIVE
vous boirez		j'avais bu, etc.		que je busse
ils boiront	IMPERFECT INDICATIVE			que tu busses
	je buvais	FUTURE PERFECT		qu'il bût
CONDITIONAL	tu buvais	j'aurai bu, etc.		que nous bussions
je boirais	il buvait			que vous bussiez
tu boirais	nous buvions	PAST CONDITIONAL		qu'ils bussent
il boirait	vous buviez	j'aurais bu, etc.		
nous boirions	ils buvaient			
vous boiriez		PAST ANTERIOR		
ils boiraient		j'eus bu, etc.		
	PRESENT SUBJUNCTIVE			
	que je boive	PASSÉ SURCOMPOSÉ		
	que tu boives	j'ai eu bu, etc.		
	qu'il boive			
	que nous buvions	PAST SUBJUNCTIVE		
	que vous buviez	que j'aie bu, etc.		
	qu'ils boivent			
		PLUPERFECT SUBJUNCTIVE		
		que j'eusse bu, etc.		

The regular and the common irregular verbs are conjugated by tenses on pages 256–73. This is practical for easy reference, but the verbs will be easier to learn if you rearrange them by stems as shown in the above conjugation of the verb **boire.**

At the end of each lesson are two verbs to be reviewed. If your instructor directs you to do so, learn to write each tense under the proper principal part as above. To find the forms you do not know, consult pages 256–73.

The conjugation of the verb

INFINITIVE AND PARTICIPLES	INDICATIVE			
	PRESENT	IMPERFECT	SIMPLE PAST	FUTURE
1. -er *verbs* **parler** (*speak*) parlant parlé	parle parles parle parlons parlez parlent	parlais parlais parlait parlions parliez parlaient	parlai parlas parla parlâmes parlâtes parlèrent	parlerai parleras parlera parlerons parlerez parleront
	COMPOUND PAST	PLUPERFECT	PAST ANTERIOR	FUTURE PERFECT
	ai parlé as parlé a parlé avons parlé avez parlé ont parlé	avais parlé avais parlé avait parlé avions parlé aviez parlé avaient parlé	eus parlé eus parlé eut parlé eûmes parlé eûtes parlé eurent parlé	aurai parlé auras parlé aura parlé aurons parlé aurez parlé auront parlé
	PRESENT	IMPERFECT	SIMPLE PAST	FUTURE
2. -ir *verbs* **finir** (*finish*) finissant fini	finis finis finit finissons finissez finissent	finissais finissais finissait finissions finissiez finissaient	finis finis finit finîmes finîtes finirent	finirai finiras finira finirons finirez finiront
	COMPOUND PAST	PLUPERFECT	PAST ANTERIOR	FUTURE PERFECT
	ai fini as fini a fini avons fini avez fini ont fini	avais fini avais fini avait fini avions fini aviez fini avaient fini	eus fini eus fini eut fini eûmes fini eûtes fini eurent fini	aurai fini auras fini aura fini aurons fini aurez fini auront fini
	PRESENT	IMPERFECT	SIMPLE PAST	FUTURE
3. -re *verbs* **perdre** (*lose*) perdant perdu	perds perds perd perdons perdez perdent	perdais perdais perdait perdions perdiez perdaient	perdis perdis perdit perdîmes perdîtes perdirent	perdrai perdras perdra perdrons perdrez perdront
	COMPOUND PAST	PLUPERFECT	PAST ANTERIOR	FUTURE PERFECT
	ai perdu as perdu a perdu avons perdu avez perdu ont perdu	avais perdu avais perdu avait perdu avions perdu aviez perdu avaient perdu	eus perdu eus perdu eut perdu eûmes perdu eûtes perdu eurent perdu	aurai perdu auras perdu aura perdu aurons perdu aurez perdu auront perdu

La conjugaison du verbe

CONDITIONAL	IMPERATIVE	SUBJUNCTIVE	

PRESENT CONDITIONAL		PRESENT	IMPERFECT
parlerais		parle	parlasse
parlerais	parle	parles	parlasses
parlerait		parle	parlât
parlerions	parlons	parlions	parlassions
parleriez	parlez	parliez	parlassiez
parleraient		parlent	parlassent

PAST CONDITIONAL		PAST	PLUPERFECT
aurais parlé		aie parlé	eusse parlé
aurais parlé		aies parlé	eusses parlé
aurait parlé		ait parlé	eût parlé
aurions parlé		ayons parlé	eussions parlé
auriez parlé		ayez parlé	eussiez parlé
auraient parlé		aient parlé	eussent parlé

PRESENT CONDITIONAL		PRESENT	IMPERFECT
finirais		finisse	finisse
finirais	finis	finisses	finisses
finirait		finisse	finît
finirions	finissons	finissions	finissions
finiriez	finissez	finissiez	finissiez
finiraient		finissent	finissent

PAST CONDITIONAL		PAST	PLUPERFECT
aurais fini		aie fini	eusse fini
aurais fini		aies fini	eusses fini
aurait fini		ait fini	eût fini
aurions fini		ayons fini	eussions fini
auriez fini		ayez fini	eussiez fini
auraient fini		aient fini	eussent fini

PRESENT CONDITIONAL		PRESENT	IMPERFECT
perdrais		perde	perdisse
perdrais	perds	perdes	perdisses
perdrait		perde	perdît
perdrions	perdons	perdions	perdissions
perdriez	perdez	perdiez	perdissiez
perdraient		perdent	perdissent

PAST CONDITIONAL		PAST	PLUPERFECT
aurais perdu		aie perdu	eusse perdu
aurais perdu		aies perdu	eusses perdu
aurait perdu		ait perdu	eût perdu
aurions perdu		ayons perdu	eussions perdu
auriez perdu		ayez perdu	eussiez perdu
auraient perdu		aient perdu	eussent perdu

The conjugation of the verb

INFINITIVE AND PARTICIPLES	INDICATIVE			
	PRESENT	IMPERFECT	SIMPLE PAST	FUTURE
4. *2d class* *-ir verbs* **dormir** *(sleep)* dormant dormi	dors dors dort dormons dormez dorment	dormais dormais dormait dormions dormiez dormaient	dormis dormis dormit dormîmes dormîtes dormirent	dormirai dormiras dormira dormirons dormirez dormiront
	COMPOUND PAST	PLUPERFECT	PAST ANTERIOR	FUTURE PERFECT
	ai dormi as dormi a dormi avons dormi avez dormi ont dormi	avais dormi avais dormi avait dormi avions dormi aviez dormi avaient dormi	eus dormi eus dormi eut dormi eûmes dormi eûtes dormi eurent dormi	aurai dormi auras dormi aura dormi aurons dormi aurez dormi auront dormi
	PRESENT	IMPERFECT	SIMPLE PAST	FUTURE
5. *-oir verbs* **recevoir** *(receive)* recevant reçu	reçois reçois reçoit recevons recevez reçoivent	recevais recevais recevait recevions receviez recevaient	reçus reçus reçut reçûmes reçûtes reçurent	recevrai recevras recevra recevrons recevrez recevront
	COMPOUND PAST	PLUPERFECT	PAST ANTERIOR	FUTURE PERFECT
	ai reçu as reçu a reçu avons reçu avez reçu ont reçu	avais reçu avais reçu avait reçu avions reçu aviez reçu avaient reçu	eus reçu eus reçu eut reçu eûmes reçu eûtes reçu eurent reçu	aurai reçu auras reçu aura reçu aurons reçu aurez reçu auront reçu
	PRESENT	IMPERFECT	SIMPLE PAST	FUTURE
6. *Intransitive verb of motion* **entrer** *(enter)* entrant entré	entre entres entre entrons entrez entrent	entrais entrais entrait entrions entriez entraient	entrai entras entra entrâmes entrâtes entrèrent	entrerai entreras entrera entrerons entrerez entreront
	COMPOUND PAST	PLUPERFECT	PAST ANTERIOR	FUTURE PERFECT
	suis entré(e) es entré(e) est entré(e) sommes entré(e)s êtes entré(e)(s) sont entré(e)s	étais entré(e) étais entré(e) était entré(e) étions entré(e)s étiez entré(e)(s) étaient entré(e)s	fus entré(e) fus entré(e) fut entré(e) fûmes entré(e)s fûtes entré(e)(s) furent entré(e)s	serai entré(e) seras entré(e) sera entré(e) serons entré(e)s serez entré(e)(s) seront entré(e)s

La conjugaison du verbe

CONDITIONAL	IMPERATIVE	SUBJUNCTIVE	

PRESENT CONDITIONAL		PRESENT	IMPERFECT
dormirais		dorme	dormisse
dormirais	dors	dormes	dormisses
dormirait		dorme	dormît
dormirions	dormons	dormions	dormissions
dormiriez	dormez	dormiez	dormissiez
dormiraient		dorment	dormissent

PAST CONDITIONAL		PAST		PLUPERFECT	
aurais dormi		aie dormi		eusse dormi	
aurais dormi		aies dormi		eusses dormi	
aurait dormi		ait dormi		eût dormi	
aurions dormi		ayons dormi		eussions dormi	
auriez dormi		ayez dormi		eussiez dormi	
auraient dormi		aient dormi		eussent dormi	

PRESENT CONDITIONAL		PRESENT	IMPERFECT
recevrais		reçoive	reçusse
recevrais	reçois	reçoives	reçusses
recevrait		reçoive	reçût
recevrions	recevons	recevions	reçussions
recevriez	recevez	receviez	reçussiez
recevraient		reçoivent	reçussent

PAST CONDITIONAL		PAST		PLUPERFECT	
aurais reçu		aie reçu		eusse reçu	
aurais reçu		aies reçu		eusses reçu	
aurait reçu		ait reçu		eût reçu	
aurions reçu		ayons reçu		eussions reçu	
auriez reçu		ayez reçu		eussiez reçu	
auraient reçu		aient reçu		eussent reçu	

PRESENT CONDITIONAL		PRESENT	IMPERFECT
entrerais		entre	entrasse
entrerais	entre	entres	entrasses
entrerait		entre	entrât
entrerions	entrons	entrions	entrassions
entreriez	entrez	entriez	entrassiez
entreraient		entrent	entrassent

PAST CONDITIONAL		PAST		PLUPERFECT	
serais entré(e)		sois entré(e)		fusse entré(e)	
serais entré(e)		sois entré(e)		fusses entré(e)	
serait entré(e)		soit entré(e)		fût entré(e)	
serions entré(e)s		soyons entré(e)s		fussions entré(e)s	
seriez entré(e)(s)		soyez entré(e)(s)		fussiez entré(e)(s)	
seraient entré(e)s		soient entré(e)s		fussent entré(e)s	

The conjugation of the verb

INFINITIVE AND PARTICIPLES	INDICATIVE			
	PRESENT	**IMPERFECT**	**SIMPLE PAST**	**FUTURE**
7. *Reflexive verb*	me lave	me lavais	me lavai	me laverai
	te laves	te lavais	te lavas	te laveras
	se lave	se lavait	se lava	se lavera
se laver	nous lavons	nous lavions	nous lavâmes	nous laverons
(*wash*	vous lavez	vous laviez	vous lavâtes	vous laverez
oneself)	se lavent	se lavaient	se lavèrent	se laveront
se lavant				
lavé	**COMPOUND PAST**	**PLUPERFECT**	**PAST ANTERIOR**	**FUTURE PERFECT**
	me suis lavé(e)	m'étais lavé(e)	me fus lavé(e)	me serai lavé(e)
	t'es lavé(e)	t'étais lavé(e)	te fus lavé(e)	te seras lavé(e)
	s'est lavé(e)	s'était lavé(e)	se fut lavé(e)	se sera lavé(e)
	nous	nous	nous	nous
	sommes lavé(e)s	étions lavé(e)s	fûmes lavé(e)s	serons lavé(e)s
	vous êtes lavé(e)(s)	vous étiez lavé(e)(s)	vous fûtes lavé(e)(s)	vous serez lavé(e)(s
	se sont lavé(e)s	s'étaient lavé(e)s	se furent lavé(e)s	se seront lavé(e)s
	PRESENT	**IMPERFECT**	**SIMPLE PAST**	**FUTURE**
8. *Auxiliary verb*	ai	avais	eus	aurai
	as	avais	eus	auras
	a	avait	eut	aura
avoir	avons	avions	eûmes	aurons
(*have*)	avez	aviez	eûtes	aurez
ayant	ont	avaient	eurent	auront
eu				
	COMPOUND PAST	**PLUPERFECT**	**PAST ANTERIOR**	**FUTURE PERFECT**
	ai eu	avais eu	eus eu	aurai eu
	as eu	avais eu	eus eu	auras eu
	a eu	avait eu	eut eu	aura eu
	avons eu	avions eu	eûmes eu	aurons eu
	avez eu	aviez eu	eûtes eu	aurez eu
	ont eu	avaient eu	eurent eu	auront eu
	PRESENT	**IMPERFECT**	**SIMPLE PAST**	**FUTURE**
9. *Auxiliary verb*	suis	étais	fus	serai
	es	étais	fus	seras
	est	était	fut	sera
être	sommes	étions	fûmes	serons
(*be*)	êtes	étiez	fûtes	serez
étant	sont	étaient	furent	seront
été				
	COMPOUND PAST	**PLUPERFECT**	**PAST ANTERIOR**	**FUTURE PERFECT**
	ai été	avais été	eus été	aurai été
	as été	avais été	eus été	auras été
	a été	avait été	eut été	aura été
	avons été	avions été	eûmes été	aurons été
	avez été	aviez été	eûtes été	aurez été
	ont été	avaient été	eurent été	auront été

La conjugaison du verbe

CONDITIONAL	IMPERATIVE	SUBJUNCTIVE	

PRESENT CONDITIONAL		PRESENT	IMPERFECT
me laverais		me lave	me lavasse
te laverais	lave-toi	te laves	te lavasses
se laverait		se lave	se lavât
nous laverions	lavons-nous	nous lavions	nous lavassions
vous laveriez	lavez-vous	vous laviez	vous lavassiez
se laveraient		se lavent	se lavassent

PAST CONDITIONAL		PAST	PLUPERFECT
me serais lavé(e)		me sois lavé(e)	me fusse lavé(e)
te serais lavé(e)		te sois lavé(e)	te fusses lavé(e)
se serait lavé(e)		se soit lavé(e)	se fût lavé(e)
nous		nous	nous
serions lavé(e)s		soyons lavé(e)s	fussions lavé(e)s
vous seriez lavé(e)(s)		vous soyez lavé(e)(s)	vous fussiez lavé(e)(s)
se seraient lavé(e)s		se soient lavé(e)s	se fussent lavé(e)s

PRESENT CONDITIONAL		PRESENT	IMPERFECT
aurais		aie	eusse
aurais	aie	aies	eusses
aurait		ait	eût
aurions	ayons	ayons	eussions
auriez	ayez	ayez	eussiez
auraient		aient	eussent

PAST CONDITIONAL		PAST	PLUPERFECT
aurais eu		aie eu	eusse eu
aurais eu		aies eu	eusses eu
aurait eu		ait eu	eût eu
aurions eu		ayons eu	eussions eu
auriez eu		ayez eu	eussiez eu
auraient eu		aient eu	eussent eu

PRESENT CONDITIONAL		PRESENT	IMPERFECT
serais		sois	fusse
serais	sois	sois	fusses
serait		soit	fût
serions	soyons	soyons	fussions
seriez	soyez	soyez	fussiez
seraient		soient	fussent

PAST CONDITIONAL		PAST	PLUPERFECT
aurais été		aie été	eusse été
aurais été		aies été	eusses été
aurait été		ait été	eût été
aurions été		ayons été	eussions été
auriez été		ayez été	eussiez été
auraient été		aient été	eussent été

The conjugation of the verb

INFINITIVE AND PARTICIPLES	INDICATIVE			
	PRESENT	IMPERFECT	SIMPLE PAST	COMPOUND PAST
10. acquérir (*acquire*) acquérant acquis	acquiers acquiers acquiert acquérons acquérez acquièrent	acquérais acquérais acquérait acquérions acquériez acquéraient	acquis acquis acquit acquîmes acquîtes acquirent	ai acquis as acquis a acquis avons acquis avez acquis ont acquis
11. aller (*go*) allant allé	vais vas va allons allez vont	allais. allais allait allions alliez allaient	allai allas alla allâmes allâtes allèrent	suis allé(e) es allé(e) est allé(e) sommes allé(e)s êtes allé(e)(s) sont allé(e)s
12. asseoir* (*seat*) asseyant assis	assieds assieds assied asseyons asseyez asseyent	asseyais asseyais asseyait asseyions asseyiez asseyaient	assis assis assit assîmes assîtes assirent	me suis assis(e)* t'es assis(e) s'est assis(e) nous sommes assis(es) vous êtes assis(e)(s) se sont assis(es)
assoyant	assois assois assoit assoyons assoyez assoient	assoyais assoyais assoyait assoyions assoyiez assoyaient		
13. battre (*beat*) battant battu	bats bats bat battons battez battent	battais battais battait battions battiez battaient	battis battis battit battîmes battîtes battirent	ai battu as battu a battu avons battu avez battu ont battu
14. boire (*drink*) buvant bu	bois bois boit buvons buvez boivent	buvais buvais buvait buvions buviez buvaient	bus bus but bûmes bûtes burent	ai bu as bu a bu avons bu avez bu ont bu

* This verb is usually used in its reflexive form **s'asseoir** (*to sit*). For this reason, the reflexive forms of the compound past and imperative are given.

Certain tenses of this verb have two forms.

La conjugaison du verbe

	CONDITIONAL	IMPERATIVE	SUBJUNCTIVE	
FUTURE			PRESENT	IMPERFECT
acquerrai	acquerrais		acquière	acquisse
acquerras	acquerrais	acquiers	acquières	acquisses
acquerra	acquerrait		acquière	acquît
acquerrons	acquerrions	acquérons	acquérions	acquissions
acquerrez	acquerriez	acquérez	acquériez	acquissiez
acquerront	acquerraient		acquièrent	acquissent
irai	irais		aille	allasse
iras	irais	va	ailles	allasses
ira	irait		aille	allât
irons	irions	allons	allions	allassions
irez	iriez	allez	alliez	allassiez
iront	iraient		aillent	allassent
assiérai	assiérais		asseye	assisse
assiéras	assiérais	assieds-toi*	asseyes	assisses
assiéra	assiérait		asseye	assît
assiérons	assiérions	asseyons-nous	asseyions	assissions
assiérez	assiériez	asseyez-vous	asseyiez	assissiez
assiéront	assiéraient		asseyent	assissent
assoirai	assoirais		assoie	
assoiras	assoirais	assois-toi	assoies	
assoira	assoirait		assoie	
assoirons	assoirions	assoyons-nous	assoyions	
assoirez	assoiriez	assoyez-vous	assoyiez	
assoiront	assoiraient		assoient	
battrai	battrais		batte	battisse
battras	battrais	bats	battes	battisses
battra	battrait		batte	battît
battrons	battrions	battons	battions	battissions
battrez	battriez	battez	battiez	battissiez
battront	battraient		battent	battissent
boirai	boirais		boive	busse
boiras	boirais	bois	boives	busses
boira	boirait		boive	bût
boirons	boirions	buvons	buvions	bussions
boirez	boiriez	buvez	buviez	bussiez
boiront	boiraient		boivent	bussent

* This verb is usually used in its reflexive form **s'asseoir** (*to sit*). For this reason, the reflexive forms of the compound past and imperative are given.

The conjugation of the verb

INFINITIVE AND PARTICIPLES	INDICATIVE			
	PRESENT	IMPERFECT	SIMPLE PAST	COMPOUND PAST
15. **conduire** (*lead*) conduisant conduit	conduis conduis conduit conduisons conduisez conduisent	conduisais conduisais conduisait conduisions conduisiez conduisaient	conduisis conduisis conduisit conduisîmes conduisîtes conduisirent	ai conduit as conduit a conduit avons conduit avez conduit ont conduit
16. **connaître** (*be acquainted*) connaissant connu	connais connais connaît connaissons connaissez connaissent	connaissais connaissais connaissait connaissions connaissiez connaissaient	connus connus connut connûmes connûtes connurent	ai connu as connu a connu avons connu avez connu ont connu
17. **courir** (*run*) courant couru	cours cours court courons courez courent	courais courais courait courions couriez couraient	courus courus courut courûmes courûtes coururent	ai couru as couru a couru avons couru avez couru ont couru
18. **craindre** (*fear*) craignant craint	crains crains craint craignons craignez craignent	craignais craignais craignait craignions craigniez craignaient	craignis craignis craignit craignîmes craignîtes craignirent	ai craint as craint a craint avons craint avez craint ont craint
19. **croire** (*believe*) croyant cru	crois crois croit croyons croyez croient	croyais croyais croyait croyions croyiez croyaient	crus crus crut crûmes crûtes crurent	ai cru as cru a cru avons cru avez cru ont cru
20. **devoir** (*owe, have to*) devant dû, due*	dois dois doit devons devez doivent	devais devais devait devions deviez devaient	dus dus dut dûmes dûtes durent	ai dû as dû a dû avons dû avez dû ont dû

* The masculine singular form of the past participle is written with the circumflex accent to distinguish it from the word **du.** All other forms are written without the accent (**dû, due, dus, dues**).

La conjugaison du verbe

FUTURE	CONDITIONAL	IMPERATIVE	SUBJUNCTIVE PRESENT	IMPERFECT
conduirai	conduirais		conduise	conduisisse
conduiras	conduirais	conduis	conduises	conduisisses
conduira	conduirait		conduise	conduisît
conduirons	conduirions	conduisons	conduisions	conduisissions
conduirez	conduiriez	conduisez	conduisiez	conduisissiez
conduiront	conduiraient		conduisent	conduisissent
connaîtrai	connaîtrais		connaisse	connusse
connaîtras	connaîtrais	connais	connaisses	connusses
connaîtra	connaîtrait		connaisse	connût
connaîtrons	connaîtrions	connaissons	connaissions	connussions
connaîtrez	connaîtriez	connaissez	connaissiez	connussiez
connaîtront	connaîtraient		connaissent	connussent
courrai	courrais		coure	courusse
courras	courrais	cours	coures	courusses
courra	courrait		coure	courût
courrons	courrions	courons	courions	courussions
courrez	courriez	courez	couriez	courussiez
courront	courraient		courent	courussent
craindrai	craindrais		craigne	craignisse
craindras	craindrais	crains	craignes	craignisses
craindra	craindrait		craigne	craignît
craindrons	craindrions	craignons	craignions	craignissions
craindrez	craindriez	craignez	craigniez	craignissiez
craindront	craindraient		craignent	craignissent
croirai	croirais		croie	crusse
croiras	croirais	crois	croies	crusses
croira	croirait		croie	crût
croirons	croirions	croyons	croyions	crussions
croirez	croiriez	croyez	croyiez	crussiez
croiront	croiraient		croient	crussent
devrai	devrais		doive	dusse
devras	devrais	dois	doives	dusses
devra	devrait		doive	dût
devrons	devrions	devons	devions	dussions
devrez	devriez	devez	deviez	dussiez
devront	devraient		doivent	dussent

The conjugation of the verb

INFINITIVE AND PARTICIPLES	INDICATIVE			
	PRESENT	IMPERFECT	SIMPLE PAST	COMPOUND PAST
21. **dire** (*say, tell*) disant dit	dis dis dit disons dites disent	disais disais disait disions disiez disaient	dis dis dit dîmes dîtes dirent	ai dit as dit a dit avons dit avez dit ont dit
22. **écrire** (*write*) écrivant écrit	écris écris écrit écrivons écrivez écrivent	écrivais écrivais écrivait écrivions écriviez écrivaient	écrivis écrivis écrivit écrivîmes écrivîtes écrivirent	ai écrit as écrit a écrit avons écrit avez écrit ont écrit
23. **envoyer** (*send*) envoyant envoyé	envoie envoies envoie envoyons envoyez envoient	envoyais envoyais envoyait envoyions envoyiez envoyaient	envoyai envoyas envoya envoyâmes envoyâtes envoyèrent	ai envoyé as envoyé a envoyé avons envoyé avez envoyé ont envoyé
24. **faire** (*do, make*) **faisant*** **fait**	fais fais fait faisons faites font	faisais* faisais faisait faisions faisiez faisaient	fis fis fit fîmes fîtes firent	ai fait as fait a fait avons fait avez fait ont fait
25. **falloir**** (*be necessary*) fallu	il faut	il fallait	il fallut	il a fallu
26. **fuir** (*flee*) fuyant fui	fuis fuis fuit fuyons fuyez fuient	fuyais fuyais fuyait fuyions fuyiez fuyaient	fuis fuis fuit fuîmes fuîtes fuirent	ai fui as fui a fui avons fui avez fui ont fui
27. **lire** (*read*) lisant lu	lis lis lit lisons lisez lisent	lisais lisais lisait lisions lisiez lisaient	lus lus lut lûmes lûtes lurent	ai lu as lu a lu avons lu avez lu ont lu

* The **ai** of the stem of these forms is pronounced like mute **e** [ə].
** Used in third person singular only.

La conjugaison du verbe

| FUTURE | CONDITIONAL | IMPERATIVE | SUBJUNCTIVE | |
			PRESENT	IMPERFECT
dirai	dirais		dise	disse
diras	dirais	dis	dises	disses
dira	dirait		dise	dît
dirons	dirions	disons	disions	dissions
direz	diriez	dites	disiez	dissiez
diront	diraient		disent	dissent
écrirai	écrirais		écrive	écrivisse
écriras	écrirais	écris	écrives	écrivisses
écrira	écrirait		écrive	écrivît
écrirons	écririons	écrivons	écrivions	écrivissions
écrirez	écririez	écrivez	écriviez	écrivissiez
écriront	écriraient		écrivent	écrivissent
enverrai	enverrais		envoie	envoyasse
enverras	enverrais	envoie	envoies	envoyasses
enverra	enverrait		envoie	envoyât
enverrons	enverrions	envoyons	envoyions	envoyassions
enverrez	enverriez	envoyez	envoyiez	envoyassiez
enverront	enverraient		envoient	envoyassent
ferai	ferais		fasse	fisse
feras	ferais	fais	fasses	fisses
fera	ferait		fasse	fît
ferons	ferions	faisons	fassions	fissions
ferez	feriez	faites	fassiez	fissiez
feront	feraient		fassent	fissent
il faudra	il faudrait		il faille	il fallût
fuirai	fuirais		fuie	fuisse
fuiras	fuirais	fuis	fuies	fuisses
fuira	fuirait		fuie	fuît
fuirons	fuirions	fuyons	fuyions	fuissions
fuirez	fuiriez	fuyez	fuyiez	fuissiez
fuiront	fuiraient		fuient	fuissent
lirai	lirais		lise	lusse
liras	lirais	lis	lises	lusses
lira	lirait		lise	lût
lirons	lirions	lisons	lisions	lussions
lirez	liriez	lisez	lisiez	lussiez
liront	liraient		lisent	lussent

The conjugation of the verb

INFINITIVE AND PARTICIPLES	INDICATIVE			
	PRESENT	IMPERFECT	SIMPLE PAST	COMPOUND PAST
28. mettre (*put*) mettant **mis**	mets mets met mettons mettez mettent	mettais mettais mettait mettions mettiez mettaient	mis mis mit mîmes mîtes mirent	ai mis as mis a mis avons mis avez mis ont mis
29. mourir (*die*) mourant mort	meurs meurs meurt mourons mourez meurent	mourais mourais mourait mourions mouriez mouraient	mourus mourus mourut mourûmes mourûtes moururent	suis mort(e) es mort(e) est mort(e) sommes mort(e)s êtes mort(e)(s) sont mort(e)s
30. naître (*be born*) naissant né	nais nais naît naissons naissez naissent	naissais naissais naissait naissions naissiez naissaient	naquis naquis naquit naquîmes naquîtes naquirent	suis né(e) es né(e) est né(e) sommes né(e)s êtes né(e)(s) sont né(e)s
31. ouvrir (*open*) ouvrant ouvert	ouvre ouvres ouvre ouvrons ouvrez ouvrent	ouvrais ouvrais ouvrait ouvrions ouvriez ouvraient	ouvris ouvris ouvrit ouvrîmes ouvrîtes ouvrirent	ai ouvert as ouvert a ouvert avons ouvert avez ouvert ont ouvert
32. peindre (*paint*) peignant peint	peins peins peint peignons peignez peignent	peignais peignais peignait peignions peigniez peignaient	peignis peignis peignit peignîmes peignîtes peignirent	ai peint as peint a peint avons peint avez peint ont peint
33. plaire (*please*) plaisant plu	plais plais plaît plaisons plaisez plaisent	plaisais plaisais plaisait plaisions plaisiez plaisaient	plus plus plut plûmes plûtes plurent	ai plu as plu a plu avons plu avez plu ont plu
34. pleuvoir* (*rain*) pleuvant plu	il pleut	il pleuvait	il plut	il a plu

* Used only in third person singular.

La conjugaison du verbe

FUTURE	CONDITIONAL	IMPERATIVE	SUBJUNCTIVE PRESENT	IMPERFECT
mettrai	mettrais		mette	misse
mettras	mettrais	mets	mettes	misses
mettra	mettrait		mette	mît
mettrons	mettrions	mettons	mettions	missions
mettrez	mettriez	mettez	mettiez	missiez
mettront	mettraient		mettent	missent
mourrai	mourrais		meure	mourusse
mourras	mourrais	meurs	meures	mourusses
mourra	mourrait		meure	mourût
mourrons	mourrions	mourons	mourions	mourussions
mourrez	mourriez	mourez	mouriez	mourussiez
mourront	mourraient		meurent	mourussent
naîtrai	naîtrais		naisse	naquisse
naîtras	naîtrais	nais	naisses	naquisses
naîtra	naîtrait		naisse	naquît
naîtrons	naîtrions	naissons	naissions	naquissions
naîtrez	naîtriez	naissez	naissiez	naquissiez
naîtront	naîtraient		naissent	naquissent
ouvrirai	ouvrirais		ouvre	ouvrisse
ouvriras	ouvrirais	ouvre	ouvres	ouvrisses
ouvrira	ouvrirait		ouvre	ouvrît
ouvrirons	ouvririons	ouvrons	ouvrions	ouvrissions
ouvrirez	ouvririez	ouvrez	ouvriez	ouvrissiez
ouvriront	ouvriraient		ouvrent	ouvrissent
peindrai	peindrais		peigne	peignisse
peindras	peindrais	peins	peignes	peignisses
peindra	peindrait		peigne	peignît
peindrons	peindrions	peignons	peignions	peignissions
peindrez	peindriez	peignez	peigniez	peignissiez
peindront	peindraient		peignent	peignissent
plairai	plairais		plaise	plusse
plairas	plairais	plais	plaises	plusses
plaira	plairait		plaise	plût
plairons	plairions	plaisons	plaisions	plussions
plairez	plairiez	plaisez	plaisiez	plussiez
plairont	plairaient		plaisent	plussent
il pleuvra	il pleuvrait		il pleuve	il plût

The conjugation of the verb

INFINITIVE AND PARTICIPLES	INDICATIVE			
	PRESENT	IMPERFECT	SIMPLE PAST	COMPOUND PAST
35. pouvoir (*be able*) pouvant pu	peux, puis peux peut pouvons pouvez peuvent	pouvais pouvais pouvait pouvions pouviez pouvaient	pus pus put pûmes pûtes purent	ai pu as pu a pu avons pu avez pu ont pu
36. prendre (*take*) prenant pris	prends prends prend prenons prenez prennent	prenais prenais prenait prenions preniez prenaient	pris pris prit prîmes prîtes prirent	ai pris as pris a pris avons pris avez pris ont pris
37. rire (*laugh*) riant ri	ris ris rit rions riez rient	riais riais riait riions riiez riaient	ris ris rit rîmes rîtes rirent	ai ri as ri a ri avons ri avez ri ont ri
38. savoir (*know*) sachant su	sais sais sait savons savez savent	savais savais savait savions saviez savaient	sus sus sut sûmes sûtes surent	ai su as su a su avons su avez su ont su
39. suivre (*follow*) suivant suivi	suis suis suit suivons suivez suivent	suivais suivais suivait suivions suiviez suivaient	suivis suivis suivit suivîmes suivîtes suivirent	ai suivi as suivi a suivi avons suivi avez suivi ont suivi
40. tenir (*hold, keep*) tenant tenu	tiens tiens tient tenons tenez tiennent	tenais tenais tenait tenions teniez tenaient	tins tins tint tînmes tîntes tinrent	ai tenu as tenu a tenu avons tenu avez tenu ont tenu

La conjugaison du verbe

	CONDITIONAL	IMPERATIVE	SUBJUNCTIVE	
FUTURE			PRESENT	IMPERFECT
pourrai	pourrais		puisse	pusse
pourras	pourrais		puisses	pusses
pourra	pourrait		puisse	pût
pourrons	pourrions		puissions	pussions
pourrez	pourriez		puissiez	pussiez
pourront	pourraient		puissent	pussent
prendrai	prendrais		prenne	prisse
prendras	prendrais	prends	prennes	prisses
prendra	prendrait		prenne	prît
prendrons	prendrions	prenons	prenions	prissions
prendrez	prendriez	prenez	preniez	prissiez
prendront	prendraient		prennent	prissent
rirai	rirais		rie	risse
riras	rirais	ris	ries	risses
rira	rirait		rie	rît
rirons	ririons	rions	riions	rissions
rirez	ririez	riez	riiez	rissiez
riront	riraient		rient	rissent
saurai	saurais		sache	susse
sauras	saurais	sache	saches	susses
saura	saurait		sache	sût
saurons	saurions	sachons	sachions	sussions
saurez	sauriez	sachez	sachiez	sussiez
sauront	sauraient		sachent	sussent
suivrai	suivrais		suive	suivisse
suivras	suivrais	suis	suives	suivisses
suivra	suivrait		suive	suivît
suivrons	suivrions	suivons	suivions	suivissions
suivrez	suivriez	suivez	suiviez	suivissiez
suivront	suivraient		suivent	suivissent
tiendrai	tiendrais		tienne	tinsse
tiendras	tiendrais	tiens	tiennes	tinsses
tiendra	tiendrait		tienne	tînt
tiendrons	tiendrions	tenons	tenions	tinssions
tiendrez	tiendriez	tenez	teniez	tinssiez
tiendront	tiendraient		tiennent	tinssent

The conjugation of the verb

INFINITIVE AND PARTICIPLES	INDICATIVE			
	PRESENT	IMPERFECT	SIMPLE PAST	COMPOUND PAST
41. vaincre (*conquer*) vainquant vaincu	vaincs vaincs vainc vainquons vainquez vainquent	vainquais vainquais vainquait vainquions vainquiez vainquaient	vainquis vainquis vainquit vainquîmes vainquîtes vainquirent	ai vanicu as vaincu a vaincu avons vaincu avez vaincu ont vaincu
42. valoir (*be worth*) valant valu	vaux vaux vaut valons valez valent	valais valais valait valions valiez valaient	valus valus valut valûmes valûtes valurent	ai valu as valu a valu avons valu avez valu ont valu
43. venir (*come*) venant venu	viens viens vient venons venez viennent	venais venais venait venions veniez venaient	vins vins vint vînmes vîntes vinrent	suis venu(e) es venu(e) est venu(e) sommes venu(e)s êtes venu(e)(s) sont venu(e)s
44. vivre (*live*) vivant vécu	vis vis vit vivons vivez vivent	vivais vivais vivait vivions viviez vivaient	vécus vécus vécut vécûmes vécûtes vécurent	ai vécu as vécu a vécu avons vécu avez vécu ont vécu
45. voir (*see*) voyant vu	vois vois voit voyons voyez voient	voyais voyais voyait voyions voyiez voyaient	vis vis vit vîmes vîtes virent	ai vu as vu a vu avons vu avez vu ont vu
46. vouloir (*wish, want*) voulant voulu	veux veux veut voulons voulez veulent	voulais voulais voulait voulions vouliez voulaient	voulus voulus voulut voulûmes voulûtes voulurent	ai voulu as voulu a voulu avons voulu avez voulu ont voulu

La conjugaison du verbe

FUTURE	CONDITIONAL	IMPERATIVE	SUBJUNCTIVE PRESENT	IMPERFECT
vaincrai	vaincrais		vainque	vainquisse
vaincras	vaincrais	vaincs	vainques	vainquisses
vaincra	vaincrait		vainque	vainquît
vaincrons	vaincrions	vainquons	vainquions	vainquissions
vaincrez	vaincriez	vainquez	vainquiez	vainquissiez
vaincront	vaincraient		vainquent	vainquissent
vaudrai	vaudrais		vaille	valusse
vaudras	vaudrais	vaux	vailles	valusses
vaudra	vaudrait		vaille	valût
vaudrons	vaudrions	valons	valions	valussions
vaudrez	vaudriez	valez	valiez	valussiez
vaudront	vaudraient		vaillent	valussent
viendrai	viendrais		vienne	vinsse
viendras	viendrais	viens	viennes	vinsses
viendra	viendrait		vienne	vînt
viendrons	viendrions	venons	venions	vinssions
viendrez	viendriez	venez	veniez	vinssiez
viendront	viendraient		viennent	vinssent
vivrai	vivrais		vive	vécusse
vivras	vivrais	vis	vives	vécusses
vivra	vivrait		vive	vécût
vivrons	vivrions	vivons	vivions	vécussions
vivrez	vivriez	vivez	viviez	vécussiez
vivront	vivraient		vivent	vécussent
verrai	verrais		voie	visse
verras	verrais	vois	voies	visses
verra	verrait		voie	vît
verrons	verrions	voyons	voyions	vissions
verrez	verriez	voyez	voyiez	vissiez
verront	verraient		voient	vissent
voudrai	voudrais		veuille	voulusse
voudras	voudrais	veuille	veuilles	voulusses
voudra	voudrait		veuille	voulût
voudrons	voudrions		voulions	voulussions
voudrez	voudriez	veuillez	vouliez	voulussiez
voudront	voudraient		veuillent	voulussent

Verbs with Spelling Changes

A. Verbs in **-cer**

Since **c** is pronounced like **s** only before **e** and **i** and like **k** before **a, o,** and **u,** verbs whose infinitives end in **-cer** change **c** to **ç** when the **c** is followed by **a, o,** or **u,** in order to preserve the *s* sound of the **c.** Changes are made then in the tenses below and in the imperfect subjunctive.

EXAMPLE: **effacer.**

PRESENT PARTICIPLE	PRESENT INDICATIVE	IMPERFECT INDICATIVE	SIMPLE PAST
effaçant	j'efface	j'effaçais	j'effaçai
	tu effaces	tu effaçais	tu effaças
	il efface	il effaçait	il effaça
	nous effaçons	nous effacions	nous effaçâmes
	vous effacez	vous effaciez	vous effaçâtes
	ils effacent	ils effaçaient	ils effacèrent

B. Verbs in **-ger**

Since **g** is pronounced like *g* in *get* before **a, o,** and **u,** and like *s* in *pleasure* before **e** and **i,** verbs whose infinitives end in **-ger** insert **e** between **g** and the next vowel whenever that vowel is not **e** or **i.** Changes are made then, in the tenses below and in the imperfect subjunctive.

EXAMPLE: **changer.**

PRESENT PARTICIPLE	PRESENT INDICATIVE	IMPERFECT INDICATIVE	SIMPLE PAST
changeant	je change	je changeais	je changeai
	tu changes	tu changeais	tu changeas
	il change	il changeait	il changea
	nous changeons	nous changions	nous changeâmes
	vous changez	vous changiez	vous changeâtes
	ils changent	ils changeaient	ils changèrent

C. Verbs in **-yer**

Verbs in **-yer** (**-ayer, -oyer, -uyer**) change **y** to **i** before a mute **e** in the following syllable. This change occurs throughout the present except for the **nous** and **vous** forms and throughout the entire future and conditional.

EXAMPLE: **nettoyer.**

PRESENT INDICATIVE	PRESENT SUBJUNCTIVE	FUTURE	CONDITIONAL
je nettoie	que je nettoie	je nettoierai	je nettoierais
tu nettoies	que tu nettoies	tu nettoieras	tu nettoierais
il nettoie	qu'il nettoie	il nettoiera	il nettoierait
nous nettoyons	que nous nettoyions	nous nettoierons	nous nettoierions
vous nettoyez	que vous nettoyiez	vous nettoierez	vous nettoieriez
ils nettoient	qu'ils nettoient	ils nettoieront	ils nettoieraient

D. Verbs in **-e-** $+ \begin{cases} \text{a single} \\ \text{consonant} \end{cases} +$ **-er**

Many verbs, such as **mener, lever,** and **acheter,** whose stems end in unaccented **e** plus a single consonant, place a grave accent (`) over this **e** whenever the following syllable also has a mute **e**. This indicates that the pronunciation of the **e** [ə] of the stem becomes **è** [ɛ]. The grave accent is found throughout the singular and in the third person plural of the present indicative and subjunctive and throughout the entire future and conditional of all these verbs.

EXAMPLE: **mener.**

PRESENT INDICATIVE	PRESENT SUBJUNCTIVE	FUTURE	CONDITIONAL
je mène	que je mène	je mènerai	je mènerais
tu mènes	que tu mènes	tu mèneras	tu mènerais
il mène	qu'il mène	il mènera	il mènerait
nous menons	que nous menions	nous mènerons	nous mènerions
vous menez	que vous meniez	vous mènerez	vous mèneriez
ils mènent	qu'ils mènent	ils mèneront	ils mèneraient

E. Verbs in **-é-** + {a single / consonant} + **-er**

Verbs whose stems end in **é** followed by a single consonant change this **é** to **è** throughout the singular and in the third person plural of the present indicative and present subjunctive, that is, in those forms in which the following syllable has a mute **e**. In the future and conditional the **é** is retained in writing, but this **é** is usually pronounced **è** because a vowel tends to open in a closed syllable.[1]

EXAMPLE: **espérer**

PRESENT INDICATIVE	PRESENT SUBJUNCTIVE	FUTURE	CONDITIONAL
j'espère	que j'espère	j'espérerai	j'espérerais
tu espères	que tu espères	tu espéreras	tu espérerais
il espère	qu'il espère	il espérera	il espérerait
nous espérons	que nous espérions	nous espérerons	nous espérerions
vous espérez	que vous espériez	vous espérerez	vous espéreriez
ils espèrent	qu'ils espèrent	ils espéreront	ils espéreraient

F. Verbs in **-eler** and some in **-eter**

Verbs in **-eler** and a few verbs in **-eter** double the **l** or **t** when the next syllable contains a mute **e**. This change takes place in the singular and third person plural of the present indicative and of the present subjunctive and throughout the future and conditional.

EXAMPLE: **appeler.**

PRESENT INDICATIVE	PRESENT SUBJUNCTIVE	FUTURE	CONDITIONAL
j'appelle	que j'appelle	j'appellerai	j'appellerais
tu appelles	que tu appelles	tu appelleras	tu appellerais
il appelle	qu'il appelle	il appellera	il appellerait
nous appelons	que nous appelions	nous appellerons	nous appellerions
vous appelez	que vous appeliez	vous appellerez	vous appelleriez
ils appellent	qu'ils appellent	ils appelleront	ils appelleraient

---

[1] The fact that the mute **e** of the infinitive drops out in pronunciation closes the preceding syllable, thus tending to open the **e**; e.g., j'espérerai [ʒɛspɛrre]; il espérerait [ilɛspɛrrɛ]; tu céderas [tysɛdra].

French-English Vocabulary

ABBREVIATIONS

adj.	adjective	*irr. sp.*	irregular spelling	*pers.*	person
adv.	adverb	*m.*	masculine	*prep.*	preposition
cond.	conditional	*n.*	noun	*pres.*	present
conj.	conjugated	*obj.*	object	*pron.*	pronoun
conjunc.	conjunction	*p.*	page	*rel.*	relative
f.	feminine	*part.*	participle	*sing.*	singular
fut.	future	*pl.*	plural	*sp*	simple past
inf.	infinitive	*pp*	past participle	*subjunc.*	subjunctive
interrog.	interrogative			*v.*	verb

*aspirate *h*   (2) -**ir** verbs that do not insert -**iss**-; all other -**ir** verbs insert -**iss**-.

Verbs whose principal parts are given are irregular, and their conjugations may be found on pp. 256–73. The use of the principal parts is explained on page 255. Verbs followed by (*conj. like* . . .) are irregular and follow the pattern of the verb indicated.

Verbs followed by (*irr. sp.* **A** to **F**) undergo a spelling change in certain forms. The letter refers to the appropriate type of change explained on pp. 274–76.

This vocabulary contains all words used in the text and in the *Manual* except words that have the same form in English and French and words whose French spelling is so near to the English that they are easily recognizable.

Adverbs ending in *-ment* are omitted when the corresponding adjective is included and when the English adverb ends in *-ly*.

A

à at; with; in; by; **à votre accent** from (by) your accent; **c'est à lui** it is up to him

a (*pres. of* avoir) has; **il y a** there is, there are; **il y a un an** a year ago

abandonner abandon; **s'abandonner** give way (to)

abattre (*conj. like* battre) tear down

abondamment abundantly

abord: d'abord at first; from the very beginning; **tout d'abord** first of all

aboyer (*irr. sp.* C) bark

abri *m.* shelter; **se mettre à l'abri** take shelter

abrupt steep

absolu absolute

Académie *f.* Academy; **Académie française** the French Academy, founded in 1635, made up of 40 prominent personalities, mainly writers; **Académie Goncourt** a group of writers which each year awards a prize for works that depart from traditional patterns

accablé overwhelmed; weary

accent *m.* accent; **à votre accent** from (by) your accent
accompagner accompany
accomplir accomplish; **accomplir un mouvement** make a movement
accomplissement *m.* accomplishment
accord *m. agreement;* **être d'accord** agree; **se mettre d'accord** come to an agreement
accueillir receive, welcome
accusé *m.* defendant
acheter (*irr. sp.* **D**) buy
acquitter pay
acteur *m.* actor
actif (*f.* **active**) active
actrice *f.* actress
actuel (*f.* **actuelle**) present-day
addition *f.* check (in a restaurant)
adieu *m.* goodbye; **faire ses adieux** say goodbye
admettre (*conj. like* **mettre**) admit
adresser (**s'**) (**à** + *n.*) go to; ask at; apply
aéroport *m.* airport
affaire *f.* affair; thing; deal; business; **les affaires** business; one's things; **tirer quelqu'un d'affaire** get someone out of trouble
affectueusement affectionately
affiche *f.* poster; bulletin
affirmer affirm
affolement *m.* panic
affreux (*f.* **affreuse**) horrible
afin de in order to; **afin que** in order that
Afrique *f.* Africa; **Afrique du Nord** North Africa
agacer (*irr. sp.* **A**) provoke
âgé old
agence *f.* agency
agent *m.* policeman; **agent de change** stock broker
aggloméré *m.* conglomerate
agir act; **s'agir de** be a question of, be about
agitation *f.* movement
agneau *m.* lamb
agrandir enlarge
agréable pleasant, agreeable
aider (+ *person* + **à** + *inf.*) help
aïeul *m.* ancestor
aile *f.* wing; **à grands coups d'ailes** with powerful flaps of the wings
aille (*pres. subjunc. of* **aller**) go
ailleurs elsewhere; **d'ailleurs** besides; **nulle part ailleurs** nowhere else
aimer (+ *inf.*) like; love
ainsi thus; so; as; **pour ainsi dire** so to speak
air *m.* air; appearance; look; **air libre** open air; **avoir l'air** (+ *adj.*) look; seem; **avoir l'air de** (+ *inf.*) seem to; **d'un air** with a look
aise *f.* ease; **être à l'aise** be comfortable; **mal à l'aise** ill at ease
ait (*pres. subjunc. of* **avoir**) has; have
ajouter add
alcool *m.* alcohol
algèbre *m.* algebra

Alger Algiers, a city on the seacoast of North Africa, capital of Algeria
Algérie *f.* Algeria
allée *f.* lane
Allemagne *f.* Germany
allemand German
aller (**allant, allé, je vais, j'allai**) (+ *inf.*) go; **aller voir** go and see, visit; **ça va de soi** that goes without saying; **cette robe vous va bien** this dress fits you well, this dress looks very becoming on you; **quelque chose ne va pas** there's something wrong; **s'en aller** go away, leave; start on one's way
allergie *f.* allergy
allié *m.* ally
allô hello (in answering the telephone)
allonger (**s'**) (*irr. sp.* **B**) stretch out
allons bon there now
allumer light; turn on the lights
alors then; **alors que** when; whereas
Alpes *f. pl.* Alps
alpiniste *m. or f.* mountain climber
âme *f.* soul
amer (*f.* **amère**) bitter
américain American
Amérique *f.* America; **Amérique du Sud** *f.* South America
amertume *f.* bitterness
ami *m.* friend
amie *f.* friend; **bonne amie** girlfriend
amitié *f.* friendship; **faites-lui mes amitiés** give him my best regards
amollir (**s'**) soften
amour (*m. in sing., f. in pl.*) love
amoureusement lovingly
amoureux *m. s. or pl.* people in love
amoureux (*f.* **amoureuse**) in love
ampleur *f.* magnitude
amusant entertaining; amusing
amuser entertain; **s'amuser** (**à** + *inf.*) have fun; have a good time; amuse oneself
an *m.* year
analogue similar
ancêtre *m. or f.* ancestor
ancien (*f.* **ancienne**) old; former
âne *m.* donkey, ass
anéantir (**s'**) be destroyed
anglais English
Angleterre *f.* England
angoissant anguished, distressed
angoissé in a state of anxiety
animé animated, lively
année *f.* year
anniversaire *m.* anniversary; birthday
annonce *f.* announcement
annoncer (*irr. sp.* **A**) announce; say; herald
anxiété *f.* anxiety, worry
anxieux (*f.* **anxieuse**) anxious, worried
apercevoir (*conj. like* **recevoir**) (+ *n.*) notice; catch sight of; **s'apercevoir** (**de** + *n.;* **que** + *clause*) notice, realize

Irregular verbs are conjugated on pp. 256–273.

apparaître (*conj. like* connaître) appear (physically)

appareil *m.* apparatus; machine; **appareil de photo** camera

appartement *m.* apartment

appartenir (*conj. like* tenir) belong

appeler (*irr. sp.* F) call; s'appeler be called, be named

appétissant appetizing

applaudir applaud

appliquer (s') apply oneself; work hard at

apporter bring

apprécier appreciate

appréhender seize

apprendre (*conj. like* prendre) (*thing* + à + *person;* à + *inf.*) learn; teach; **apprendre par cœur** memorize, learn by heart

apprêter (s') get ready

approcher (de + *n.*) approach; s'approcher (de + *n.*) approach

approfondir delve into

approuver approve

appuyer (*irr. sp.* C) lean; support; s'appuyer lean

après after; afterwards; **d'après** according to; after

après-midi *m. or f.* afternoon

arbre *m.* tree; **arbre fruitier** fruit tree

Arc de Triomphe *m.* Arch of Triumph

ardemment ardently

ardeur *f.* enthusiasm, ardor

ardoise *f.* slate

argent *m.* money; silver; **papier d'argent** aluminum foil

armé armed

armée *f.* army

armoire *f.* cupboard; a large piece of furniture used as a wardrobe

arracher snatch, grab

arrangé set

arranger (*irr. sp.* B) fix; arrange; s'arranger come out all right; manage

arrêt *m.* stop; stoppage; **sans arrêt** without stopping, ceaselessly

arrêter (de + *inf.*) stop; arrest; fix; s'arrêter (de + *inf.*) stop

arrière: **en arrière** behind

arrivé: **les nouveaux arrivés** the people who have just arrived

arrivée *f.* arrival

arriver arrive, reach; happen

arroser water

art *m.* art; **beaux-arts** fine arts

ascenseur *m.* elevator

asile *m.* insane asylum

aspirateur *m.* vacuum cleaner

asseoir (asseyant, assis, j'assieds, j'assis) sit; seat; s'asseoir sit down

assez enough; rather

assiette *f.* plate

assis (*pp and sp of* asseoir) seated; sitting

assister (à + *n.*) attend, be present at

assombri darkened

assurance *f.* insurance; **bureau d'assurance** insurance office

assurer guarantee; s'assurer make sure, assure oneself

astiquer polish

atomique atomic, nuclear

attacher (s') attach; become fond of; **s'attacher aux pas** follow closely

attaquer attack

atteindre (*conj. like* peindre) reach; affect; damage

attendre (+ *n.*) wait; wait for; expect; s'attendre (à + *n.*) expect

attente *f.* wait

attentif (*f.* attentive) attentive

attention *f.* attention; **faire attention à** watch out for; pay attention to; **faire bien attention** pay special attention to; be very careful about; **faites attention** look out

atténué subdued

atterrir land

attirer attract; s'attirer attract to oneself

attraper catch

au to the; **au revoir** goodbye

aube *f.* dawn

aubergiste *m. or f.* innkeeper

aucun any; **ne . . . aucun** no; none

audacieux (*f.* audacieuse) audacious; bold

au-dehors outside

au-delà beyond

au-dessus above

augmentation *f.* raise

augmenter increase; raise

auparavant formerly

auprès near; **auprès de** at the side of, near; compared with

aurai, aurais (*fut. and cond. of* avoir) will have; would have

aussi also; (when at beginning of sentence) so, therefore

aussitôt at once, immediately; **aussitôt que** as soon as

autant as much; **d'autant plus que** all the more because

auteur *m.* author

auto *f.* car, auto; **parc à autos** parking lot

autobus *m.* (city) bus

autocar *m.* (interurban) bus

automne *m.* autumn, fall

autoriser authorize

autoritaire dominating, bossy

autoroute *f.* freeway

autour around

autre other

autrefois formerly

autrement differently; otherwise

Autriche *f.* Austria

auxiliaire auxiliary

avance: **d'avance** in advance

Verbs with spelling changes are explained on pp. 274–276.

avancer (*irr. sp.* A) advance, move forward;
s'avancer advance; approach

avant before; ahead; formerly; avant-dernier
next to the last; avant-hier the day before
yesterday; avant tout above all

avare *m.* miser

avec with

avenir *m.* future

aventure *f.* adventure

aventurer (s') venture

avertir warn; inform

avertissement *m.* notice, indication

aveugle (*adj.*) blind; (*n.*) blind person

aveuglément blindly

avez (avoir) have

aviateur *m.* flier

avion *m.* airplane

avis *m.* opinion; changer d'avis change one's
mind; être de l'avis de be of the opinion
that

avocat *m.* lawyer

avoir (ayant, eu, j'ai, j'eus) (à + *inf.*) have;
avoir beau faire quelque chose do
something in vain, avoir de la chance be
lucky; ce qu'il y a the trouble is; il y a there
is, there are; ago

avouer confess; admit

ayant (*pres. part. of* avoir) having

azur blue; Côte d'Azur French Riviera

B

baccalauréat *m.* baccalaureat (state examination
given to secondary school students)

bagage *m.* baggage; faire les bagages pack

bague *f.* ring

baigné suffused

bain *m.* bath

baissé lowered

baisser lower

bal *m.* dance

balancer (*irr. sp.* A) swing

balayer (*irr. sp.* C) sweep away, push away

ballon *m.* ball

ballot *m.* bundle

Balzac, Honoré de (1799–1850) French realistic
novelist, author of *La Comédie humaine*

bande *f.* strip; tape (for tape recorder); bande
de fleurs flower bed

banlieue *f.* suburbs

banque *f.* bank; billet de banque banknote

banquier *m.* banker

baptisé baptized

barbe *f.* beard

barrière *f.* fence

bas (*f.* basse) low; en bas downstairs; tout bas
in a whisper

Bastille *f.* a square in Paris, formerly the site of
the state prison that was taken and
destroyed by the people on July 14, 1789

bataille *f.* battle

bateau *m.* boat; bateau à moteur motorboat;
faire du bateau take a boatride; go boating;
traversée en bateau boat trip

bâtiment *m.* building

bâtir build

bâton *m.* stick; cane

Baton Rouge capital of Louisiana

battre (battant, battu, je bats, je battis) beat; se
battre fight

bavarder talk; chat

bazar *m.* department store

beau (*before vowel sound* bel; *f.* belle)
beautiful; handsome; avoir beau faire
quelque chose do something in vain; il fait
beau the weather is good; un beau jour one
fine day; a certain day

beaucoup much, many, a great deal, a great
many, a lot

beaux-parents *m. pl.* parents-in-law

bébé baby

bec *m.* beak, bill (of a bird)

belette *f.* weasel

Belge *m. or f.* Belgian

Belgique *f.* Belgium

belle (*f. of* beau) beautiful; de belle taille huge
(referring to a dog); la belle saison the
summer months

belle-fille *f.* daughter-in-law

berger *m.* shepherd; l'étoile du Berger Venus

besoin *m.* need; avoir besoin (de + *n;* de +
inf.) need; être dans le besoin be poverty-
stricken

bêta *m.* blockhead

bête *f.* beast; animal

bêtement stupidly

bêtise *f.* foolish action; faire des bêtises do
something foolish

beurre *m.* butter

bibelots *m. pl.* curios

bibliothèque *f.* library

bicyclette *f.* bicycle

bien well; well-off; comfortable; good; indeed;
really; very; very much; right; bien en face
straight in the eye; bien que although; bien
se porter be well; faire du bien do good; ou
bien or else; qu'on est bien how
comfortable we are; vouloir bien be willing;
vous comprenez bien you must understand

bienfaiteur *m.* benefactor

bienheureux blessed; blissful; fortunate

bientôt soon

bienveillance *f.* kindness, benevolence

bière *f.* beer

bifteck *m.* steak

bigot narrow-minded

bijou *m.* jewel

bijouterie *f.* jewelry store

bilingue bilingual

billet *m.* ticket; billet de banque banknote

bistrot *m.* a small café or restaurant (patronized
principally by the working class)

Irregular verbs are conjugated on pp. 256–273.

bizarre odd, strange; outlandish **bizarrement** strangely

blanc (f. blanche) white

blé m. wheat

blessé m. the wounded man

blesser wound

bleu blue

boire (buvant, bu, je bois, je bus) drink

bois m. wood

boîte f. box

bon (f. bonne) good; fit; allons bon there now; bon marché cheap; il fait bon it is cozy; it is comfortably warm

bonbon m. candy

bondir jump

bonheur m. happiness

bonhomme m. man; fellow; bonhomme de neige snowman

bonjour good morning, hello

bonne f. maid

bonnet m. cap

bord m. edge

bordé (de) lined (with)

Bordeaux city in southwestern France near the Atlantic

borner limit

bosquet m. grove; thicket

bouche f. mouth

boucher stop one's ears

bouclé curled

boudin m. black pudding

bouger (irr. sp. B) move

bougie f. candle

boulanger m. baker; chez le boulanger at the bakery

boule f. ball

boulette f. pellet

bourgeois middle-class

bourse f. stock exchange

bout m. end; tip

bouteille f. bottle

boxe f. boxing

Brahma m. Hindu god

brahmin m. priest of Brahma

bras m. arm

brave worthy; fine

Brésil m. Brazil

brève (f. of bref) short

brillant brilliant; bright

broder embroider

brosser brush

bruit m. noise; rumor

brûlant burning; passionate

brûler burn

brume f. haze; mist

brun brown; dusky

brune f. brunette

brusque blunt; brusk

brusquement suddenly; bruskly

brutalement brutally

bruyant noise

bu, bus (pp and sp of boire) drunk; drank

bureau m. desk; office; bureau d'assurance insurance office; bureau de tabac tobacco shop

buste m. bust

but m. aim

buvant (pres. part. of boire) drinking

C

ça that; it; çà et là here and there

cabane f. hut

cacher hide

cacheter (irr. sp. F) seal

cadeau m. gift; faire un cadeau give a present

café m. coffee; café, coffee house, tavern

cahier m. notebook

calcul m. calculation

calculer calculate; estimate

calme m. peace; calm; (adj.) calm

calmement calmly

camarade m. or f. friend; pal; camarade de classe classmate; camarade d'études school friend

camion m. truck

camp m. camp; team

campagne f. country; countryside, landscape; maison de campagne country home

campement m. camping site

camper camp

Camus, Albert (1913–1960) well-known philosopher, novelist, and playwright, winner of the Nobel Prize for Literature

Cannes town on the French Riviera

capable capable, able; capable de tout capable of anything

capitaine m. captain

car for

caractère m. character (attributes or features that distinguish a person)

cardiologue m. or f. heart specialist

caresser caress, fondle

carnet m. small notebook; carnet de route traveler's notebook

carré square

carrefour m. crossing; crossroad

carrière f. career

carte f. card; map; carte d'identité identification card; carte postale postcard; carte de visite visiting card

cas m. case; en tout cas in any case; faire grand cas de attach much importance to

casser break; se casser break

Caucase m. the Caucasus, a mountainous area in southern Russia

cause f. cause; à cause de because of

causer talk; chat; cause

cave f. cellar

ce (adj.) this; that; (pron.) this; that; it; he; she; they

céder (irr. sp. E) yield

Verbs with spelling changes are explained on pp. 274–276.

cela that
célèbre famous
célibataire *m.* bachelor
celui (*f.* celle) this one, that one; the one; celui-ci this one, that one; the latter
cendrier *m.* ashtray
censure *f.* censorship
cent hundred
centaine *f.* about a hundred
cependant however
cerise *f.* cherry
certain some; certain
certainement certainly
certes certainly
cesse: sans cesse constantly, ceaselessly
cesser (de + *inf.*) stop, cease
cet this; that
cette (*f. of* ce) this, that
chagrin *m.* sorrow; chagrin
chaise *f.* chair
chalet cottage
chaleur *f.* heat
chambre *f.* bedroom; robe de chambre gown
champignon *m.* mushroom
Champs-Elysées avenue in Paris leading from the Place de la Concorde to the Place Charles de Gaulle
chance *f.* luck; avoir de la chance be lucky
change *m.* exchange; agent de change stockbroker
changement *m.* change
changer (*irr. sp.* B) change; changer d'avis change one's mind
chanson *f.* song
chant *m.* song
chantant melodious
chanter sing
chanteur *m.* singer
chanteuse *f.* singer
chapeau *m.* hat
chaque each
chargé loaded; overloaded; chargé de filled with
charger (se) (de + *inf.*) take care
charmant charming
Chartres town southwest of Paris, famous for its Gothic cathedral
chasse *f.* hunt, hunting; aller à la chasse go hunting
chasser hunt; throw out; chase away; blow around
chat *m.* cat; chat de gouttière alley cat; chat perché children's game of tag
château *m.* castle
Chateaubriand, René de (1769–1848) early nineteenth-century Romantic writer
chaud hot; warm; j'ai chaud I am warm; il fait chaud it is warm; it is hot
chauffeur *m.* driver; chauffeur
chaussé shod, wearing shoes
chaussette *f.* sock
chaussure *f.* shoe; *pl.* footwear; shoes

chauve bald
chef *m.* head, leader; chief
chemin *m.* road; path; way; chemin faisant on one's way
cheminée *f.* fireplace
chemise *f.* shirt
chèque *m.* check
cher (*f.* chère) dear; expensive
chercher (+ *n.*) look for; meet; go and get; pick up; (à + *inf.*) try to, seek to; envoyer chercher send for
chérie *f.* dear
cheval *m.* (*pl.* chevaux) horse; faire du cheval go horseback riding
chevelure *f.* head of hair
cheveux *m. pl.* hair
chez at; with; in; at the house of; in the case of; allez chez vous go home; chez le directeur to the director's office; chez nous at our house; in our country; chez qui at whose home
chien *m.* dog; chien-loup *m.* German shepherd
chiffre *m.* figure
chimie *f.* chemistry
Chine *f.* China
chinois Chinese
choc *m.* shock
chœur *m.* choir
choisir choose
choix *m.* choice
chômage unemployment
Chopin, Fréderic (1810–1849) nineteenth-century Romantic composer
chose *f.* thing; pas grand-chose not much, not very much
chouette *f.* owl
Cid *m. Le Cid* a well-known play by Pierre Corneille (1636)
ci-dessus above
ciel *m.* sky
cigale *f.* a sort of grasshopper
cinéma *m.* movie; movies
cinq five
cinquante fifty
cinquième fifth
cirer wax; shine
cirque *m.* circus
cité *f.* city
citer quote; mention
citron *m.* lemon
clair clear, light; obvious; clair de lune *m.* moonlight
clairvoyante *f.* seer
classe *f.* class; classroom; camarade de classe classmate; faire une classe teach
classique classical
clé *f.* key; fermer à clé lock
client *m.* client; customer; patron
climatiser air-condition
clinique *f.* private hospital
cloche *f.* bell

Irregular verbs are conjugated on pp. 256–273.

clochette *f.* small bell
clos (*pp of* clore) shut
clou *f.* nail
clown *m.* [klun] clown
cochon *m.* pig, hog
cœur *m.* heart; apprendre par cœur memorize; au cœur de in the middle of; avoir mal au cœur be nauseated
coffre *m.* safe; coffre-fort *m.* safe
cognac *m.* brandy
cogner (se) bump into
coiffeur *m.* hairdresser; barber
coiffure *f.* hairdo
coin *m.* corner
colère *f.* anger; en colère angry; se mettre en colère get angry
colis *m.* package
collaborer collaborate
collation *f.* light meal; snack
colle *f.* glue
collé pressed; collé au corps pressed against the body
collectionner collect
collectionneur *m.* collector
collégien *m.* secondary school student
coller (+ *person*) (*colloquial*) fail (someone in a test or a course)
collier *m.* necklace
colline *f.* hill
colon *m.* colonist
colonne *f.* column
colosse *m.* colossus, a huge figure
combien how much; how many; tous les combien how often
combiner plan; draw up; figure out
comédie *f.* comedy; play
comédien *m.* actor; comedian
commander order (a meal); require
comme as; like; as well as; since; comme si as if; comme d'habitude as usual; comme il faut properly
commencement *m.* beginning
commencer (irr. sp. A) begin
comment how; what; What!; What do you mean?; comment trouvez-vous what do you think of
commerce *m.* business
commettre (*conj. like* mettre) commit
commissaire *m.* police commissioner
commission *f.* errand; faire des commissions go shopping
commode convenient
commun common
compagnie *f.* company; firm
compagnon *m.* companion
complètement completely
compliqué complicated
complot *m.* plot; conspiracy
comportement *m.* behavior; attitude
comporter require; include; comprise; se comporter behave

composé compound; passé composé compound past
composition *f.* composition; theme
comprendre (*conj. like* prendre) understand; comprise
comprenez (*from* comprendre) understand; vous comprenez bien you must understand
comptable *m. or f.* bookkeeper, accountant
compte *m.* account; se rendre compte (de + *n.*) realize
compter count; (+ *inf.*) expect; intend; include; sans compter que besides the fact that
comptoir *m.* counter
concierge *m. or f.* house-porter; janitor; caretaker
concilier reconcile
conclure (*irr. v.*) conclude; l'affaire sera conclue the deal will be closed
Concorde *m.* supersonic Anglo-French plane
concours *m.* competitive examination
condamnable seriously questionable
condamner condemn
condition *f.* condition; social level; à condition que provided that
conduire (conduisant, conduit, je conduis, je conduisis) drive; take; se conduire behave
conduite *f.* behavior
conférence *f.* lecture; en conférence in conference, at a meeting
conférencier *m.* speaker, lecturer
confiance *f.* trust; faith
confier à trust (someone with)
confiture *f.* jam
conflit *m.* conflict
confort *m.* comfort
conjonction *f.* conjunction
connaissance *f.* acquaintance; knowledge; faire connaissance avec get acquainted with, meet; faire la connaissance de get acquainted with, meet
connaître (connaissant, connu, je connais, je connus) know, be acquainted with
connu well-known, famous
consciencieux (*f.* consciencieuse) conscientious
conseil *m.* piece of advice; *pl.* advice; tenir conseil have a meeting
conseiller (à + *person* + de + *inf.*) advise
conservateur *m.* curator
consolant consoling
consommer accomplish
conspiration *f.* conspiracy
constamment constantly
construction *f.* construction work
construire (*conj. like* conduire) build
conte *m.* short story
contempler view; observe
contenir (*conj. like* tenir) contain
contenter satisfy; se contenter de be satisfied with
contestataire *m. or f.* protester

Verbs with spelling changes are explained on pp. 274–276.

contestation *f.* protest
conteur *m.* story teller
continuellement continually; incessantly
continuer (à + *inf.*) continue; keep on
contraire *m.* contrary; au contraire on the
   contrary
contrebandier *m.* smuggler
contribuer contribute
convaincre (*conj. like* vaincre) convince
convaincu (*pp of* convaincre) convinced
convenable proper, fitting
convenir (*conj. like* venir) agree; be proper; be
   suiting; convenir de accept; quelque chose
   convient something is proper, something is
   suitable
convenu agreed; OK; agreed upon
convertir convert
convive *m. or f.* guest
copain *m.* pal. chum, close friend
copie *f.* paper (to hand in); (school) exercise
copier copy
copieux (*f.* copieuse) copious, plentiful
coq *m.* rooster
coquille *f.* shell
corps *m.* body
correctement correctly
corriger (*irr. sp.* B) correct
cortège *m.* procession
cosmique cosmic, vast
costume *m.* suit
côte *f.* coast; côte à côte side by side; Côte
   d'Azur French Riviera
côté *m.* side; à côté de near, beside, alongside
   of; in addition to; in the direction of;
   nearby; on the side of; du côté de toward;
   near; mettre de côté save; tout à côté right
   near
cou *m.* neck
couchant *m.* sunset
couché stretched out
coucher put to bed; spend the night; se
   coucher go to bed; (*n.*) *m.* bedtime;
   coucher de soleil sunset
couleur *f.* color
couloir *m.* corridor
coup *m.* blow; "coup"; à grands coups d'ailes
   with powerful flaps of the wings; coup
   d'œil glance; coup de tonnerre thunderclap;
   tout à coup all of a sudden; tout d'un coup
   all of a sudden
coupable guilty; (*n.*) *m or f.* the guilty one
couper cut; cut down
cour *f.* yard; courtyard; court; faire la cour
   make love; court
courageux (*f.* courageuse) brave
courant running; au courant informed; dans le
   courant de during; tenir au courant keep
   informed
courber lean
courir (courant, couru, je cours, je courus) run
couronne *f.* crown

courrier *m.* mail
cours *m.* course; au cours de during; cours de
   vacances summer courses
course *f.* errand; race
court short
courtisan *m.* courtier
couteau *m.* knife
coûter cost; coûter cher be expensive
coûteux (*f.* coûteuse) expensive
couturière *f.* seamstress
couvert (*pp of* couvrir) covered; (*n.*) *m.* cover;
   knives, forks, and spoons used for eating;
   enlever le couvert clear the table; (*adj.*)
   covered
couverture *f.* blanket
couvrir (se) become covered
craie *f.* chalk
craignais (*imperfect of* craindre) feared
craindre (craignant, craint, je crains, je
   craignis) fear
crâne *m.* skull; head
crayon *m.* pencil
créancier *m.* creditor
créateur *m.* creator
créer create
crème *f.* cream
crêpe *f.* pancake
crépuscule *m.* twilight
creux (*f.* creuse) hollow
crevette *f.* shrimp
cri *m.* cry; screaming; pousser un cri utter a cry
crier yell; cry out
critique *f.* criticism; review
critiquer criticize
crochet *m.* hook
croire (croyant, cru, je crois, je crus) believe;
   croire bon deem fit
croisade *f.* crusade
croisé crossed; mots croisés crossword puzzle
croiser cross
croissant *m.* crescent-shaped French pastry
croyant *m.* believer
cru harsh
cru, crus (*pp and sp of* croire) believed
cueillir pick
cuir *m.* leather
cuire (cuisant, cuit, je cuis, je cuisis) cook
cuisine *f.* cooking; kitchen
cuisinière *f.* cook
cultivé educated
cultiver cultivate.
curieux (*f.* curieuse) curious; odd; strange;
   inquisitive; eager; (*n. pl.*) curious people

D

d'abord at first; tout d'abord first of all
d'ailleurs besides
dame *f.* lady; dame! (*interjection*); why, of
   course
Danemark *m.* Denmark

Irregular verbs are conjugated on pp. 256–273.

dans in, on

danse *f.* dancing; leçon de danse dancing lesson

danser dance

danseuse *f.* dancer

dater date

d'avance in advance

de of; from; by; in; out of; with

débarrasser (se) (de + *n.*) get rid of

débattre (se) resist, struggle

déborder overflow

debout standing; puisque vous êtes debout since you are up

débrouiller (se) get along; figure a way out

début *m.* beginning

décapotable *f.* convertible (car)

décence *f.* decency

décerner award

décès *m.* death

déchirer tear up

décider (de + *inf.*) decide; se décider (à + *inf.*) make up one's mind

décisif (*f.* décisive) decisive

décision *f.* decision; prendre une décision make a decision, make up one's mind

décor *m.* setting

décorateur *m.* interior decorator

découper cut; cut out

décourager (*irr. sp.* B) discourage

découverte *f.* discovery

découvrir (*conj. like* ouvrir) discover

déçu disappointed

défaut *m.* defect; shortcoming

défendre defend; (à + *person* + de + *inf.*) forbid

défilé *m.* march; procession; parade

définir define

définitivement definitely

défunt *m.* deceased person

dehors outside

déjà already

déjeuner have breakfast; have lunch; (*n*) *m.* noon meal (main meal in France); petit déjeuner breakfast

délicatesse *f.* consideration

délicieux (*f.* délicieuse) delightful

délivrance *f.* emancipation

délivrer free

demain tomorrow; à partir de demain from tomorrow on

demander ask; (à + *person* + de + *inf.*) ask someone to; (à + *inf.*) ask to

démarche *f.* step

déménager (*irr. sp.* B) move

demeurer remain

demi half; demi-heure half an hour; demi-obscurité *f.* semi-darkness; shadowy light

demoiselle *f.* young lady; maiden lady

démission *f.* resignation

démolir demolish

dent *f.* tooth

dentelle *f.* lace

d'entre of

départ *m.* departure

dépasser go beyond; go around

dépêcher (se) (de + *inf.*) hurry

déplacer (*irr. sp.* A) shift; (se) go around

déplaire (*conj. like* plaire) displease

déposer (se) be found; settle

dépourvu without

dépression *f.* hollow; fall

déprimant depressing

depuis since; from; for; depuis peu recently, since not very long ago

déranger (*irr. sp.* B) disturb, bother

dernier (*f.* dernière) last; latter

dérouler (se) unfold; develop; take place

derrière behind; la porte de derrière the back door

dès from; dès l'aube from early dawn; dès que as soon as; dès que possible as soon as possible

désagréable unpleasant

désastre *m.* disaster

désastreux (*f.* désastreuse) disastrous

descendre come down; go down; descend

désert deserted

désespéré desperate

désespérer (se) dispair

désintéresser (se) lose interest

désirer (+ *inf.*) wish, desire

désolé sorry

désoler grieve, distress

désordonné disordered; wild

désordre *m.* disorder; en désordre in a mess

désormais from now on

dessin *m.* drawing

dessus upstairs; on it; prendre le dessus prevail

détourner turn away from

détruire (*conj. like* conduire) destroy

dette *f.* debt

deuil *m.* mourning

deux two; à deux the two of us; together; tous deux both; vous deux both of you

devant before

devenir (*conj. like* venir) become

deviner guess

devoir (*pp. 199–204*) (devant, dû, je dois, je dus) have to, must, ought to; should probably + *verb;* (*n.*) *m.* duty; exercise; devoir connaître be able to, know

dévorer devour

devrais (*cond. of* devoir) should, ought to

diable *m.* devil

diamant *m.* diamond

diapositive *f.* (photographic) slide

dictionnaire *m.* dictionary

Dieu *m.* God

difficile difficult

diffuser broadcast

Dijon city in eastern France between Paris and Lyons

Verbs with spelling changes are explained on pp. 274–276.

dimanche *m.* Sunday
diminuer diminish
dîner dine, have dinner
dire (disant, dit, je dis, je dis) (à + *person* + de + *inf.*) say; tell; **c'est-à-dire** that is to say; **en dire trop** say too much; **on dirait** one would say; it seems; **pour ainsi dire** so to speak; **vouloir dire** mean
directeur *m.* director; manager
dirigeant *m.* leader
diriger (*irr. sp.* B) direct; **se diriger** go
disant (*pres. part. of* dire) saying
discours *m.* speech
discuter discuss; argue about; talk something over
disparaître (*conj. like* connaître) disappear
dispenser give out, distribute
disposé arranged
disposer have available
disque *m.* (phonograph) record
dissimuler hide
distingué distinguished
dit (*pres. and pp of* dire) say; said; so-called
divers various, different
divertir amuse
divertissement *m.* passtime
docteur *m.* doctor
doigt *m.* finger
doit (*pres. of* devoir) must; has to; is to; probably does
domaine *m.* estate; grounds
domestique *m. or f.* servant
dominer reign over
dommage too bad
don *m.* gift
donc then; thus; therefore; now; **allez donc voir** be sure and see; **entrez donc** do come in; **pensez donc** think of it; **qui donc** who is that?; whom do you mean?
donner give; **donner raison** justify one's action, prove that one is right; **donner sur** look out upon
doré gilded; golden
dormir (2) sleep
dos *m.* back
dossier *m.* file
Dostoïevski, Féodor (1821–1881) nineteenth-century Russian novelist
douane *f.* customs
doucement gently; softly
douceur *f.* softness
doué gifted
douleur *f.* pain; suffering; sorrow
douloureux (*f.* douloureuse) painful
doute *m.* doubt; **sans doute** probably
douteux (*f.* douteuse) doubtful
doux (*f.* douce) mild, soft
douzaine *f.* dozen
doyen *m.* dean; oldest member
dramaturge *m. or f.* dramatist
drame *m.* drama
drapeau *m.* flag

dresser raise; **dresser les oreilles** prick up one's ears; **se dresser** straighten oneself up; get up
drogue *f.* drug
droit *m.* study of law; justice; law; (*adj.*) right; straight; **tout droit** erect; straight ahead
droite *f.* right; **à ma droite** to my right
drôle funny; odd
drôlement in a peculiar manner
du of the; some
dû, due (*pp of* devoir) had to, etc.; due to
Dumas, Alexandre (1802–1870) nineteenth-century novelist and dramatist, author of *Les Trois mousquetaires*
dur hard; **dur d'oreille** hard of hearing
durer last

E

eau *f.* water; **eau de vie** brandy; **troubler l'eau** make the water murky
écart: à l'écart aside
écarter pull aside; ward off
échange *m.* exchange
échanger (*irr. sp.* B) exchange
échapper (à + *n.*) escape, avoid; **s'échapper (de + *n.*)** escape
écharpe *f.* scarf
échecs *m. pl.* chess
échelle *f.* ladder
éclabousser splash
éclairage *m.* light; lighting
éclaircir explain, clarify
éclairer light
éclat *m.* gleam; brightness
éclater burst; break out; flash; **éclater de rire** burst out laughing
école *f.* school
économies *f. pl.* savings; **faire des économies** save
économiser save
écouler (s') elapse, pass
écouter (+ *n.*) listen; listen to
écrasé crushed; overwhelmed
écrire (écrivant, écrit, j'écris, j'écrivis) write; **machine à écrire** *f.* typewriter
écris (*m. pl.*) writings
écrit: par écrit in writing
écrivain *m.* writer
édifice *m.* building; framework, structure
éducation *f.* education; bringing up; **éducation poussée** college education
effacer (*irr. sp.* A) erase; obliterate; draw in
effet *m.* effect; **en effet** in fact; **exercer un effet** have an effect; **faire cet effet** have this effect; **par l'effet de** because of
effort *m.* effort
effrayer (*irr. sp.* C) scare, frighten; **s'effrayer (de)** become frightened (at)
effroyable frightful
égal equal; **cela m'était égal** it did not make any difference to me
également also

Irregular verbs are conjugated on pp. 256–273.

égard: à tous les égards in all respects

égarer (s') wander; lose one's way

église *f.* church

égoïste selfish

égratignure *f.* scratch

élancer (s') (*irr. sp.* A) dart forth

élargir (s') widen

électricité *f.* electricity; **panne d'électricité** power failure

élève *m. or f.* pupil

élevé high; brought up; **bien élevé** well-mannered; **mal élevé** ill-mannered, ill-bred

élever raise; s'élever rise, get up

élire (*conj. like* lire) elect

éloigner keep away; s'éloigner go off, go away

élu (*pp of* élire) elected

émaner emanate; proceed

emballer wrap up

embarrassé embarrassed

embêter annoy

emboîter: emboîter le pas fall into step

embouteillage *m.* traffic jam

émerger (*irr. sp.* B) emerge

émigré *m.* migrant

émigrer emigrate

éminent prominent

emmener (*irr. sp.* D) take away; take along

emparer (s') (de + *n.*) seize

empêcher (*n.* + de + *inf.*) hinder, prevent; **il n'empêche pas** that doesn't prevent

empereur *m.* emperor

empiéter encroach

emplir fill

emploi *m.* use; job

employé *m.* clerk; employee; **petit employé** minor office clerk

employer (*irr. sp.* C) use

empoigner seize, grab

emporter take away (a thing); take along (a thing); l'emporter prevail

emprunter borrow

ému moved

en in; to; as; while; by; **en dehors** outside; **en vis-a-vis** opposite each other

encercler encircle

enchanté delighted

enchanteur *m.* enchanter; magician

encore again; still; yet; **encore un mot** one more word

encourageant encouraging

encre *f.* ink

encrier *m.* inkwell

endormi asleep; sleeping

endormir (s') (2) fall asleep

endroit *m.* place

endurci hardened; confirmed

énergie *f.* energy; power

enfance *f.* childhood

enfant *m. or f.* child

enfantin childish

enfermer fence in

enfin finally, at last; in short, anyway; well

s'enfuir (*conj. like* fuir) flee; run

engagé engaged, involved

engagement *m.* involvement

engager (*irr. sp.* B.) hire; start

enivrant intoxicating

enjoué sprightly, lively

enlever (*irr. sp.* D) take away; take off; **enlever le couvert** clear the table

ennui *m.* boredom; trouble

ennuyer (*irr. sp.* C) bore; bother; s'ennuyer get bored; be lonesome; be bored

ennuyeux (*f.* ennuyeuse) annoying; boring

énorme enormous

énormément very much; considerably

enregistrer record; register; check (baggage)

enregistreur *m.* tape recorder

enseigner (*thing* + à + *person; person* + à + *inf.*) teach

ensemble together; whole; **exercices d'ensemble** summing-up exercises, review exercises

ensuite then

entassé packed

entasser stack up

entendre hear; mean; **entendre dire que** hear that; s'entendre be heard; get along

entendu agreed

entente *f.* understanding; agreement; harmony

enterrement *m.* burial

entier (*f.* entière) entire; whole **tout entier** completely

entièrement entirely

entouré surrounded

entourer (de + *n.*) surround; cover over

entre between; **d'entre** of

entrée *f.* entrance; beginning

entreprendre (*conj. like* prendre) undertake

entrer (dans + *n.*) enter; penetrate

entrevoir (*conj. like* voir) imagine

envahir invade; come over

enveloppe *f.* envelope

envelopper wrap; wrap up

envers toward

envie *f.* wish, desire; **avoir envie de** feel like

envier envy

environ about, approximately

environs *m. pl.* surroundings; surrounding territory

envisager (*irr. sp.* B) consider

envoi *m.* parcel

envoyer (envoyant, envoyé, j'envoie, j'envoyai) send; **envoyer chercher** send for

épais (*f.* épaisse) thick

épaisseur *f.* depth

épargner spare

épatant wonderful; stunning

épaule *f.* shoulder; **hausser les épaules** shrug one's shoulders

éperdu in a panic

épidémie *f.* epidemic

épigraphe *f.* epigraph, a quotation at the beginning of a book

Verbs with spelling changes are explained on pp. 274–276.

époque *f.* time; period
épouser (+ *person*) marry
épouvantable appalling, frightful
éprouver feel; experience
épuisé exhausted
épuiser (s') wear oneself out
errer wander
erreur *f.* mistake
érudit *m.* scholar; learned person
escale *f.* port of call; faire escale stop at (a port)
escroc *m.* swindler
espace *m.* space
espacé spaced
Espagne *f.* Spain
espagnol Spanish
espèce *f.* kind
espérer (*irr. sp.* E) (+ *inf.*) hope; expect
espion *m.* spy
espoir *m.* hope
esprit *m.* spirit; wit; mind
essai *m.* essay
essayer (*irr. sp.* C) (de + *inf.*) try
essayiste *m.* essayist
essence *f.* essence; gasoline
essuyer (*irr. sp.* C) wipe
estimer think, consider
et and
établir establish
étage *m.* floor; le premier étage the second floor
étaler display
étant (*pres. part. of* être) being
état *m.* state; shape
États-Unis *m. pl.* United States
été (*v.*) (*pp of* être) been; (*n.*) *m.* summer
éteindre (*conj. like* peindre) turn off; s'éteindre come to an end; die out
étoffe *f.* fabric; material; cloth
étoile *f.* star; l'étoile du Berger Venus
étonnant astonishing; remarkable; surprising
étonné surprised
étonnement *m.* surprise
étonner astonish; surprise; s'étonner be surprised
étouffé stifled
étouffer choke, smother
étrange strange
étranger *m.* foreigner, strange man; stranger; à l'étranger abroad; (*adj.*) (*f.* étrangère) foreign; strange
étrangeté *f.* strangeness
étrangler strangle
être (étant, été, je suis, je fus) be; être à l'aise be comfortable; ne pas être en reste be equal to the situation; vous n'en seriez pas là you wouldn't be in such a fix; (*n.*) *m.* being
étroit narrow; close
étude *f.* study; camarade d'étude school friend
étudiant *m.* (college) student
eu, eus (*pp and sp of* avoir) had

européen (*f.* européenne) European
eux *m.* them
évader (s') escape
évanouir (s') faint
éveiller awaken; arouse
événement *m.* event
évidemment obviously
évident obvious
éviter (de + *inf.*) avoid
évocateur suggestive; meaningful, inspiring
évoluer develop; evolve; change
évoquer evoke, bring up
exact true; correct
exactement exactly
examen *m.* examination; passer un examen take an examination
examiner examine
exaucer grant; fulfill
excepté except
excès *m.* excess; faire des excès "go overboard"
excuser (s') apologize
exécuter (s') take place
exemple *m.* example; servir d'exemple serve as an example
exempt free
exercer (*irr. sp.* A): exercer un effet have an effect
exercice *m.* exercise; exercices d'ensemble summing-up exercises; review exercises
exigeant demanding
exiger (*irr. sp.* B) require; call for; demand
existence *f.* existence; life
existentialiste existentialist; referring to the philosophy of existentialism
exotisme *m.* exoticism; being from another and strange land
expérience *f.* experience; experiment
explication *f.* explanation
expliciter make explicit; develop
expliquer explain
exposer exhibit
exposition *f.* fair
exprès on purpose; par exprès special delivery
exprimer express
extase *f.* ecstasy
extraire extract
extrêmement extremely

F

fabriquer make; manufacture
fabuliste *m. or f.* writer of fables
face *f.* face; bien en face straight in the eye; d'en face on the opposite side (of the street); face à facing; face à face facing each other; faire face à face up to; accept
fâché angry; sorry
fâcher (se) (contre + *person*) get angry
fâcheux (*f.* fâcheuse) unfortunate, annoying

Irregular verbs are conjugated on pp. 256–273.

facilement easily

façon *f.* manner; way; de la même façon in the same way

facteur *m.* mailcarrier

faculté *f.* college or school of a university, including buildings and teaching staff

faible weak

faim *f.* hunger; avoir faim be hungry

faire (faisant, fait, je fais, je fis) (+ *inf.*) do; make; carry out; have (done)*

faisant: chemin faisant on one's way

fait *m.* fact

falloir (—, fallu, il faut, il fallut) (+ *inf.*) must; be necessary; comme il faut properly; il faut it takes; one must; il me faut I need

familial (*adj.*) family

familier (*f.* familière) familiar; intimate

famille *f.* family; famille nombreuse large family

faner (se) wilt

fantaisiste whimsical; fanciful

fantassin *m.* foot-soldier

fantastique *m.* the fantastic, the fanciful; the fantastic quality

farce *f.* farce; faire des farces play tricks; play jokes

farine *f.* flour

fasciner fascinate

fasse (*pres. subjunc. of* faire) make; do

fatigant tiring; tiresome

fatiguer tire

faut (*pres. of* falloir) must, has to; il faut one must; it takes; comme il faut properly; il me faut I need

faute *f.* mistake; sans faute without fail

fauteuil *m.* armchair

fauve tawny; wild

faux (*f.* fausse) false

faveur *f.* favor

favori (*f.* favorite) favorite

favoriser favor

féliciter congratulate

femme *f.* woman; wife; femme de ménage cleaning woman; *Les Femmes savantes The Learned Women,* a play by Molière (1672)

fenêtre *f.* window

fente *f.* crack, slit

ferai, ferais (*fut. and cond. of* faire) will make, will do; would make, would do

ferme *f.* farm; (*adj.*) firm; tenir ferme hold fast

fermement firmly

fermer close; fermer à clé lock

fermier *m.* farmer

féroce ferocious

fervent (*n.*) *m.* enthusiastic fan

fête *f.* holiday; festivity; celebration; birthday

feu *m.* fire; en feu on fire; feu rouge red light; traffic light

feuille *f.* leaf; sheet

feuillet *m.* leaf

ficelle *f.* string; piece of string

fidèle faithful

fidélité *f.* loyalty

fier (se) trust; have confidence in

fier (*f.* fière) proud

figure *f.* face

fil *m.* wire

fille *f.* daughter; girl; jeune fille *f.* girl

fillette *f.* young girl; little girl

fils *m.* son

fin *f.* end

finalement finally

finesse *f.* subtlety; finesse; fineness

finir finish; finir mal end up badly; finir par end up by; il n'en finit pas he never stops

fixer fix; retain

flairer sniff

flamand Flemish

flambé bright-colored

flanc *m.* side

flatter satisfy

flatteur (*f.* flatteuse) flattering; (*n.*) *m.* flatterer

Flaubert, Gustave (1821–1885) well-known nineteenth-century French novelist, author of *Madame Bovary*

flèche *f.* arrow

fleur *f.* flower; fleur d'eau water flower

fleuriste *m. or f.* florist

foie *m.* liver

fois *f.* time; à la fois at the same time; une fois pour toutes once and for all; maintes fois many times

folie *f.* folly; joke

folle (*f. of* fou) crazy, reckless

follement wildly; ardently

foncé dark

fonctionnaire *m. or f.* government employee

fond *m.* bottom; background; end; au fond deep down inside; indeed; essentially; in the depths of

fonder found

fondre melt

fontaine *f.* fountain

football *m.* football; ball; soccer

force *f.* strength; force; de toutes ses forces with all her strength

forêt *f.* forest

formation *f.* development

formidable marvelous

fort (*adj.*) loud; strong; (intellectually) good; (*adv.*) hard; very

fou (*before vowel sound* fol, *f.* folle) crazy; reckless

fouet *m.* whip

fouille *f.* search; faire des fouilles dig, excavate

fouine *f.* marten

---

* Expressions beginning with faire are defined under the other significant word(s) of the expression.

Verbs with spelling changes are explained on pp. 274–276.

foule *f.* crowd
fouler sprain
fourchette *f.* fork
fournir furnish; provide
fourrure *f.* fur
foyer *m.* fireplace
fraîcheur *f.* freshness
frais (*f.* fraîche) fresh; cool
fraise *f.* strawberry
framboise *f.* raspberry
franc (*f.* franche) frank
Français *m.* Frenchman
français French
franchement frankly
frappant striking
frapper strike; knock
fraternité *f.* fraternity; brotherhood
frémir quiver; shudder; **il en frémit** it made
  him shudder
fréquemment frequently
fréquenté visited; **peu fréquenté** not very often
  visited
fréquenter frequent, go to regularly
frère *m.* brother
frigidaire *m.* refrigerator
frissonner shiver
froid *m.* cold; **avoir froid** be cold; **il fait froid**
  it is cold
froidement coldly; cooly
front *m.* forehead
fugitif (*f.* fugitive) fleeting
fuir (fuyant, fui, je fuis, je fuis) flee; avoid
fumer smoke
furieux (*f.* furieuse) furious
furtivement furtively
fus, fut (*sp of* être) was
fusil *m.* gun; rifle
fusse, fût (*pres. subjunc. of* être) was
fuyant (*pres. part. of* fuir) fleeing

G

gâcher spoil
gagner win; gain; earn
gai cheerful
gaillard *m.* a vigorous, strapping fellow
galerie *f.* gallery; **Galeries Lafayette** a well-
  known chain of French department stores
Gange *m.* the Ganges, sacred river of India
gant *m.* glove
garagiste *m. or f.* auto mechanic; garage owner
garçon *m.* boy; waiter
garde *m.* watchman; guard; **être de garde** be on
  duty
garder keep; watch
gardien *m.* watchman
gare *f.* station; railroad station
gare à lui! he'd better look out
Garonne *f.* river in southwestern France
gâteau *m.* cake

gâter spoil
gauche *f.* left
gazon *m.* lawn
gelée *f.* jelly
gêné embarrassed
gêner disturb; bother; embarrass
génie *m.* genius
genou *m.* knee
genre *m.* type
gens *m. pl.* people; **braves gens** fine people; **les
  gens de dessus** the people who live above;
  jeunes gens young men; young people
gentil (*f.* gentille) nice
gentiment in a friendly way, in a nice way
geste *m.* gesture
gifler slap
gisement *m.* mineral field
glissement *m.* sliding; sliding noise; swishing
glisser slip
gloire *f.* glory; **valoir la gloire** bring glory
glorieux (*f.* glorieuse) glorious
Goncourt, Edmond (1822–1896) et Jules
  (1830–1870) nineteenth-century naturalist
  writers
gonfler swell
gorge *f.* throat
gorgée *f.* spoonful (*lit.* throatful)
goût *m.* taste
goûter taste
gouverner govern
gracieux (*f.* gracieuse) graceful; gracious
grammaire *f.* grammar
grand great; large; main; **il est grand temps** it is
  high time
grand-chose much; **votre idée ne vaut pas
  grand-chose** your idea isn't worth much
grands-parents *m. pl.* grandparents
grand-père *m.* grandfather
grandir grow
grange *f.* barn
gras (*f.* grasse) fat
gratter scratch
Grèce *f.* Greece
grenier *m.* attic
grève *f.* strike; beach
grille *f.* iron gate
grillé toasted
gris gray
griser intoxicate
gronder scold; grumble; rumble
gros (*f.* grosse) big; fat; important
grossir get fat
grotte *f.* grotto; cave
guère scarcely, hardly
guéri cured; healed
guéridon *m.* small round table
guérison *m.* recovery; cure
guerre *f.* war; **faire la guerre** wage war
guitare *f.* guitar
gymnastique *f.* exercise; **faire de la
  gymnastique** exercise

Irregular verbs are conjugated on pp. 256–273.

H

*indicates an aspirate *h*

habileté *f.* cleverness; ability
habiller dress; s'habiller dress
habiter (+ *place;* à + *place*) live; inhabit
habitude *f.* habit; comme d'habitude as usual
habituer (s') (à + *inf.*) get used to
*haine *f.* hate
haleine *f.* breath
*haletant breathless, panting
*hameau *m.* hamlet
*hanté haunted
hardi bold
*haricots verts *m. pl.* greenbeans
harmonieux (*f.* harmonieuse) harmonious
*hasard *m.* hazard; chance; au hasard at random
*hâte *f.* haste; avoir hâte be in a hurry
*hausser raise; hausser les épaules shrug one's
   shoulders
*haut high; à haute voix aloud
*hauteur *f.* height; level
*Haye, La *f.* The Hague, capital of the
   Netherlands
*hélas alas
héritier *m.* heir
*héros *m.* hero
hésiter hesitate
heure *f.* hour; o'clock; time; à l'heure on
   time; de bonne heure early tout à l'heure in
   a little while; a little while ago
heureux (*f.* heureuse) happy
*heurter (se) (à + *n.*) run up against
hier yesterday; avant-hier the day before
   yesterday
histoire *f.* story; history; trouble; quelle
   histoire! what a fuss!
hiver *m.* winter
*hocher nod; hocher la tête nod one's head
homme *m.* man; homme politique politician
*Hongrois *m.* Hungarian
honneur *m.* honor; faire honneur honor
*honteusement in embarrassment
*honteux (*f.* honteuse) ashamed
*hors outside; hors de lui beside himself
hôte *m.* guest; host
hôtel *m.* hotel; hôtel de ville city hall
huiler oil
huître *f.* oyster
humain human
humble *m.* humble person, meek person
humeur *f.* humor; mood; de mauvaise humeur
   in a bad mood
hurler howl
hypocrite (*adj.*) hypocritical
hypothèse *f.* hypothesis

I

ici here
idée *f.* idea

identité *f.* identification; carte d'identité
   identification card
ignorer not to know; be unaware of
île *f.* island
illusoire illusory
illustre illustrious
illustré illustrated
ilôt *m.* small island; small block
image *f.* picture
imbécile *m. or f.* fool
immédiatement immediately
immobile motionless
imparfait *m.* imperfect (tense)
impatienter (s') become impatient
imperméable *m.* raincoat
impertinent bad
importe: n'importe quoi anything
importer matter; be important
impôt *m.* tax
imprévu unforeseen
imprimer print
inaltérable unchangeable
inattendu unexpected
incendie *m.* fire
incendier set fire
incertitude *f.* uncertainty
incliné sloping
incliner bend
inconnu *m.* stranger; (*adj.*) unknown
incroyable unbelievable
inculpé *m.* accused one
indécis irresolute, indecisive
indemne untouched, unharmed
Inde *f.* India
indien (*f.* indienne) Indian
indiquer indicate; show
individu *m.* person; individual (often with an
   unfavorable connotation)
inébranlable unshakable
inestimable priceless
inexplicable unexplainable
inextricable inextricable, difficult to solve
infiniment infinitely
infirmier *m.* male nurse; infirmière *f.* female
   nurse
influent influential
influer influence
informé informed
informer (s') (sur + *n.*) inquire for information;
   get information about
ingénieur *m.* engineer
ingrat *m.* ungrateful man; (*adj.*) dull; thankless
inhabituel (*f.* inhabituelle) unaccustomed; out
   of the ordinary
injuste unjust
innombrable innumerable
inoffensif (*f.* inoffensive) harmless
inondation *f.* flood
inonder flood
inquiet (*f.* inquiète) uneasy, worried
inquiétant alarming

Verbs with spelling changes are explained on pp. 274–276.

inquiéter (s') (*irr. sp.* E) worry
inquiétude *f.* uneasiness; worry
inscrire (*conj. like* écrire) inscribe
insignificant unsignificant
insister (sur + *thing;* pour + *inf.;* pour que + *subjunc.*) insist
inspecteur *m.* detective
instant *m.* instant; moment; à l'instant même où at the very moment when
instantanément suddenly; instantly
institutrice *f.* woman teacher
instruire (s') learn
insuffisant insufficient
insupportable unberable
intention *f.* intention; avoir l'intention de intend to
interdire (*conj. like* dire) forbid
intéressé self-seeking
intéresser interest; s'intéresser (à + *n.*) be interested in
intérêt *m.* interest
intérieur *m.* inside
intime intimate; journal intime diary
intoxiqué *m.* addict
introduire (*conj. like* conduire) introduce (somthing into); insert
intrus *m.* intruder, trespasser
inutile useless
invendable unsaleable
inverse inverted
inversé inverted; upside down
invité *m.* guest
inviter (à + *inf.*) invite; entice
involontaire involuntary
invoquer invoke
irai, irais (*fut. and cond. of* aller) will go; would go
ironique ironical
Isle-Adam a town near Paris
isoler isolate
issue *f.* exit; sans issue impassable
italien (*f.* italienne) Italian
italique *m.* italics
itinéraire *m.* itinerary

J

jadis [ʒadis] formerly
jaloux (*f.* jalouse) jealous
jamais ever; never; à jamais forever; ne . . . jamais never
jambe *f.* leg
Japon *m.* Japan
japonais Japanese
jardin *m.* garden; park; jardin zoologique zoo
jardinage *m.* gardening
jardinier *m.* gardener
jaunâtre yellowish
jaune yellow
Jeannot Johnnie
jet *m.* flow

jeter (*irr. sp.* F) throw; jeter les yeux glance; jeter le trouble disrupt; se jeter throw oneself; empty
jeu *m.* game; play; jeu de cartes deck of cards; jeu de mots play on words, pun; jeu video video game
jeudi *m.* Thursday
jeune young; jeune fille *f.* girl; jeunes gens *m.* young men; young people
jeunesse *f.* youth
joie *f.* joy
joindre (*conj. like* craindre) join
joli pretty
joliment nicely
jongleur *m.* juggler
joue *f.* cheek
jouer (de + *instrument;* à + *game*) play; jouer de make use of; turn on
jouet *m.* toy
joueur *m.* player
jouir enjoy
jour *m.* day; au jour le jour day by day; from one day to the other; un beau jour one fine day; a certain day; dans les beaux jours during the summer months; de nos jours in our days; in our time
journal *m.* newspaper; magazine; journal intime diary; journal de sport sports magazine
journaliste *m.* newspaper man; journalist
journée *f.* day
jovial fun-loving
joyeusement joyfully
juge *m. or f.* judge
juger (*irr. sp.* B) deem; judge; examine; scan; juger bon deem advisable
jugement *m.* judgment
juin June
jumelles *f. pl.* twin sisters; field glasses
jurer swear
jus *m.* juice
jusqu'à up to; as far as; to the point of
jusqu'à ce que (+ *subjunc.*) until
juste just; exact
justice *f.* justice; palais de justice courthouse

K

kilo *m.* kilogram (2.2 pounds)
kiosque *m.* newspaper stand

L

là there; here; çà et là here and there
là-bas over there
lac *m.* lake
lâcher let go
Lafayette: Galeries Lafayette a well-known chain of French department stores

Irregular verbs are conjugated on pp. 256–273.

lâcher let go
laine *f.* wool
laisser (+ *inf.*) let; leave
lait *m.* milk
laitier *m.* milk dealer; milkman
lamentable woeful
lancer (*irr. sp.* A) throw
langage *m.* manner of speech
langue *f.* tongue; language
lapin *m.* rabbit
large *m.* open sea; (*adj.*) wide
largement widely
lasser (se) get tired
Lausanne town situated on Lake Geneva in the French part of Switzerland
laver wash; se laver wash oneself
le, la, les (*definite article*) the; (*personal pron.*) him; her; it; them
leçon *f.* lesson; leçon de danse dancing lesson
lecteur *m.* reader
lecture *f.* reading
léger (*f.* légère) light; slight
lendemain *m.* next day; le lendemain matin the next morning
lent slow
lequel (*f.* laquelle) (*interrog.*) which; which one; (*rel.*) whom; which
lettre *f.* letter; faire une lettre write a letter; homme (femme) de lettres writer; papier à lettre stationery, writing paper
leur (*pron.*) them; to them; (*adj.*) their; le leur, etc. theirs
lever: lever du soleil *m.* sunrise
lever (*irr. sp.* D) raise; lift; se lever get up
lèvre *f.* lip
lézard *m.* lizard
libérer free, liberate
liberté *f.* freedom
libertin *m.* libertine; nonconformist
libraire *m.* bookseller
libre free; open
lier link; tie; se lier avec form a friendship with
lieu *m.* place; spot; s'il y a lieu if necessary; au lieu de instead; avoir lieu take place
ligne *f.* line; continuity; outline; manner; pilote de ligne *m.* commercial pilot
limbes *f. pl.* limbo
linge *m.* dirty clothes; linen; laundry
lire (lisant, lu, je lis, je lus) read
lisant (pres. part. of lire) reading
lisse smooth
lit *m.* bed
litre *m.* liter (about 1.06 quarts)
livre *m.* book *f.* pound
livrer (se) à have recourse to
loger (*irr. sp.* B) lodge, live
loi *f.* law
loin far; de loin by far
lointain distant
Loire *f.* river in central and western France
loisir *m.* leisure time

Londres *m.* London
long (*f.* longue) long; le long de along
longer (*irr. sp.* B) go along the edge of
longtemps a long time
longuement at length
louable praiseworthy
louer rent; reserve (a seat); hire
Louisiane *f.* Louisiana
loup *m.* wolf
lourd heavy
Louvre *m.* famous museum in Paris
lu, lus (*pp and sp of* lire) read
luisant shiny
lui him, to him; to her; it, to it; bien à lui typical, characteristic
lumière *f.* light; mettre en lumière throw light upon
lundi *m.* Monday
lune *f.* moon; clair de lune *m.* moonlight
lutte *f.* struggle; wrestling
luxe *m.* luxury
lycée *m.* French secondary school, somewhat equivalent to American high school and junior college combined
Lyon Lyons, largest city of France located on the Rhône
lyrique lyrical
lyrisme *m.* lyricism

M

machine *f.* machine; machine à écrire typewriter; taper à la machine typewrite
madrigal *m.* a short love poem
magasin *m.* store
magnétophone *m.* tape recorder
magnifique magnificent
maigre very thin, skinny; low (salary); poor
maigrir get thin
main *f.* hand; porter la main à put one's hand on; se tenir par la main hold hands
maintenant now
maintes: maintes fois many times
maire *m.* mayor
mairie *f.* city hall; town hall
mais but; mais non why, no; mais oui certainly; why, yes
maïs *m.* corn
maison *f.* house; home; maison de campagne country home
maître *m.* teacher; master; leader; title given to lawyers and to country residents of a certain stature
maîtriser control; master
majorité *f.* majority
mal *m.* evil; sickness, (*adv.*) badly; not well; avoir mal be sore; ache; avoir mal au cœur feel nauseated; avoir mal à la tête have a headache; avoir un terrible mal de tête have a terrible headache; finir mal end up badly;

Verbs with spelling changes are explained on pp. 274–276.

mal à l'aise ill at ease; **mal élevé** ill-bred; **se faire mal** hurt oneself; **se sentir mal** feel sick; **se trouver mal** faint; feel sick

malade *m. or f.* patient; sick person; (*adj.*) *sick;* tomber malade get sick

maladie *f.* sickness

malaise *m.* uneasiness; discomfort

malédiction *f.* curse

malgré in spite of; **malgré lui** in spite of himself

malheur *m.* misfortune

malheureux (*f.* malheureuse) unhappy

malin smart

manche *f.* sleeve

manger (*irr. sp.* B) eat; **salle à manger** dining room

manie *f.* mania

manière *f.* manner, way

manifestation *f.* demonstration

manifeste obvious

manquer (pp. 106–07) miss; lack; **elle manqua de savon** she was short of soap

mansarde *f.* attic, garret

manteau *m.* overcoat

manuscrit *m.* manuscript

marchand *m.* merchant; storekeeper

marche *f.* walking; progress

marché *m.* market; **bon marché** cheap

mardi *m.* Tuesday; **le Mardi gras** the last Tuesday before Lent

marée *f.* tide; flood

mari *m.* husband

mariage *m.* wedding; marriage

marier (*perscn* + à + *person*) marry; **se marier** (avec + *person*) marry; get married

Maroc *m.* Morocco

marquer mark; measure; indicate

marquise title given to the wife of a **marquis**

mars *m.* March

Marseille *f.* Marseilles, the second largest city in France, situated on the Mediterranean

marteau *m.* hammer

masse *f.* juggler's club

massif (*f.* massive) massive; large and heavy

match *m.* game

matin *m.* morning

maudit cursed; damned

mauvais bad

me me, to me

mécanique *f.* mechanics

mécanicien *m.* mechanic

méchant mean, vicious; bad; naughty

mécontent displeased, dissatisfied

médecin *m.* doctor

méfiance *f.* distrust

méfier (se) (de + *n.*) mistrust; distrust

meilleur better; best; **meilleur marché** cheaper; **de meilleure heure** earlier

mélancolie *f.* melancholy

mélancolique melancholy

mélange *m.* mixture

mélanger (*irr. sp.* B) mix

mêlé mixed; involved in

mêler mix; **se mêler** be mixed; be blended; make oneself a part; mingle

mélomane *m. or f.* music lover

même self; same; even; itself; mere; very; **quand même** even so, just the same; **tout de même** all the same; exactly as, just as

mémoire *f.* memory

mémoires *m. pl.* memoirs

menace *f.* threat

menacer (*irr. sp.* A) (de + *inf.*) threaten

ménage *m.* household; housework; **femme de ménage** *f.* cleaning woman

mener (*irr. sp.* D) lead, take (a person)

mensonge *m.* lie

mentir lie

menu small, tiny

menuisier *m.* carpenter

mer *f.* sea; **revenir de la mer** come back from the seaside

mercredi *m.* Wednesday

mère *f.* mother

mériter deserve

merveilleux *m.* marvelous quality; **ouvert à son merveilleux** aware of its marvelous qualities

merveilleux (*f.* merveilleuse) marvelous

messieurs (*pl. of* monsieur) gentlemen

mesure *f.* measure; **à mesure que** as; **au fur et à mesure** gradually

mesurer measure; look over

méthodique methodical

métier *m.* trade; type of work

mètre *m.* meter (39.37 inches)

métro (*abbreviation for* métropolitain) *m.* subway

mettre (mettant, mis, je mets, je mis) put, put on; **mettre à la poste** mail; **mettre en lumière** throw light on; **mettre en œuvre** apply; illustrate; **mettre la table** set the table; **se mettre** become; **se mettre à** begin; **se mettre à l'abri** take shelter; **se mettre à table** sit down at the table; **se mettre au travail** set oneself to work; **se mettre d'accord** agree; **se mettre en colère** get angry; **se mettre en quête** set out in search of

meuble *m.* (piece of) furniture

meubler furnish

Mexique *m.* Mexico

mi-corps: à mi-corps halfway into

midi *m.* noon

miel *m.* honey

mieux better; best; **faire de son mieux** do one's best

milieu *m.* middle

milieu mondain high society

militaire *m.* soldier; (*adj.*) militaire military

militant militant

mille thousand

millier *m.* thousand

mine *f.* looks, appearance

Irregular verbs are conjugated on pp. 256–273.

ministre *m.* minister
minute *f.* minute; **une minute** just a minute
minutie *f.* attention to minute detail
miraculeux (*f.* miraculeuse) miraculous
miroir *m.* mirror
mis (*pp and sp of* mettre) put
Misanthrope, Le The Misanthrope, a play by
   Molière (1666)
misérable *m. or f.* scoundrel; unfortunate
   person
mode *f.* fashion; style
modéré moderate; subdued
modifier modify
mœurs *f. pl.* mores; customs
moi me, to me; self; I
moindre least; slightest
moins less; **de moins en moins** less and less; **du
   moins** at least; **à moins que** (+ *subjunc.*)
   unless
moisson *f.* harvest
moitié *f.* half
Molière (1622–1673) French dramatist, writer
   of comedies
molle (*f. of* mou) soft; weak
mollet *m.* calf of the leg
moment *m.* moment; time; **ce n'est pas le
   moment** it isn't the proper time; **d'un
   moment à l'autre** from one minute to the
   next, at any time
monarque *m.* monarch
mondain fashionable; **milieu mondain** high
   society
monde *m.* world; people; **tout le monde**
   everybody
monsieur *m.* (*pl.* messieurs) sir, Mr.; gentleman
monstrueux (*f.* monstrueuse) monstrous
mont *m.* small mountain
Mont Blanc *m.* highest peak of the French Alps
montagne *f.* mountain
montée *f.* rise
monter go up; go up to; rise; climb; bring up;
   monter dans une chambre go to a room;
   monter dans un train get on a train
montre *f.* watch
Montréal largest city in French Canada
   (Québec)
montrer show; **se montrer** appear
moquer (se) (de + *n.*) make fun of; not care
   about
morale *f.* moral; lesson
morceau *m.* piece
mordre bite
mort (*pp of* mourir) died; dead
mort *f.* death
mortel (*f.* mortelle) mortal
Moscou *m.* Moscow
mot *m.* word; **encore un mot** one more word;
   jeu de mots play on words, pun; **mots
   croisés** crossword puzzle; **mot de passe**
   password
moteur *m.* motor; **bateau à moteur** motor boat

moto *f.* motorcycle; **en moto** on a motorcycle
motocyclette *f.* motorcycle
mou (*before vowel sound* mol; *f.* molle) weak;
   soft
moucher (se) blow one's nose
mouchoir *m.* handkerchief
mouillé wet
mouiller wet, moisten; **se mouiller** get wet
mourir (mourant, mort, je meurs, je mourus)
   die
moustique *m.* mosquito
mouton *m.* sheep
mouvement *m.* movement; **rentrer en
   mouvement** be on the move again
moyen *m.* means; way
muet (*f.* muette) silent
mur *m.* wall
mûre *f.* mulberry
musée *m.* museum
musicalité *f.* musical quality
musique *f.* music; **faire de la musique** play
   music
mystère *m.* mystery
mystérieux (*f.* mystérieuse) mysterious

N

nager (*irr. sp.* B) swim
naïf (*f.* naïve) naïve
naissance *f.* birth
naître (naissant, né, je nais, je naquis) be born
narrateur *m.* narrator
narratrice *f.* narrator
natif (*f.* native) native
nationalité *f.* nationality
natte *f.* braid of hair; pigtail
naturellement naturally
navire *m.* ship
né (*pp of* naître) born
néanmoins nevertheless
négatif *m.* negative
négligemment absent-mindedly
négliger (*irr. sp.* B) neglect
neige *f.* snow; **bonhomme de neige** *m.*
   snowman
neiger (*irr. sp.* B) snow
nerveusement nervously
nerveux (*f.* nerveuse) nervous
netteté *f.* sharpness; clearness
nettoyage *m.* cleaning; **faire un grand
   nettoyage** do a thorough cleaning
nettoyer (*irr. sp.* C) clean
neuf nine
neuf (*f.* neuve) new; **à neuf** anew
neutre neutral; impersonal
neuve (*f. of* neuf) new
neveu *m.* nephew
nez *m.* nose
ni neither; **ni . . . ni** neither . . . nor
Nice resort on the French Riviera

Verbs with spelling changes are explained on pp. 274–276.

nigaud *n.* dummy
noblesse *f.* nobility; nobleness
Noël *m.* Christmas
noir *m.* dark; darkness; night; *(adj.)* black
nom *m.* name
nombre *m.* number
nombreux *(f.* nombreuse) many; numerous;
   famille nombreuse large family
nord *m.* north
normand pertaining to Normandy
Normandie *f.* Normandy, a province in
   northwestern France
Norvège *f.* Norway
nos *(pl. of* notre) our
nostalgie *f.* nostalgia; longing
notaire *m.* notary
notamment especially
note *f.* check; bill; grade; note
noter note; notice
notre *(possessive adj.)* our
nôtre *(possessive pron.)* ours
Notre-Dame famous Gothic cathedral in Paris
nourrir feed; give substance to
nourrissant nourishing
nourriture *f.* food
nouveau *(before vowel sound* nouvel; *f.*
   nouvelle) new; à nouveau again; de
   nouveau again, once more; les nouveaux
   arrivés the people who have just arrived
nouvel, nouvelle *(m. and f. of* nouveau) new
nouvelle *f.* a piece of news; novelette; les
   nouvelles *f. pl.* news; nous avons de ses
   nouvelles we've heard from him
Nouvelle-Orléans, la *f.* New Orleans
nu bare
nuage *m.* cloud
nuit *f.* night; table de nuit night stand
nul *(pron.)* no one; *(adj.)* nul *(f.* nulle): nulle
   part ailleurs nowhere else
numéro *m.* number
nuque *f.* nape of the neck

O

obéir (à + *n.*) obey
obéissant obedient
objet *m.* object
obligatoire compulsory
obliger *(irr. sp.* B) force; oblige
observation *f.* remark; observation
observer watch; observe
obstruer obstruct
occasion *f.* opportunity
occupé busy
occuper (s') (de + *n.*) take care of; turn one's
   attention to; take charge of; busy oneself
   with
odeur *f.* odor, smell
œil *m. sing. (m. pl.* yeux) eye; coup d'œil
   glance

œillet *m.* carnation
œuf *m.* egg
œuvre *f.* work; mettre en œuvre make use of
offenser offend
officier *m.* officer
offre *f.* offer
offrir *(conj. like* ouvrir) offer
oiseau *m.* bird; oiseau de mer sea bird
olivier *m.* olive tree
ombre *f.* shade; shadow
on *(indefinite pron.)* one; we; you; they;
   people
oncle *m.* uncle
ondulation *f.* ripple; wave
ongle *m.* nail
opéra *m.* opera; opera house
opérer operate; work
opinion *f.* opinion, view
opposé opposite
or *m.* gold; *(conj.)* it so happens
orage *m.* storm
oralement orally
orange *(adj.)* orange-colored
oranger *m.* orange tree
ordinaire: d'ordinaire usually
ordinateur *m.* computer
ordonner (à + *person* + de + *inf.*) order
ordre *m.* order; à vos ordres at your orders
oreille *f.* ear; dur d'oreille hard of hearing
organiser organize; plan; utilize
orgueil *m.* pride
originaire native
original original; odd, strange, eccentric
Orléans French city on Loire between Paris and
   Tours
oser (+ *inf.*) dare
ou or
où where; in which; when; au moment où at
   the time when; où que wherever
oubli *m.* oblivion
oublier (de + *inf.*) forget
ouf! phew! (with a sigh of relief)
oui yes; mais oui certainly; why, yes
ours [urs] *m.* bear
outre besides, in addition to
outre-tombe beyond the grave
ouvert open; exposed to; aware; ouvert à son
   merveilleux aware of its marvelous qualities
ouverture *f.* opening
ouvrage *m.* work
ouvrier *m.* worker, workingman
ouvrir (ouvrant, ouvert, j'ouvre, j'ouvris) open;
   s'ouvrir lay open one's heart; get open

P

paie, paient (payer) pay
paille *f.* straw
pain *m.* bread
paix *f.* peace

Irregular verbs are conjugated on pp. 256–273.

palais *m.* palate; palace; **palais de justice** courthouse

pâle pale

pancarte *f.* sign

panier *m.* basket

panne *f.* breakdown; **panne d'électricité** power failure; **tomber en panne** have a (mechanical) breakdown

papier *m.* paper; **papier à lettre** stationery; writing paper; **papier d'argent** aluminum foil

Pâques *f. pl.* Easter

paquet *m.* package; pack

par through; by; with; for; per; **par ce temps** in such weather; **par jour** per day, each day

paraître (*conj. like* connaître) look, seem; appear

parallèlement parallel

parc *m.* park; **parc à autos** parking lot

parcourir (*conj. like* courir) travel; go through

pardonner (à + *person* + de + *inf.*) pardon; forgive

pareil (*f.* pareille) same, identical; such a

pareillement similarly

parent *m.* parent; relative

parfaitement perfectly

parfois sometimes

parfum *m.* perfume

parler (à + *person;* de + *n.*) speak; talk

parmi among

paroi *f.* wall

parole *f.* (spoken) word

part *f.* part; **à part** except; **de ma part** for me, in my behalf; **nulle part** nowhere; **nulle part ailleurs** nowhere else

partager (*irr. sp.* B) share

parti *m.* party; **prendre le parti de** side with

participe *m.* participle

participer participate, take part

particulier (*f.* particulière) particular; peculiar; **rien de particulier** nothing particular

particulièrement particularly

partie *f.* part; **faire partie de** belong to, be a part of

partir (2) leave; go away; depart; **lui parti** once he had left (*lit.* he having left); **à partir de demain** from tomorrow on

partout everywhere

paru, parus (*pp. and sp. of* paraître) seemed, looked, appeared

pas *m.* step; footstep; gait; **avancer d'un pas** take one step forward; **pas à pas** step by step; **s'attacher aux pas** follow closely; **faire quelques pas, faire un pas** take a step

passage *m.* passage; passing

passant *m.* passer-by

passé *m.* past; **passé composé** compound past; (*adj.*) past

passe-partout *m.* master key

passer pass; pass by; give; spend (time); advance; be shown; go down; **j'ai passé par** là I've gone through that; **passer** (à + *inf.*) spend time; **passer un examen** take an examination; **se passer** happen; take place; be done; **il se passe quelque chose** something is happening; **se passer de** do without

passif (*f.* passive) passive

passionnant fascinating

passionné ardent

pasteur *m.* minister (in church)

Pasteur, Louis (1822–1895) French scientist

pâtissier *m.* owner of a pastry shop

patron *m.* boss; owner

patte *f.* paw; foot

pauvre *m.* poor man; (*adj.*) poor

payer (*irr. sp.* C) pay; pay for

pays *m.* country

paysage *m.* countryside; landscape

peau *f.* skin

pêche *f.* fishing

peindre (peignant, peint, je peins, je peignis) paint; portray

peine *f.* trouble; difficulty; pain; grief; **à peine** slightly, scarcely; not very; **cela me fait de la peine** I am sorry; **valoir la peine** be worthwhile

peiner hurt

peint (*pp of* peindre) painted

peintre *m.* painter

peinture *f.* painting; portrayal

pelouse *f.* lawn

penché: la tête penchée his head cocked

pencher lean

pendant during; **pendant que** while

pendule *f.* clock

pénétrant sharp; searching

pénétrer fill; enter

penser (à + *n.*) think; think of; believe; (+ *inf.*) intend; (à + *inf.*) consider; (de + *n.*) have an opinion of

pension *f.* boarding house; boarding school

pensionnaire *m. or f.* boarder

pente *f.* slope

perché perched; **chat perché** children's game of tag

perçois (*pres. of* percevoir) perceive

perdre lose

père *m.* father

période *f.* period; **faire une période militaire** do a short tour of military duty

périodiquement periodically

permettre (*conj. like* mettre) (à + *person* + de + *inf.*) permit, allow

permis *m.* license; **permis de conduire** driver's license

Pérou *m.* Peru

perpendiculairement perpendicularly

perpétuer perpetuate

perron *m.* porch

personnage *m.* character (in a literary work)

personne *f.* person

Verbs with spelling changes are explained on pp. 274–276.

personne no one, nobody; **ne . . . personne** no one, nobody
personnellement personally
perspective *f.* prospect
peser (*irr. sp.* D) weigh; **peser lourd** be heavy; be important
peste *f.* plague
petit *m.* baby; little boy; (*adj.*) small, little; **petit déjeuner** breakfast; **petit employé** minor office clerk; **un petit cognac** a small glass of brandy; **petits pois** *m. pl.* peas
petit-fils *m.* grandson
pétrole *m.* oil
peu little; **à peu près** about, approximately; **depuis peu** recently, since not very long ago; **un peu** a little, a bit; **peu fréquenté** not very often visited; **quelque peu** somewhat
peuple *m.* people; masses
peupler inhabit; throng
peur *f.* fear; **avoir peur** be afraid; **de peur** for fear; **faire peur** scare
peut, peuvent, peux (**pouvoir**) can
pharmacien *m.* druggist; pharmacist
philosophie *f.* philosophy; **faire sa philosophie** study philosophy, carry on one's studies in philosophy
philosophique philosophical
photo *f.* photograph; snapshot
photographier photograph
phrase *f.* sentence
physique physical
pièce *f.* play; room; coin
pied *m.* foot; **à pied** on foot
piège *m.* trap
pierre *f.* stone
Pierre Peter; **Pierre le Grand** (1672–1725) eighteenth-century czar of Russia
Pierrot (*diminutive of* **Pierre**) little Peter
pilote *m.* pilot; **pilote de ligne** commercial air pilot
pilule *f.* pill
pionnier *m.* pioneer
pire (*comparative of* **mauvais**) worse
pis worse; worst; **tant pis** so much the worse
pisciculture *f.* pisciculture (fish raising)
piscine *f.* swimming pool
Pise Pisa, town in central Italy famous for its Leaning Tower
piste *f.* trail
place *f.* seat; public square; place (space); spot; job; **sur place** on the spot
placer (*irr. sp.* A) place; find a home for; **se placer** take place
plage *f.* beach
plaindre (*conj. like* **craindre**) pity; feel sorry for; **se plaindre** (**de** + *n.*) complain
plaire (**plaisant, plu, je plais, je plus**) (**à** + *person*) please
plaisanter joke
plaisir *m.* pleasure; **faire plaisir à** please, give pleasure to

plaît (*pres. of* **plaire**) pleases; **s'il vous plaît** please; **si ça vous plaît** if you wish
plan *m.* plan; map (of a city)
planter plant
plat flat
plein full; **en plein exotisme** in the middle of an exotic land; **en pleine poitrine** right in the chest, in the middle of the chest
pleinement fully
pleurer cry
pleut (*pres. of* **pleuvoir**) it is raining; it rains
pleuvoir (**pleuvant, plu, il pleut, il plut**) rain
plombier *m.* plumber
plonger (*irr. sp.* B) plunge
plu, plut (*pp and sp of* **pleuvoir**) rained
plu, plus (*pp and sp of* **plaire**) pleased
pluie *f.* rain
plupart *f.* majority
pluriel *m.* plural
plus more; most; **de plus** moreover; **de plus en plus** more and more; **ne . . . plus** no more; no longer; **non plus** either; neither; **not . . . either**; **qui plus est** what's more
plusieurs several
plutôt rather
poche *f.* pocket
poids *m.* weight; responsibility
poignant gripping
point *m.* point; period; **point de vue** point of view; **être sur le point de** be about to; (*adv.*) **ne . . . point** not at all
pointu sharp
poire *f.* pear
pois *m.* pea; **petits pois** *m. pl.* peas
poisson *m.* fish
poitrine *f.* chest; **en pleine poitrine** right in the chest, in the middle of the chest
poli polite
policier *m.* policeman; **roman policier** *m.* detective story
politique *f.* politics
Pologne *f.* Poland
polonais Polish
pomme *f.* apple; **pomme de terre** potato
pommier *m.* apple tree
Pompéi Pompeii
pompeux (*f.* **pompeuse**) pompous
pompier *m.* fireman
pont *m.* bridge
populaire popular; well liked by the masses
population *f.* people
port *m.* seaport; port
porte *f.* door; doorway; **porte de derrière** back door; **prendre la porte** get out
portefeuille *m.* billfold
porte-monnaie *m.* pocket book
porter carry; bear; lift; raise; wear; **porter la main à** put one's hand on; **se porter bien** be well
porto *m.* port wine
portrait *m.* picture, portrait

portugais Portuguese
posé resting
poser put; pose; put down; rest; **poser une question** ask a question; **un problème se pose** a problem presents itself
posséder (*irr. sp.* E) possess
possible possible; **dès que possible** as soon as possible
poste *m.* position, job
poste *f.* post office; **mettre à la poste** mail
poudre *f.* powder
poule *f.* hen
poulet *m.* chicken
poupée *f.* doll
pour for; in order to; **pour que** in order that
pourquoi why
pourrai, pourrais (*fut. and cond. of* pouvoir) will be able to; would be able to
poursuivre (*conj. like* suivre) continue; pursue
pourtant however; yet
pourvu que provided that
poussé: **éducation poussée** college education
pousser push; grow; incite; **pousser un cri** utter a cry
poussière *f.* dust
pouvoir (pouvant, pu, je peux, je pus) (+ *inf.*) can, be able to; may; **il se peut** it is possible; **puis-je** can I; may I; **sauve qui peut!** look out! run for your life!
pouvoir *m.* power
pratiquant practicing
pré *m.* meadow
précédent preceding; **le jour précédent** the day before
précéder (*irr. sp.* E) precede
précieux (*f.* précieuse) precious
précipitamment precipitately, in a hurry
précipité hasty
précipiter (se) rush
prédilection *f.* preference
prédire (*conj. like* dire) predict
préféré favorite
préférence *f.* preference; **de préférence** preferably
premier (*f.* première) first; prime
prendre (prenant, pris, je prends, je pris) (+ *thing* + à [*from*] + *person*) take; have; catch; **comment s'y prendre** how to go about it; **prendre une décision** make a decision; **prendre le dessus** prevail; **prendre le parti de** side with; **prendre la porte** leave the room; get out; **prendre au sérieux** take seriously; **prendre sa source** (of river) begin; **prendre ses responsabilités** assume some responsibility; **prendre un verre** have a drink
prénom *f.* first name
près (de + *n.*) near; **à peu près** about, approximately
présent *m.* gift; (*adj.*) present
présenter (*person* + à + *person*) introduce

presque almost
presser press; weigh; rush; **le temps presse** time is getting short; **se presser** crowd; peer
prêt (à + *inf.*) ready
prétendre claim
prêter lend
preuve *f.* proof
prévenir (*conj. like* venir) warn; inform; let someone know; call (the doctor)
prévoir (*conj. like* voir *except in fut. and conditional*) foresee
prier (*person* + de + *inf.*) pray; ask; beg; **je vous prie** please
printemps *m.* spring
pris (*pp and sp of* prendre) taken; took
prisonnier *m.* prisoner
priver (de + *n.*) deprive
prix *m.* price; prize
problème *m.* problem; **poser un problème** present a problem
procédé *m.* process; method, procedure
prochain next
proche near
procurer give
producteur *m.* producer
produire (*conj. like* conduire) produce; create; **se produire** happen
produit *m.* product
professeur *m.* professor; teacher
profil *m.* profile; side; **de profil** in profile
profit *m.* profit; **tirer profit de** profit from
profiter (de + *n.*) take advantage of
profond deep
profondeur *f.* depth
programmeur *m.* programmer
progrès *m.* progress
progresser progress, advance
projet *m.* plan; project
prolonger (se) (*irr. sp.* B) last
promenade *f.* walk; **faire une promenade** take a walk
promener (se) (*irr. sp.* D) take a walk
promeneur *m.* stroller
promesse *f.* promise
promettre (*conj. like* mettre) (à + *person* + de + *inf.*) promise
promis (*pp and sp of* promettre) promised
pronom *m.* pronoun
prononcer (*irr. sp.* A) pronounce
propos *m.* remark; **à propos de** concerning
proposer propose; suggest
proposition *f.* proposition; proposal
propre own; clean
propriétaire *m. or f.* owner; landlord, landlady
protestataire *m. or f.* protester
protestation *f.* protest
prouver prove
Provence *f.* a region of southern France
provisoire temporary
provoquer challenge; set into motion
prudence *f.* prudence, care

Verbs with spelling changes are explained on pp. 274–276.

prudent cautious; prudent
psychologique psychological
pu, pus (*pp and sp of* pouvoir) could, was able
public *m.* audience; people
publier publish
puis then
puis, puisse (*pres. indic. and pres. subjunc. of* pouvoir) can, am able; may
puissance *f.* power
puissant powerful; all-powerful, overwhelming
puits *m.* well
pull-over *m.* sweater
pûmes (*1st pers. pl. sp of* pouvoir) could
punir punish
pur pure
pus (*sp of* pouvoir) could
Pyrénées *f. pl.* Pyrenees

Q

quadrillé ruled in squares
quai *m.* wharf; quay; bank
quand when; quand même just the same, even so
quant à as for
quarante forty
quart *m.* quarter
quartier *m.* district
quatorze fourteen
que that; which; what; whom; how; when; than; que (vous ayez ou non) whether (you have or not); qu'on est bien! how comfortable one is!
Québec province in eastern Canada; also capital of the province
quel (*f.* quelle) which; what; quel que soit whatever is
quelconque some sort of
quelque some; en quelque sorte somehow; quelque peu somewhat
quelque chose something
quelqu'un someone
quereller (se) (*irr. sp.* F) quarrel
question *f.* question; poser une question ask a question
questionner question; inquire
quête *f.* quest
qui who; whom; that; which; à qui le dites-vous! you're telling me! à qui que ce soit to anyone at all qui que ce soit whoever he is
quiconque whoever
quinze fifteen
quitter (+ *n.*) leave; ne pas quitter quelqu'un des yeux not to take one's eyes off someone
quoi what; de quoi the money; the wherewithall; n'importe quoi anything, anything whatever; quoi que whatever; quoi qu'il en soit however that may be, however the case may be
quoique although
quotidiennement daily

R

racommoder mend
raconter tell
radiateur *m.* radiator
rage *f.* rabies; fury
raison *f.* reason; à plus forte raison all the more; avoir raison de overcome; donner raison justify, prove to be right
raisonnable reasonable
raisonner (se) reason with oneself; try to be reasonable
ramener (*irr. sp.* D) bring back
rang *m.* row; au premier rang of the first rank; en rang in a row
rangé dutiful; of regular habits
ranger (*irr. sp.* B) put in order; arrange; put away
ranimer (se) regain consciousness, come to
rapide fast
rappeler (*irr. sp.* F) remind; call back se rappeler (+ *n.*) remember
rapport *m.* report
rapporter bring back; relate
rapprocher (se) draw near
raser shave; se raser shave oneself
rasoir *m.* razor
rassurant reassuring
rassurer reassure
ratine *f.* woolen cloth
rattacher à associate with
ravi delighted
ravissant delightful, ravishing
rayon *m.* ray
réagir react
réaliser (se) happen
rebelle *m. or f.* rebel
rebondir bounce back
récemment recently
récepteur (radio or TV) set
recette *f.* recipe
recevoir (recevant, reçu, je reçois, je reçus) receive; entertain
recherche *f.* research; à la recherche de in search of
rechercher search for
récit *m.* story
réclame *f.* advertisement
réclamer ask for
récolter harvest
recommencer (*irr. sp.* A) do over; begin again; resume; make a fresh start
récompenser reward
réconfortant comforting
reconnaître (*conj. like* connaître) recognize
reconsidérer reconsider; take another long look at
recouvert de covered with
reçu, reçus (*pp and sp of* recevoir) received
recul *m.* recoil, withdrawal, drawing back; prendre du recul withdraw

Irregular verbs are conjugated on pp. 256–273.

redécouvrir discover again
redemander ask again
redescendre go down again; lower again
redevenir become again
rédiger (*irr. sp.* B) write; compose
redire (*conj. like* dire) repeat
redonner give again
redouter fear
réduire (*conj. like* conduire) reduce
refermer close up
réfléchir think; reflect
refléter (se) (*irr. sp.* E) be reflected
réflexion *f.* reflection; **faire des réflexions** think about, reflect on
réfugié *m.* refugee; (*adj.*) alone; withdrawn
refuser (de + *inf.*) refuse
regagner regain
regard *m.* look; glance; observation; **jeter un regard** glance
regarder (+ *n.*) look; look at
régime *m.* regime; diet; **régime de faveur** privileged status
règlement *m.* rule
régler (*irr. sp.* E) settle
régner (*irr. sp.* E) reign; exist
regret *m.* regret; grief; **comme à regret** as if he regretted it
régulier (*f.* régulière) regular
rejeter (*irr. sp.* F) reject
rejoindre (*conj. like* craindre) meet again; join
relatif (*f.* relative) relative
relique *f.* relic
relire (*conj. like* lire) read again
relu, relus (*pp and sp of* relire) read again
remarier (se) marry again
remarquable remarkable
remarque *f.* remark
remarquer notice
remboursement *m.* reimbursement; **contre remboursement** C.O.D.
rembourser pay back
remède *m.* remedy; medicine
remercier (*person* + de *or* pour + *thing; person* + de + *inf.*) thank
remettre (*conj. like* mettre) put back on again; hand in; turn in; put back; postpone; **en mémoire** remind; **se remettre** go back
remis (*pp and sp of* remettre) put back on; handed in; postponed
remonter go up; go up again; raise again; **remonter la rue** go up the street
remplacer (*irr. sp.* A) replace
remplir fill; fill up; fill out; fulfill
renard *m.* fox
rencontre *f.* meeting
rencontrer meet (by chance)
rendez-vous *m.* date; appointment
rendre return (something); (+ *adj.*) make; **se rendre** go; **se rendre compte** realize; **se rendre malade** make oneself sick
rêne *f.* rein

renommé famous
renoncement *m.* renouncing
renoncer (*irr. sp.* A) give up; renounce
renouveler (*irr. sp.* F) change; be renovated
renseignement *m.* information
renseigner give information; **se renseigner** ask for information: get information, inform oneself
rentrer return; come back home; go back home; come back in
renverser overthrow; tip over
renvoyer (*conj. like* envoyer) dismiss
répandre spread; **se répandre** spread out
répandu common
réparation *f.* repair
réparer repair, fix
repartir start on one's way again
repas *m.* meal
repeindre (*conj. like* peindre) paint again
répondre (à + *n.*) answer, reply to
reposer (se) rest
repousser push aside; push back
reprendre (*conj. like* prendre) resume; take again; regain; continue
représentation *f.* show; performance
représenter (se) imagine
repris (*pp and sp of* reprendre) resumed; regained; continued
reproche *m.* reproach
république *f.* republic
réputé famous; well known
réserver reserve; make a reservation
résister (à + *n.*) resist
respectueux (respectueuse) respectful
respirer breathe; take a breath; feel relieved
responsabilité *f.* responsibility; **prendre ses responsabilités** assume some responsibility
ressembler (à + *n.*) look like, resemble
ressortir (*conj. like* sortir) take out
ressource *f.* resource
reste *m.* remainder; **ne pas être en reste** be equal to the situation; not be backward
rester remain; stay; stand; **il me reste à** I'll have to; **il me reste une inquiétude** I still have a worry; **il ne me reste rien** I have nothing left
résultat *m.* result
résumer sum up
retard *m.* delay; **avoir du retard** be late; **être en retard** be late
retarder delay
retenir (*conj. like* tenir) reserve; hire in advance·
retirer (se) withdraw
retour *m.* return; **à ton retour** when you return; **être de retour** be back
retourner return, go back; turn again; turn around; **se retourner** turn around; look back; **s'en retourner** go back
retraite *f.* retreat; retirement; **prendre sa retraite** retire

Verbs with spelling changes are explained on pp. 274–276.

retraverser cross again

retrouver find; discover; find once more; **j'ai retrouvé le calme** peace came over me again

réunion *f.* meeting

réussi successful

réussir (à + *n.;* à + *inf.*) succeed

réussite *f.* success

revanche *f.* revenge; **en revanche** on the other hand

rêve *m.* dream; **faire un rêve** have a dream

réveil *m.* waking up; **au réveil** on awakening

réveiller awaken; **se réveiller** wake up

révéler (*irr. sp.* E) reveal; discover; **se révéler** prove to be

revenant *m.* ghost

revendication *f.* demand

revenir (*conj. like* venir) return; come back

revenu *m.* income

rêver (de + *n.;* de + *inf.*) dream

rêverie *f.* daydream

rêveur *m.* dreamer

reviendrai, reviendrais (*fut. and cond. of* revenir) will, would come back

revivre (*conj. like* vivre) live again; relive; come back to life

revoir (*conj. like* voir) see again; **se revoir** meet again; **au revoir** goodbye

révoltant revolting

revue *f.* magazine

rez-de-chaussée *m.* ground floor, first floor

Rhin *m.* Rhine

Rhône *m.* Rhone, a river whose source is in Switzerland, and which flows through France and empties into the Mediterranean near Marseilles

rhume *m.* cold

ri, rit (*pp, pres., sp of* rire) laughed; laughs; laughed

riche rich

ridé wrinkled

rideau *m.* curtain

rien nothing; **ne . . . rien** nothing; **servir à rien** be useless

rigolo very funny

rire (riant, ri je ris, je ris) (de + *n.*) laugh; **éclater de rire** burst out laughing; **rire de quelqu'un** make fun of someone

rivière *f.* river; stream; tributary

robe *f.* dress; **robe de chambre** gown

roc *m.* rock

roche *f.* rock

rocheux (*f.* rocheuse) rocky

rôder prowl about

rôle *m.* role; part

roman *m.* novel; **roman policier** detective story; (*adj.*) Romance

romancier *m.* novelist

romancière *f.* woman novelist

rompre break

rond *n.* circle; **tourner en rond** run around in circles; go round and round; (*adj.*) round

ronronner purr

rosée *f.* dew

rosier *m.* rosebush

rôti *m.* roast beef; a roast; (*adj.*) roasted

rôtir roast

rouet *m.* spinning wheel

rouge red; **feu rouge** red light; traffic light

rougeole *f.* measles

rouleau *m.* roll

rouler drive; go; roll; move

Roumanie *f.* Romania

route *f.* way; road; **carnet de route** *m.* traveller's notebook; **en route** on the way; **se tromper de route** take the wrong road

roux (*f.* rousse) (referring to hair) red, reddish

rude hard, harsh, severe

rue *f.* street

ruiner (se) ruin oneself

ruisseau *m.* brook

rusé sly; tricky

russe Russian

S

sa (*f. of* son) his; her; its

sable *m.* sand

sac *m.* bag; handbag; knapsack

saccadé jerky

sachant (*pres. part. of* savoir) knowing

sache, sachiez (*pres. subjunctive of* savoir) know

sacré sacred; damned

sacrifier (se) sacrifice oneself

sage wise; (speaking of behavior) good, well-behaved

sagesse *f.* wisdom

saigner bleed

sain healthy

sais, sait (*pres. of* savoir) know

saisir seize

saison *f.* season; **la belle saison** the summer months

sale dirty; (*fig.*) "lousy"

salé salted

sali soiled

salle *f.* room (for meetings); **salle à manger** dining room; **salle de séjour** living room

salon *m.* drawing room; living room

saluer greet; say "hello"

salut *m.* salute; salvation

samedi *m.* Saturday

sans without; **sans compter que** besides the fact; **sans doute** probably

santé *f.* health

satisfaire (*conj. like* faire) satisfy

sauf except; but

saule *m.* willow tree

saurai, saurais (*fut. and cond. of* savoir) will know; would know

sauvage wild

Irregular verbs are conjugated on pp. 256–273.

sauver save; **sauve qui peut!** look out!, run for your life!; **se sauver** escape, flee
savane *f.* savannah, prairie
savant *m.* scientist; (*adj.*) learned; trained; *Les Femmes savantes* The Learned Women, a play by Molière (1672)
savoir (**sachant, su je sais, je sus**) know; (+ *inf.*) know how to; **savoir bien** know very well
savon *m.* soap
savourer enjoy
savoureux (*f.* **savoureuse**) tasty
scène *f.* scene; stage
scie *f.* saw
science *f.* science; **homme de science** scientist
scolaire of the school
sec (*f.* **sèche**) dry
secheresse *f.* drought, dry spell
secondaire secondary
secouer shake off
secrétaire *m. or f.* secretary
secrètement secretly
séduisant extremely attractive
seigneur *m.* lord
sein *m.* breast
Seine *f.* French river which crosses Paris
séjour *m.* stay, sojourn; **salle de séjour** living room
sel *m.* salt
selon according to
semaine *f.* week
semblable similar; (*n.*) *m. or f.* fellow being
sembler (+ *inf.*) seem
sens [sãs] *m.* way; direct; meaning; **dans un sens** in a way
sensibilité sensitiveness
sensible sensitive
sensiblement more or less; perceptibly, noticeably
sentier *m.* path
sentiment *m.* feeling; sensation
sentir (2) feel; smell; **se sentir** feel; **se sentir mal** feel sick
séparer separate
serai, serais (*fut. and cond. of* être) will be; would be
serein serene; satisfied
série *f.* collection
sérieux (*f.* **sérieuse**) serious; **au sérieux** seriously
serré crowded
serrer shake; press; **serrer les dents** clench one's teeth
serrure *f.* lock
serviable obliging, willing to help
service *m.* service; silverware
serviette *f.* towel; briefcase
servir (2) serve; **ne servir à rien** be useless; **servir de** use as; **servir d'exemple** serve as an example; **se servir de** use; make use of
serviteur *m.* servant

seul alone; lonely; only; solely; single; **être seul à** be the only one to
seulement only
sévère strict
sévèrement in a stern manner
si so; yes; **si riches qu'ils soient** however rich they are
siècle *m.* century
siège *m.* seat
sien (*f.* **sienne**) his; hers; its
sieste *f.* siesta
siffler whistle
signal (*pl.* **signaux**) signal
signaler point out
signe *m.* sign; **faire signe** signal
signification *f.* signification, meaning
signifier mean
silencieusement silently
silencieux (*f.* **silencieuse**) silent
simple: simple soldat *m.* private
simplement simply
singe *m.* monkey
singulier *m.* singular; (*adj.*) (*f.* **singulière**) singular; strange
sinon otherwise
sirène *f.* siren; factory whistle
sitôt que as soon as
ski *m.* ski; **faire du ski** go skiing
sobre sober
société *f.* society; firm, company
sœur *f.* sister
soi oneself; **en soi** in itself; **ça va de soi** it goes without saying
soif *f.* thirst; **il a soif** he is thirsty
soigner take care of, care for· treat (a patient)
soigneusement carefully
soin *m.* task; care; worry
soir *m.* evening
soirée *f.* evening; party
soixante sixty
soldat *m.* soldier
soleil *m.* sun; **coucher de soleil** *m.* sunset; **lever du soleil** *m.* sunrise
solidarité *f.* solidarity
sombre dark; **il fait sombre** it is dark
somme *f.* sum (of money); amount
sommeil *m.* sleep; **avoir sommeil** be sleepy
sommet *m.* peak; top
son, sa, ses his; her; its; one's
songer (*irr. sp.* B) think
songeur (*f.* **songeuse**) pensive, dreamy
sonner ring
sonnerie *f.* ring; doorbell; ringing
Sorbonne *f.* building that formerly housed the *Faculté des Lettres et des sciences* of the University of Paris
sort *m.* fate
sorte *f.* sort; **de sorte que** so that, in such a way that; **en quelque sorte** somehow
sortie *f.* exit; **à la sortie de l'école** after school
sortilège *m.* magic spell; charm

Verbs with spelling changes are explained on pp. 274–276.

sortir (2) leave, go out
sot (*f.* sotte) foolish; silly; (*n.*) dumb person; fool
sottement foolishly; sheepishly
sou *m.* penny, cent
souci *m.* worry; care; se faire du souci worry
soucieux (*f.* soucieuse) eager
soucoupe *f.* saucer
soudain (*adj.*) sudden; (*adv.*) suddenly
souffrir (*conj. like* ouvrir) suffer
souhaiter wish
soulagement *m.* relief
soulever raise
soulier *m.* shoe
souligner underline
soupçon *m.* suspicion
soupe *f.* soup
souper *m.* supper; evening meal
soupirer sigh
souple supple, pliant
source *f.* source; prendre sa source (of a river) begin
sourcil *m.* eyebrow
sourd deaf
souriant smiling
sourire (*conj. like* rire) (à + *n.*) smile; (*n.*) *m.* smile
souris *f.* mouse
sous-sol *m.* basement
soutenir (*conj. like* tenir) support; insist
souterrain *m.* underground passage, cavern
souvenir (se) (*conj. like* venir) (de + *n.*; de + *inf.*) remember; (*n.*) *m.* souvenir; memory; remembrance; recollection; keepsake
souvent often
spectacle *m.* show; sight
spectateur *m.* spectator
splendide marvelous
spontané spontaneous
sport *m.* sport; faire des sports participate in sports; journal de sport sports magazine
sportif (*f.* sportive) sport loving; inclined toward sports
squelette *m.* skeleton
stationner park
statistique *f.* statistics
stéréotypé stereotyped
stoïquement stoically
stopper stop
strictement strictly
stupéfaction *f.* amazement
stupéfait amazed
stylo *m.* fountain pen
su, sus (*pp and sp of* savoir) known; knew; learned, found out
subit sudden
subjonctif *m.* subjunctive
subordonné subordinate
subtil subtle
subtilement subtly
succéder (à) take the place of; inherit from

succomber succumb; die
sucre *m.* sugar
sud *m.* south
Suède *f.* Sweden
suédois Swedish
suffire (suffisant, suffi, je suffis, je suffis) suffice; be enough
suffisamment enough
suggérer (*irr. sp.* E) suggest
suis (*pres. of* être) I am; (*pres. of* suivre) I, you follow
Suisse *f.* Switzerland
suite *f.* continuation; aftermath, consequence; à la suite as a result; à sa suite after them, following them; tout de suite right now, right away, immediately; in succession
suivant (*adj.*) following; next; (*prep.*) according to
suivi successful; popular
suivre (suivant, suivi, je suis, je suivis) follow; suivre un cours take a course
sujet *m.* subject; au sujet de about, concerning
superflu superfluous
supermarché *m.* supermarket
supportable bearable
supporter put up with, stand for
supprimer suppress
sur on; out of
sûr sure; firm
sûrement surely
sûreté *f.* confidence
surgir appear suddenly
surnaturel (*f.* surnaturelle) supernatural
surprenant surprising
surprise *f.* surprise, astonishment
surtout especially; above all; mostly
surveillant *m.* guard
surveiller watch over; keep an eye on
survenir (*conj. like* venir) appear
sus (*sp of* savoir) knew; learned
suspendre (*conj. like* pendre) suspend
suspens *m.* suspense; en suspens hanging
symbole *m.* symbol
sympathique nice

T

tabac *m.* tobacco; bureau de tabac tobacco shop
table *f.* table; mettre la table set the table; se mettre à table sit down at the table; table de nuit night stand
tableau *m.* picture; painting; tableau noir blackboard
tache *f.* spot; une tache de soleil a bit of sun
tâche *f.* task; duty
tâcher try
Tahiti French island in the South Pacific
taille *f.* height; de belle taille huge
tailler cut
taire (se) be quiet, keep still
tandis que while, whereas

Irregular verbs are conjugated on pp. 256–273.

tant so much; **tant pis** so much the worse
tante *f.* aunt
taper type, typewrite; **taper à la machine** typewrite
tapis *m.* rug
tard late
tarder (à + *inf.*) be late; delay, put off
tari dried up
tasse *f.* cup
taudis *m.* slum; hovel, shack
tel (*f.* telle) such, such a
téléphoner (à + *person*) telephone
téléspectateur *m.* television viewer
télévision *f.* television; television set
tellement so; so much
témérité *f.* recklessness
temoignage *m.* testimony
témoigner show; witness
témoin *m.* witness
temps *m.* time; weather; tense; **de temps en temps** from time to time; **en même temps** at the same time; **il est grand temps** it is high time; **le temps presse** time is getting short; **par ce temps** in this weather; **le temps de** long enough to
tendance *f.* tendency
tendre (*v.*) hold out; extend; give; stretch; **tendre la main** hold out one's hand; (*adj.*) tender
tendresse *f.* tenderness
ténèbres *f. pl.* obscurity
tenez look here!
tenir (tenant, tenu, je tiens, je tins) hold; keep; **tenir à** insist on; be eager to; care; **tenir au courant** keep informed; **tenir conseil** have a meeting; **tenir de** inherit from; **tenir ferme** hold fast; **se tenir** be; stand; **se tenir par la main** hold hands
tenter try; tempt
terminer finish
terrain *m.* ground; land; tract of land; field
terrasse *f.* terrace
terre *f.* earth; land; **pomme de terre** *f.* potato
terreur *f.* terror
terriblement terribly
testament *m.* will
tête *f.* head; **hocher la tête** nod one's head
thé *m.* tea
théorie *f.* theory
thèse *f.* thesis; dissertation
tiens look
tige *f.* stem
tigre *m.* tiger
timbre *m.* stamp
timidité *f.* timidity
tire-lire *f.* piggy bank
tirer take out; pull; shoot; pull the trigger; (sur + *person*) shoot at; **tirer profit** profit by; **tirer quelqu'un d'affaire** get someone out of trouble
tiret *m.* dash

tiroir *m.* drawer
toile *f.* linen; canvas, painting; **toile cirée** oilcloth
toit *m.* roof
tomber fall; **tomber en panne** have a (mechanical) breakdown; **tomber malade** get sick
ton *m.* tone
tondre mow
tonnerre *m.* thunder; **coup de tonnerre** thunder clap
tort *m.* wrong; **avoir tort** be wrong
torturant terrifying
tôt early; soon
totalement completely
touchant concerning
toucher touch
toujours always; still; continually
tour *m.* stroll: trip; trick; turn; **à son tour** in turn; **faire le tour du monde** take a trip around the world; *f.* tower
Touraine *f.* French province southwest of Paris
touriste *m. or f.* tourist; (*adj.*) tourist; for tourists
tourmenter torment; bother
tourner turn; **tourner à** become **tourner en rond** turn around in circles
tournoyer (*irr. sp.* C) circle around
Tours French city southwest of Paris in Loire valley
tousser cough
tout (*m. pl.* tous) (*adj.*) all, every; whole; **tout le monde** everyone; **tous les samedis** every Saturday
tout (*pron.*) everything; **avant tout** above all; **capable de tout** capable of anything; **en tout cas** in any case; **une fois pour toutes** once and for all; **pas du tout** not in the least, not at all; **tous deux** both
tout (*adv.*) very, quite; **tout à côté** right near; **tout à coup** all of a sudden; **tout à fait** quite, completely; **tout à l'heure** in a little while; a little while ago; **tout bas** in a whisper; **tout d'abord** first of all; **tout droit** erect; straight ahead; **tout de même** all the same; exactly as, just as; **tout de suite** immediately, right now; **tout en lisant** while reading
tracasser (se) worry
tracer (*irr. sp.* A) lay out
traduction *f.* translation
traduire (*conj. like* conduire) translate
trahison *f.* treason
train *m.* train; **en train de** in the act of
traînant languid, slow
traîneau *m.* sleigh
traité *m.* treaty
traiter treat; **traiter de** call
traître *m.* traitor
tranquille quiet, calm; **nous avons été tranquilles** we were in peace

Verbs with spelling changes are explained on pp. 274-276.

tranquillement calmly
tranquillisant (*n.*) tranquilizer; (*adj.*) tranquilizing
tranquillité *f.* calm
transatlantique *m.* ocean liner
transmettre (*conj. like* mettre) transmit
transport *m.* transportation
transporter carry
travail *m.* work; job; **se mettre au travail** set to work
travailleur (*f.* travailleuse) hard working; industrious; (*n.*) *m.* worker
travers: à **travers** across; through; **en travers** across
traversée *f.* crossing; **traversée en bateau** boat trip
traverser cross
treize thirteen
tremblant shivering
trembler shake; tremble
tremper wet; soak; dunk
trente thirty
très very
trésor *m.* treasure
trêve *f.* truce; solace
trimestre *m.* trimester; (school) quarter
trinquer clink glasses; toast
triste sad
tristesse *f.* sadness
troïka *f.* Russian sleigh with three horses
trois three
tromper deceive; **se tromper de route** take the wrong road
trompette *f.* trumpet
trop too much; **trop tard** too late
trottoir *m.* sidewalk
trou *m.* hole
troublant upsetting, troubling
trouble *m.* trouble; **jeter le trouble** perturb
troubler trouble; move; **troubler l'eau** make the water murky; **troubler (se)** become upset; become embarrassed
troupe *f.* flock
trouver find; **comment trouvez-vous** what do you think of; **se trouver** be found, be located; lie; find oneself; **se trouver mal** faint; **se trouver mieux** feel better
tuer kill
Tunisie *f.* Tunisia
turc *m.* Turk
tus (*sp of* taire) was silent, kept still
tutoyer (*irr. sp.* C) use the "tu" form in speaking to someone
type *m.* fellow; guy; person

U

un a, an; one
universel (*f.* universelle) universal; versatile and universal

usé worn out
user (s') wear oneself out
usine *f.* factory
utile useful
utiliser use

V

va (*pres. of* aller) goes; **ça va de soi** it goes without saying
vacances *f. pl.* vacation; **cours de vacances** summer courses; **en vacances** on a vacation
vaccin *m.* vaccine
vache *f.* cow
vaciller stagger
vague *f.* wave
vaguement vaguely
vaille (*pres. subjunc. of* valoir) be worth
vainement in vain
vaisselle *f.* dishes; **faire la vaiselle** do the dishes
valeur *f.* value
valide valid, good
valise *f.* suitcase; **faire une valise** pack a suitcase
vallée *f.* valley
valoir (valant, valu, je vaux, je valus) be worth; **valoir la gloire** bring glory; **il vaut mieux** it is better; **valoir la peine** be worth the trouble; **votre idée ne vaut pas grand-chose** your idea isn't worth much
valve *f.* valve (a half shell)
vanter (se) boast
vapeur *f.* steam
Vatican *m.* Vatican, papal headquarters in Rome
vaut (*pres. of* valoir) is worth
veau *m.* calf; veal
vécu, vécus (*pp and sp of* vivre) lived
veille *f.* watch
veiller watch; **veiller sur quelqu'un** watch over someone
vélo *m.* bicycle
velours *m.* velvet
vendeuse *f.* saleswoman
vendre sell
vendredi *m.* Friday
venir (venant, venu, je viens, je vins) come; **faire venir** send for; **venez me voir** come and see me; **venir de** have just (il vient d'arriver he has just arrived); **il en vint à conclure** he finally concluded
Venise *f.* Venice
vent *m.* wind
vente *f.* sale; **en vente** on sale
ventre *m.* belly; abdomen; stomach; **le ventre plein** on a full stomach
ventru potbellied
verdure *f.* grass; green meadows
verglas *m.* ice
véritable real

Irregular verbs are conjugated on pp. 256–273.

véritablement really; truly

vérité *f.* truth; resemblance; **en vérité** in fact

Verlaine, Paul (1844–1896) French symbolist poet

verni varnished; shiny

vernir varnish

verrai, verrais (*fut. and cond. of* voir) will see; would see

verre *m.* glass; **prendre un verre** have a drink

vers toward; around; about; *n. m.* verse; **faire des vers** write poetry

verser pay (a sum of money)

vert green

vertu *f.* virtue

vestiaire *m.* cloak room

veston *m.* suitcoat; jacket

vêtu dressed

veuf *m.* widower

veut (*pres. of* vouloir) wants, wishes

vexer vex; hurt

viande *f.* meat

victorieux (*f.* victorieuse) victorious

vide empty

vider empty

vie *f.* life; **eau de vie** brandy

vieillard *m.* old man; *m. pl.* old people

vieillir grow old

Vienne *f.* Vienna

viens, vient, viennent (*pres. of* venir) comes; come

vierge *f.* virgin; (*adj.*) untouched

vieux (*before vowel sound* vieil; *f.* vieille) old

vif (*f.* vive) alert; quick

vilain ugly; bad

villa *f.* country home

ville *f.* city; town; **en ville** downtown; **hôtel de ville** city hall

vin *m.* wine

vingt twenty

vingtaine *f.* about twenty

violent violent; very strong

violet purple

violon *m.* violin; **faire du violon** play the violin

virtuose *m. or f.* virtuoso

visage *m.* face

vision *f.* vision; point of view

visiter visit (a place)

visiteur *m.* visitor

vit (*sp of* voir) saw (*pres. of* vivre) lives

vite quick; quickly, fast

vitesse *f.* speed

vitre *f.* window pane

vitrine *f.* store window; show window

vivant living; merry; alive; (*n.*) *m.* living person

vivre (vivant, vécu, je vis, je vécus) live

vœu *m.* wish

voici here is, here are; **et voici que** and now; **voici que** then

voie *f.* way; direction; lane

voie (*1st person pres. subjunc. of* voir) see

voilà there is, there are; here it is; **les voilà** here they come

voile *m.* veil; *f.* sail

voiler hide

voir (voyant, vu, je vois, je vis) see; notice; **aller voir** go and see; visit; **faire voir** show; **venez me voir** come and see me

voisin *m.* neighbor; (*adj.*) near

voisinage *m.* vicinity

voiture *f.* car

voix *f.* voice; **à haute voix** aloud; **à trois voix** between three people

vol *m.* flight; theft

volant flying; (*n.*) *m.* steering wheel

voler fly; rob

volet *m.* shutter

voleur *m.* thief

volontairement willingly; voluntarily

volonté *f.* will

volontiers willingly; with pleasure

Voltaire (1694–1778) eighteenth-century writer of philosophical novels, essays, poems, and plays

vont (*pres. of* aller) go

vos (*pl. of* votre) your

votre (*pl.* vos) your

vôtre (*pron.*) yours

voudrai, voudrais (*fut. and cond. of* vouloir) will want; would like

vouloir (voulant, voulu, je veux, je voulus) want; wish; desire; **voulez-vous** will you please; **vouloir bien** be willing; **vouloir dire** mean

vous you; **vous deux** both of you

voyage *m.* trip; **faire un voyage** take a trip

voyager (*irr. sp.* B) travel

voyageur *m.* traveler; passenger

voyant (*pres. part of* voir) seeing

voyante *f.* clairvoyant, seer

voyons (voir) we see; come now; look here

voyou *m.* hoodlum

vrai true; real

vraiment really; truly

vu (*pp of* voir) seen

vue *f.* view; sight; **en vue** prominent

Y

y there; in it

yeux (*m.; pl. of* œil) eyes; **jeter les yeux** glance; **quitter quelqu'un des yeux** take one's eyes off someone

Z

zoologique zoological; **jardin zoologique** zoo

Verbs with spelling changes are explained on pp. 274–276.

English-French Vocabulary

ABBREVIATIONS

adj.	adjective	*irr. sp.*	irregular spelling	*pers.*	person
adv.	adverb	*m.*	masculine	*prep.*	preposition
cond.	conditional	*n.*	noun	*pres.*	present
conj.	conjugated	*obj.*	object	*pron.*	pronoun
conjunc.	conjunction	*p.*	page	*rel.*	relative
f.	feminine	*part.*	participle	*sing.*	singular
fut.	future	*pl.*	plural	*sp*	simple past
inf.	infinitive	*pp*	past participle	*subjunc.*	subjunctive
interrog.	interrogative			*v.*	verb

* aspirate *h* (2) -ir verbs that do not insert -iss-; all other -ir verbs insert -iss-.

Page references immediately following the English word refer to explanations of the word in question.

Verbs whose principal parts are given are irregular, and their conjugations may be found on pp. 256–73. The use of the principal parts is explained on pp. 254–55. Verbs followed by (*conj. like* . . .) are irregular and follow the pattern of the verb indicated.

Verbs followed by (*irr. sp.* A to F) undergo a spelling change in certain forms. The letter refers to the appropriate type of change explained on pp. 274–76.

A

a un, une
able capable; be able pouvoir (pouvant, pu, je peux, je pus) (+ *inf.*)
about (pp. 238–39) de; sur; environ; à peu près; vers; au sujet de; à propos de; about that à ce sujet; be about to être sur le point de; talk about parler de; tell about parler de
above (p. 239) sur; au-dessus de
abroad à l'étranger; from abroad de l'étranger
absence absence *f.*; in the absence en l'absence
absent absent

absolutely absolument
accent accent *m.*
accept accepter
accident accident *m.*
according to (p. 239) selon, suivant, d'après
accused (*n.*) accusé *m.*
accustomed get accustomed to s'habituer (à + *inf.*)
ache (*v.*) faire mal; I have a headache j'ai mal à la tête
acquaintance connaissance *f.*; relation *f.*

309

across (p. 240) à travers; de l'autre côté de; **run across** traverser en courant; **travel across** traverser

act agir

action action *f.*

actress actrice *f.*

actually (pp. 9–10) vraiment, réellement; en fait, à vrai dire

address adresse *f.*

admire admirer

admit admettre (*conj. like* mettre)

adopt adopter

adore adorer

adventure aventure *f.*

advice (p. 10) conseil *m.;* **a piece of advice** un conseil *m.*

advise conseiller (à + *person* + de + *inf.*); **advise against** déconseiller

affair affaire *f.*

afraid **be afraid** avoir peur, craindre; **became afraid** *compound past of* avoir peur, prendre peur; avoir peur

Africa Afrique *f.*

after (pp. 224, 234, 240) après; d'après; **after hearing** après avoir entendu

afternoon après-midi *m. or f.*

again (p. 10) encore, encore une fois, de nouveau, à nouveau; re- + *verb*

against contre; **advise against** déconseiller

age âge *m.;* **old age** vieillesse *f.,* vieux jours *m. pl.*

ago il y a; **a little while ago** tout à l'heure; **a month ago** il y a un mois

agree (p. 11) s'accorder; consentir (à + *inf.*); être d'accord

agreed d'accord, c'est entendu, entendu

aim but *m.*

air air *m.;* **in the air** en l'air

air conditioner climatiseur *m.*

airplane avion *m.*

airport aéroport *m.*

alarm clock réveil *m.*

Albert Albert

Alexander Alexandre

all tout (*f.* toute, *m. pl.* tous); **all the same** quand même; **all the while** (pp. 103–4) tout en; **come out all right** finir bien; **not at all** pas du tout

allow laisser (*person* + *inf.*); permettre (à + *person* + de + *inf.*); **I was allowed** j'ai pu

almost presque

alone seul; **leave me alone** laissez-moi tranquille

along (p. 240) le long de; **get along** se débrouiller; **go along the road** suivre le chemin

already déjà

although bien que, quoique

always toujours

amateur amateur *m.*

ambassador ambassadeur *m.*

ambitious ambitieux (*f.* ambitieuse)

America Amérique *f.*

American Américain *m.;* **South American** Sud-Américain *m.*

amuse amuser; **amuse oneself** s'amuser (à + *inf.*)

amusing amusant

Andrew André

anger colère *f.*

angry fâché; en colère; vexé; **get angry** se mettre en colère; se fâcher

animal animal *m.*

Anne Anne

anniversary anniversaire *m.*

announcement annonce *f.*

announcer speaker *m.*

annoying ennuyeux (*f.* ennuyeuse)

another encore un(e)

answer (*v.*) répondre (à + *n.*) (*n.*) réponse *f.*

any du, de la, des; quelque; (*obj. pron.*) en; **any at all** pas du tout; **in any case** en tout cas; **not any** pas de, ne . . . aucun; **not any more** ne . . . plus

anyone quelqu'un; **not . . . anyone** ne . . . personne

anything quelque chose; **not . . . anything** ne . . . rien

apartment appartement *m.*

approach approcher (de + *n.*); s'approcher (de + *n.*)

April avril

Arabic (*n.*) arabe *m.*

architect architecte *m. or f.*

ardent ardent

are sont; se trouvent; **are to** doivent; **there are** il y a

area région *f.*

aren't you n'est-ce pas

arm bras *m.*

armchair fauteuil *m.*

army armée *f.*

around: **get around** se déplacer (*irr. sp.* A)

arrest arrêter

arrive arriver

art art *m.*

artist artiste *m. or f.*

as (pp. 19, 234–35) comme; **as . . . as** aussi . . . que; **as for** quant à; **as long as** tant que; **as soon as** dès que

ashamed: **be ashamed** avoir honte

ask demander (*thing* + à + *person; à + person* + de + *inf.*); **ask a question** poser une question; **ask for something** demander quelque chose; **ask of someone** demander à quelqu'un; **he asked my pardon** il m'a demandé pardon

asleep: **be asleep** dormir (2)

aspirin aspirine *f.*

assistant assistant *m.*

astronaut astronaute *m. or f.*

at (pp. 212–14, 241) à; chez; **at length** longuement; **at once** tout de suite; **not at all** pas du tout

Athens Athènes

Irregular verbs are conjugated on pp. 256–273.

attend (p. 80) aller à; assister à
attention attention *f.*
attentively attentivement
attitude attitude *f.*
aunt tante *f.*
author auteur *m.*
automatically automatiquement
awaken réveiller; se réveiller
away: go away s'en aller, partir (2); **right away** tout de suite

B

baby bébé *m.*
back (*n.*) dos *m.*
back: come back revenir; come back home rentrer; go back retourner
bad (*n.*) mauvais *m.* (*adj.*) mauvais
ball danse *f.,* bal *m.*
ball (point) pen stylo à bille *m.;* bic *m.*
Balzac Balzac
bank banque *f.*
barber coiffeur *m.*
bare nu
bark aboyer (*irr. sp.* C)
bathe se baigner
be être (étant, été, je suis, je fus); be able pouvoir (pouvant, pu, je peux, je pus); be asleep dormir (2); be better aller mieux; être mieux; valoir mieux; be bored s'ennuyer (*irr. sp.* C); be careful! attention!; be mistaken se tromper; be warm avoir chaud; be well aller bien; be willing vouloir bien
beach plage *f.*
beautiful beau (*before vowel sound* bel; *f.* belle)
beauty beauté *f.*
because (p. 235) parce que; because of à cause de
become (pp. 23–4, 69) devenir (*conj. like* venir); become afraid prendre peur; become frightened s'effrayer; become interested in s'intéresser à; it became cold il a fait froid
bed lit *m.;* go to bed se coucher
bedtime: at bedtime avant de se coucher, à l'heure de se coucher
before (pp. 224, 235, 242) (time) avant (+ *n. or pron.*), avant de (+ *inf.*), avant que (+ *subjunc.*); (place) devant
begin commencer (à + *inf.*) (*irr. sp.* A), se mettre (à + *inf.*)
beginning commencement *m.*
believe croire (croyant, cru, je crois, je crus) (+ *inf.;* + *person;* à + *thing;* en + *person* [with the sense of *to have faith in*])
belong appartenir (*conj. like* tenir)
best (*adj.*) meilleur; (*adv.*) mieux
better (pp. 24–5) (*adj.*) meilleur; (*adv.*) mieux; be better valoir mieux, être mieux; (referring to health) aller mieux
between entre
big grand
billfold portefeuille *m.*

bird oiseau *m.*
bit: a bit un peu
blame blâmer
blanket couverture *f.*
blue bleu
boat bateau *m.,* sailboat bateau à voiles
book livre *m.;* telephone book annuaire *m.*
bored ennuyé; be bored s'ennuyer (*irr. sp.* C)
boring ennuyeux (*f.* ennuyeuse)
born: be born naître (naissant, né, je nais, je naquis); he was born il est né
boss patron *m.*
both les deux, tous les deux; both of you vous deux
bother déranger (*irr. sp.* B); ennuyer (*irr. sp.* C)
boy garçon *m.*
brave courageux (*f.* courageuse)
break casser; se casser; break down être en panne
bridge (*over river*) pont *m.;* (*game*) bridge *m.*
briefcase serviette *f.*
brilliantly brillamment
bring (p. 25) (*a thing*) apporter; (*a person*) amener (*irr. sp.* D)
brother frère *m.;* brother-in-law beau-frère *m.,;* oldest brother aîné *m.,* frère aîné
brush brosser
Brussels Bruxelles
build construire (*conj. like* conduire)
building immeuble *m.;* bâtiment *m.,* édifice *m.*
bus (*within city*) autobus *m.;* (*between cities*) autocar *m.*
business affaire *f.;* les affaires *f. pl.;* businessman homme d'affaires *m.;* talk business parler affaires, parler des affaires
busy (p. 104) occupé; be busy être en train de; he was busy writing il était occupé à écrire, il était en train d'écrire
but (p. 235) (*conjunc.*) mais; (*prep.*) sauf, excepté
buy acheter (*irr. sp.* D)
by par; de; en; by falling en tombant; by plane par avion, en avion; by the time quand; go by passer

C

café café *m.*
call appeler (*irr. sp.* F); téléphoner (à + *person*)
can (pp. 25–6) pouvoir (pouvant, pu, je peux, je pus); (*know how*) savoir (sachant, su, je sais, je sus)
Canada Canada *m.*
candidate candidat *m.*
capable capable
car voiture *f.,* auto *f.,* automobile *f.*
care soin *m.,* prudence *f.*
careful: be careful! attention!
carefully attentivement
careless négligent
carnation œillet *m.*
carol: Christmas carol cantique de Noël *m.*

Verbs with spelling changes are explained on pp. 274–276.

carpenter menuisier *m.*

case cas *m.; in any case* en tout cas; *in case of* en cas de

cash (*a check*) toucher (un chèque)

cat chat *m.*

catastrophe catastrophe *f.*

catch attraper; *catch sight of* apercevoir (*conj. like* recevoir)

Catholic catholique

caught pris

celebrate célébrer

center: *shopping center* centre commercial *m.*

certain certain

chair chaise *f.*

change (pp. 37–8) (*v.*) (*irr. sp.* B) changer; *change one's mind* changer d'avis; *m.* changement *m.; (small) change* monnaie *f.*

character (pp. 38–9) personnage *m.;* caractère *m.*

charge prendre (prenant, pris, je prends, je pris)

charm charme *m.*

charming charmant

chat bavarder

chauffeur chauffeur *m.*

cheap bon marché

check chèque *m.*

chess échecs *m. pl.*

child enfant *m. or f.*

Chinese chinois

Christmas Noël *m.; Christmas carol* cantique de Noël *m.*

church église *f.*

cider cidre *m.*

cigaret cigarette *f.*

city ville *f.; city hall* hôtel de ville *m.,* mairie *f.*

claim prétendre

class classe *f.; conversation class* classe de conversation *f.*

classmate camarade de classe *m. or f.*

cleaner teinturier *m.; to the cleaner's* à la teinturerie; chez le teinturier

cleaning woman femme de ménage *f.*

clear évident

clear the table débarrasser la table

climate climat *m.*

clock: *alarm clock* réveil *m.*

close (*v.*) fermer (*adj.*) proche; *a close friend* un ami intime *m.*

clothes habits *m. pl.;* vêtements *m. pl.*

club club *m.,* cercle *m.*

coat (*overcoat*) manteau *m.; (suitcoat)* veste *m.*

coffee café *m.*

cold (*n.*) rhume *m.; (adj.)* froid; *it became cold* il a fait froid; *it was cold* il faisait froid

Colette Colette

colleague collègue *m. or f.*

collection collection *f.*

colonel colonel *m.*

come venir (venant, venu, je viens, je vins); *come back* revenir (*conj. like* venir); *come back home* rentrer; *come and see me* venez me voir; *come in* entrer; *come to dinner* venir dîner; *come out all right* finir bien

comfortable confortable

company compagnie *f.;* maison *f.;* société *f.*

completely complètement

computer ordinateur *m.*

concern: *concern onself with* s'occuper (de + *n.*)

concerning (pp. 238–9) au sujet de; sur; *concerning them* à leur sujet

concert concert *m.*

condemn condamner

condition condition *f.; on the condition that* à (la) condition que

conditioner: *air conditioner* climatiseur *m.*

confess avouer

considerable considérable

construct construire (construisant, construit, je construis, je construisis)

contest concours *m.*

continue continuer (à + *inf.*); *continue on our way* continuer notre route

convention congrès *m.*

conversation conversation *f.; a conversation class* une class de conversation *f.*

convince convaincre (*conj. like* vaincre)

cook faire la cuisine

cookie biscuit *m.*

copy copier; *copy again* recopier

correct (*v.*) corriger (*irr. sp.* B); *(adj.)* exact

corridor corridor *m.;* couloir *m.*

Corsica Corse *f.*

cost prix *m.*

count compter (+ *inf.*)

country pays *m.; (opposite of city)* campagne *f.*

courage courage *m.*

course cours *m.; take a course* suivre un cours; *course (of action)* démarche *f.; drop a course* abandonner un cours, laisser tomber un cours

cousin cousin *m.;* cousine *f.*

cream crème *f.; ice cream* glace *f.*

crime crime *m.*

criminal criminel *m.*

criticize critiquer

cross traverser

crossword puzzle mots croisés *m. pl.*

crowd foule *f.*

cry pleurer

cultured cultivé

curious curieux (*f.* curieuse)

curtain rideau *m.*

cut couper; *cut down* couper

cute mignon (*f.* mignonne)

D

dance danse *f.;* bal *m.*

danger danger *m.*

dangerous dangereux (*f.* dangereuse)

dark brun; sombre

date rendez-vous *m.*
daughter fille *f.*
dawn aube *f.*
day (p. 39) jour *m.;* journée *f.;* the day after tomorrow après-demain; the next day le lendemain, le jour suivant, le jour après
daylight jour *m.*
dead mort
deal: a great deal beaucoup
December décembre *m.*
decide décider (de + *inf.*), se décider (à + *inf.*)
decision décision *f.;* make a decision prendre une décision
decorator: interior decorator décorateur *m.;* décoratrice *f.*
deep profond
deep-seated profond
defend défendre
defendant inculpé *m.*
delegate délégué *m.;* déléguée *f.*
delighted enchanté
demanding exigeant
democracy démocratie *f.*
Denmark Danemark *m.*
dentist dentiste *m. or f.*
describe décrire (*conj. like* écrire)
desk bureau *m.*
destiny destinée *f.*
detective inspecteur *m.;* detective story roman policier *m.*
diamond diamant *m.*
die mourir (mourant, mort, je meurs, je mourus)
difference différence *f.*
different différent
difficult difficile
difficulty difficulté *f.*
dinner dîner *m.;* come to dinner venir dîner; have dinner dîner
directly directement
director directeur *m.;* directrice *f.*
discuss discuter
discussion discussion *f.*
dishes vaisselle *f. sing.* wash the dishes faire la vaisselle
disillusion désillusion *f.*
distance distance *f.;* in the distance au loin
distribute distribuer
do faire (faisant, fait, je fais, je fis); do without se passer de; do wrong faire du tort
doctor docteur *m.,* médecin *m.*
doctorate doctorat *m.*
dog chien *m.*
dollar dollar *m.*
door porte *f.*
dormitory dortoir *m.,* résidence *f.*
doubt douter (de + *n.*)
doubtful douteux (*f.* douteuse)
down (p. 242) en bas; cut down couper; go down descendre; slow down ralentir
drawer tiroir *m.*
dream rêver (de + *n.;* de + *inf.*)

dress robe *f.*
drink boire (buvant, bu, je bois, je bus)
drive conduire (conduisant, conduit, je conduis, je conduisis)
drop (*a course*) abandonner, laisser tomber
duck canard *m.*
duty devoir *m.*

E

each chacun; each other se . . . l'un l'autre
earlier plus tôt; de meilleure heure
early (pp. 52–3) tôt, de bonne heure; en avance
earn gagner
ease facilité *f.*
easily facilement
Easter Pâques *m.*
easy facile; easy-going indulgent
eat manger (*irr. sp.* B)
egg œuf *m.*
Egypt Égypte *f.*
eight huit
either non plus
elbow coude *m.*
election élection *f.*
elegant élégant
else: something else autre chose
elsewhere ailleurs, autre part
emergency urgence *f.*
encourage encourager (*irr. sp.* B)
end (p. 53) fin *f.;* bout *m.*
energetically énergiquement
engineer ingénieur *m.*
England Angleterre *f.*
English (*n.*) Anglais *m.;* (*adj.*) anglais
enough assez
enter entrer (dans + *n.*)
entertaining amusant
erase effacer (*irr. sp.* A)
error erreur *f.,* faute *f.*
escape (pp. 53–54) échapper (à + *n.*); s'échapper (de + *n.*)
especially surtout
Europe Europe *f.*
even même; even though bien que, quoique; tout en (+ *pres. participle*)
evening (pp. 39, 135) soir *m.;* soirée *f.;* evening party soirée *f.;* last evening hier soir
event événement *m.*
ever jamais
every (pp. 54–5) chaque; tous les; every other year tous les deux ans
everyone (p. 54) tout le monde
everything (pp. 54–5, 128) tout; n'importe quoi; everything that tout ce qui, tout ce que
everywhere partout
evident évident
examination examen *m.*
excellent excellent
except (p. 242) sauf, à part, excepté

Verbs with spelling changes are explained on pp. 274–276.

exchange (p. 38) échanger (*irr. sp.* **B**)
exercise devoir *m.,* exercice *m.*
exist exister; régner
exotic exotique
expect (pp. 66–67) attendre (+ *n.*); s'attendre (à
    + *n.*); compter (+ *n.*) what do you expect
    que voulez-vous
expensive cher (*f.* chère); be expensive coûter
    cher
experience expérience *f.*
explain expliquer
explosion explosion *f.*
exterior extérieur *m.*
extraordinary extraordinaire
eye œil *m.* (*pl.*) yeux

F

face figure *f.*
factory usine *f.*
fail (pp. 67–68) manquer (de + *inf.*); échouer (à
    un examen); coller (quelqu'un)
fair exposition *f.*
fall tomber; fall out tomber de
family famille *f.*
famous célèbre, connu
far loin
farmer fermier *m.*
fast rapide; vite
fate sort *m.*
father père *m.*
father-in-law beau-père *m.*
faucet robinet *m.*
favorite préféré
February février
feel (p. 68) sentir; se sentir; feel well se sentir
    bien; How do you feel? Comment allez-
    vous?
few peu; a few quelques
field champ *m.;* domaine *m.*
fifty cinquante
fight se battre (battant, battu, je bats, je battis)
fill remplir (de + *n.*)
film film *m.*
finally enfin, finalement
find trouver; find again retrouver; find out
    découvrir (*conj. like* ouvrir), apprendre
    (*conj. like* prendre)
fine excellent; beau (*before vowel sound* bel; *f.*
    belle); those fine people ces braves gens *m.*
    pl.
finger doigt *m.*
finish finir
fire incendie *m.*
first premier (*f.* première); on the first floor au
    rez-de-chaussée
fish poisson *m.*
five cinq
fix réparer
floor plancher *m.;* étage *m.;* on the first floor
    au rez-de-chaussée

Florida Floride *f.*
florist fleuriste *m. or f.*
flower fleur *f.* ˙
fluently couramment
follow suivre (suivant, suivi, je suis, je suivis)
foolish stupide
foot pied *m.;* on foot à pied
football ballon *m.;* football *m.;* football game
    un match de football, une partie de football
for (pp. 236, 242) (*conjunc.*) car (*prep.*) pour;
    pendant; depuis, il y a . . . que, voilà . . .
    que
forbid défendre (à + *person* + de + *inf.*)
foreign étranger (*f.* étrangère)
foreigner étranger *m.* (*f.* étrangère)
forget oublier (de + *inf.*)
former ancien (*f.* ancienne); the former celui-là
formerly autrefois
fortune fortune *f.*
forty quarante
fountain pen stylo *m.*
four quatre
France France *f.*
Frances Françoise *f.*
Francis François *m.*
frankly franchement
Frederick Frédéric
free libre
French français; French class classe de français
    f.
Friday vendredi *m.*
friend ami *m.,* amie *f.;* a close friend un ami
    intime
frightened effrayé; become frightened s'effrayer
    (*irr. sp.* **C**)
frigidaire réfrigérateur *m.;* frigidaire *m.*
from de; keep from empêcher (+ *person* + de
    + *inf.*)
front: in front of devant
fruit fruit *m.*
full plein
fun: make fun of se moquer (de + *n.*)
funny amusant
fur fourrure *f.*
furious furieux (*f.* furieuse)

G

gain gagner; gain ground avancer (*irr. sp.* **A**)
game match *m.,* partie *f.;* a football game une
    partie de football, un match de football
garden jardin *m.*
general général *m.*
generous généreux (*f.* généreuse)
George Georges
German (*adj.*) allemand
Germany Allemagne *f.*
get (pp. 68–9) chercher; recevoir; prendre;
    faire; avoir; obtenir; atteindre; get along se
    débrouiller; get angry se fâcher; get around
    se déplacer; get into entrer dans; get

married se marier; **get out of** sortir de; **get pale** pâlir; **get somewhere** arriver; **get tired** se fatiguer; **get up** se lever (*irr. sp.* D); **it got warm** il a fait chaud

gift cadeau *m.;* **give a gift** faire un cadeau

girl jeune fille *f.*

give donner; consacrer; **give a lecture** faire une conférence

glad content, heureux (*f.* heureuse)

glance regard *m.*

go (pp. 79–80, 246) aller (allant, allé, je vais, j'allai); **go and see** aller voir; **go away** partir (2), s'en aller; **go back** retourner; **go by** passer; **go down** descendre; **go for a walk** aller se promener; **go out** sortir (2); **go to bed** se coucher; **go through** passer par; **go up** monter; remonter

going: **easy-going** indulgent

golf golf *m.*

good (*n.*) bon *m.;* bien *m.* (*adj.*) bon; (*well-behaved*) sage; **good looks** beauté *f.;* **have a good time** s'amuser

goodbye au revoir

grandchild petit-fils *m.;* petite-fille *f.;* petits-enfants *m. or f. pl.*

grandmother grand-mère *f.*

grandparents grands-parents *m. pl.*

grapefruit pamplemousse *m.*

grave grave

great grand; **a great deal** beaucoup; **a great many** beaucoup

Greece Grèce *f.*

green vert

ground: **gain ground** avancer (*irr. sp.* A)

group groupe *m.*

H

hair cheveux *m. pl.*

hairdresser coiffeur *m.;* coiffeuse *f.*

half (*n.*) moitié *f.* (*adj.*) demi; **a half hour** une demi-heure

hall: **city hall** hôtel de ville *m.,* mairie *f.*

hand main *f.* **shake hands** se serrer la main

hand in remettre (*conj. like* mettre)

happen (pp. 80–1) se passer; arriver; se trouver; **it happened to me** cela m'est arrivé

happiness bonheur *m.*

happy heureux (*f.* heureuse), content; **Happy New Year** Bonne Année, une Bonne Nouvelle Année

hard (*adj.*) dur; difficile

hard (*adv.*) dur

hateful méchant

have avoir (ayant, eu, j'ai, j'eus); (pp. 192–94, 201–4) (*causative*) faire (+ *inf.*) **have dinner** dîner; **have a good time** s'amuser, bien s'amuser; **have lunch** déjeuner; **have to** devoir, falloir, être obligé de

head tête *f.*

headache mal de tête *m.;* **have a headache** avoir mal à la tête

hear (p. 82) entendre; **hear of** entendre parler de; **hear that** entendre dire que

heartily de bon cœur

heaven ciel *m.*

heavy lourd

Helen Hélène

hell enfer *m.*

help (*v.*) aider (*person* + à + *inf.*); (*n.*) aide *f.*

her (*direct obj.*) la; (*indirect obj.*) lui; (*with prep.*) elle; (*adj.*) son, sa, ses

here ici; **here is, here are** voici

hero *héros *m.*

hesitate hésiter

high élevé; *haut

hill colline *f.*

him (*direct obj.*) le; (*indirect obj.*) lui; (*with prep.*) lui

hire engager (*irr. sp.* B)

his (*adj.*) son, sa, ses; (*pron.*) le sien, la sienne, etc.

history histoire *f.*

hold tenir (tenant, tenu, je tiens, je tins); avoir lieu

home maison *f.;* **at home** chez soi; chez nous; **be home** être chez soi; **come back home** rentrer; **return home** rentrer

homework devoir *m.*

honor honneur *m.*

hope espérer (+ *inf.*) (*irr. sp.* E); **hope for** espérer (+ *n.*)

horrified scandalisé

horseback: **go horseback riding** faire du cheval, faire une promenade à cheval

hostile hostile

hotel hôtel *m.*

hour heure *f.;* **a half hour** une demi-heure

house maison *f.;* **at your house** chez vous

housework ménage *m.*

how comment; **how often** tous les combien; **know how to do something** (p. 94) savoir faire quelque chose

however cependant, pourtant; si (+ *adj.*); **however rich he is (may be)** si riche qu'il soit; **however that may be** quoi qu'il en soit

humble humble

hundred (*n.*) centaine *f.;* (*adj.*) cent

hurry se dépêcher (de + *inf.*)

hurt (*v.*) faire mal (à + *person*); **hurt oneself** se faire mal; (*adj.*) vexé

husband mari *m.*

hypothesis hypothèse *f.*

I

I je; moi

ice glace *f.;* **ice cream** glace *f.;* **ice water** eau glacée

idea idée *f.*

if si
illness maladie *f.*
illustrated illustré
imagine imaginer
immediate immédiat
immediately immédiatement
import importer
important important
impression impression *f.*
in (pp. 212–14, 243–44) dans; en; à; de; **eight
    in the evening** huit heures du soir; **in that
    manner** de cette façon; **in the theater** au
    théâtre; **in two hours** dans deux heures; en
    deux heures
in spite of (p. 244) malgré
indifference indifférence *f.*
information information *f.;* renseignements *m.
    pl.*
initiative initiative *f.*
inquire se renseigner
inspect inspecter
instead of (pp. 244–45) au lieu de
insult insulte *f.*
intelligence intelligence *f.*
intelligent intelligent
intend (p. 92) avoir l'intention de; compter (+
    inf.); penser (+ *inf.*)
interest (*v.*) intéresser; s'intéresser (à + *n.*); (*n*)
    intérêt *m.;* **take an interest in** s'intéresser (à
    + *n.*)
interested: **become interested in** s'intéresser (à
    + *n.*)
interesting intéressant
interior intérieur *m.;* **interior decorator**
    décorateur *m.;* décoratrice *f.*
interrupt interrompre
intervene intervenir (*conj. like* venir)
into dans; en
introduce (p. 92) présenter
invitation invitation *f.*
invite inviter (à + *inf.*)
Ireland Irlande *f.*
Irene Irène
is est
isn't it? n'est-ce pas?
it (*subject*) il; elle; ce; ça; (*direct obj.*) le, la
Italian (*n.*) Italien *m.* (*adj.*) italien (*f.* italienne)
Italy Italie *f.*

J

Jack Jacques
Japan Japon *m.*
Japanese japonais
Jean Jeanne
job (p. 168) place *f.;* travail *m.;* position *f.;*
    situation *f.*
Johnnie Jeannot
joke plaisanterie *f.*
joy joie *f.*

Irregular verbs are conjugated on pp. 256–273.

judge juge *m.*
Julia Julie
July juillet *m.*
June juin *m.*
just juste; **I have just done something** je viens
    de faire quelque chose; **just now** tout à
    l'heure

K

keep garder; **keep from** empêcher (*n.* + de +
    inf.)
key clé *f.*
kilometer kilomètre *m.* (⅝ of a mile)
kind aimable
kindness bonté *f.*
king roi *m.*
knife couteau *m.*
knock frapper; **there was a knock** (p. 92) on a
    frappé
know (pp. 93–4) (*something*) savoir (sachant,
    su, je sais, je sus); (*be acquainted with
    someone or something*) connaître
    (connaissant, connu, je connais, je connus);
    know how to savoir (+ *inf.*)

L

laboratory laboratoire *m.*
lack (pp. 106–7) manquer (de + *n.*)
ladder échelle *f.*
lady dame *f.;* femme *f.*
lake lac *m.*
lamp lampe *f.*
language langue *f.*
large grand; gros (*f.* grosse)
last dernier (*f.* dernière); **last evening** hier soir;
    last night (p. 107) cette nuit; la nuit dernière
late (p. 107) (*not early*) tard; (*not on time*) en
    retard
latter: **the latter** celui-ci; ce dernier
laugh (*v.*) rire (riant, ri, je ris, je ris) (de + *n.*);
    laugh at rire de, se moquer de; (*n.*) rire *m.*
Laura Laure
Lawrence Laurent
lawyer avocat *m.*
lazy paresseux (*f.* paresseuse)
learn apprendre (*conj. like* prendre)
leather cuir *m.*
leave (pp. 108–9) (*something somewhere*)
    laisser; (*a place*) quitter; partir (de + *n.*) (2);
    sortir (de + *n.*) (2); **leave me alone** laissez-
    moi tranquille
lecture conférence *f.*
leg jambe *f.;* (*of an animal*) patte *f.*
lend prêter
length longueur *f.;* **at length** longuement
lesson leçon *f.*
letter lettre *f.*

library bibliothèque *f.*
lie mentir (2)
lieutenant lieutenant *m.*
life vie *f.*
light lumière *f.*
like (*v.*) aimer; vouloir; (*prep.*) comme
lip lèvre *f.*
listen écouter; listen to écouter (+ *n.*)
little (*adj.*) petit; (*adv.*) (p. 121) peu; un peu
live (p. 122) habiter (+ *n.* or: à + *n.*, or: dans
    + *n.*); vivre (vivant, vécu, je vis, je vécus)
living room salle de séjour *f.*; salon *m.*
lock fermer à clé
London Londres *m.*
long (pp. 122–23) long (*f.* longue); a long time
    longtemps; as long as tant que; how long
    depuis quand, depuis combien de temps;
    combien de temps, pendant combien de
    temps
longer (time) plus longtemps; no . . . longer ne
    . . . plus
look regarder; look after s'occuper (de + *n.*);
    look at regarder (*n.*); look for chercher (+
    n.); look well on someone aller bien à
    quelqu'un
looking: good looking joli; beau
looks: good looks beauté *f.*
lose perdre
lot: a lot beaucoup
loud fort
Louvre Louvre *m.*
love aimer
luck chance *f.*
Lucy Lucie
lunch déjeuner *m.*; have lunch déjeuner
Lyons Lyon

M

machine machine *f.*
magazine revue *f.*; magazine *m.*
mail mettre à la poste
main principal
majority plupart *f.*; majorité *f.*
make faire (faisant, fait, je fais, je fis); make +
    adj. (p. 123) rendre + *adj.*; make fun of se
    moquer de; make a decision prendre une
    décision; make a trip faire un voyage
man homme *m.*; businessman homme
    d'affaires; old man vieil homme *m.*, vieillard
    m.; homme âgé *m.*; (*adj. used as n.*) vieux
    m.; young man jeune homme; (*pl.*) jeunes
    gens
manage to s'arranger pour
manager gérant *m.*
many beaucoup; a great many beaucoup;
    énormément, des tas de; many times bien
    des fois

March mars *m.*
Margaret Marguerite
Mark Marc
marriage mariage *m.*
married marié; get married se marier
marry (p. 132) épouser; se marier avec; marier
    (quelqu'un à quelqu'un)
Martha Marthe
marvelous superbe; merveilleux (*f.*
    merveilleuse)
master maître *m.*
mathematics mathématiques *f. pl.*
matter: what is the matter with me ce que j'ai
mayor maire *m.*
me me, moi
meager maigre
meal repas *m.*
mean vouloir dire; signifier
meet (p. 93) (*by appointment*) retrouver; (*by
    chance*) rencontrer; (*make the acquaintance
    of*) faire la connaissance de, connaître
meeting réunion *f.*
mention mentionner
Mexico Mexique *m.*
Michael Michel
Michelle Michelle
midnight minuit *m.*
military militaire
milk lait *m.*
milliner modiste *f.*
mind esprit *m.*; change one's mind changer
    d'avis
mine le mien, la mienne, etc.; à moi
minister (of the gospel) pasteur *m.*
minute minute *f.*
miss (p. 133) manquer; regretter
mission mission *f.*
mistake faute *f.*; erreur *f.*
mistaken: be mistaken se tromper
model mannequin *m.*
modern moderne
money argent *m.*
monster monstre *m.*
month mois *m.*
moon lune *f.*
more (pp. 133–34) plus; more and more de
    plus en plus; the more . . . the more plus
    . . . plus; no longer ne . . . plus; not any
    more ne . . . plus
morning (p. 39) matin *m.*; matinée *f.*; the next
    morning le lendemain matin, le matin
    suivant; yesterday morning hier matin
most plus; le plus
mother mère *f.*
mother-in-law belle-mère *f.*
motorcycle motocyclette *f.*, moto *f.*; on a
    motorcycle en moto
mountain montagne *f.*
mouth bouche *f.*
move bouger (*irr. sp.* B); remuer; (*change
    dwellings*) déménager (*irr. sp.* B)

Verbs with spelling changes are explained on pp. 274–276.

movie cinéma *m.;* film *m.;* **movies** cinéma *m.*
much beaucoup; **so much** tellement; tant; **very much** (p. 227) beaucoup
music musique *f.*
musical musicien (*f.* musicienne)
must (pp. 201–4) devoir (devant, dû, je dois, je dus) (+ *inf.*); falloir (—, fallu, il faut, il fallut) (+ *inf.*); être obligé (de + *inf.*)
my mon, ma, mes

N

nasty désagréable
native natal; (*language*) maternel (*f.* maternelle)
natural naturel (*f.* naturelle)
nature nature *f.*
near près de, à côté de
necessary nécessaire; **it is necessary** il faut
necklace collier *m.*
need (*v.*) avoir besoin de; (*n.*) besoin *m.*
neighbor voisin *m.;* (*biblical sense*) prochain *m.*
neither . . . nor ni . . . ni
nervous nerveux (*f.* nerveuse)
never jamais; ne . . . jamais
new nouveau (*before vowel sound* nouvel; *f.* nouvelle)
news nouvelles *f. pl.;* informations *f. pl.;* **piece of news** nouvelle *f.*
newscast informations *f. pl.*
newspaper journal *m.*
next (pp. 134–35) prochain; suivant; **the next day** le lendemain, le jour suivant, le jour après; **the next morning** le lendemain matin, le matin suivant
nice (*of persons*) gentil; (*of things*) joli; beau; **he is nice to us** il est gentil avec nous; **it is nice of him** c'est gentil de sa part
niece nièce *f.*
night nuit *f.*
nine neuf
no (*adj.*) aucun; ne . . . aucun; **no longer** ne . . . plus; **no more** ne . . . plus; (*adv.*) non
no one personne; ne . . . personne
noise bruit *m.*
noon midi *m.*
not ne . . . pas; **not any** pas de
nothing rien; ne . . . rien
notice (p. 152) remarquer; voir; s'apercevoir (*conj. like* recevoir)
novel roman *m.*
now maintenant; **just now** tout à l'heure; **right now** immédiatement, tout de suite; **up to now** jusqu'à présent
number nombre *m.;* (*street, telephone*) numéro *m.*
numerous nombreux (*f.* nombreuses); beaucoup de
nylon nylon *m.*

O

obey obéir (à + *person*)
obliged obligé (de + *inf.*)
observe observer
obviously évidemment
o'clock heure *f.*
of de; **both of you** vous deux
office bureau *m.;* (*doctor's*) cabinet *m.*
often souvent; **how often** tous les combien
old vieux (*before vowel sound* vieil; *f.* vieille); âgé; **I was four years old** j'avais quatre ans; **old age** vieillesse *f.;* vieux jours *m. pl.;* **old man** vieil homme *m.,* vieillard *m.;* homme âgé *m.;* (*adj. used as n.*) vieux *m.*
oldest: **oldest brother** aîné, frère aîné; **oldest daughter** aînée, fille aînée
Oliver Olivier
on sur; dans; en; pour; à; **on the condition** à (la) condition; **on foot** à pied; **on a motorcycle** en moto; **on Saturdays** le samedi; **on the telephone** au téléphone; **on the way** en route; **try on** essayer (*irr. sp.* C)
once une fois; **at once** de suite; tout de suite
one un; on; **the one** celui qui; **no one** ne . . personne
only seulement, ne . . . que
open (*v.*) ouvrir (ouvrant, ouvert, j'ouvre, j'ouvris); (*adj.*) ouvert
opera opéra *m.*
operation opération *f.*
opinion opinion *f.;* avis *m.*
opportunity (p. 153) occasion *f.;* possibilité *f.*
optimistic optimiste
or ou
orange orange *f.*
order (*v.*) ordonner; (*meal*) commander; (*prep.*); **in order to** pour
other autre; **each other** se; l'un l'autre; **every other year** tous les deux ans; **others** (*pron.*) les autres
ought to (p. 203) devrais, devrait, etc. (*conditional form of verb* devoir)
out (p. 245) dehors; **fall out** tomber de; **go out** sortir (2); **one out of three** un sur trois; **out of** hors de; **out of money** sans argent
overtake rattraper

P

pack one's suitcase faire sa valise
package colis *m.*
page page *f.*
paint peindre (peignant, peint, je peins, je peignis)
painter *m.* peintre
painting tableau *m.;* peinture *f.*
pale pâle

paper (pp. 153–54) papier *m.;* copie *f.;* composition *f.;* (*newspaper*) journal *m.*

parade défilé *m.*

pardon pardon *m.;* **he asked my pardon** il m'a demandé pardon

parent parent *m.*

part partie *f.;* (*in a play*) rôle *m.*

partner associé *m.*

party soirée *f.*

pass passer; **pass an examination** réussir à un examen

passport passeport *m.*

past passé *m.*

patient *m.* patient; (*adj.*) patient

pay (*v.*) payer (*irr. sp.* A); (*n.*) salaire *m.;* paie *f.*

peace paix *f.;* **in peace** en paix; **Peace Street** rue de la Paix

peaceful tranquille, calme, paisible

pen plume *f.;* **fountain pen** stylo *m.*

pencil crayon *m.*

people (pp. 154–55) gens *m. pl.;* on; personnes *f. pl.;* (*nation*) peuple *m.;* **those fine people** ces braves gens; **young people** jeunes gens *m. pl.*

per par; à; de; le; la

percent pourcent *m.*

perfume parfum *m.*

perhaps peut-être

permit permettre (*conj. like* mettre) (à + *person* + de + *inf.*)

permission permission *f.*

person personne *f.*

personal personnel (*f.* personnelle)

piano piano *m.;* **play the piano** jouer du piano

pick up ramasser; cueillir

picture tableau *m.;* peinture *f.*

picturesque pittoresque

piece (p. 167) morceau *m.;* bout *m.;* (*of advice*) conseil *m.;* (*of paper*) feuille *f.*

pilot pilote *m.*

place (p. 168) endroit *m.;* lieu *m.;* place *f.;* espace *m.;* **at their place** chez eux

plain: **in plain daylight** en plein jour

plane avion *m.*

plant plante *f.*

play (*v.*) jouer (de + *instrument;* à + *game*); (*n.*) pièce *f.*

pleasant agréable

please plaire (plaisant, plu, je plais, je plus) (à + *person*); faire plaisir à; s'il vous plaît

pleasure plaisir *m.*

pocket poche *f.*

poetry poésie *f.*

point point *m.*

poker poker *m.*

Poland Pologne *f.*

police police *f.*

policeman agent *m.;* agent de police *m.;* policier *m.*

polite poli

poli.ics politique *f. sing.*

pool (swimming) piscine *f.*

poor pauvre

popular populaire

portrait portrait *m.*

Portugal Portugal *m.*

Portuguese portugais

position place *f.;* position *f.;* situation *f.*

possible possible

postcard carte postale *f.*

powerful puissant

practice pratique *f.*

preach prêcher

prefer préférer (*irr. sp.* E); aimer mieux

prepare préparer

present (*time*) présent *m.;* (*gift*) cadeau *m.*

president président *m.*

pressed together serré

pretty joli

prince prince *m.*

prison prison *f.*

prize prix *m.*

probable probable

probably probablement

problem problème *m.*

prodigy prodige *m.*

product produit *m.*

professor professeur *m.*

program programme *m.*

progress progrès *m.;* **make progress** faire des progrès

promise promettre (*conj. like* mettre) (à + *person* + de + *inf.*)

proper convenable

proud fier (*f.* fière)

prove prouver

provided that pourvu que (+ *subjunc.*)

public public, publique *f.*

publish publier

publisher éditeur *m.*

punish punir

pupil élève *m. or f.*

purple mauve

purse sac *m.*

put mettre (mettant, mis, je mets, je mis); **put away** ranger (*irr. sp.* B); **put down** baisser; **put on** mettre

puzzle: **crossword puzzle** les mots croisés *m. pl.*

Pyrenees Pyrénées *f. pl.*

Q

quality qualité *f.*

question (*v.*) questionner; interroger (*irr. sp.* B); (*n.*) question *f.;* **ask a question** poser une question

quickly vite

quiet tranquille, calme

Verbs with spelling changes are explained on pp. 274–276.

R

radio radio *f.*

rain (*v.*) pleuvoir (pleuvant, plu, il pleut, il plut); (*n.*) la pluie (*f.*)

raise (*v.*) lever (*irr. sp.* D); (*n.*) augmentation *f.*

rapidly vite; rapidement

rare rare

rarely rarement

rather (p. 169) plutôt; plutôt que de; assez; aimer mieux; au lieu de

read lire (lisant, lu, je lis, je lus)

real vrai

realize se rendre compte

really vraiment

reason (pp. 169–170) raison *f.*; the reason for la raison de; the reason that la raison pour laquelle

reassure rassurer

reassured rassuré

receive recevoir (recevant, reçu, je reçois, je reçus)

recently récemment

reception réception *f.*

recognize reconnaître (*conj. like* connaître)

recommend recommander

recommendation recommandation *f.*

record disque *m.*

red rouge

refuse refuser (de + *inf.*)

regret (*v.*) regretter; (*n.*) regret *m.*

relate raconter

relative parent *m.*

religion religion *f.*

remain rester

remarkable remarquable

remember se souvenir (*conj. like* venir) (de + *n.*; de + *inf.*); se rappeler (*irr. sp.* F) (+ *n.*)

repair réparer

repent se repentir (2)

reply (*v.*) répondre (à + *n.*); (*n.*) réponse *f.*

republic république *f.*

require exiger (*irr. sp.* B)

resemble ressembler (à + *n.*)

reserve réserver, louer

resignation démission *f.*

resist résister (à + *n.*)

report rapport *m.*, compte rendu *m.*

rest se reposer

restaurant restaurant *m.*

restful reposant

result résultat *m.*

résumé résumé *m.*

retire prendre (sa) retraite

retirement retraite *f.*

return (*v.*) (pp. 179–80) (*come back*) revenir (*conj. like* venir); (*go back*) retourner; (*go back home*) rentrer; (*give back*) rendre; (*n.*) retour *m.*

reward récompenser

Rhone Rhône *m.*

rich riche

ridiculous ridicule

riding: go horseback riding faire du cheval, faire une promenade à cheval

right bon; juste; right away tout de suite; right now immédiatement, tout de suite; be right avoir raison

ring (*v.*) sonner; (*n.*) bague *f.*

river fleuve *m.*; rivière *f.*

Riviera Côte d'Azur *f.*

road route *f.*; chemin *m.*; go along the road suivre la route (le chemin)

roast rôti *m.*

roasted rôti

room (pp. 180–81) (*in general*) pièce *f.*; (*bedroom*) chambre *f.*; (*room for meetings*) salle *f.*; (*living room*) salle de séjour *f.*; salon *m.*; (*space*) place *f.*

rose rose *f.*

row rang *m.*

rub frotter

rule règle *f.*

rummage around fouiller

run courir (courant, couru, je cours, je courus); run across traverser en courant

rush se précipiter

Russia Russie *f.*

Russian russe

S

sad triste

sailboat bateau à voiles *m.*

salesman vendeur *m.*; représentant *m.*

same même; all the same quand même

sample échantillon *m.*

sandwich sandwich *m.*

satisfied content; satisfait

Saturday samedi *m.*

save (p. 181) sauver; économiser; faire des économies; garder; mettre de côté

say dire (disant, dit, je dis, je dis) (á + *person* + de + *inf.*)

scarcely à peine

scarf écharpe *f.*

school école *f.*; to, in, at school à l'école

scientific scientifique

scientist savant *m.*

season saison *f.*

secretary secrétaire *m. or f.*

see voir (voyant, vu, je vois, je vis) see again revoir (*conj. like* voir); come and see me venez me voir

seem sembler (+ *inf.*); paraître (*conj. like* connaître) (+ *inf.*); avoir l'air (+ *adj.*; de + *inf.*)

sell vendre

senator sénateur

Irregular verbs are conjugated on pp. 256–273.

send envoyer (envoyant, envoyé, j'envoie, j'envoyai)
sentence phrase *f.*
separate séparer
serious sérieux (*f.* sérieuse)
servant serviteur *m.;* domestique *m.* or *f.*
serve servir (2)
service service *m.*
set (*v.*) (*the sun*) se coucher; (*n.*) (*television*) télévision *f.*
seven sept
several plusieurs
shake secouer; serrer; shake hands se serrer la main
sharp: at one o'clock sharp à une heure précise
sheet drap *m.*
shirt chemise *f.*
shopping center centre commercial *m.*
short court, bref (*f.* brève); short story conte *m.*
shortcoming défaut *m.*
should (p. 203) devrais, devrait, etc.; *conditional form of verb*
shoulder épaule *f.*
show montrer
shrug hausser; shrug one's shoulders hausser les épaules
shut fermer
sick malade
sight vue *f.;* catch sight of apercevoir (*conj. like* recevoir) (+ *n.*)
sign signer
silk soie *f.*
silly bête; sot (*f.* sotte)
silver argent *m.*
silverware argenterie *f.*
since (pp. 43, 236) puisque; comme; depuis que; depuis
single seul
sister sœur *f.;* sister-in-law belle-sœur *f.*
sit, sit down (p. 182) s'asseoir (s'asseyant, assis, je m'assieds, je m'assis) (*imperative*) asseyez-vous; sitting assis
situate situer; be situated se trouver
situation situation *f.*
six six
sixteen seize
skin peau *f.*
sleep dormir (2)
sleepy: be sleepy avoir sommeil
slight léger (*f.* légère)
slightest moindre
slow down ralentir
small petit
smile sourire *m.*
smoke (*v.*) fumer; (*n.*) fumée *f.*
snapshot photo *f.;* photographie *f.*
snow (*v.*) neiger; (*irr. sp.* B) (*n.*) neige *f.*
so si; tant; tellement; le; so much tant, tellement; so that pour que
soap savon *m.*
sofa sofa *m.;* canapé *m.*

soft doux (*f.* douce)
solve résoudre; (*pp*) résolu
soldier soldat *m.;* militaire *m.*
somber sombre
some (*adj.*) du, de, la, de l', des; quelque; (*pron.*) quelques-uns; en
someone quelqu'un
something quelque chose; something else autre chose
sometimes quelquefois, parfois
somewhere quelque part
son fils *m.*
song chanson *f.*
soon (pp. 195–96) tôt; bientôt; as soon as dès que
sooner plus tôt
sore douloureux (*f.* douloureuse); I have a sore throat j'ai mal à la gorge
sorrow chagrin *m.;* to my great sorrow à mon vif regret
sorry désolé; be sorry regretter; I'm sorry pardon
sort sorte *f.*
soundly profondément
south sud *m.*
South American Sud-Américain *m.*
Spain Espagne *f.*
Spanish espagnol
speak parler
special particulier (*f.* particulière); spécial
specialist spécialiste *m.*
spend (p. 196) (*money*) dépenser; (*time*) passer
spite: in spite of (p. 244) malgré
sport sport *m.*
spring printemps *m.*
spy espion *m.*
square place *f.*
stamp timbre *m.*
stand se tenir, se tenir debout; (*bear*) supporter
state état *m.*
station gare *f.*
stay rester
step (*course of action*) démarche *f.*
still encore; toujours
stocking bas *m.*
stop (pp. 196–97) cesser (de + *inf.*); arrêter (+ *n.; de + inf.*); s'arrêter (de + *inf.*) without stopping sans arrêt
store magasin *m.*
storm orage *m.*
story histoire *f.;* detective story roman policier *m.;* short story conte *m.*
strange étrange; curieux (*f.* curieuse)
stranger étranger *m.*
street rue *f.;* on the street dans la rue
stretch étendre; stretched out tendu; étendu
strict sévère
strong fort
stubborn entêté, têtu
student (*college*) étudiant *m.,* étudiante *f.;* (*grade and high school*) élève *m.* or *f.*

Verbs with spelling changes are explained on pp. 274–276

study (*v.*) travailler; étudier; (*n.*) étude *f.*
style style *m.*
succeed réussir (à + *inf.*)
success succès *m.*
such (p. 197) tel (*f.* telle); aussi; comme ça; pareil (*f.* pareille)
suddenly soudain; tout à coup; tout d'un coup
suffer souffrir (*conj. like* ouvrir)
sugar sucre *m.*
suit costume *m.*
suitcase valise *f.;* pack one's suitcase faire sa valise
sum somme *f.;* somme d'argent *f.*
summer été *m.*
sun soleil *m.;* there is sun il fait du soleil, il y a du soleil; the sun set le soleil s'est couché
Sunday dimanche *m.*
sunlight soleil *m.*
surprise étonner
surprised étonné
surprising étonnant
Susan Suzanne
suspect suspect *m.*
Sweden Suède *f.*
swim nager (*irr. sp.* B)
swimming pool piscine *f.*

T

table table *f.;* clear the table débarrasser la table
tail queue *f.*
take (pp. 205–7) prendre (prenant, pris, je prends, je pris); mener (*irr. sp.* D); emmener (*irr. sp.* D); amener (*irr. sp.* D); apporter; (= *subscribe to*) s'abonner à, être abonné à; take a course suivre un cours; take an interest in s'intéresser (à + *n.*); take a walk se promener (*irr. sp.* D), faire une promenade
talent talent *m.*
talk (*v.*) parler; (*n.*) causerie *f.;* give a talk faire une causerie; talk business parler affaires, parler des affaires
taxi taxi *m.*
tea thé *m.*
teach (pp. 207–8) enseigner; apprendre (*conj. like* prendre)
teacher professeur *m.;* maître *m.*
team équipe *f.*
teenagers les jeunes, les adolescents, les «teenagers,» les moins de vingt ans
telephone (*v.*) téléphoner (à + *person*); (*n.*) téléphone *m.;* telephone book annuaire *m.;* telephone number numéro de téléphone
televison télévision *f.,* la télé, la TV; television set télévision *f.*
tell dire (disant, dit, je dis, je dis) (à + *person* + de + *inf.*); raconter; tell about parler de
ten dix

tender tendre
terrible terrible
than que; (*before numerals*) de
thank remercier (de *or* pour + *thing;* de + *inf.*)
that (*conjunc.*) que; so that pour que; (*demonstrative*) ce, cet, cette, ces; celui, etc., cela; (*relative*) qui; que
the le, la, l', les
theater théâtre *m.;* in the theater au théâtre
their leur
then ensuite, puis; alors
theory théorie *f.*
there y; là; from there en; de là; there is, there are il y a; voilà
these ces
they ils; on; eux
thief voleur *m.*
thing chose *f.*
think penser (à + *n.*); croire (croyant, cru, je crois, je crus)
third troisième
thirty trente
this ce, cet, cette
though bien que, quoique; even though quoique; bien que; tout en (+ *pres. participle*)
thought pensée *f.*
three trois
throat gorge *f.;* I have a sore throat j'ai mal à la gorge
through par; go through passer par; parcourir (*conj. like* écrire)
Thursday jeudi *m.*
tie cravate *f.*
tied up attaché
time (pp. 208–9) temps *m.;* fois *f.;* heure *f.,* époque *f.;* moment *m.;* by the time quand; for a long time longtemps; from time to time de temps en temps; have a good time s'amuser, bien s'amuser; in time à temps; many times bien des fois; on time à l'heure
tired fatigué
title titre *m.*
to à; chez; dans; en
today aujourd'hui
together ensemble; pressed together serré
tomorrow demain; the day after tomorrow après-demain
tonight ce soir
too trop
tool outil *m.*
top sommet *m.*
tourist touriste *m.* or *f.*
tournament tournoi *m.*
toward (p. 245) vers; envers
town ville *f.*
toy jouet *m.*
traffic (*adj.*) de la circulation
train train *m.;* by train en train, par le train
translate traduire (*conj. like* conduire)

Irregular verbs are conjugated on pp. 256–273.

travel (*v.*) voyager (*irr. sp.* B) (pp. 213–14);
travel across traverser; (*n.*) voyage *m.*
traveller voyageur *m.*
tray plateau *m.*
trip voyage *m.;* take a trip faire un voyage
troop troupe *f.*
trouble histoire *f.;* ennuis *m. pl.;* difficultés *f. pl.*
true vraie
truly vraiment
truth vérité *f.*
try essayer (*irr. sp.* C) (de + *inf.*); chercher (à + *inf.*); try on essayer
turn around se retourner
twelve douze
twenty vingt
twice deux fois
twist tordre
two deux
type taper à la machine, écrire à la machine
typewrite taper à la machine, écrire à la machine

U

ugly vilain
unbearable insupportable
under (pp. 245–46) sous; au-dessous de
understand comprendre (*conj. like* prendre)
undeveloped sous-développé
uneasiness malaise *m.*
unfortunately malheureusement
United States États-Unis *m. pl.*
university université *f.*
unless à moins que (+ *subjunc.*)
until (pp. 236–37) (*conjunc.*) jusqu'à ce que (+ *subjunc.*); (*prep.*) jusqu'à
up (p. 246) dessus; sur; en haut; go up remonter; monter; up to now jusqu'à présent
use se servir (de + *n.*); employer (*irr. sp.* C); used to (pp. 73–4) *a form of the imperfect tense*
useful utile
useless inutile

V

vacation vacances *f. pl.*
valuable précieux (*f.* précieuse); de prix; de valeur
vase vase *m.*
very très; very much (p. 227) beaucoup beaucoup; énormément, un tas de, des tas de
vicious méchant
village village *m.*
violin violon *m.*

visit (p. 228) (*a place*) visiter; (*a person*) aller voir; rendre visite à; faire une visite à
visitor visiteur *m.*
voice voix *f.*

W

wait attendre; wait for attendre (+ *n.*)
waiter garçon *m.*
wake up réveiller; se réveiller
walk (*v.*) marcher; se promener (*irr. sp.* D); (*n.*) promenade *f.;* go for a walk, take a walk aller se promener, faire une promenade, se promener (*irr. sp.* D)
want vouloir (voulant, voulu, je veux, je voulus) (+ *inf.*)
war guerre *f.;* world war guerre mondiale *f.*
warm chaud; be warm avoir chaud
wash laver; wash the dishes faire la vaisselle
waste perdre; gaspiller
watch (*v.*) regarder, observer; surveiller; (*n.*) montre *f.*
water eau *f.;* ice water eau glacée
way route *f.;* manière *f.;* façon *f.;* continue on our way continuer notre route; in that way de cette façon; on the way en route
wear porter
weather temps *m.;* the weather is good il fait beau
wedding mariage *m.*
week semaine *f.*
weekend week-end *m.*
well bien; well known connu, célèbre; bien connu
what (*interrog.*) qu'est-ce qui; que, qu'est-ce que; quoi; quel, quelle; comment; (*relative*) ce qui; ce que
whatever quoi que; quel que (*f.* quelle que)
when (p. 131) quand; où
where où
whereas tandis que
wherever où . . . que (+ *subjunc.*)
whether si
which (*interrog.*) quel, quelle; lequel, laquelle; (*rel.*) qui; que; lequel; quoi
while (pp. 103–4, 228–29) (*at the same time*) pendant que; (*whereas*) tandis que; a little while ago tout à l'heure; all the while tout en (+ *pres. participle*)
white blanc (*f.* blanche)
who (*interrog.*) qui; (*rel.*) qui; que
whoever qui que; quel que; whoever he is (may be) qui que ce soit; quel qu'il soit
whole tout (*m. pl.* tous)
why pourquoi
wife femme *f.*
willing: be willing vouloir bien
win gagner; remporter

Verbs with spelling changes are explained on pp. 274–276.

window fenêtre *f.*; vitre *f.*
windowpane vitre *f.*
wine vin *m.*
winner gagnant *m.*
winter hiver *m.*
Wisconsin Wisconsin *m.*
wish (pp. 139, 229) vouloir (voulant, voulu, je veux, je voulus) (+ *inf.*); désirer (+ *inf.*); souhaiter
with (pp. 246–47) avec; sur; de; chez
without sans; do without se passer de
woman femme *f.*; cleaning woman femme de ménage *f.*
wonder se demander
wonderful merveilleux (*f.* merveilleuse)
won't ne pas vouloir (+ *inf.*)
wood bois *m.*
word mot *m.* (*spoken word*) parole *f.*
work (*v.*) travailler; (*n.*) travail *m.*; out of work sans travail
workman ouvrier *m.*; travailleur *m.*
world monde *m.*; world war guerre mondiale *f.*
worried inquiet (*f.* inquiète)
worry inquiéter; s'inquiéter (*irr. sp.* E)
would (pp. 49, 50, 73–4, 249) vouloir; *as auxiliary verb:* (*in conditional*) *conditional of main verb;* (= *used to*) *imperfect of main verb*

write écrire (écrivant, écrit, j'écris, j'écrivis)
writer écrivain *m.*
wrong faux (*f.* fausse); be wrong avoir tort; do wrong faire du tort

Y

yawn bailler
year (p. 250) an *m.*; année *f.*; Happy New Year Bonne Année, Bonne Nouvelle Année; I was ten years old j'avais dix ans; twice a year deux fois par an; every year tous les ans; youthful years années de jeunesse *f. pl.*
yes (p. 250) oui; si
yesterday hier; yesterday evening hier soir; yesterday morning hier matin
you tu; vous; both of you vous deux
young jeune
young men (p. 251) jeunes gens *m. pl.*
your votre, vos
yours le vôtre, la vôtre, etc.
yourself vous-même
youthful jeune; youthful years années de jeunesse *f. pl.*

Irregular verbs are conjugated on pp. 256–273.

Index

à
à + de verbs 219
characteristic 247
with cities 212–13
with countries 213–14
être à to show possession 91
with expressions such as à pied, à bicyclette 165
à l'heure 164
before infinitive 217
à mesure que 234–35
meaning *with* 247
about 238–39
above 239
abstract nouns 158–59
according to 239
across 240
actually 9–10
adjectives
beau, nouveau, vieux, etc. 16–17
c'est + adjective + infinitive 222
comparison of equality 19
comparison of inequality 17–18
de + adjective + plural noun 174
demonstrative 113
descriptive 20–21
feminine 15–17
il est + adjective + infinitive 222
interrogative 2–3, 7
irregular 17
limiting 21
of material 178
plural 14–17
position 20–22
possessive 86–87
adverbs
à peine 31
aussi (meaning *therefore*) 31
formation 28–29
irregular 29
negative 32–35
peut-être 31
position 30–31
of quantity 176–77
advice 10
after
après vs. après que 233–34
d'après 240
+ verb + *-ing* 224
again 10
agent (with par and de) 187–88

agree 11
agreement
of past participle
with en 98
of faire followed by the infinitive 194
of verb in passive voice 187
of reflexive verbs 100–01
of verbs conjugated with avoir 98
of verbs of motion 99
with preceding vous 100
of possessive adjective 86
of present participle 103
-aine 239
along 240
an vs. année 250
appositives 160–61
après
après vs. après que 234
après + compound infinitive 47–48, 224
article (uses and omission)
with appositives 160–61
with cities 164
with countries and continents 163
with dates 159
with days of week 159
after dont 130
after en 161
forms of 158
with languages 159–60
with means of locomotion 165
with given names 161
with nouns of nationality, profession, religion 165
with nouns used in general sense 158–59
with nouns of material 178
partitive 173–74
with parts of body 87–89
with seasons 159
with streets and avenues 164
with titles 161–62
with units of measure 164–65
with units of time 165
as 234–35
as . . . as 19
as long as 122
at
à 241
chez 241
with cities 212–13
dans 241
au, aux with countries 213–14

325

aussi (*therefore*) (word order) 31
auxiliaries 97–101
avant
  avant vs. avant que 235
  avant vs. devant 242
  avant de + infinitive 224
  avant de vs. avant que 146
avec + abstract noun 175
avenues
  use and omission of article with 164
  use of preposition with 164
avoir
  as auxiliary 97
  conjugation 260
  idiomatic expressions with 175
-ayer verbs 275

because, because of 235
beaucoup
  as adverb of quantity 176
  cannot modify meilleur 24–25
  cannot be modified by très 227
  very much 227
become 23–24
before
  avant vs. avant que 235
  avant vs. devant 242
  avant de vs. avant que 146
  + -*ing* 224
better 24–25
bien des 176
body (parts of)
  attitude or manner with 89–90, 247
  possession with 87–89
bring 25
but (preposition) 235
by (agent after passive) 187–88

can 25–26
causative
  agreement of past participle of faire 194
  definition of 192
  formation of 192
  with one object 192
  with two objects 193
  with pronoun objects 194
ce
  adjective 113
  pronoun
    indefinite 117–18
    introductory 118–19
    pleonastic 117
ceci, cela, ça 114–15
-cer verbs 274
c'est
  + adjective + à + infinitive 222
  with adjective 117
  with disjunctive pronoun 62, 118–19
  with noun or pronoun 118–19
  with superlative 119
ce qui, ce que 128

change 37–38
character 38–39
chez 241, 246
-ci, -là
  after nouns 113–14
  after demonstrative pronouns 115–16
cities
  use of article with 164
  at, in, to 212–14
comme
  meaning *as* 234
comment (meaning *What?*) 5
comparison of adjectives 18–19
  of equality 19
  of inequality 18–19
compound infinitive 223–24
compound past (also called PASSÉ COMPOSÉ and
    "past indefinite")
  auxiliaries 97
  uses 71, 73–74
compound subject with disjunctive pronoun 62
compound tenses
  auxiliaries 97
  future perfect 48–49
  PASSÉ COMPOSÉ 71, 73–74, 97
  PASSÉ SURCOMPOSÉ 47
  past anterior 47
  pluperfect 46–47
conditional
  in conditional sentences 49–51
  as past of future 45
  in softened statements 45
conditional sentences 49–51
conjugations
  irregular verbs 260–73
  based on principal parts 254–55
  regular verbs 256–59
  verbs with spelling changes 274–76
continents (prepositions used with) 213, 214
countries
  from 215
  gender 213
  in, to 213–14

dans
  vs. en 243
  with modified place names 214
dates (use of article with) 159
day 39
days of week (use of article with) 159
de
  about 238–39
  after certain adjectives and verbs 246–47
  before adjective + plural noun 174
  in adjectival phrase 178
  as preposition of agent after passive 188
  de l'heure 164
  from (with place names) 215
  before infinitive 217, 219
  with nouns of material 178
  in phrases of manner 243, 246–47

after **heure** in telling time 244
instead of partitive 174, 176–78
after superlative 19
meaning *than* 18
meaning *with* 246–47
definite article (also see "article") 158–65
definition (asking for) 8
demonstrative adjectives 113–14
demonstrative pronouns
  ce 117–19
  ceci, cela, ça 114–15
  celui, etc. 115–16
  with **-ci** and **-là** 115–16
depuis
  vs. **depuis que** 236
  with imperfect 46
  vs. **pendant** and **pour** 242–43
  with present 43–44, 242
dernier
  ce dernier = *the latter* 116
  with subjunctive 149
dès que
  with future 44
  with future perfect 49
  with PASSÉ SURCOMPOSÉ 47
  with past anterior 47
devoir 201–204
  compound past 203
  conditional 203
  imperfect 202
  past conditional 203
  present 201
direct object pronouns 58, 60
disjunctive pronouns 61–64
dont 129–30
down (*come down, go down*) 242

each other 58, 100–01
early 52–53
en
  agreement of past participle with 98
  to express *as* 234–35
  use with and without definite article 161
  with countries and continents 213
  vs. **dans** 243
  de + thing = **en** 63
  with languages 159–60
  with means of locomotion 165
  with nouns of material 178
  position 60
  with present participle 103, 224
  as pronoun 59, 63
  with seasons 159
  tout en 103–04
en train de 43, 104–05
end 53
escape 53–54
être
  with **à** to show possession 91
  as auxiliary 97
  conjugation 260–61

with reflexive verbs 97, 100–01
with verbs of motion 97, 99
evening
  the next evening 135
  soir vs. **soirée** 39
every 54
everyone 54
everything 54
everything that 54–55, 128
except 242
exchange 38
expect 66–67

fail 67–68
faire
  agreement of past participle of **faire** followed
    by infinitive 194
  causative 192–94
  conjugation 266–67
faut (il)
  to express *must* 204
  with subjunctive 143
feel 68
feminine of adjectives 15–17
first names (use of article with) 161
for
  depuis vs. **pendant** vs. **pour** 43–44, 242–43
  pour vs. **car** 236
former, latter 116
from (with place names) 215
future
  with **pendant** and **pour** 242–43
  expressed by present 43
  with **quand,** etc. 44
  with **tant que** 44, 122
  use 44
future perfect (also called FUTUR ANTÉRIEUR) 48–49

gender
  of countries 213
  of languages 160
general sense (nouns used in) 158–59
-ger verbs 274
get 68–69
given names (use of article with) 161
go 79–80
go out of 245
go up 246

happen 80–81
have
  have something done (causative) 192–94
  have to = *must* 201–204
  have a good time 209
hear 82
how long 122

il est
  + adjective 118
  + adjective + infinitive 118, 222
il y a . . . que + present 43

il y avait . . . que + imperfect 46
imperative (word order of pronoun objects) 60
imperfect
  in conditional sentences 49
  with depuis and il y avait . . . que 46
  uses 72–75
impersonal expressions
  il est + adjective + infinitive 118, 222
  followed by indicative or subjunctive 142
in
  dans vs. en 243
  after heure in telling time 243
  in the 243
  in the morning, etc. 243
  in phrases of manner 243
  with place names 212–14
  after superlative 19
in spite of 244
indefinite
  indefinite antecedent followed by subjunctive
    148
  indefinite article (also see "article") 158, 161,
    164–65
  indefinite ce 117
  indefinite noun 173–78
    after avec 175
    after de 176–78
    in expressions with avoir 175
    after ni . . . ni 175
    after sans 175
    after verbs and adjectives followed by de 177
  indefinite + que + subjunctive 149–50
indicative
  in clauses with definite antecedent 148
  function of 139
  after certain impersonal expressions 143
indirect object pronouns 58, 60
infinitive
  with pour 225
  after prepositions 216–17, 224
  preceded by c'est + adjective + à 222
  preceded by il est + adjective + de 118, 222
  simple and compound 223–24
  instead of subjunctive 142, 146–47
instead of 244–45
intend 92
interrogatives
  adjectives 2–3, 7–8
  pronouns 4–8
intransitive verbs of motion 97, 99
introduce 92
introductory ce 118–19
inverted word order
  after à peine, aussi, peut-être 31
irregular verbs (conjugation of) 260–273

jusqu'à 236–37
jusqu'à ce que
  vs. jusqu'à 236–37
  with subjunctive 145–46

knock (a) 92
know 93–94

là vs. y 59
lack 106–07
languages
  with and without article 159–60
  with en 159–60
  gender 160
last night 107
late 107
latter, former 116
leave 108–09
length (at) 123
lequel, etc.
  interrogative 6–7
  relative 127–28, 129
limiting adjectives 22
little vs. *a little* 121
live 122
long 122–23

make + adjective 123
marry 132
material (nouns of) 178
measure (preposition and article with units of)
  164–65
meet 93
meilleur
  comparative of bon 18
  vs. mieux 24–25
  much better 24–25
mental states 72–73
-ment 30
mieux
  comparative of bien 29
  vs. meilleur 24–25
  much better 24–25
miss 133
modes (indicative vs. subjunctive) 138–39, 143,
  144–45, 148
more
  more and more 133
  the more . . . the more 133–34
morning
  matin vs. matinée 39
  in the morning 243
  the next morning 135
motion (intransitive verbs of) 97, 99
much
  much better 24–25
  very much, very many 227
must
  meanings of 201
  ways of saying in French 204

names (use of article with first names) 161
nationality (nouns of) 119, 165

ne
  ne . . . que (position) 34
  omission 35
  position 34
negative
  combinations 34
  position 32–35
  in sentence without verb 35
next 134–35
ni . . . ni
  with indefinite nouns 175
  position 35
night (last) 107
notice 152
nouns
  used as adjectives in English 178
  the noun alone 175–78
  in apposition 160–61
  used in general sense 158–59
  indefinite 173–78
  of material 178
  of nationality, profession, religion, etc. 119,
    165

object pronouns 58–60
  direct 58, 60
  en 59
  indirect 58, 60
  order and position 60
  y 59, 60
obligé de (être) 204
on + ing 103, 224
  used to avoid passive 189–90
  used to mean *people* 154–55
opportunity 153
orthographical changing verbs 274–76
où (relative) 131
ought to 203
out of 245
-oyer verbs 275

paper 153–54
par
  preposition of agent 187–88
  with units of time 165
participles
  past 97–101
  present 102–05
partitive
  article 173
  construction 173, 176–77
  de used instead 174, 176–78
parts of body
  attitude or manner with 89–90, 247
  possession with 87–90
pas
  followed by de 177
  followed by partitive 177
  position
    in sentence 32–33

PASSÉ COMPOSÉ (also called "compound past" and
    "past indefinite")
  auxiliary 97
  uses 43–44, 71, 73–74
PASSÉ SIMPLE (also called "simple past" and "past
    definite") 76–77
PASSÉ SURCOMPOSÉ
  formation 47
  use 46–47
passive voice
  agent 187–88
  agreement of past participle 187
  nature of 186–87
  ways of avoiding
    by use of active voice 189–90
    by use of on 189
    by use of reflexive verb 191
    when subject of English passive is indirect
      object of active 190
past anterior (also called PASSÉ ANTÉRIEUR) 47
past conditional 49
past definite (called "simple past" and PASSÉ SIM-
    PLE) 76–77
past indefinite (called "compound past" and PASSÉ
    COMPOSÉ) 43–44, 71, 73–74, 97
past participle (agreement of)
  with auxiliary avoir 98
  with auxiliary être
    in passive voice 187
    in reflexive verbs 100–01
    verbs of motion 99
past subjunctive 141
past tenses in narration 71–77
peine (à) (word order) 31
pendant (vs. depuis and pour) 242–43
people 154–55
per (+ units of time and measure) 165
personal pronouns
  direct object 58, 60
  disjunctive 61–64
  indirect object 58, 60
  order and position 60
  reciprocal 58, 100–01
  reflexive 41, 100–01
personne 34
peut-être (word order) 31
peux (vs. puis) 25
piece 167
place 168
place
  adverbs of 31
  article with place names 163–64
  prepositions of 212–15
pleonastic ce 117
plupart (la) 177
pluperfect (also called "past perfect" and PLUS-
    QUE-PARFAIT)
  in conditions 49–51
  expressed by French imperfect 46
  use 46
  when not to use 46–47

plural (of adjectives) 14–17
plus
    used in comparisons 18
    followed by **que** and **de** 18
position
    of adjectives 20–22
    of adverbs 30–31
    of **en** 60
    of negative words 32–35
    of object pronouns 60
    of **y** 60
possession
    with **appartenir à** and **être à** 91
    with parts of body 87–90
possessive adjectives 86–87
possessive pronouns 90–91
pour
    to express *to* in *enough to, too much to* 225
    with future 243
    as preposition 236
    to express purpose 225
premier (followed by subjunctive) 149
prepositions
    with cities 212, 215
    with countries 213–15
    with disjunctive pronouns 62
    before infinitive 216–17, 224
    with means of locomotion 165
    with **rue, avenue, place** 164
    with seasons 159
    with units of measure and time 164–65
    after verbs and before nouns 220–21
present
    with **depuis**, etc. 43–44
    for future 43
    uses 42–43
present participle
    agreement 103
    with **en** 103
    formation 102
    nature of 102
    with **tout en** 103–04
ways of expressing English present participle in
        French 104–05
principal parts (of verbs) 254–55
profession (nouns of) 119, 165
pronouns (also see types of pronouns)
    demonstrative 114–19
    direct object 58, 60
    disjunctive 61–64
    en 59
    indirect object 58, 60
    interrogative 4–8
    où (relative) 131
    possessive 90–91
    reciprocal 58
    reflexive (**se**) 58, (**soi**) 62
    relative 126–31
    y 59, 60
puis (vs. **peux**) 25

purpose
    with **pour** + infinitive 225
    with **pour que** + subjunctive 145–46

quand
    with future 44
    with future perfect 48–49
    vs. **où** 131
    with PASSÉ SURCOMPOSÉ 46–47
quantity (adverbs of) 176–77
que
    interrogative 4–8
    vs. **qu'est-ce que** 5
    relative 127, 129
quel, etc.
    adjective 2–3
    quel est . . . , etc. 3, 7–8
    as exclamation 2–3
qu'est-ce que and **qu'est-ce que c'est que** 8
quoi
    interrogative 5–6
    relative 128–29

rather 169
reason 169–170
reciprocal
    pronouns (**se**) 58
    verbs 100–01
reflexive pronouns (**se**) 58, (**soi**) 62
reflexive verbs
    agreement of past participle 100–01
    auxiliary 97
    to express English passive 191
    types 100–01
relative pronouns
    definition 127
    dont 129–30
    forms 127–31
    où 131
    table 129
    what 128
return 179–80
rien (position in compound tenses) 34
room 180–81

sans
    before an unmodified indefinite noun 175
sans que 145–47
save 181
seasons (use of article and preposition) 159
sequence of tenses
    in conditional sentences 49–51
    after present and past of indicative 45
    in subjunctive 141
seul (followed by subjunctive) 149
should, should have 203
si
    in conditions 49–51

meaning *if* and *whether* 50–51
meaning *yes* 250
simple past (also called PASSÉ SIMPLE and "past definite") 76–77
since
depuis vs. depuis que 236
puisque 236
sit 182
soi 62
soon 195–96
spelling changes in verbs 274–76
spend 196
spite: in spite of 244
stop 196–97
subject (compound) 62
streets (use of article and preposition with) 164
subjunctive
its basic problems 138
vs. indicative 138–39, 143, 148
vs. infinitive 142, 146–47
nature of 139
tenses (present and past) 141
uses
in clauses with indefinite antecedent 148
in clauses introduced by qui que, quel que, si . . . que, etc. 149–50
after certain impersonal expressions 143
after superlatives, seul, premier, dernier 149
after certain subordinate conjunctions 145–46
after verbs of thinking and believing 144–45
after verbs of wishing, doubting, and emotion 139–40
such 197
superlative
after c'est 119
formation and use 18–19
followed by *in* 19
with subjunctive 149

take 205–07
teach 207–08
tenses (also see name of tense)
use of past tenses 71–77
sequence of
in conditional sentences 49–51
after present and past of indicative 45
in subjunctive 141
than 18
this and *that* 113–14
time 208–09
titles of address (use of article with) 161–62
to
with cities 214
with countries and continents 214
to express purpose 225
tout ce qui, tout ce que 54–55, 128
tout en + present participle 103
toward 245
train: en train de 43, 104–05

under 245–46
until 236–37
up: go up 80
used to 73
-uyer verbs 275

verbs (also see "passive," "subjunctive," and names of various tenses and other parts of verbs)
à + de verbs 219
auxiliaries 97
classification 253
conjugations
irregular verbs 260–73
under principal parts 255
regular verbs 256–60
verbs with spelling changes 274–76
of motion 97, 99
passive voice 186–91
prepositions with
before infinitive 216–17, 225
before nouns 220
principal parts 254–55
reciprocal 100–01
reflexive 97, 100–01
spelling changes 302–304, 274–76
stems 253
very much, very many 227
visit 228
voice (passive) 186–91
vous (agreement of past participle with) 100

what
interrogative adjective 2–3
interrogative pronoun 3–5, 7–8
relative pronoun 128
what is, what are
to ask for a definition (qu'est-ce que, etc.) 8
to ask which of a number of possibilities (quel est, etc.) 2–3, 7–8
when
with future 44
with future perfect 48–49
with PASSÉ SURCOMPOSÉ 46–47
quand vs. où 131
which 126–29
while 228–29
who 127
whose 129–30
wish 229
with 246–47
word order
of adjectives 20–22
of adverbs 30–31
of interrogative pronouns 4–5
inverted
after aussi (therefore) 31
after à peine and peut-être 31
negative 32–35
of pronoun objects 60

would
  to express customary action in the past 73, 249
  in conditions 49–51, 249
  to express the past of the future 45

y
  à + thing = y 64

  used with **aller** 79–80
  vs. là 59
  position 60
year 250
yes 250
young men 251